GO»
AHEAD
REALSCHULE BAYERN

Go Ahead · Band 7

Im Auftrag des Verlages konzipiert und erarbeitet von	Rebecca Robb Benne, Kopenhagen, Dänemark; Ursula Fleischhauer, Hannover (Language file); Petra Ullrich, Bessenbach (Skills file)
unter Mitarbeit und beratender Mitwirkung von	Annette Baader, Nürnberg; Klaus Berold, Kulmbach; Gerlinde Eberhardt, Surberg; Christina Forstner, Lenggries; Martin Fritze, Bad Abbach; Oliver Kosina, Regensburg; Carmen Lux-Younts, Lauf a. d. Pegnitz; Petra Ullrich, Bessenbach
in Zusammenarbeit mit der Englischredaktion	Klaus Unger (Projektleitung); Jutta Seuren (koordinierende Redakteurin); Michael Dunkel, Undine Griebel, Mara Leibowitz, Michaela Schmidt, Kathrin Spiegelberg, Frederike Stapelmann, Olivia Wintgens, Silja Wollburg
Vokabelanhänge	Ingrid Raspe, Düsseldorf
Lizenzmanagement	Ina Gafarova, Rebekka Gerlach
Illustrationen	Bildbad, Jutta Melsheimer & Kai Hofmann, Berlin
Layoutkonzept	finedesign, Büro für Text & Gestaltung, Berlin; designcollective, Team für Mediengestaltung, Berlin
Technische Umsetzung	designcollective, Team für Mediengestaltung, Berlin
Umschlaggestaltung	Cornelsen Schulverlage Design unter Verwendung der Entwürfe von hawemannundmosch, Berlin

www.cornelsen.de

Für die freundliche Unterstützung danken wir der Mount Kelly School, Tavistock und der Immanuel-Kant-Schule, Hamburg.

Dieses Werk berücksichtigt die Regeln der reformierten Rechtschreibung und Zeichensetzung. Ausnahmen bilden Originaltexte, bei denen lizenzrechtliche Gründe einer Änderung entgegenstehen.

1. Auflage, 1. Druck 2019

Alle Drucke dieser Auflage sind inhaltlich unverändert und können im Unterricht nebeneinander verwendet werden.

Im Lernmittel wird in Form von Symbolen auf eine CD verwiesen; diese enthält – bis auf die Hörverstehensübungen – ausschließlich optionale Unterrichtsmaterialien. Die CD unterliegt nicht dem staatlichen Zulassungsverfahren.

Druck: Firmengruppe APPL, aprinta Druck, Wemding

ISBN 978-3-464-31117-2 (Schülerbuch)
ISBN 978-3-464-33913-6 (E-Book)

PEFC
PEFC/04-32-0928

PEFC zertifiziert
Dieses Produkt stammt aus nachhaltig bewirtschafteten Wäldern und kontrollierten Quellen.

www.pefc.de

GO »
AHEAD

REALSCHULE BAYERN

7

Cornelsen

Dein Englischbuch enthält folgende Teile:

Unit 1 bis 5	Die fünf Kapitel des Buches
Revision	Üben und Vertiefen
Partner pages	Aufgaben für Partnerarbeit
More ideas	Weitere Redemittel für einige Übungen
Fast finishers	Weitere Aufgaben
Wordbank	Zusätzliche Wörter zu bestimmten Themen
Text file / TF	Interessante Texte, passend zu den Units 1 bis 5
Language file / LF	Zusammenfassung wichtiger Sprachregeln
Skills file / SF	Beschreibung wichtiger Lern- und Arbeitstechniken
Vocabulary	Wörterverzeichnis zum Lernen der neuen Wörter
Dictionary	Alphabetisches Wörterverzeichnis zum Nachschlagen (*English-German* und *German-English*)

Die Units bestehen aus diesen Teilen:

W & P Words and pictures	Einstieg in die neue Unit
Text 1 / Text 2	Neue Texte und Themen mit vielen Aktivitäten und Übungen
Introduction 1 / Introduction 2	Texte und Aufgaben zum Entdecken von Regeln und Üben wichtiger Strukturen
Skills training	Listening – Reading – Speaking – Writing – Mediation – Viewing
Study skills	Lern- und Arbeitsmethoden
YOUR CHECK	Lernfortschritt feststellen
YOUR TASK	Gelerntes kreativ anwenden

In den Units findest du diese Symbole:

	Partnerarbeit
	Gruppenarbeit
	Text auf CD und MP3
VIEWING	Filmclip auf DVD
More ideas → *p. 119*	Zu dieser Übung findest du unterstützende Redemittel im Anhang.
	Frage deinen Lehrer / deine Lehrerin nach einer Kopiervorlage.
Fast finishers 2 → *p. 124*	Nachdem diese Übung erarbeitet wurde, gibt es eine zusätzliche Übung im Anhang.
WB 1-2, p. 8	Auf dieser Seite im Workbook findest du passgenaue Übungen zur Schülerbuchseite.

Verweise in den Units:
LF = Language file
SF = Skills file
TF = Text file
WB = Workbook

Für deine Arbeit mit den Units ist außerdem wichtig:

- Am Anfang jeder Unit findest du auf der rechten Seite eine Liste mit Lernzielen. So weißt du, was du nach dieser Unit auf Englisch kannst.
- Unten auf den Unit-Seiten findest du Sätze mit einem grünen Häkchen. Sie zeigen dir, was du nach der Erarbeitung dieser Seite kannst.

Unit 1 – Away at school

	Thema	Kompetenzen	Sprachliche Mittel
8	W & P **Away at school**	Ein britisches Internat kennen lernen und darüber sprechen *The most famous school:* Filmszenen über ein Internat verstehen	Wortfeld *school activities*
10	TEXT 1 **Boarding school life**	Britische und deutsche Internate vergleichen Informationen in einem Brief verstehen und mit Informationen aus einem Hörtext vergleichen Seine Meinung zu den Vor- und Nachteilen des Internatslebens äußern	persönliche Meinungsäußerung *verbs with two objects*
12	INTRODUCTION 1 **People and places**	Menschen und Orte beschreiben	*relative pronouns* *who, which, that, whose, where* *Revision: present tenses*
14	SKILLS TRAINING **Starting and finishing a conversation**	Unterhaltungen angemessen beginnen und beenden	Wortfeld *starting and finishing a conversation*
15	**Filling in forms**	Ein Formular ausfüllen	*Instructions in an application form*
16	INTRODUCTION 2 **We're all different**	Etwas über ein geflüchtetes Mädchen erfahren Über multikulturelle Schulen sprechen *The school that turned Chinese:* Filmszenen zu einem britischen Schulexperiment verstehen und seine Meinung dazu äußern	*contact clauses*
18	STUDY SKILLS **Paraphrasing**	Unbekannte oder vergessene Wörter umschreiben	*It's a type of sport that you play ...*
19	SKILLS TRAINING **At the school shop**	Informationen in einem Laden höflich vermitteln	*polite phrases* *Could I have ...?*
20	TEXT 2 **A strange code**	Einen authentischen Auszug aus einem Jugendroman verstehen Informationen zu einer Person sammeln Über Hintergründe spekulieren	unbekannten Wortschatz erschließen
22	YOUR CHECK	Sprachliche und methodische Lernfortschritte prüfen und üben	
23	YOUR TASK	Sein Wunsch-Internat beschreiben und präsentieren	

Unit 2 – Jesse's world

	Thema	Kompetenzen	Sprachliche Mittel
24	W & P **Jesse's world**	Über seinen Alltag und das Hobby Musik sprechen Freizeitbeschäftigungen in den USA und D vergleichen	Wortfeld *daily activities*
26	TEXT 1 **Superheroes**	Einen Artikel über Superhelden verstehen und seine Meinung zu Superhelden äußern Einen Superhelden beschreiben Wortbildungsgesetze anwenden	Vergleiche mit *like* Vorsilbe *super-* Wortfeld *describing people*
28	INTRODUCTION 1 **How to be super**	Ein Wiki verstehen und verfassen Beschreiben, wie etwas gemacht wird	*adverbs of manner*
30	SKILLS TRAINING **The Red Thunder**	*The Red Thunder:* Szenen eines Superhelden-Films vorhersagen und verstehen	Wortfeld *film phrases*
31	**A scene in a film script**	Einen Drehbuchauszug verstehen Eine Filmszene verfassen	Wortfeld *parts of a script*
32	INTRODUCTION 2 **Doing chores**	Sagen, wie man zu Hause hilft Regeln, die zu Hause gelten, diskutieren Eine Klassenumfrage durchführen	Wortfeld *jobs at home* *modal verbs* *(don't) have to / must(n't) / needn't*

	Thema	Kompetenzen	Sprachliche Mittel
34	STUDY SKILLS **Taking notes**	Über *potluck dinner* reden Beim Telefonieren nachfragen und sich Notizen machen	Wortfeld *American food* *What time ...? / What do we have to ...?*
35	SKILLS TRAINING **Asking for information**	Textnachrichten verstehen, aufnehmen und sich auf eine gemeinsame Unternehmung einigen	*Can you repeat that, please?*
36	TEXT 2 **Mo's bow ties**	Einen Artikel über einen jungen Unternehmer verstehen Sich über Mo und seine Ratschläge austauschen *Mo can tie a bow:* Handlungsorte in einem Film benennen und seine Meinung zum Film und zum Thema Mode äußern	Wortfeld *business words*
38	YOUR CHECK	Sprachliche und methodische Lernfortschritte prüfen und üben	
39	YOUR TASK	Eine Filmszene schreiben, präsentieren und dazu Feedback bekommen	

40	*REVISION 1	Üben und Vertiefen	*Use of English:* sich als Gastschüler verständigen *Vocabulary: going to the cinema, chores*

Unit 3 – People of Britain

	Thema	Kompetenzen	Sprachliche Mittel
42	W & P **People of Britain**	Wissen über Großbritannien teilen Informationen über die britische Geschichte einordnen	Wortfeld *history* *The Vikings came to ... and built ...*
44	TEXT 1 **The Romans and Vikings in Britain**	*The Romans in Britain:* ein Quiz zu den Römern in Großbritannien mithilfe eines Films lösen Sich mit der Geschichte der Stadt York beschäftigen Notizen machen und Informationen präsentieren	Wortfeld *materials* *leather/linen/metal/...*
46	INTRODUCTION 1 **Vikings in York today**	Den Inhalt einer Museumsbroschüre verstehen Von Museumsbesuchen und Festivals erzählen	*Revision past tenses (simple past, past progressive, present perfect)*
48	SKILLS TRAINING **Writing a story**	Verstehen, was einen Text interessant macht Eine Bildergeschichte erzählen	*linking words: although/because/ but/ so that /until/...*
49	**Expressing opinions and feelings**	Seine Meinung zum Ausdruck bringen, zustimmen und widersprechen	Wortfeld *expressing opinions and feelings*
50	INTRODUCTION 2 **People in Britain today**	Informationen verstehen und überprüfen Fragen beantworten und Smalltalk halten Mehr über andere Schüler/innen herausfinden	*question tags* *aren't you? / don't you? / did we?*
52	STUDY SKILLS **Giving a short talk**	*Two short talks:* Erkennen, was einen guten Vortrag ausmacht Einen Vortrag vorbereiten und halten	*phrases to give a talk:* *I'd like to talk about ...* *Do you have any questions?*
53	SKILLS TRAINING **Mediation: The British royal family**	Mithilfe von Notizen Informationen über die königliche Familie sinngemäß auf Deutsch wiedergeben	*talking about famous people*
54	TEXT 2 **Time Flyer**	Einen Auszug aus einer Lektüre verstehen Eine Mindmap über die Charaktere erstellen Eine Geschichte weitererzählen	persönliche Meinungsäußerung *In my opinion, ...*
56	YOUR CHECK	Sprachliche und methodische Lernfortschritte prüfen und üben	
57	YOUR TASK	Eine Zeitkapsel für die Zukunft planen und füllen	

*Fakultativ

INHALT

Unit 4 – Irish stories

	Thema	Kompetenzen	Sprachliche Mittel
58	W & P **Irish stories**	Irland und seine Besonderheiten entdecken *A tour of Dublin:* Filmszenen über Dublin verstehen Irische Traditionen kennenlernen	Wortfeld *Ireland*
60	TEXT 1 **Leaving Ireland**	Einen Artikel über die große Hungersnot und die Emigration nach Nordamerika verstehen Unterschiedliche Lesestrategien anwenden Zahlen wiederholen und eine Infografik erstellen Wortmuster üben und vertiefen	Wortfeld *numbers* *Word patterns: chunks with verb + to-infinitive* *The ship managed to take … / I'd like to do … / …*
62	INTRODUCTION 1 **Two countries, one history**	Ausdrücken, was früher geschehen war Sich mit der irischen Geschichte befassen	*past perfect*
64	SKILLS TRAINING **Asking for and giving directions**	Nach dem Weg fragen und Wegbeschreibungen geben	Wortfeld *giving directions* *Excuse me, how do I get to … / Go straight. / Walk across …*
65	**Helping tourists**	Touristen helfen, sich zurechtzufinden	Wortfeld *helping tourists*
66	INTRODUCTION 2 **Tips for tourists in Ireland**	Etwas über eine typische irische Stadt und Kobolde erfahren Sagen, was passiert, wenn … Ein Rezept verstehen und irisches Brot backen	*if-sentences type 0 / type 1* Wortfeld *in the kitchen* *bake / bowl / teaspoon / …*
68	STUDY SKILLS **Understanding body language**	Körpersprache verstehen	Wortfeld *body language* *tap your fingers / shrug / frown / …*
69	SKILLS TRAINING **Viewing**	*Yu Ming is ainm dom*: einen Film über einen chinesischen Jungen in Irland verstehen	Wortfeld *feelings*
70	TEXT 2 **It's a tech thing**	Eine Geschichte über das Engagement eines irischen Mädchens verstehen Sich mit der eigenen Haltung zum Thema moderne Technologien auseinandersetzen	Wortfeld *technology* *Word patterns: chunks with verb + ing-form* *Keela started coding …*
72	YOUR CHECK	Sprachliche und methodische Lernfortschritte prüfen und üben	
73	YOUR TASK	Einen Aspekt Irlands für eine Gruppenpräsentation vertiefen	
74	*REVISION 2	Üben und Vertiefen Notizen machen	*Use of English:* einen Artikel vervollständigen *Vocabulary: museums, holidays, directions*

Unit 5 – It's my life

	Thema	Kompetenzen	Sprachliche Mittel
76	W & P **It's my life**	Herausfinden, welche Interessen drei Freunde teilen und mit den eigenen Hobbys vergleichen Diskutieren, was einen glücklich macht Unterschiede zwischen offline- und online-Freunden benennen	Wortfeld *interests and activities* *I like cooking.* Wortfeld *friendship* *I can tell my online friends things …*
78	TEXT 1 **Video stars**	Über Lieblingsvideos im Internet sprechen Einen Artikel verstehen und mithilfe des Kontextes vervollständigen Wortbildung: Zusammensetzungen Das Profil eines Internet-Stars erstellen	Wortfeld *internet videos* *compound nouns*
80	INTRODUCTION 1 **Social media and other interests**	Berichten, was neulich oder gerade geschehen ist und bis jetzt andauert	*the present perfect progressive with for and since*
82	SKILLS TRAINING **Explaining games**	Über Lieblingsspiele sprechen, Spielregeln verstehen und diese auf Deutsch erklären	Wortfeld *games*

	Thema	Kompetenzen	Sprachliche Mittel
83	**Understanding opinions**	*Coach:* wesentliche Filmszenen und unterschiedliche Meinungen verstehen	sich in andere hineinversetzen *In David's shoes, I'd ...*
84	INTRODUCTION 2 **If I were you**	Ratschläge verstehen und erteilen	*if-sentences type 2* *If I were you, ...*
86	STUDY SKILLS **Understanding and learning words**	Unbekannten Wortschatz erschließen Elektronische Nachschlagewerke und Vokabeltrainer-Apps nutzen	Wortfeld *skateboarding*
87	SKILLS TRAINING **A letter to me**	Einen Brief verstehen Einen eigenen Brief verfassen Eigene Texte überprüfen und korrigieren	*Dear ... / Love ...*
88	TEXT 2 **Girl Online**	Einen authentischen Romanauszug verstehen Die Hauptperson des Textes beschreiben Einen Kommentar zum Thema Mobbing verfassen	Wortfeld *adjectives to describe people*
90	YOUR CHECK	Sprachliche und methodische Lernfortschritte prüfen und üben	
91	YOUR TASK	Webpages für ein Jugendmagazin schreiben und gestalten	

ANHÄNGE

92 PARTNER PAGES (UNITS 1–5)

97 MORE IDEAS (UNITS 1–5)

104 *FAST FINISHERS (UNITS 1–5)

109 *WORDBANK 1–7

116 *TEXT FILE

116 TF 1 STORY A school trip (Unit 1)
118 TF 2 POEM The Ant-Eater (Unit 2)
120 TF 3 COMIC The Bridge of Swords (Unit 3)
125 TF 4 LEGENDS Scary fairies (Unit 4)
127 TF 5 SONG Mama said (Unit 5)

128 LANGUAGE FILE

128 LF 1 Relative clauses
129 LF 2 Revision: The simple present and the present progressive
130 LF 3 Contact clauses
131 LF 4 Adverbs of manner
132 LF 5 *must – (to) have to*
134 LF 6 Revision: The simple past
134 LF 7 Revision: The past progressive
135 LF 8 Revision: The present perfect
137 LF 9 Question tags
139 LF 10 The past perfect
140 LF 11 Revision: The *will*-future
140 LF 12 *If*-sentences (1)
141 LF 13 The present perfect progressive
143 LF 14 The present perfect and the present perfect progressive
143 LF 15 *If*-sentences (2)

144 Grammatical terms

146 SKILLS FILE

146 SF 1 Learning words
147 SF 2 Understanding new words
148 SF 3 Using an online dictionary
149 SF 4 Doing (internet) research
150 SF 5 Listening
151 SF 6 Reading a text
152 SF 7 Marking up a text and note-taking
153 SF 8 Filling in forms
154 SF 9 How to write good texts
156 SF 10 Writing an email / a letter
157 SF 11 Being polite
158 SF 12 Expressing opinions and feelings
159 SF 13 Giving a talk
160 SF 14 Paraphrasing
160 SF 15 Describing pictures
161 SF 16 Mediation
162 SF 17 Doing better in tests
164 SF 18 Working with charts and diagrams
165 SF 19 Viewing

166 VOCABULARY

194 DICTIONARY ENGLISH–GERMAN

219 DICTIONARY GERMAN–ENGLISH

242 SOUNDS & ALPHABET

243 COUNTRIES AND CONTINENTS

244 IRREGULAR VERBS

246 LIST OF NAMES / ENGLISH-SPEAKING COUNTRIES

248 CLASSROOM ENGLISH

250 Answers to YOUR CHECK

256 QUELLENVERZEICHNIS

*Fakultativ

Unit 1 Away at school

Victoria School

– one of the UK's best boarding schools

1

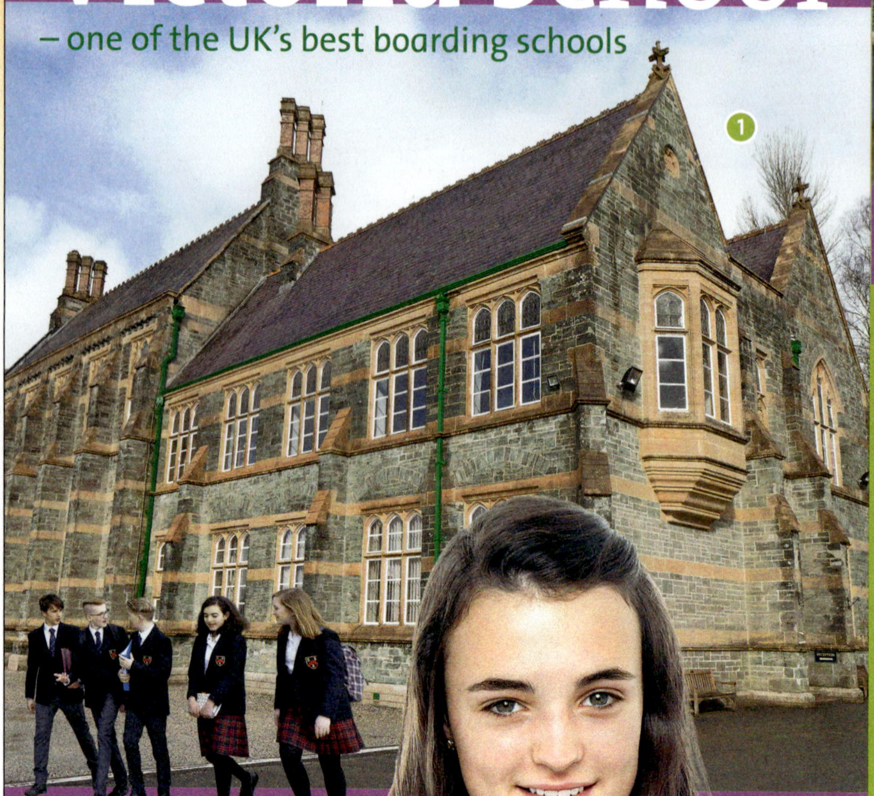

2

Our boarders love spending their free time together.

3

Some of our activities this year

- *Chinese*
- *Choir*
- *Coding*
- *Drama*
- *Fencing*
- *Knitting*
- *Orchestra*
- *Self-defence*
- *Sign language*
- *Yoga*

Ella Stephens, year 7

The bedrooms in the boarding houses are for two roommates.

Lacrosse – one of our traditional sports. Our school has great sports facilities!

In this unit you'll learn to
- talk about different types of schools.
- describe people, places and things.
- start and finish conversations.
- fill in forms.

➔ At the end of the unit you'll present your dream school.

1 LISTENING A new boarding school

a **Look at the pictures of a boarding school in England. Think about these questions, make notes and then share your ideas with a partner.**

1 How is a boarding school different to other schools?
2 What do students do at a boarding school?
3 What do you think boarding schools are like?

1.1 **b** **Listen to the school principal and to Ella. Complete the sentences and say why.**

I find the school *interesting / fun / hard / ...* because ...
I think Ella sounds *nervous / nice / happy / ...*

1.1 **c** **Listen again and complete the information.**

Another great school year at Victoria School!
New activities: Chinese, ... , ...
Sports facilities: ..., tennis courts, ..., playing fields
New arts centre: theatre for ... and ..., new ...
Wi-Fi: where: ..., when: ...
Ella Stephens
New student in year ...; boarder in Wilton House
Age: ... From: ... Why here: ...
Favourite subjects: ... Hobbies: ...

2 VIEWING The most famous school

Fara

James

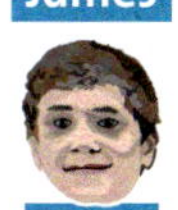
Theo

a **Fara, James and Theo have started at Eton, a famous boarding school for boys.**
Partner B: Look at page 92.
Partner A: Watch the video and take notes.
What do you find out about:
getting up • chapel • exams • snacks

b **Tell Partner B what you found out.**

c **Watch the film again. Then talk to your partner.**
What do James and Fara think about Eton?
And you? Would you like to go to a boarding school? Why (not)? SF 19 → p. 165

➔ I can give my opinion about boarding schools. ✔

Boarding school life

1 LISTENING A Skype call from Africa

1.2 **a** **Listen to Ella and her mum. What does Ella say? Choose the right answers.**

1. She's made *lots of / no* friends.
2. There are *lots of / not too many* rules.
3. She gets up *earlier / later* than at home.
4. Lacrosse is *strange / fun*.
5. The food is *very / not very* good.
6. She's always careful not to eat *nuts / eggs*.
7. She *is / isn't* homesick.
8. She *has been / hasn't been* worried about her parents.

ACROSS CULTURES

Compare the information about the UK and Germany.

UK
- 9.5 %
- 1 %

Germany
- 10.2 %
- 0.75 %

private schools — boarding schools

Price of boarding schools for a year:

£ 20,000–30,000 — € 4,800–14,400

b **How do Ella's mum and dad feel about living in Africa? What are their jobs there?**

2 Ella's letter

a **Do you ever send letters? If yes, go to the back of the class. Talk about who to and why. If no, go to the front of the class. Talk about why not.**

b **Look at the picture. Why do you think Ella is writing a letter and not an online message?**

c **Now read Ella's letter to her best friend Riya in London. What Ella tells Riya is different to what she told her mum. How?**

Ella tells her mum that everything is … But she tells Riya that … Fast Finishers 1 → p. 104

Dear Riya
Thanks for your message! I miss you and all our friends from home.
I'm sending you a letter because we can only use Wi-Fi sometimes in my boarding house. I'm writing this at night with a torch!
You asked if the school is like Hogwarts. Well, we don't play Quidditch, but we do some sports that I've never done before – like lacrosse. It's a strange sport which you play with nets on sticks! The school food is good too, but it doesn't appear by magic – and I miss my dad's curries, and takeaway pizza ☺. There's a school shop where you can buy sweets, but you can't buy chocolate frogs. And the uniform isn't as cool as at Hogwarts!
I've made lots of friends here. Roxy, the girl who shares my room, is showing me the school. It's nice to have a roommate, but I miss my own room at home where I can read and be alone. I miss my mum and dad too. Maybe everybody is homesick in the beginning and then it goes away.
There are lots of rules here. We also have to get up early at weekends – and you know I like to stay in bed until 12 o'clock! They give us a lot of homework too. I've written my school day for you – what do you think?
I must sleep now. Say hi to everyone at school from me! But don't say I'm homesick – that's our secret. Ok?
Love Ella xx

7.00	wake-up time (a very loud bell!)
7.30	breakfast (8.30 at weekends!)
8.30	morning lessons start
12.30	lunch in dining room (hot food)
13.15	afternoon lessons
15.30	end of lessons, snack time (cake and sandwiches)
16.00	sports and activities
18.00	dinner – hot food again
18.45	homework for 1.5 hours, then free time
21.30	get ready for bed
22.00	bedtime (lights out)

3 What do you think?

Talk about the questions.

More ideas → p. 97

1 Ella told her parents some lies. Why? Was she right to do that?

> I think Ella told her parents some lies because ...

2 Ella is homesick, but she tells Riya to keep it a secret. Why?

> She doesn't want her friends to ...

3 What do you think about Ella's school day? Compare it to your day.
I get up earlier than Ella, at 6 o'clock / at 6.30 am.

4 For and against

a **Think:** Collect your notes about boarding schools from 1 and 2 on p. 9. Read Ella's letter and timetable again and add more information about boarding schools.

b **Pair:** Look at your notes. Put your information into two lists: the advantages of boarding schools (for) and the disadvantages (against). Then decide on the three most important things in each list.

c **Share:** Discuss your lists. Explain why you chose your top three in each list. Do you all have the same top three?

5 Class opinions

a Make a line on the floor of the classroom. Then stick a piece of paper at each end with these sentences:
Boarding schools are good for students.
Boarding schools are bad for students.

b Stand on the line according to your opinion. Tell your class why you are standing there.

People and places

1.3 1 At the drama club

Read the conversation between Ella and her roommate Roxy. Find Tara, Nikolai and Harry in the picture.

Roxy: The drama club is very popular. This is the new school theatre where the drama club is going to meet now. Our play is *Romeo and Juliet* this year.

Ella: Great! I love the film – not the old film which has Claire Danes in it, the new film with ... er, the girl whose name I always forget!

Roxy: You mean Hailee Steinfeld. Yeah, she's good. In our play Tara is Juliet. Tara's the girl who has curly brown hair. She's standing near Nikolai – you know, the tall Russian boy that is in our year.

Ella: And who's Romeo in the play?

Roxy: That's Harry – the blond boy with the glasses and the hair that looks really cool. Don't worry – you'll know everybody's names soon.

LOOK AT LANGUAGE: relative clauses

Look at the words *who, which, that, where* and *whose* in 1 and 2. These are relative pronouns. Complete the rules.

Relative clauses describe people, things and places.
We use ... or ... for people.
We use ... when things or people belong together.
We use ... or ... for things.
We use ... for places.

LF 1 → p. 128

2 Who is it? What is it?

Match the two parts of the sentences to describe the drama club and the students.

1 Roxy is the student
2 The drama club is one of the clubs
3 The new theatre is the place
4 *Romeo and Juliet* is a play
5 Tara is the girl
6 Nikolai is the boy in year 7
7 Harry is the boy
8 Hailee Steinfeld was in a film

a which is about a famous love story.
b who is from Russia.
c who has glasses.
d that are very popular with students.
e that tells the *Romeo and Juliet* story.
f whose hair is very long and curly.
g who shares a room with Ella.
h where the drama club is going to meet.

3 Romeo and Juliet

a Complete the description of the story with *who, which, whose* or *where.*

Romeo Montague and Juliet Capulet are two young people (1) … live in Verona, Italy and (2) … families are old enemies. The Capulets plan a party for Juliet and a rich man (3) … wants to marry her. Romeo goes to the party (4) … he meets Juliet. The next day they marry in secret. Romeo leaves Verona after he was in a fight (5) … goes wrong. Later he hears that Juliet is dead and kills himself. But the story (6) … Romeo heard wasn't true. When Juliet finds Romeo dead, she kills herself too.

b Look at the pronouns in a again. Where can you use *that*?

4 Describing people

a Read the box and complete the sentences with the correct form of the verb. Which boy in the photo is Alex?

LOOK AT LANGUAGE: present tenses (revision)

We use the **simple present** for regular activities and unchanging situations. We use the **present progressive** for activities now and describing pictures. LF 2 → p. 129

Alex is the boy who …

1 often (talk) in a loud voice.
2 usually (wear) a red hoodie.
3 (wear) a grey hoodie today.
4 (smile) in this photo.
5 (not like) dancing.
6 (not wear) his glasses in this photo.

b Think of famous people or people in books and films.
horrible teacher, Harry Potter films, long black hair Wordbank 1 → p. 109

c Tell your partner about the person. Does your partner know his or her name?
A *It's the horrible teacher in the Harry Potter films who has long black hair.*
B *That's easy! It's … / I don't know. Can you give me more information, please?*

5 Great people and places

a **Think:** Make notes about two great people and one great place and why you like them. **Pair:** Tell your partner.
Niklas Süle is a great football player who is very tall.
My neighbour tells funny jokes that always make me laugh.
My grandparents' house is the place where I go every summer.
More ideas → p. 97 SF 7 → p. 152

people: coach • neighbour • person in your family • famous person • …

places: cinema • park • pool • stadium • zoo • …

b **Share:** Tell the class. Then write sentences and put them in My file.

→ I can describe people, places and things. ✔

Starting and finishing a conversation

1.4

1 LISTENING At school

a Listen to two conversations at Ella's school and do the tasks.

1 Match the students with a description. There are two extra descriptions.

1 Ella and Lucy	are roommates.
2 Landon and Ella	don't know each other.
3 Landon and Roxy	are relatives.
	are classmates.
	are boyfriend and girlfriend.

2 What do the students talk about in the conversations? Choose four topics.

being ill • food • tests • teachers • out-of-school activities • homework • sport

b Listen again. Copy and complete the phrases in the phrase box. SF 5 → p. 150

2 SPEAKING Your conversation

a Partner A: Choose situation 1 or 2 and start a conversation. Use the phrases in the box. SF 11 → p. 157

1 You're in a shop. You see a friend from your sports club.

2 You see a friend of a friend in town. You think you remember the person's name, but the person doesn't remember you.

b Partner B: Choose the other situation and start a conversation.

c Find a new partner and have a new conversation: You're at a concert or a sports match and your partner is sitting next to you.

PHRASE BOX

Say hello
Hey / Hi / Hello.
You're Roxy, ...?
How do you ... *(Roxy)*?

Ask how somebody is
How is ...?
What's ...?
How ...?

Check names
Sorry, I didn't get ...
Can you say ...?

Say goodbye
Sorry, I need to ...
See you t...
Say hi ... *(Liam)*.
... to meet you.
See you l...

I can start and finish a conversation. ✔

Filling in forms

1 The Fencing Club
Ella filled in a form for the Fencing Club at school. Look at the form. Which two instructions didn't Ella follow?

The Fencing Club
Application form

Please write clearly. Use CAPITALS for part A.

PART A

First name *Ella*

Last name *Stephens*

Date of birth *01.10.2*

Gender male ☐ female ☐ unspecified ☐

Contact information

Mobile

Name and mobile of parent or guardian
Chris Stephens (father)

PART B

Reasons for joining the club
I love trying new sports, and fencing sounds very exciting. I think you need to be very fast and think a lot when you do this sport. I'm also looking forward to making some new friends in the club.

Other information
I have no health problems and I am very fit. I play basketball and do gymnastics.

Signature (full name)
Ella

Signature of parent or guardian
C.W. Stephens

2 WORDS Look at the form again. Which words or phrases mean:

1 when you were born
2 if you are a man/boy or woman/girl
3 address or phone number or email address
4 a person who looks after you (but isn't your mother or father)
5 your name in your writing

3 Your application form

a You want to join an English club outside school where you can practise the language and learn about the UK. Fill in the form. SF 8 → p. 153

> Read the form carefully.
> Check you understand the instructions.
> Check you understand the language in the form.

b CHECK Give your form to your partner. Your partner checks it and says what could be better.

> Has he/she filled in everything?
> Has he/she followed the instructions?
> Has he/she given good reasons?
> Has he/she used the right spelling?

c Correct your form.

We're all different

1 Jumana's story

At Ella's last school in London, there were lots of students from different cultures. Jumana was a refugee from Syria. Read her story and answer the questions.

1 Why did Jumana leave her country?
2 How long did it take her to get to the UK?
3 What problems did she have in the beginning?
4 How do you feel when you read Jumana's story?

ACROSS CULTURES

In British schools there are students from many different cultures. People have come to Britain as immigrants from countries like India, Bangladesh and Pakistan, the Caribbean, Kenya and Europe. Some have also come as refugees from countries like Iraq and Afghanistan. In some London schools, two thirds of the students have a first language which is not English. What about German schools?

I came here from Syria when I was eleven. The government killed my father, and my mother and I wanted to live in a country that is safe. We left family and friends we will never see again. It took five months to get to the UK. We walked and travelled by boat and by lorry. We nearly froze in the food lorry which took us through the Channel Tunnel.

It was hard to come to a country which I didn't know. In the beginning it was hard to learn English and to make friends but now I'm happy at my school. I don't talk about the bad things that I saw in Syria and on the journey as a refugee. I can't forget them, but I want to enjoy the new life I have here.

LOOK AT LANGUAGE: relative clauses without a relative pronoun (contact clauses)

a **The relative pronoun can be the subject or the object of a sentence. Look at these sentences from Jumana's story. A subject pronoun comes directly before the verb.**

My mother and I wanted to live in a country **that** (subject) **is** (verb) safe.

I don't talk about the bad things **that** (object) **I** (subject) **saw** (verb).

Find one more sentence with a subject pronoun and one with an object pronoun in her story.

b **Now look at these sentences. The relative pronoun is missing. Write it in the right place. Is it the subject or the object of the relative clause?**

We left family and friends we will never see again. I want to enjoy the new life I have here.

c **Choose the correct word for the rule:**

We can leave out the relative pronoun when it is the subject / object of the relative clause.

LF 3 → p. 130

2 At a London school

Read what students in the London school say. Decide which pronouns you can leave out.

3 An interview at a London school

Match the sentence parts and add a relative pronoun if you need it.

1	We learn about different countries and the people	a	we don't usually celebrate.
2	We eat amazing food	b	we don't speak.
3	We listen to bands	c	come from different places.
4	We learn some words from languages	d	live there.
5	We make friends with students	e	play different types of music.
6	We go to festivals	f	we've never tried before.

Fast Finishers 2 → p. 104

4 VIEWING The school that turned Chinese

a Watch the video (until 2:09) and complete the notes. SF 19 → p. 165

Where? *... School, Hampshire*
How long? *For one ...*
Who? *... students in year ...*
What? *Lessons with ...*
Why? *British students will be in competition with ... in the future.*
Exams *in ..., ... and Mandarin*

b Watch the whole video. Which of these things change in Chinese school? Write the correct letters in your exercise book. If you can, add information for each point.

a way of teaching b school books c school uniform d assembly/start of school day e lunch

1.5 c Now listen and find out what happened. How did the students do in their exams? Are you surprised by the results? Is this a good way of learning for you?

I can describe different classes and students. ✔ WB 1-2, p. 9

Paraphrasing

'Paraphrasing' means explaining words when you don't know (or have forgotten) an English word or phrase.

1.6 1 SOUNDS & STRESS Useful phrases

When you don't know a word, don't stop talking – use one of these phrases.
Listen to them, then listen again and repeat.

What's the word?
How do you say it?
I've forgotten the word.
I don't know the English word.
Just a minute ...
Let me think ...

2 Umbrella words

Remember: you can use an umbrella word when you have forgotten a word: *It's a type of ...*
What are the umbrella words for these things? Copy and complete the umbrella pictures.

SPORT	?	?	?	?
lacrosse fencing	lunch dinner	gym swimming pool	English Arabic	Syria Italy

3 More information

a Sometimes umbrella words don't give enough information. You can add more specific information with relative clauses. For example:
It's a type of sport ***that you play with a ball and sticks that have a net on them.***
Can you think of other descriptions for lacrosse? Find as many as you can in the class.
... that you play on / in / with ...
... that ... usually play.

b Write one or more explanations for each word.

boarder • choir • lorry • male • nut • refugee

c Compare your explanations.

4 GAME What's the word?

1.7 a You're going to play a game in two teams. First listen to Ella's class playing the game. Say the right words.

b Now play the game in your class. One person from each team sits in front of the board. The rest of the team explains the word on the board.

Step by step: paraphrasing
- Say you don't know a word.
- Think of the umbrella word.
- Add more information.

SF 14 → p. 160

→ I can explain words that I don't know in English. ✔

At the school shop

1 MEDIATION Help another student

a You're on a language course in England. You visit a school and buy sweets in the school shop. Another German student is too shy to speak and asks you for help. Complete the conversation.

b Practise the conversation with two partners.

Remember: paraphrase when you don't know a word (see p. 18).

Student:	Kannst du etwas für mich kaufen?
You:	Klar. Was hättest du gern?
Student:	Fünf von den Colaflaschen bitte und fünf von den Schnullern.
You:	*Hello. Could my friend have five ... and ..., please.*
Assistant:	Ah, you mean the dummies. Here you are.
Student:	Kannst du fragen, was die weißen Dinger in dem Glas links sind?
You:	*Ok. What are ...?*
Assistant:	They're fish and chips.
Student:	Schmecken die auch nach *fish and chips?*
You:	*Do they ...?*
Assistant:	Oh no, they're just white chocolate.
Student:	Sind da Nüsse drin? Ich darf keine Nüsse essen.
You:	...
Assistant:	Oh no, there are no nuts. We're very careful about that.
Student:	Also, dann nehme ich 100 Gramm von denen und auch 100 Gramm von den Schokoladendingern mit den bunten Krümeln.
You:	...
Assistant:	Here you are. That's six pounds twenty, please.

SF 16 → p. 161

2 SPEAKING Your sweets

a Work with a partner.
Partner A: Ask for the sweets that you want.
Partner B: You're the shop assistant.

b Swap roles.

Fast Finishers 3 → p. 104
SF 11 → p. 157

ACROSS CULTURES

Remember: it's important to be polite in English. Use *Could I have ...?* or *I'd like ...* (**not** *I want*). Say *please* and *thank you*.

I can help other students at school. ✔

A strange code *(by Lauren Child)*

1 Ruby Redfort

a The *Ruby Redfort* books are Ella's favourite books. Look at the book cover and the file.
What type of books do you think these are? Why?

RUBY REDFORT

age:	13
lives in:	Twinford, USA
description:	very clever, independent
likes:	writing in notebooks (she has 622), codes
favourite clothes:	jeans and T-shirts with slogans
best friend:	Clancy Crew (very clever, he's bad at French, but good at codes and keeping secrets)
worst enemy:	Vapona Begwell (the school bully)

b Read the story. Was your answer in 1a correct? Explain why.

It was the usual school day at Twinford Junior High. Ruby had the usual conversation with her enemy Vapona Begwell:

VAPONA: *Hey Ruby, can you see out of those glasses? Don't look in the mirror if you don't want to get scared.*

RUBY: *Why, you gonna be standing behind me?*

There was an interesting geography lesson followed by a boring French class (Ruby's French was so good that she spent the lesson reading a book in Russian). [...]

At lunch Ruby got into an argument with her teacher Mrs Arthur over the T-shirt she was wearing. Mrs Arthur told Ruby to turn her T-shirt inside out or get a month of detention.

Ruby said goodbye to Clancy who had to take his French vocab test again. 'You'll be fine, Clance,' said Ruby. 'Copy this list onto your arm and you'll have no problem.'
The piece of paper had all the test answers in their code. To the person on the street it just looked like gobbledygook.

Yes, everything was normal. Things only started to get strange when Ruby got home.

The front door to the house was standing open and a police car was in the drive. As she walked upstairs to the kitchen, she could hear the voice of Sheriff Bridges. *Now what is he doing here?* It didn't take Ruby long to find the answer. She stood in the living room with her mouth open.
Everything was gone. Well, nearly everything. The phone was still plugged in and was sitting on the floor. The rest of the house was empty.
'Yes,' said her mother Sabina. 'Every room is full of nothing'. [...]

The phone rang. 'It's good that we still have the phone!' said Sabina. 'Answer that please, Ruby.' [...]
'I am looking for Ruby Redfort,' said a voice.
'Well, you found her,' said Ruby.
'Good. So now I've found you, you need to find me.'
'Excuse me?' said Ruby. 'What is this, a quiz?'
'Well,' the voice said, 'somebody told me that you notice everything – but do you notice everything Ruby Red?'
'The name's Ruby Red*fort*', said Ruby.
'As I was saying,' said the voice, 'I hear that you notice the smallest things. I'm sure *you* can see when something is in the wrong place, while everyone else just walks past. You can see that something ordinary could mean something extraordinary. Am I right?'
'I can crack a code,' said Ruby.
'Good,' said the voice, and the line went dead.
'So what's the code?' said Ruby to herself.
[...]

All evening Ruby waited to hear again from the strange caller – but the phone didn't ring. When Ruby went to bed that night, she thought about the conversation.
Who was this strange caller? You want a person to crack a code – so why don't you give that person the code? But then, when it was 4.43 am, Ruby suddenly sat up in bed. Of course! The whole conversation was a code! ◇

2 More about Ruby

Add more information to Ruby's file in 1a.

3 New words in the story

Decide what these words and phrases from the story mean. Check in the dictionary.

1 enemy (line 3)
2 get into an argument (line 13)
3 detention (line 16)
4 gobbledygook (line 23)
5 notice (line 49)
6 crack a code (line 59) SF 2-3 → p. 147f.

4 Normal and strange

a What was normal at school? Complete the sentences.

1 Ruby had a conversation with ...
2 Ruby had a boring ...
3 Ruby had an argument ...
4 Ruby helped ...

b What was strange at home?

1 The police was ...
2 The house ...
3 A strange caller phoned and ...
4 The strange caller didn't ...

5 The strange caller

a Think: Who was the caller? What do you think happened next?
Pair: Discuss ideas. Share: Then tell the class.

I think the caller is ...
- the person who took the family's furniture.
- Vapona Begwell who is playing a trick.
- somebody who is playing a trick
- somebody who knows that Ruby is very clever.
- somebody who wants help from Ruby.

After Ruby understood the conversation was a code, ...
- she told the police.
- she told Clancy / her parents.
- she cracked the code.
- she found the caller.
- she wrote it in her notebook and forgot about it.

1.8 b Listen. Find out who the caller was and why this person phoned Ruby. TF 1 → p. 116f.

Do the tasks and then check your answers on page 250 at the back of the book. Did you get most of the answers right? Well done! Can you do better? Then look at the unit and at the **Vocabulary** and the **Language file** again.

1 Check your vocabulary

a Match the activities with the correct definitions.

1 Self-defence is	a when you fight back to stop others from hurting you.
2 A choir is	b when you write a computer program.
3 Coding is	c a group that plays instruments together.
4 Fencing is	d using your hands to 'talk' to people who can't hear.
5 An orchestra is	e a sport where two people fight.
6 Sign language is	f a group of people who sing together.

b A coach at a club is filling in a form for Roxy.
Complete the speech bubble with the missing words.

So, your (1) ... is female. What's your date of (2) ... ?
I need your (3) ... information. What's your address and phone number?
Do you live with a parent or with a (4) ...?
That's it. Could you please write your (5) ... here?

2 Check your language

Complete the school magazine article with the correct relative pronouns (*who, which, that, where* or *whose*). If two pronouns are correct, write both. If you don't need a relative pronoun, write (–).

Ella is a London girl (1) ... parents are in Africa. She's really enjoying all the activities (2) ... she is doing and she's started two sports (3) ... are new for her. Ella is very happy in Wilton House (4) ... she is a boarder and she loves the room (5) ... she shares with Roxy. Ella would like to say thank you to all the students in Wilton House (6) ... have been very friendly to her.

3 Check your speaking

Put this conversation in the right order.

1 Yes, I am. How do you know Ethan?
2 Sorry, it's Ari.
3 We're in the football team together. I'm Ari.
4 Hi, you're Noah, right? Ethan's brother.
5 Nice to meet you, Ari.
6 Sorry, I didn't get your name. Could you say it again, please?

4 Check your writing

Complete this letter. Use one word for each number.

(1) ... Ella
(2) ... are you? (3) ... for your letter. I'm (4) ..., thanks. Here's some school (5) ...: we have a new (6) ... His name is Mr Planter and he (7) ... history. He's very nice and (8) ... give (9) ... too much homework.
Write (10) ... !
Love Riya

Present your dream boarding school

GET READY

Make groups (4–6 students).
You're going to present your dream boarding school to the class. First brainstorm ideas in your group for these topics.

the school
- type of school (sports / film / technology/...)
- the building (old / new)
- school facilities (Wi-Fi / swimming pool /...)
- activities and sports
- uniform
- dream teachers (famous people /...)

the boarding houses
- facilities in the houses
- the bedrooms

the school day
- wake-up time and bedtime
- start and finish of lessons
- school subjects
- meals (when/what?)
- time for activities and free time
- homework

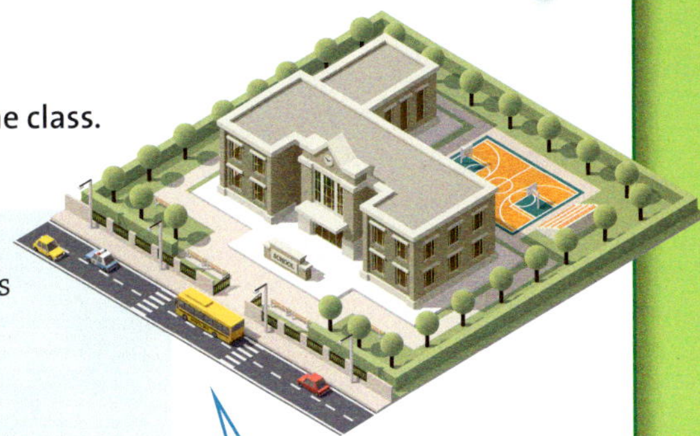

> What about a film school? Our school could have its own cinema which has a big screen and a popcorn machine.

GO AHEAD

In your group, decide if your presentation is a slide or a poster presentation. Decide who is going to present each part.

- Prepare your part. Explain what things should be like and why.
- Make drawings or find photos and pictures.
- Discuss your parts and make slides or a poster.
- Practise your part at home.

FINISH

Your group presents your dream boarding school.

- Say hello to the class and introduce your group.

> Hello everybody. How are you? We're group 4: Mia, Chiara, Moritz and Theo. Our dream boarding school is a film school. All the teachers are actors who have been in famous films and series.

- If you forget a word – paraphrase! (see page 18)
- At the end say why this is your dream school.
- Give feedback on the other groups' schools and ask questions.

> We think your film school is really cool, group 4! We liked the teachers that you chose. We have some questions that we'd like to ask you.
> Can you tell us more about ...?
> Why did you say that ...?
> Can you explain ...?

Unit 2

Jesse's world

In this unit you will

- compare the daily lives of some American teenagers with your own.
- exchange opinions about music, TV and films.
- describe how people do things.
- do a survey of chores at home.
- ask for information and take notes.

At the end of the unit you'll write a scene for a film script.

6

7

1 Jesse's life and activities

Look at the photos. Describe what is important in Jesse's world. Fast Finishers 4 → p. 105

2 LISTENING An interview with Jesse

1.9 **a** **Now listen to Jesse on a music radio programme. Were you right about Jesse's life and activities? What else is important to him?**

1.9 **b** **Listen again. Are the sentences true or false? Correct the false sentences.**

1 Music helps Jesse to relax when he is at home.
2 Jesse thinks that chores are boring without music.
3 Jesse doesn't listen to music when he does homework because he can't concentrate.
4 He likes listening to different types of music.
5 He's very good at playing the guitar.
6 He sings in the choir at church.

c **Think about when and why you play music or listen to it. Then tell your partner.**

ACROSS CULTURES

Describe the graph.
Ask students in your group how many hours they spend on these activities.
Make a graph for your group.
Present your graph and compare with the other groups.

How US school students spend their time each week

	weekdays	weekends
Music, TV, video games, internet, texting	2.3 hours	4.3 hours
Hobbies and meeting friends	1.4 hours	1.9 hours
Playing sports	0.7 hours	0.9 hours

Source: U.S. Department of Health

SF 18 → p. 164

I can discuss and compare students' daily activities. ✔ WB 1-2, p. 17

Superheroes

1.10 **1 American superheroes**

Jesse loves superheroes. Look at the article: which of the superheroes do you know?

Our top American superheroes

Superman and Supergirl

Clark Kent works as a newspaper reporter and wears a suit. But as the superhero Superman, he wears a blue costume and a red cape. He fights against evil and saves the world! Superman is superstrong, can run fast and fly like a bird. His cousin Supergirl (Kara Zor-El) has the same amazing powers, but because she is so young, her powers aren't as strong.

Ms. Marvel

Kamala Khan is a Pakistani-American teenager. She sees the world differently from other people and has problems at school and with her parents. Kamala loves superhero video games, so she's very happy when she becomes Ms. Marvel and can catch the bad guys in real life! Ms. Marvel's costume is a blue and yellow dress over a red T-shirt with a red scarf. To escape from dangerous situations, Ms. Marvel can become bigger or smaller and even change how she looks.

CRASH!

Black Panther

Black Panther is the first black superhero. Prince T'Challa can speak many languages and is an amazing fighter. When he became King of Wakanda, he ate a special food which gave him amazing superpowers: he can see, smell and hear so well that he can see when it's dark, notice when a person's smell changes and hear every noise. He wears a special black suit, black boots and a black face mask, and he has long claws like a cat.

ICEMAN

Iceman is supercool! He can change his whole body into hard ice, so that his enemies can't hurt him and in an emergency he can use water in the air around him to make ice weapons. He can also move very quickly through water. He usually wears a blue suit. In real life Iceman's name is Bobby Drake, he's an accountant and he's the first gay superhero.

POW!

Wonder Woman

In the past Wonder Woman's name was Diana. The young Diana behaved kindly to people and wanted to make peace in the world, but later she became a fighter. Wonder Woman wears a short dress, boots and special bracelets. She carries a magic lasso: when she catches people with it, they must tell the truth. Wonder Woman can speak all languages and understand and talk to animals.

SPLASH!

 WB 1-2, p. 18

2 Six superheroes

Scan the article and complete the information.

Scan (= look at) each paragraph for these points only. SF 6 → p. 151

superhero	real name and life	costume	powers
Superman	Clark Kent, reporter, wears a suit	?	?
...			

3 What do you think?

Discuss the questions.

1 Do you enjoy watching or reading about superheroes? Why (not)?

2 Why do you think superheroes are so popular?

4 WORDS Superpowers

a Complete these phrases from the first two paragraphs.

Superheroes
1 fight against ...
2 save the ...
3 have amazing ...
4 catch the bad ...
5 escape from ...

b Superman flies 'like a bird'. Complete these phrases with your own ideas. Then compare.

1 hear like a ...
2 run like a ...
3 jump like a ...
4 swim like a ...
5 see like a ...
6 fight like a ...

c WORD BUILDING You can add *super* to the start of words (e.g. superhero, supercool). Find five other words with *super* in a dictionary. What types of words are they (adjectives, verbs, nouns, ...)? SF 2-3 → p. 147f.

5 Your hero

a Do real-life heroes exist? How are they the same as or different to superheroes? Discuss.

b Choose A or B.

A Write a short description of your favourite superhero. Look at 2 to help you: think of his/her real name and life, costume and superpowers.

The name of ...
In real life he/she ...
He/She wears ...
He/She can ...

B Write a short description of your real-life hero (someone you know or a famous person). Give reasons for your choice.

My real-life hero is ...
He/She is an amazing/awesome ...
My hero helps/fights for/helped/saved/...
I chose him/her because ...

Philipp Lahm

c Put your description in My file.

→ I can understand and write descriptions. ✓

How to be super

1 How to become a superhero

Read the wiki. Which three tips are the most important?

How to become a superhero

- Think of a good superhero name.
- Buy a suit and a cape or make your own costume. (It should fit comfortably.)
- Quick ideas can save your life, so learn to think quickly!
- Learn to run fast and move quietly.
- Eat healthily – healthy foods make you strong.
- Train hard every day to get fit and become a good fighter.
- Always behave well: never behave badly (even to the really bad guys).

2 GAME Mime it!

Choose one word from each word group. Mime the activity. The class guesses.

– You're smiling crazily.

Right! Now you! / No, sorry, that's wrong.

walk • smile • fight • speak • fly • run • write • eat • jump • laugh • swim • hurt

crazily • clearly • cleverly • loudly • badly • quietly • excitedly • fast • carefully • dangerously • happily

LOOK AT LANGUAGE: adverbs of manner

a **Look at this sentence from the wiki. Answer the questions.**

Quick ideas can save your life: learn to think quickly.

quick is an adjective. What word does it describe? Is it a noun or a verb?

quickly is an adverb. What word does it describe? Is it a noun or a verb?

b **Find the adverbs in 1 for the adjectives in the table. Complete the rules.**

adjective	adverb	adjective	adverb
quick	quickly	healthy	...
quiet	...	comfortable	...
bad	...		

We usually add ... to adjectives to make adverbs. But sometimes the spelling changes:

-y → ...	consonant + le → ...

c **Find the irregular adverbs for these adjectives in 1.**

fast – ... hard – ... good – ...

LF 4 → p. 131

3 Be a superhero!

Correct the mistakes in the descriptions of the superheroes.

1 Supermouth talks very ~~loud~~.
2 Superfish swims very ~~quick~~.
3 Supersmile laughs ~~happy~~.
4 Superturtle does everything ~~slow~~.
5 Superbaby can't talk ~~clear~~.
6 Superbat can see really ~~good~~.

4 How to be a superhero at school

a Complete the wiki. Use the right form of the words in the box.

careful • hard • kind • loud • nice • tidy

Work (1) ...
Do your homework (2) ...
Write (3) ...
Behave (4) ... to the other students.
Don't talk (5) ... in class.
Smile (6) ... at your teacher.

b Add two more instructions.

Fast Finishers 5 → p. 105

5 How to be a ...

a Choose one of the wiki titles in the box or write your own title. Think of some adverbs and make a short wiki like the one in 4.
Behave ..., Talk ..., Listen ..., Don't shout ...

How to be a super brother/sister
How to be a super parent
How to be a super teacher
How to be super friend
How to be a super ...

b Swap wikis. Say if you like your partner's ideas. Are the adverbs correct?

6 Your superhero

a Create your own superhero. Draw a picture and write a description. Remember:
- superhero name / real-life person
- costume and description
- superpowers *(can fly quickly / fight well / ...)*

b WALK AROUND Look at everybody's superheroes. Put a tick (✔) or a sticky dot on the three you like best.

Tam-An Nguyen, Erlangen

I can describe how people do activities. ✔

The Red Thunder

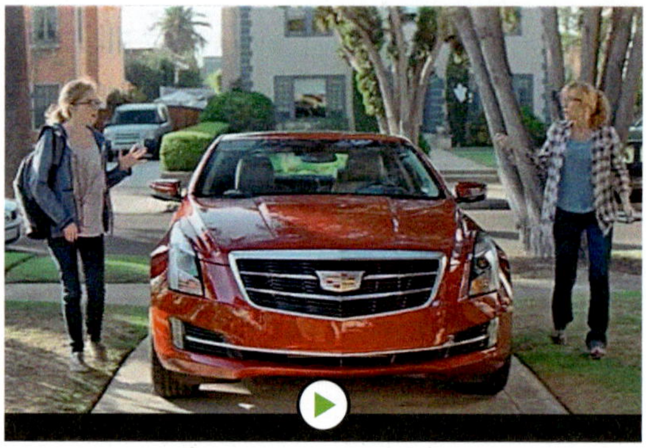

1 The beginning of the film

a Look at the picture. What do you think the mother and daughter are talking or arguing about?

b Read the information. Watch the first part of the film (until 1:59) and complete the information.

The film's setting is (1) ..., one of the most dangerous cities in America. Recently crime is down (2) ... %.
Danny wants to go to (3) ... with Sarah Thun, but somebody stole his car. Sarah has a car, but (4) ... Sarah's mom is a (5) ... who looks after people's feet.
Sarah wants to (6) ..., but her mom says no because (7) ...

SF 19 → p. 165

c How do Sarah and her mother feel at the end of this part?

Watch and listen carefully to **the beginning** of a film and find out information about:
- the place (the setting)
- the people (the characters)
- what the video is about (the plot)

Remember to look at people's faces and body language and listen to their voices.

2 What happens next?

a Watch the second part of the video (until 2:48) and find out:
- what Sarah's mum is doing and what Sarah does
- what happens when Sarah gets in the car
- what happens when Sarah stops the car

b Discuss what you think happens next.
I think ... / Maybe ... / In the end ... / ...

More ideas → p. 98

c Watch the third part (until 4:17). Were you right?

3 The end

a Watch the end and discuss the questions.
1 Who is the Red Thunder? Explain the name.
2 How does Sarah feel about her mother now?
3 What did you like or not like about the film?
4 Is the Red Thunder a typical superhero? Why (not)?

b Choose one task.
A Write a diary entry for Sarah for this day.
B Write a description of the Red Thunder for a website about superheroes.

Put your work in My file.

I can understand and discuss a short film. ✔

A scene in a film script

1 Your favourite film

a Think about your favourite film and why you like it. The ideas in the box can help you.

characters • clever dialogue • jokes • music/soundtrack • plot • setting • exciting/funny/sad scenes

b Explain to your partner why it's your favourite film.

2 Parts of a script

a Look at the script for a scene from The Red Thunder. How is it different from other texts (for example an article)?

b Match the descriptions in the box (a–f) to the correct parts in the script (1–6).

- a character description (what a person looks like / is like)
- b character name
- c description of setting (the place)
- d dialogue
- e instructions (how people do or say things)
- f time of day

c Describe what parts are in *italics*, in CAPITAL LETTERS or in brackets (...).

THE RED THUNDER, Scene 1

(1) In the afternoon. (2) Outside a college. (3) SARAH THUN, (4) a student who is wearing glasses and carrying a backpack, walks into DANNY, a student from her class with a bike.

(5)
SARAH
Oh my god!
DANNY
Sorry, sorry.
SARAH
It's OK, I'm sorry.

DANNY (6) *(nervously)*
Hey, I really liked what you were saying in class earlier about changing the world.

SARAH *(smiles)*
Oh, yeah, I think you were probably the only one who was listening.
(tries to leave)

DANNY *(sadly)*
Well, erm. I actually, I bought these tickets to a show, and I was gonna see if you wanted to go with me ... erm, but then they stole my car. So ...

SARAH *(happily)*
Oh ... I have a car.

DANNY *(hopefully)*
You have a car?

3 Your script SF 9 → p. 154

a Watch the scene where Sarah talks to her mother without the sound. Take notes.

b Write a simple script for the scene. Include everything in the box in 2b. More ideas → p. 98

c CHECK Swap scripts with another pair. Check and give them feedback.

Are all the parts of the script there?
Are the character descriptions and the setting clear?
Are the instructions useful?

d Act out your script for the class or record it or film it and present it to the class.

I can write a short scene for a film script. ✔

WB 1-2, p. 21

Doing chores

1 Kimani's worst chores

Read about the chores that Jesse's sister hates. Which chore do you think is the worst?

SHaRE

Hi guys. Our question today: What chores do you have to do? What chores do you really hate?

These are my top 5 worst chores!

Making my bed My mom says 'You must make your bed every day'. But it just gets untidy again when I sleep!

Cleaning the bathroom I really hate cleaning the bathroom. It's so gross! Yesterday I had to clean the shower, it was really dirty. But I didn't have to clean the toilet – my twin had to do that!

Vacuuming I hate vacuuming, but I don't have to do it, that's my brother's job. He has to vacuum every day because of our cats.

Setting the table I have to set the table for dinner and my brothers have to load the dishwasher after dinner. Setting the table is so boring!

Taking out the trash I had to do this when I was small – it was my first chore. I thought it was fun – but not now!

2 What do you have to do?

Tell a partner what you have to do at home and what you don't have to do.

Wordbank 2 → p. 110

I have to clean ... / tidy ... / vacuum / help with ... / look after ... / ...
I don't have to ... – my brother / dad / ... does that.

LOOK AT LANGUAGE: *must, have to* and *don't have to*

Read Kimani's list in 1 again and complete the rules.

When we **need to** do something, we use *must* or **...** .

There isn't a past form of *must*. We use ... as the **past form** for both verbs.

When we **don't need to** do something, we use ... in the present, and ... in the past.

LF 5 → p. 132

3 When you were younger

Talk about what chores you didn't have to do when you were younger, but have to do now.

4 Comments and questions

a Complete the comments with the correct form of *(not) have to*.

I (1) … take the dog to the park every day. It's nice when it's sunny, but it's horrible when it's raining. I (2) … do other chores at home because we have a cleaner. Yesterday at my grandma's house I (3) … help with the cooking – it was fun. She has a dishwasher, so I (4) … do the washing-up. ☺

My mom (5) … work in the evening, so I (6) … look after my little brother. I don't mind looking after him, but my big brother (7) … do anything. It's not fair!

b Discuss the question and agree on an answer:
Should your parents give you money for chores?

I think kids should get money for chores – it's work, right?

I don't agree. Everybody in a family should help.

5 Instructions and rules

1.11 a Kimani's mother is giving her some instructions. Listen and complete the reasons.

1 Kimani needn't set the table because …
2 The kids mustn't get pizza on the sofa because …
3 The kids needn't wait for their parents to come home because …
4 They mustn't go to bed late because …
5 They mustn't play loud music because …

b Look at the sentences in 5a and complete the tip with the correct words.

When somebody **doesn't have to do** something, you can say *you* …
When somebody **shouldn't do** something because it's a rule, you can say *you* …
LF 5b → p. 133

c Do your parents have rules? What mustn't you do at home? Tell your partner.
More ideas → p. 99

6 A class survey

a What is your worst chore? What is your best or easiest chore? Tell the other students in your group.
One person should take notes.
Vacuuming is my worst chore because I have to do it every day.

b Tell the class your group's results.
Two students think that … is their worst chore. One student …

c Compare with other groups. What is the worst chore for the class?

→ I can talk about chores at home. ✔

Taking notes

1 A potluck dinner

Jesse's church sent his family an invitation to a potluck dinner. First read the information in *Across cultures*. Do you ever go to potluck dinners? What type of food do people usually bring?

2 The invitation

a Jesse's mom can't find the invitation about the potluck dinner. She asks Jesse to phone the church. What do you think she wants to know? Make a list of questions.

When ...? What time ...? How many ...? Why ...?

1.12 **b** Listen to Jesse's mom. Write her questions. Did you think of the same questions? SF 5 → p. 150

3 The phone call

1.13 **a** Listen carefully for the answers to Jesse's mom's questions in 2b and take notes. Don't write every word – use symbols and short forms.

1.13 **b** Compare with a partner. Then listen again and check.

c Role-play the conversation with Jesse and his mom. One partner asks the questions, the other gives the answers using the notes.

Fast Finishers 6 → p. 105

ACROSS CULTURES

- A potluck dinner is a party where everybody has to bring some food.
- In the USA people often bring these foods to potluck dinners:

Step by step: taking notes

- Decide what information you need.
- Listen only for the information you need.
- Take short notes.

SF 7 → p. 152

 WB 1-2, p. 24

→ I can take notes on the phone. ✔

Asking for information

1.14

1 LISTENING A voice message

a You're at a language school in the USA. You get a voice message from another student about meeting in the evening. Listen to the message and take notes.

b Listen again and check.

When: meet at ...
Where: at Beale Street Landing ...,
in ... Memphis (next to ...)
Movie: a new ... (ask Kayla)
Must bring: ...
Don't forget: ...
No food or ...
Ticket price: ...

2 SPEAKING Another evening out

You and your friend have information about two events.

a Partner B: Look at page 92. Partner A: Ask:

- what the event is
- where it is
- if it's OK for wheelchairs
- when it starts
- how much it costs
- what you must wear and what you mustn't bring

If you don't understand or can't hear clearly:

- Ask the person to repeat:
  Sorry, can you say that again? / Can you repeat that, please?
- Ask for spelling:
  Can you spell that, please?
  How do you spell that?
- Check if you understood:
  Did you say ...? / Did you mean ...?

b Partner A: Answer your partner's questions about the Memphis Music Band.

c Decide together which event sounds best.

CONCERT

The Memphis Music Band

Playing at The Concert Hall (1365 Jefferson Avenue)

Concert starts at 8pm (doors open at 7pm)

Tickets at door: $13.

All ages. Wheelchair accessible.

No weapons, no food or glass bottles, no backpacks

3 SOUNDS & STRESS Your voice message

1.15

a You want to go to the event that you chose in 2c with another friend who uses a wheelchair. Listen to an advert for your event.

b Record a voice message for your friend about the event. Then listen to your message and check your pronunciation.

c Listen to your partner's message (use headphones).

1 Does the message have all the important information?
2 Does your partner speak clearly and say the words correctly?

I can ask for information and leave a voice message. ✔

WB 1-2, p. 25

Mo's bow ties

1 Mo's style

Moziah (Mo) Bridges is a famous face in Jesse's hometown. Look at the photos of Mo and describe what he's wearing. What do you think of his style? The words in the box can help you.

cool • creative • different • fun • interesting • smart • sporty • traditional

2 Paragraph headings

1.16

a Read the article. Think: Find headings for paragraphs 1–6. More ideas → p. 99

b Pair: Agree on headings.

c Share: Compare your headings in class.

Mo's bows

1 Moziah Bridges from Memphis likes to look good. Because if you look good, you feel good. Even when he was small, Mo always wanted to express himself with his clothes. When he was four years old, he often wore a bow tie and a suit. Mo thinks bow ties are fun and make people feel happy.

2 But Mo found it hard to find bow ties that he liked. So when he was nine, he decided to make his own. His grandmother taught him to sew and to use a sewing machine and Mo chose material to make the bow ties. Soon friends and other people wanted to buy them. So Mo started his own business – he sold his bow ties online and at shops and markets in Memphis.

3 Mo is the CEO (the boss) of a company, but his mom still makes the rules at home. Mo has to clean his room and cut the grass. And he still needs help from his family – his mom (his manager), his grandma, his aunt and his cousin.

4 Mo works hard. After a day of school and homework he puts his bow ties in envelopes and sends them to his customers. He always writes a note to say thank you to every customer. Sometimes he watches TV in the evening, but he often has to practise a talk or prepare for an interview.

5 Mo's business has become very successful and makes a healthy profit. Mo has met lots of important people who have helped him and given him advice. Mo met Barack Obama when he was president. 'He told me to never give up,' says Mo.

6 In the future Mo wants to work in the fashion business and design his own clothes. He also wants to help other kids to dream. As Mo writes on his website: 'You can be anything you want – at any age'. His advice to other teenagers is: 'Find out what you like doing and why.'

3 WORDS

a Make a word web with 'business' words from the article.

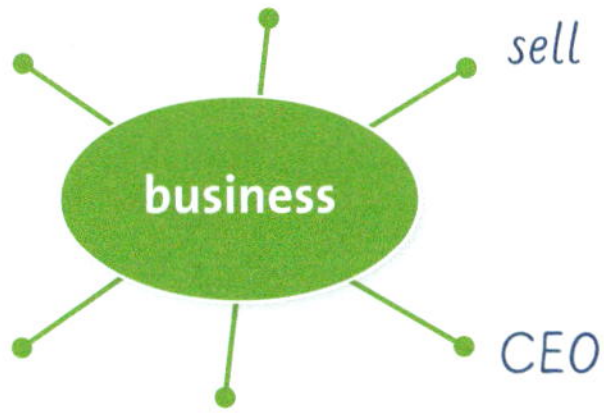

b Find words in the article that mean:

1 to say something about himself (paragraph 1)
2 to do work for something in the future (paragraph 4)
3 tips (paragraph 5)
4 not to stop what you are doing (paragraph 5)
5 clothes (paragraph 6) SF 1 → p. 146

4 How to be a CEO

a Read the article again. Who or what helped Mo to start and develop a successful business? Make a list.

b At the end of the article Mo gives some advice to other teenagers. Why is this advice important for Mo's life? Do you think it's important for your life? Why (not)?

5 VIEWING Mo can tie a bow

a When Mo was twelve, a film company made a film about him: *Mo can tie a bow*. Watch the film. Make a list of all the places where we see Mo in the film. SF 19 → p. 165

First half (until 7:16): Mo's life at home and at school
1 *at home, in the living room / sewing room*
2 *on his bike*
3 …

Second half: before and after the Christmas market
1 *at home, family night*
2 *at home, on the phone*
3 …

b Make two groups. The first group watches the first half of the film again; the second group watches the second half of the film again. Take notes about what Mo does in each place on your list in 5a.

first half	second half
1 *sews a bow tie*	1 *everyone makes bow ties*
2 *rides his bike*	2 *asks friends for help*

c Tell a partner from the other group what happens in your part of the film. Use your notes.

d Discuss the film: Did you like it? Why (not)?
What did you think of Mo?
Is fashion important to you? TF 2 → p. 118f.

→ I can find out information from an article and a film. ✔ WB 2, p. 26

You can find the answers for these tasks on page 251.

1 Check your vocabulary

a Complete the sentences.

1 Superheroes c… the bad guys.
2 They s… the world.
3 They h… amazing powers.
4 They f… against evil.
5 They e… from dangerous situations.

b Match the parts of the instructions.

1	Please vacuum	a	the table for dinner.
2	Don't forget to set	b	the trash.
3	Have you cut	c	your bed.
4	You need to take out	d	the grass?
5	Remember to make	e	the living room carpet.

c Complete the instructions for guests with *needn't* or *mustn't*.

You (1) … take off your shoes – you can wear them inside.

You (2) … sit in that chair – it's Grandad's chair.

You (3) … let the dog lie on the sofa.

You (4) … eat everything if it's too much.

2 Check your language

a Complete the script instructions. Use the adverb form of the adjectives in the box.

She sits down (1) … on the broken chair.
She doesn't shout: she speaks (2) …
He cries and looks at her (3) …
She runs out of the room (4) …
Then she smiles and laughs (5) …

careful • happy • quick • quiet • sad

b Match what the director says to the actors.

1	You sat down too fast.	a	I need to eat something.
2	You don't have to cry.	b	I had to leave without breakfast.
3	We have to do the scene again.	c	You must do it slowly.
4	But we must have lunch first.	d	We need to get it right this time.
5	I got up late this morning.	e	Just look unhappy.

3 Check your speaking

Partner A: You phone the cinema. Ask about:
- the price of the tickets
- visiting the cinema in a wheelchair
- taking drinks into the cinema

Partner B: Answer the questions.
Partner A: Check if you understood the answer to your last question.

4 Check your writing

Write two short character descriptions for a film script (25–30 words each). Choose two of these people:
- a good friend
- your mum or dad
- your favourite singer or actor

Write a scene for a film script

GET READY

Make groups (4–6 students).

First brainstorm ideas in your group for your film script. One person should take notes.

- Is it a funny/sad/action/... story? Is it about a superhero / a family / a real-life hero /...?
- Who are the characters and what are they like? You can use your own superheroes from p. 29 (or think of new characters).
- What is the setting?
- What happens in your scene?

– superhero story – lots of action
– characters:
Green Magic (green costume and cape, green boots; can disappear in the air, change people into mice and ...)
– scene:
In a dark forest, at night, Green Magic's enemy is planning ...

GO AHEAD

In your group, write the scene for your script on a computer or tablet (about one page).

- First write the setting, the time of day and the character descriptions (see p. 31).
- Write the dialogue. Remember to add instructions about how people do or say things.
- When you have finished, read your script again. Correct it and make it better.

FINISH

Introduce and read scripts.

- First give a short introduction to your script to the class.

Our script is for the first scene of an action story. The most important character is a superhero who can ...
In the scene in our script the superhero ...

- Swap scripts and read the other groups' scripts. When you read a script, decide if the characters are interesting, if the story is exciting or sad or funny, and if the instructions are clear.
- Give feedback to the other groups.
- Act out and film another group's script.
- Have a vote and give an Oscar for the best script.

We think your script is exciting.
Your superhero *Green Magic* is very clever.
We like the dialogue, but we think you sometimes need to give more information about the characters.

1.17 1 LISTENING Two different worlds

Listen to Carly and Ed, a British exchange student at Carly's American school. For each question, choose A, B or C.

1 Lunch at Carly's school is ...
- A at about the same time as at Ed's school.
- B earlier than at Ed's school.
- C later than at Ed's school.

2 At Carly's school students can ...
- A play basketball and rugby and do fencing.
- B play basketball and do fencing.
- C play basketball and rugby.

3 Ed says one of the worst things at his school is ...
- A always being with other students.
- B doing chores.
- C not being with his family.

4 You spell the name of Carly's friend ...
- A Dee Angelo.
- B D'Angelo.
- C Dangelo.

5 Carly's friend ...
- A can't come to the cafeteria.
- B isn't going to have lunch.
- C doesn't say goodbye.

2 SPEAKING Movie night

a It's Tuesday and you want to go to the cinema.
Partner B: Turn the book around.
Partner A: Ask Partner B questions about *Supercoolkid: The Movie.*

Which actor ...?
What other actors ...?
... the film on today?
What time ...?
How much ...?
... take drinks?

b Partner A: Read the poster and answer Partner B's questions.

a Partner B: Read the poster and answer Partner A's questions.

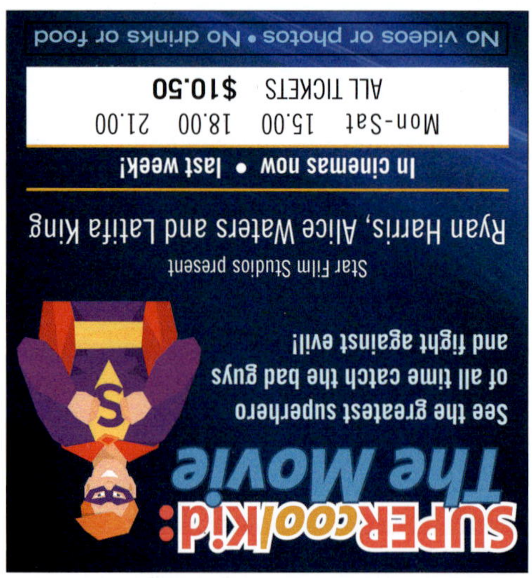

b Partner B: Ask Partner A questions about *Green Magic and the Evil Prince.*

...Green Magic?
... the film about?
Who plays the role of ...?
Where ...?
What days ...?
What time ...?

3 USE OF ENGLISH A new home

Felix is visiting Britain. Complete the conversation between Felix and his exchange family. For 1–5 choose the right letters (A–G). There are two extra letters. *1 G, 2 …*

Dad: We hope you enjoy staying here, Felix.

Felix: (1) …

Dad: Thanks. Chris will show you your room upstairs.

Felix: (2) …

Chris: Do you mean 'floor'?

Felix: (3) …

Chris: So this is your room. And this is the bathroom here.

Felix: (4) …

Chris: Ah, you mean a shower. No, we don't. A lot of English houses only have baths. Do you want something to eat, Felix?

Felix: (5) …

Chris: In English we say 'I could eat a horse'. But I like the German phrase. Let's get some food.

A Ah, so my room is on the first … er, I've forgotten the word.

B Oh, there's a window. That's nice.

C No thank you. I'm really hungry.

D Ah, you don't have a … . What's the word? You stand under the water.

E Yes please. I'm – how do you say it? I'm as hungry as a wolf.

F Yes, that's right.

G Thanks. You have a nice house.

4 VOCABULARY Chores

a Make a table and complete each group with chores.

food and eating	*cleaning and tidying*	*clothes*	*chores outside*

b In some Asian countries students must clean their classrooms and other parts of the school, even the toilets. Do you clean in your school? What chores do you think students should do?

In our school we have to / don't have to …

I think students should/shouldn't … because …

5 MEDIATION How-to Festival

You're an exchange student in Memphis. You're going to this festival in the next town on Saturday. Complete the chat with your brother.

HOW-TO FESTIVAL *in Germantown*

Do you want a new hobby? Do you want to learn something new? At the How-to Festival we have lots of experts who can teach you new skills. There is something for all ages at this free event! You can learn how to play the guitar or to knit, write poems or make smoothies. If you enjoy the outdoor life, why not find out how to keep chickens or make a bird house?

The festival will be on at Germantown Library from 1 to 4 pm. You can buy drinks and snacks.

LEO Was machst du am Samstag?

YOU Ich werde …

LEO Ist das in Memphis?

YOU Nein, …

LEO Und was kann man da machen?

YOU Also, zum Beispiel …

LEO Klingt gut, aber du musst bestimmt früh aufstehen.

YOU …

LEO Na dann, viel Spaß!

Unit 3 People of Britain

Start

Presentation

A journey through time

The ancient Britons

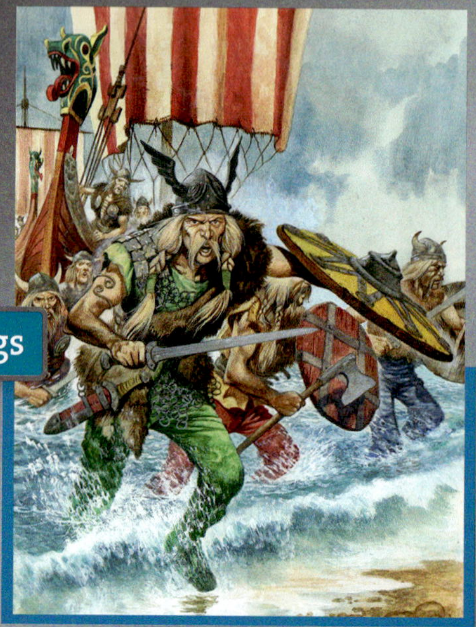

The Vikings

The Romans

The Angles and Saxons

The Normans

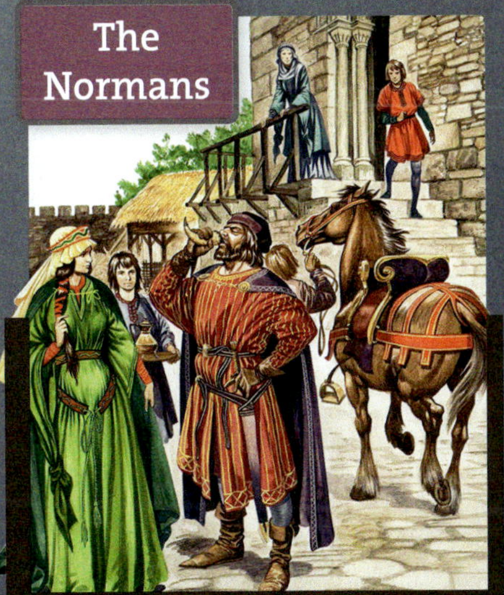

In this unit you will

- find out about the history of people in Britain.
- describe past events, link events and write a story.
- make notes and give a short talk.
- express your opinions and feelings.

➔ At the end of the unit you'll make a time capsule.

1 What do you know?

a PLACEMAT Make groups of four. Divide a big piece of paper into five parts like this:

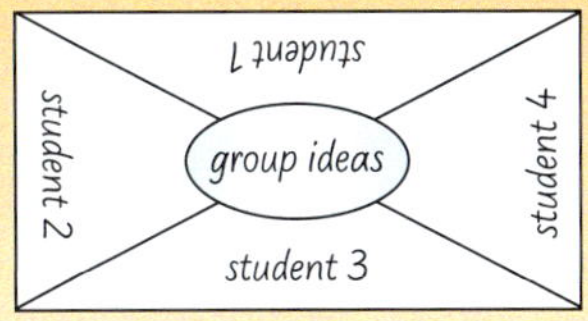

b What do you know about Britain? In your part of the paper, write ideas. For example, you can make notes about the different countries, the people, famous places and people, …

c Turn the paper around three times. Read all the ideas.

d Discuss your notes and collect your main ideas in the circle in the middle.

e Share your ideas with the class.

2 LISTENING Asha's presentation

a Look at the slides from Asha's presentation. Describe the different people and what they're doing.
Wordbank 3 → p. 111 SF 15 → p. 160

1.18 b Listen to Asha's talk and write the date when each group of people came to Britain.

1.18 c Listen again. Complete the information in the rest of the table. SF 5 → p. 150

Who?	The Britons	The Romans	The Angles & Saxons	The Vikings	The Normans
When?	Around … BC.	… AD	about …	about …	in …
Where from?	—				
What did they do in Great Britain?	• different tribes …	• built … • helped …	• took land and …	• came to … • settled in the … • con-quered …	• built … and castles • divided England into …

➔ I can understand the early history of the UK. ✔

The Romans and Vikings in Britain

1 The Romans in Britain

a Look at the map and discuss with the class:

1 What was the Roman Empire?
2 What modern countries were part of it?
3 What were the names for Roman Britain and Germany?
4 What do you know about the Romans in Germany and in your area? What did they do or build there?

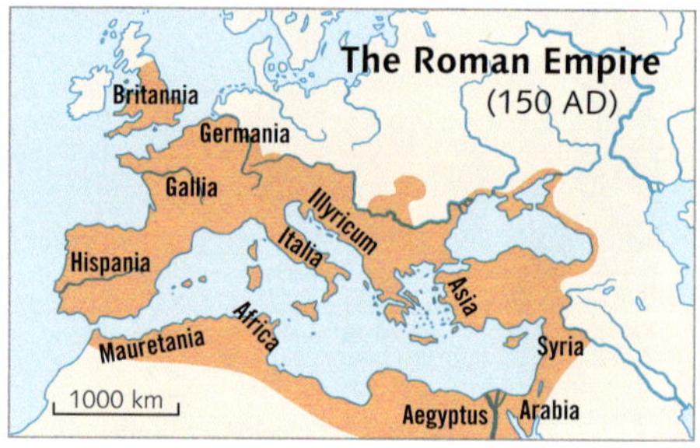

b VIEWING Read the quiz questions. Then watch the video and do the quiz. For each question there are two correct answers. *1 B and ..., 2 ...* SF 19 → p. 165

Quiz

1 What did the Romans build in Britain?
A castles B temples C baths

2 What were the Romans good at?
A sailing B fighting
C conquering other countries

3 Why did the Romans invade Britain?
A for its precious metals
B for its good land
C for its coast

4 Why didn't the Romans conquer Britain in 55 and 54 BC?
A There were lots of other people in Britain.
B The Britons were good at fighting.
C The Roman ships weren't very good.

5 Which countries became part of the Roman Empire?
A England B Scotland C Wales

6 Why did the Romans build roads?
A So that they could build stone buildings.
B So that they could trade easily.
C So that their army could stop trouble quickly.

7 Why did Emperor Hadrian build a wall across the north of Britain?
A To keep the Scots out of Britannia.
B To keep the Britons out of Caledonia (Scotland).
C To stop trouble between the Scots and Romans.

c On the internet find pictures of Hadrian's Wall and famous Roman buildings in Britain.

2 People of York

a Make five groups. Each group reads about one famous person from York on p. 45. Take notes on your person and try to remember the information. SF 7 → p. 152

b Make new groups with students who have read about the four other people. Tell the group about your person.

1.19 Famous people of York

full picture on p. 160

I am Cartimandua, Queen of the tribe of the Brigantes and daughter of a king. Before the Romans came to Yorkshire, my tribe was the biggest in Britain. I helped the Romans and became rich. Look at my fine clothes of wool and linen! I left my husband Venutius in 69 AD so I could be together with Vellocatus, one of his soldiers. After that Venutius became my enemy and took away my power.

My name is Quintus Petillius Cerialis. My army built the town of Eboracum (you call it York today) in 71 AD. The rivers on both sides kept our enemies away. They also meant we could bring materials here from the North Sea. We built stone walls around our new town and stone houses and baths.

I am Constantine the Great. When my father died, I became emperor in Eboracum in 306. I was a really great emperor! I made the Roman Empire great again. When I left Britain, I built a new Roman capital. Of course I called it after myself: Constantinople. You call my city Istanbul now.

I am Ivar the Boneless, a famous Viking. When the Romans left Eboracum, the Angles and Saxons took the town and called it Eoforwic. On November 1, 866, I conquered Eoforwic with the Viking army. We called the town Jorvik and we decided to settle there. We created objects to trade: cups from wood, knives from metal, bracelets from silver, and shoes from leather.

I am Eric Haraldsson, son of King Harald Finehair of Norway. People called me Eric Bloodaxe because I had a big axe and I liked using it! I was the King of Norway and later I was the last Viking king in Jorvik. In 954 the horrible Angles and Saxons came back to the city, conquered us, and took Jorvik back.

3 Who said it?

Read new sentences for each person and say the person's name.

1 I was a king in two different countries.
2 I'm sad that my city has a new name.
3 My people made beautiful things.
4 I did business with the enemy.
5 My soldiers and I created a great new town.

4 WORDS Materials

a Write the names of the materials.

b Look at the pictures on pp. 42–43. Find things made of the materials in a.

Fast Finishers 7 → p. 106 SF 1 → p. 146

I can understand a video and an article. ✔

Vikings in York today

1 A time capsule of York's Viking past

a Talk about a museum (or zoo/aquarium) you have visited with your class or your family (in your area or on holiday). Say:

- what kind of museum it is and when you went there
- what you did or saw while you were visiting the museum

Wordbank 4 → p. 112

Two years ago I went to the open-air museum in Bad Windsheim with my grandparents. We saw …

b Asha visited the Jorvik Viking Centre in York with her class. Read the brochure and answer the questions.

1. How is this museum special?
2. What did people find at this place?
3. What has recently changed at the museum?

Have you ever been to York? If you haven't been here yet, then come and see the Jorvik Viking Centre. It's special! Over thirty years ago we built our amazing museum over an old Viking street. You can see the old city under your feet, and travel around in a time car.

People were digging in the earth when they discovered a time capsule of York's Viking past: they found out how people lived, what they ate and how they died. They discovered thousands of objects like dishes, leather shoes and animal bones while they were working here. They even found a Viking sock!

The Jorvik Viking Centre opened in 1984 and we have just added new sights, sounds and smells. Over 18 million people have already seen the museum: why don't YOU come and see it?

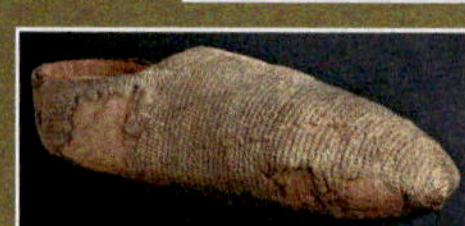

LOOK AT LANGUAGE: past tenses (revision)

Read the explanations. Find examples of simple past and past progressive in the brochure.
What time words do we use with each tense?

- We use the **simple past** for completed actions at specific times in the past.
- We use the **past progressive** for an action which was happening in the past.

LF 6-7 → p. 134f.

2 The Viking festival

Complete Asha's speech bubble with the past progressive or the simple past.

Last year I (1 visit) … York with my family when we (2 decide) … to go to the Viking Festival. While my mum and my aunt (3 watch) … the *Strongest Viking* competition, I (4 go) … to the *Best Beard* competition with my dad. Three people (5 win) …: a girl who (6 wear) … an orange beard from wool, a woman who (7 use) … her own hair to make a beard and a man who (8 have) … a real beard!

LOOK AT LANGUAGE: present perfect and simple past

Look at the explanation and example below and find three more examples of the present perfect in the brochure on page 46. What time words are in the examples?

We use the **present perfect** when something happened at a time before now. The exact time is not important.
Have you ever been to York?

⚠ Use the **present perfect** to say that something happened.
Use the **simple past** to say when it happened.
I've been to the Roman Museum in Weißenburg.
I went there last year with my class. LF 6, 8 → p. 134f.

3 Costumes and fantasy

a **Choose the correct verbs for an interview with Asha's friend Oliver.**

I (1) *started / I've started* wearing costumes when I was small. Two years ago (2) *I joined / I've joined* a Viking group. At first my mum (3) *bought / has bought* me costumes online, but now we (4) *learned / have learned* to make our own Viking clothes. (5) *I made / I've already made* some trousers and some wool socks! Some of my friends (6) *laughed / have laughed* at me when (7) *I told / I've told* them about my new hobby. But (8) *I met / I've met* some great new people. Fast Finishers 8 → p. 106

b **Interview your partner. When you answer, give more information.**

Have you ever been to a festival or market with people in costumes?
– Yes, I have. In the summer we went to a festival in Miesbach. We saw dancers in costumes.

c **Now ask a different partner three more *Have you ever …?* questions.**

Have you ever …
(wear) a costume?
(read) *Lord of the Rings*?
(watch) a fantasy film or series?
(play) a fantasy video game?

Yes, I have.
I went / saw / wore / …
last week / year / …
No, I haven't.
I don't like / have never …

I can describe events in my life. ✔

A story *(by Roald Dahl)*

1 The Mildenhall Treasure

1.20

Asha's class is reading a story by Roald Dahl about two men who discovered some amazing Roman silver in Britain in 1942. Look at the pictures, read part of the story and answer the questions.

1 What is the setting?
2 Who are the characters?
3 How did they find the treasure?
4 How did Ford feel at different parts in the story? How do you know? Find words that describe his feelings.

Ford knelt down next to the front of the plough **and** looked into the small hole Gordon Butcher had dug with his hands. He touched the green-blue metal with his finger. He scraped away a bit more earth. He leaned further forward **so that** his nose was down the hole. **Then** he stood up and said, 'Let's get the plough out of the way and dig.' **Although** fireworks were exploding in his head, Ford kept his voice very soft.

Together they moved the plough back. 'Give me the spade,' Ford said, and he started carefully to dig the earth away. **When** the hole was two feet deep, he threw away the spade and used his hands. He knelt down and scraped the earth away **until** at last a great round plate was before them. [...]

Carefully Ford took it out of the hole. He got to his feet and turned it in his hands. There was nothing much to see **because** a hard green-blue material covered it. **But** he knew that it was a very heavy plate or dish. It was about eighteen pounds!

Ford stood in the field and looked at the big plate. His hands started to shake. A great excitement was boiling up inside him and it was not easy for him to hide it. But he did his best. 'A type of dish,' he said. ◇

2 Linking words

a **Look at the words in blue in the story. Why does the writer use them? What other linking words do you know?**

b **Link the ideas with words from the story.**

(1) ... he looked in the hole (2) ... saw the metal, Ford knew it was silver. (3) ... he knew it was treasure, Ford didn't tell Butcher (4) ... he wanted to keep it himself.
He tried to hide his feelings (5) ... Butcher wouldn't find out.

3 The end of the story

a Look at the pictures on page 93 and follow the instructions. More ideas → p. 100

b CHECK Swap your story with another pair. Read their story and give feedback: have they followed the tips in the box?

c Correct your story and put it in My file.

Writing a story
- Describe the setting and characters.
- Describe what happens. Use adjectives and adverbs to make the story more interesting.
- Describe the feelings of the characters.
- Write what people say and think.
- Use linking words.

SF 9 → p. 154

→ I can write an interesting story and link ideas. ✔

Expressing opinions and feelings

1 The treasure story

1.21 **a** Listen to Asha and her friends Noah and Zahid. They're talking about the treasure story in class. Do they like the story? Why (not)? Complete their opinions.

Asha thinks the story is … because …
Noah … and he also thinks the writer …
In Zahid's opinion, the story … because …

1.21 **b** Something is wrong in each sentence. Listen again and correct the wrong information.

1 I was so angry that Mr Butcher took all the treasure for himself.
2 I don't agree with you about the treasure.
3 I don't think Mr Butcher knew Mr Ford.
4 Maybe you're right about the problems.
5 I felt upset for Mr Ford.
6 In my opinion, it wasn't nice.
7 That's true, but I think Mr Ford really loved money.
8 I'm not sure that's true. He was just stupid and greedy.
9 I can't believe that the treasure was from the fifth century.
10 I was really surprised that it was so dirty.

c Copy the table. Complete it with the phrases from b.

give your opinion	say you have the same opinion	say you have a different opinion	express a feeling
I think …	I agree	…	…

SF 12 → p. 150

d Now discuss your opinion of the story and the characters. Use phrases from 1c and give reasons.

In my opinion, … because …

2 Your opinion

a Choose a group topic from the box (or choose your own topic) and think about your opinion and feelings.

b Discuss the topic. Remember to give reasons.

c Talk about your ideas with the class. Agree or disagree with other opinions.

- It's OK not to tell the truth sometimes.
- It's hard to be a teenager today. People had easier lives in the past.
- I think it's OK to think of yourself and not other people.
- Students should choose what they learn in school.

I can express my opinions and feelings. ✔

WB 1-2, p. 34

People in Britain today

1 Asha's family history

a Asha and her parents are visiting their family in Bradford, a city in West Yorkshire. Find Bradford on the map on the inside cover.

1.22 b Asha is asking her grandparents about why they came to Britain. Listen and complete the information.

1947	…	…	When he was …	…	…
India became independent from Britain	Grandad's family came to the UK	Grandma's family came to the UK	Grandad got work in a … factory.	Grandma and Grandad …	Grandma and Grandad had …

LOOK AT LANGUAGE: question tags

a Asha and her grandparents want to check information so they use 'question tags'. Make the rule.

positive statement + … question tag	You're doing something about the Romans, aren't you? But you miss India sometimes, don't you?
negative statement + … question tag	Nobody in our family lives in India now, do they? We didn't want to move, did we?

b How can you say these question tags in German?

LF 9 → p. 137f.

2 Lewis' family history

Complete Asha's conversation with Lewis, her grandparents' neighbour. Use the correct question tags from the box. There is one extra question tag.

aren't they? • do they? • do you? • don't you? • haven't you?

Asha: Your grandparents are from Jamaica, (1) *aren't they?*
Lewis: Yes, they are. You've met them, (2) …?
Asha: Yes, I have. They were at your birthday party.
Lewis: That's right. They always come to my birthday.
Asha: But they don't live in Bradford, (3) …?
Lewis: No, they don't. They live in London, so I don't see them very often.
Asha: But you skype with them, (4) …?
Lewis: Yes, I do. We talk a lot on skype. But you don't skype with your grandparents, (5) …?
Asha: No, but I see them quite a lot.

ACROSS CULTURES

When people make small talk with strangers or friends, they talk about things that are not really important. In the UK, people often make small talk about the weather.
"It's a nice day, isn't? It's not very warm, is it?"
What do people in Germany talk about?

3 A conversation

Lewis meets Asha's grandma at the bus stop and they make small talk. Add the correct question tags.

Lewis: Hello, Mrs. Sharma. It's cold today, (1) *isn't it?*
Mrs S: Yes, it is, Lewis. It's very cold. … You saw Asha when she was here, (2) …
Lewis: Yes, I did. It was good to see her. But she didn't stay very long this time, (3) …?
Mrs S: No, she didn't. But I'm sure she'll be here again soon.
Lewis: Erm, you don't know what time the bus comes, (4) …, Mrs Sharma?
Mrs S: It usually comes at five past. But it isn't on time, (5) …?
Lewis: No, it's late. Oh wait, here it is now!

Fast Finishers 9 → p. 106

4 NOW YOU Small talk with a partner

a Find a student you know well. Complete the questions for him or her with information and a question tag.

1 You like …, …?
2 You don't like …, …?
3 You play …, …?
4 You went to … last week, …?
5 You didn't … at the weekend, …?

b Make small talk with your partner and ask your questions. How many things did you get right?

You like cats, don't you?

Yes, I do. That's right. / No, I don't. I hate cats!

5 Small talk with other students

a Think of at least three questions with question tags that you can ask other students.

b WALK AROUND
Ask different students your questions and answer theirs. SF 11 → p. 157

I can check information and make small talk. ✔

Giving a short talk

1 VIEWING Two short talks

a You're going to give a short talk on a famous person in history. Watch two talks by Sitara and Owen. Who are they talking about? Do they mention all the points in the box?

* Name and role in history
* Date and place of birth
* Life and work
* Year of death
* Why the speaker chose this person

b Watch again. Which presentation is better and why? Think about these points:

Structure: Beginning: who? • Description of the person's life • End of the presentation: sum up.
Pictures: Does the speaker point out pictures and maps on the slides?
Way of talking: Clear? • Too fast or slow? • Confident?

2 Prepare your talk

a First make notes on your person.

- Choose your person and do research. Use websites like the BBC, serious newspapers, universities, ... Check the facts on different websites.
- Make notes on the points in the box in 1a: use headings or make a mind map.
- Write down your sources. SF 4 → p. 149

Sources
Bookmark the website. Write down the name of the website and the name, the writer and the date of the article. Write the date when you used the website.

b Then prepare your notes for your talk.

- Highlight the main points in your notes.
- Structure your talk (see 1b).
- Find pictures which help people understand your talk. Remember to use pictures from 'creative commons' and give the source. Point out the pictures in your talk.

Look at this picture/map.
You can see ... in this picture / on this map.

3 Practise your talk

Practise your talk with your notes from 2b in front of the mirror or film your talk. Look at how you talk and move.

Remember:
- Look at the class and smile.
- Speak clearly and confidently.
- Try not to move around too much.

4 Give your talk

Use these tips.

- Beginning: Say who or what you're going to talk about.
- Main part: Give your information.
- End: Sum up what you've said.

To sum up, ...

Step by step: giving a talk
- Make notes.
- Structure your talk.
- Practise!
- Give your talk confidently.

SF 13 → p. 159

→ I can make notes, do research and give a short talk. ✔

The British royal family

1 Who are they?

What do you know about the British royal family? Make a family tree as a class.

2 Harry and Meghan

a Partner A: Read about Harry and Meghan on this page. Make notes on the main points.
Partner B: Read about William and Kate on page 94.

ACROSS CULTURES

The British royal family has no power – it is just a symbol of Britain. Many people in Britain love the royal family, but others say a modern country doesn't need a royal family – and shouldn't pay for it.
What do you think? Should Germany have a royal family? Discuss your opinions.

Prince Harry is the younger son of Charles, Prince of Wales and Diana, Princess of Wales. He's one of the most popular people in the royal family, although when he was younger, he often drank too much and was often in trouble. From 2005 to 2015 Harry was a soldier in the army, but now he works for the royal family. He helps charities which support soldiers and their families. In 2014 Harry created the Invictus Games, a sports competition for injured or sick soldiers. Harry's charity work also helps young people. After he had visited Lesotho in Africa, Harry started a charity to help children whose parents have died. He also works with programmes in the UK that help young people walk away from gang activities.

In 2018 Harry married Meghan Markle, a famous American actor. Before she married Harry, Meghan lived in Canada where she acted in the drama series *Suits*. She also did charity work for children. Since her marriage she has worked with many other charities.

Harry and Meghan first lived at Kensington Palace, where other members of the royal family also live, and then moved to Frogmore Cottage near Windsor Castle.

b Partner A: Tell Partner B about Harry and Meghan in German. Use your notes. Then listen to your partner. SF 16 → p. 161

c What is similar about the two brothers' lives? What is different? Discuss.

Time Flyer *(by Christina de la Mare)*

1 Past or future?

a **Think:** Imagine you can travel in time. Then answer these questions.

1. Would you like to go into the past or the future?
2. Where would you like to go?
3. Who would you like to meet?
4. What would you like to find out?

b **Pair:** Tell your partner your ideas.

c **Share:** Share your ideas with the class.

2 Alex travels in time

1.23 1.24

Read the story about Alex, who can travel in time. Answer the questions.

1. Does Alex travel into the future or the past?
2. What happens when he travels in time?
3. Has he been to this place before?
4. Who does he meet there?

In 2012 Alex and his parents visited Renton Grange, a big old empty house which was home to Mr and Mrs Renton, their twins and their daughter many years ago. Alex likes making model planes out of wood and after the visit, strange things start to happen to Alex when he works with his planes.

That evening I was making one of my planes. I put the pieces on a rug in the garden and started to work.

Only seconds later the ground started to spin and I flew down the black tunnel again. I started to ask myself why. Being at home had something to do with it. My glasses could have something to do with it too. But there must be other reasons why I travelled through time.

I arrived next to a small lake in the gardens of Renton Grange. It was quite far from the house, which I could see through some trees. First I thought I was alone there, but then I saw Freddie and Charlie in his chair. I couldn't see Alice. As the two boys came nearer, I could see that Charlie was holding a bag of bread.

This time I didn't have to hide. The boys had seen me disappear before their eyes only a few days before, so I stood in front of them and said 'Hello'.

'Hello Alex!' said Charlie, who looked happy and excited to see me. I looked at

Freddie, who looked at me seriously, then nodded his head.
'Where's Alice?' I asked.
'She's gone to visit our aunt with Mother,' said Charlie. 'They won't be back until tomorrow.' I felt disappointed.
Freddie put Charlie's chair by the lake and Charlie threw a few bits of bread into the water. A family of ducks from the other side swam quickly towards it.
'Did you know about this house before you started time travelling?' Charlie asked.
'Yes,' I answered, 'I visited it with my parents.'
'Is it open to the public in 2012?' he asked.
'Er ... yes, it is,' I said and felt nervous.
'So nobody lives there in the future,' he said, looking at the ducks at his feet.
'That's right.' I didn't know what else to say.

'Did something happen to us? I mean, will something happen to my family in the future?' asked Charlie, looking at me. He wore glasses like Freddie's, but his eyes were light blue like his sister's.

I didn't want to tell him the truth, but I couldn't think of anything else to say.

Charlie looked out at the lake. 'Don't tell me,' he said. 'I don't want to know.'

Then he looked at Freddie and said, 'Could you get me a rug, Fred? I'm cold.' Freddie wanted to say something rude, but he stopped himself. He stood up and said, 'I'll be back in a minute.' Then he ran through the trees towards the house.

Charlie and I were quiet. I had no idea what to say to him. Suddenly he spoke. 'Is the land around the house the same in 2012?'

'Yes,' I said, jumping to my feet. I pointed to the trees and the gardens behind them. 'All that looks the same.'

We stopped talking then, but I felt more relaxed and Charlie started feeding the ducks again. I decided to walk around the lake. I looked at the house in the distance and thought how beautiful it looked. I was nearly halfway round the lake when I turned and saw Charlie. He had dropped the bag of bread and was leaning out of his chair to get it. 'Stop Charlie,' I shouted. 'I'll come and get it for you.'

But it was too late. As I spoke, he fell out of his chair into the water below him. The water wasn't very deep, but Charlie couldn't keep his head over the water.

I started running towards him. If I could get to him in time, I could get him out the water and he would be all right. But suddenly the spinning was back. As I tried to run, my legs became heavier and heavier until I couldn't move. I could hardly see Charlie in the water. Then I saw a figure running through the trees. It was Freddie. But I didn't see what happened next. Everything became black around me and I couldn't do anything to help.

3 The characters

a Make a mind map about the characters.

b Read lines 43–64 again. Explain why Alex was nervous. What do you think he knew about the family's future?

In my opinion, the family had to sell their house / moved to a different country / died / …

4 What happened to Charlie?

Look at the picture and read the end of the story again. Then write a paragraph about what happened to Charlie. Use your own ideas and the tips on page 48. Put your writing in My file. More ideas → p. 100

Do you want to find out more about Charlie, Freddie, Alice and Alex? Read the Cornelsen book *Time Flyer*.

TF 3 → p. 120ff.

→ I can understand and continue part of a story. ✔

3 YOUR CHECK

You can find the answers for these tasks on page 252.

1 Check your vocabulary

a Complete the descriptions with the correct people and the right words.

1 The … were many different t…
2 The … i… Britain in 43 AD. They built roads so that they could t…
3 The … and … s… in Britain because of the land.
4 The … c… the city of York.
5 The … built lots of churches and c …

b You found these old objects in a time capsule. Describe the objects and the materials.

2 Check your language

a Write the questions. Then ask and answer them with a partner. Use the pictures.

1 you / ever / visit / Rome? (✔) *Yes, I have.*
2 you / have / nice weather?
3 what / you / see / while you / visit Rome?
4 you / ever / find / 'treasure' in the street? (✔)
5 what / you / find?
6 what / you / do / with it?

b You're at a party with your parents. Complete the questions with question tags.

1 It's a nice party, …?
2 You and your family live near here, …?
3 You were in sixth class last year, …?
4 You don't like history, …?
5 You won a prize at school, …?
6 Your parents didn't tell you about me, …?

3 Check your speaking

Complete the dialogue with a partner and then practise it.

A In my opinion, we don't need teachers. Computers can do their job.

B I don't agree with you! …

A That's …, but I think …

B I can't believe …

A I feel …

B …

4 Check your writing

Write a 50-word story about the things in the picture.

Make a time capsule

GET READY

Make groups. You're going to make a time capsule to tell somebody in the future about you, your class, your school and Germany today.
First choose at least five things to put in your time capsule. You can use some of these ideas or your own ideas.

- photos of you / your school / your area with captions
- your class 7 timetable
- one of your group's presentations from page 52
- an interview with a student about his or her family history
- a description of what you did yesterday (a typical day) or a real diary entry
- an article about something or somebody in the news
- a list of the most popular hobbies and interests of students
- a description of a popular TV programme, series or film
- your favourite song text and video
- a photo of your favourite object and a description of it
- ...

Everybody in the group should do something: decide who does what.

GO AHEAD

In your group, write, record, make or find the things for your time capsule.

- Write a letter together to the group who will open the time capsule:
  Say what is in your capsule and why it is important.
- Find a box for your things and decorate it. SF 10 → p. 156

FINISH

Put everything in your time capsule and close it.

- Write your names and the date on it.
- As a class decide when you will open the time capsules (In one year? At the end of your time at school?).
  Write the date for opening on the box. Decide on a good place to keep the box.
- Tell the class about your time capsule. Say what you thought was important in your group and if you enjoyed creating the time capsule.

Unit 4 Irish stories

1

Me! – Conor O'Brien

2

4

Some people speak Gaelic.

3

Beautiful Connemara on the west coast

6

A traditional pub

5

'Silicon Docks' (the old docks with new buildings in Dublin)

7

8

My friends in coding class

I ♥ Irish stew and soda bread.

9

In this unit you will

- find out what is similar and what is different in Ireland and Germany.
- read and listen to Irish stories.
- ask for help and help tourists.
- learn to understand people's body language.
- give instructions and express rules.

➔ At the end of the unit you'll present snapshots of Ireland.

1 Conor and Ireland

a **What can you say about Conor and Ireland when you look at the photos and the map?**

2.1 **b** **Moritz, a German student, is coming to stay with Conor in Ireland. Conor has recorded some information for his photos. Listen to his message and write two pieces of information for each picture.**

2 VIEWING A tour of Dublin

a **Watch the video. Match the activities (a–j) with the places (1–7). For two places there is more than one activity.**

1. St Stephen's Green
2. Grafton Street
3. Temple Bar
4. the River Liffey
5. Moore Street
6. O'Connell Street
7. Dublin Bay

a buy flowers, fruit and vegetables
b see the Jeanie Johnston
c see the statue of Molly Malone
d go to shops, cafes and clubs
e see old and modern monuments
f see the sea
g take a break from the city
h walk over the Ha'penny Bridge
i watch musicians and dancers and maybe meet a leprechaun
j see the Famine Memorial

b **Watch the part about the Famine Memorial again and take notes:**

The famine was from … to … There was a big problem … … people died. Many people went to … But on the way …

3 A trip to Ireland

Decide which activities in Dublin or in the photos are most interesting for you. Then compare with a partner and agree on three things to do together.

Leaving Ireland

1 The famine

What do you remember from the Dublin video about the Great Famine in Ireland?

2.2 **2 The journey**

Skim the text from a history book as quickly as you can: what is the text about?

Skim (= read quickly) for the main ideas. Don't worry about new words. SF 6 → p. 151

Life and death on the way to the New World

A fresh start

Even before the Great Famine, many people had already left Ireland. In the thirty years before the famine, over one million Irish people had decided to leave their home country. Ireland was a very poor country. People had heard about the New World and wanted to make a fresh start.

The Great Famine

Then came the terrible famine in 1845. For a third of the population, potatoes were their main source of food. But a disease meant that most of the potatoes went bad. Many Irish people chose to leave their country – and not to stay and die. Starving and sick with terrible diseases, thousands of people waited on the docks for the ships to North America.

Coffin ships

The ships themselves were very crowded. The passengers had only a very small area each below deck and they usually couldn't go on deck to get fresh air. There were no bathrooms: people couldn't wash and had to use a bucket to go to the toilet. And there wasn't much food or clean water. Since passengers ate, slept and went to the toilet in the same area, disease spread quickly. People called these ships 'coffin ships' because 25–30% of the passengers died. They threw so many bodies into the sea that sharks often followed the ships.

The Jeanie Johnston

For the lucky passengers on the Jeanie Johnston the story was very different. The ship travelled sixteen times to Canada and managed to take more than 2,500 people safely to their new home. The ship had its own doctor and a strict captain who made sure that the ship wasn't crowded and that passengers had food and clean water. Not one person died on the Jeanie Johnston.

Actually, on its first journey, the ship arrived in North America with one more passenger: Nicholas Johnston Ryal was born on the Jeanie Johnston. His happy parents gave him the name of one of the owners of the ship and the name of the ship itself.

Irish roots

Today over four and a half million Canadians have Irish roots and there are over thirty-four million Irish Americans. Do you know that there are nine cities and

3 On the ships

a Partner A: Read the part about coffin ships.
Partner B: Read the part about the Jeanie Johnston.

b Partner A: Explain how disease spread on the coffin ships and why many people died.
Partner B: Explain how and why the Jeanie Johnston was different to the other ships.

4 Emigration in numbers

a Now scan the article for all the dates and numbers (in figures and words). Write them down and add what they mean.
For example: *1845: the famine* SF 6 → p. 151
Make an infographic with the numbers. Use different colours and sizes for the numbers and add small drawings and icons. You can also use an online infographic maker.

b Compare your infographic with other students. How are they similar or different?

5 WORDS Word patterns

a Look at this sentence from the text. What comes after the verb 'manage'?
The ship managed to take more than 2,500 people safely to their new home.

b Find three more verbs with the same pattern in the text on p. 60.

c Ask and answer with a partner.

1 What do you plan to do this evening?
2 What would you like to do at the weekend?
3 What have you learned to do this week?
4 What do you hope to do this year?

Remember to learn words with their patterns! SF 1 → p. 146

Two countries, one history

2.3 **1 Fighting and peace**

Read the conversation and answer the questions.

1 When did southern Ireland become an independent country? Why?
2 What do people call the time in Ireland when there was fighting and violence?
3 When did peace come to Ireland?

Moritz: Why are there two countries?

Mum: Well, you know, Ireland was a part of Britain in the past. After so many people had died in the potato famine, a lot of people in Ireland were very angry. They were angry with the British government because Britain hadn't helped the Irish people. Most people in southern Ireland are Catholics, and they wanted independence from Britain.

Moritz: So the Catholics in the south didn't want to be a part of Britain – is that right?

Mum: Yes, that's right. Most people in the north are Protestants – that means they belong to the Church of England. They wanted to stay a part of Britain. So in 1922 southern Ireland became an independent country. But not everybody was pleased that Ireland had become two countries. And in the 1970s the Troubles started.

Moritz: The Troubles? What were the Troubles?

Mum: There was fighting and violence in Ireland. In 1999, after lots of people had died, everybody agreed to stop fighting and make peace.

Moritz: So everything is OK now?

Mum: Well, not everyone is happy. Some people want Ireland to be one country again, so there still are some problems.

LOOK AT LANGUAGE: the past perfect

a Look at these sentences. Which event happened first in each sentence? Make a table.

1 After so many people had died, a lot of people in Ireland were very angry.
2 They were angry with the British government because Britain hadn't helped the Irish people.
3 Not everybody was pleased that Ireland had become two countries.
4 After lots of people had died, everybody agreed to stop fighting.

event 1	event 2 (simple past)
so many people had died	people in Ireland were very angry

b Look at your table in a. For events that happen before another event in the past, we use *the past perfect*. Complete the explanation.

We make the past perfect with *had/hadn't* + …

Irregular verbs → p. 244f.
LF 10 → p. 139

2 The Troubles

Complete the sentences with the past perfect.

1 Conor and Moritz (not be born) *hadn't been born* yet when the Troubles started.
2 Conor wanted to explain, but he (forgot) … some of the dates.
3 Moritz was puzzled because he (not hear) … about the Troubles.
4 Moritz understood after Conor's mum (explain) … everything.
5 When Moritz visited Conor, the Troubles (be) … already … over for more than twenty years.
6 But even after both sides (agree) … to stop fighting, there still were problems.

3 The story of Saint Patrick

2.4

Copy the table and read the sentences. Then listen and put the sentences in the right order. Write the letters.

1	2	3	4	5	6	7	8
e	…	…	…	…	…	…	…

a When he was a teenager, Irish pirates took him to Ireland as a slave. He prayed to God to help him.
b St Patrick died on March 17th around 460 AD.
c After he had been there for six years, he managed to escape and went home to study as a Catholic priest.
d He decided to go back to Ireland to teach about God.
e St Patrick was born in Britain in about 385 AD and his parents were Romans. They called him Maewyn.
f St Patrick used the shamrock in his teaching because he had noticed that a shamrock has three parts, like God – the Father, the Son and the Holy Ghost.
g The first St Patrick's Days celebrated that Patrick had helped most of Ireland to become Catholics. Today people wear green clothes and funny hats.
h In 1903 March 17th became St Patrick's Day, a public holiday in Ireland and Northern Ireland.

ACROSS CULTURES

Saint Patrick's Day is Ireland's national day and people celebrate it in Ireland, in Northern Ireland and also in the USA. The USA has a national day, but Britain doesn't have one. What is your national day? Do you know other national days and their traditions?

4 Saint Patrick and the snakes

2.5

a Complete the story with the past perfect and the simple past. Then listen and check.

After some snakes (1 attack) … Saint Patrick, he (2 decide) … to drive all the snakes out of Ireland. He (3 stand) … on a hill and (4 drive) … them into the sea. One clever snake (5 be) … left. But after Patrick (6 catch) … it in a box, he (7 throw) … the last snake into the sea. It's a great story, isn't it? But it's not true. Scientists say that there (8 not be) … any snakes in Ireland before Saint Patrick (9 go) … there!

b Now look at the cartoon. Write a modern story about what happened when Saint Patrick drove the snakes out of Ireland.

More ideas → p. 101   Fast Finishers 10 → p. 107

St Patrick driving the snakes out of Ireland.

Well, here's the ferry terminal, fellas. That'll be 20 euro, please.

Asking for and giving directions

1 Directions in Dublin

2.6 **a** Moritz is in Dublin with two students from his exchange group. He asks Karla, the virtual assistant on his phone, for directions. Find the arrow on the map. Then listen and follow the directions. Where is Moritz?

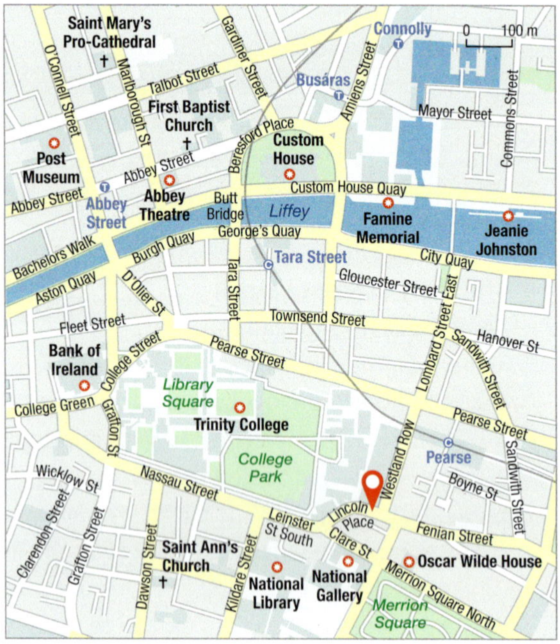

2.6 **b** Look at the map. Listen again and choose the right words.

1 Tell me the *way / road* to …
2 Go *straight / right* on.
3 Turn *right / left* into Leinster Street South.
4 So not *through / past* the college gardens?
5 Go *past / along* Nassau Street, *near / past* the college.
6 We're going *under / across* the bridge.
7 Let's walk *up / down* the street.

c Copy and complete the phrase box.

PHRASE BOX

Give directions

Go straight …

Go … the college.

Go … the college gardens.

… right.

Go … the bridge.

Go … Nassau Street.

It's … the left.

2 You're in Dublin

You're in Dublin on an exchange.

a Partner B: Look at page 95.
Partner A: Ask for directions from your partner. Follow the directions on the map.

1 You're at the National Library and you want to go to the Famine Memorial.
2 You're at the Famine Memorial and you want to go to the Abbey Theatre.

b Swap roles. Give your partner directions.

1 You're at the Post Museum.
2 You're at the Jeanie Johnston.

Fast Finishers 11 → p. 107 SF 11 → p. 157

ACROSS CULTURES

Remember: when you ask people for directions, it's important to be polite.
Use *Excuse me* and polite questions:
Excuse me, how do I get to …?
Could you tell me the way to …?
(**Not:** *Tell me …*)
Say thank you:
Thanks for your help. / Thank you.

 WB 1-2, pp. 47-48

I can ask for and give directions. ✔

Helping tourists

1 In your home town

a You're visiting your grandparents in another town. A tourist asks you for help. SF 16 → p. 161

Tourist: Excuse me. Do you speak English?
You: Yes, I do. Can I help you?
Tourist: Is there a bank near here?
You: Erm … Opa, sie fragt nach einer Bank.
Opa: Naja, es gab früher hier eine um die Ecke, aber die hat geschlossen. Die nächste ist drei Straßen weiter in der Thomasstraße. Das dauert nur ein paar Minuten zu Fuß.
You: My grandad says the nearest one …
Tourist: Oh good. Do you know how long it's open?
You: …?
Opa: Ich glaube, sie hat heute bis 16 Uhr geöffnet. Wenn die Dame sich beeilt, kann sie das gerade noch schaffen.
You: …
Tourist: Great, thanks for your help.
You: No problem. Have a nice day!

When you don't want to repeat a noun, you can use *one* or *ones*:
the nearest one (= the nearest bank)
the best ones (= the best sunglasses)

b Another tourist asks you for help.

Tourist: Excuse me. Can you help me, please? I'm looking for a shop where I can buy some sunglasses.
You: Hello. Let me just ask my grandad. Opa, …?
Opa: Die besten kriegt er bei Zimmermann. Und die Bedienung ist dort sehr gut.
You: You can buy the best ones at …
Tourist: Oh, good. Can you tell me the way to the shop, please?
You: …
Opa: Hinter dem Dom, neben der Buchhandlung. Am besten geht er hier links an dem Kaufhaus vorbei und dann rechts. Das ist der schnellste Weg.
You: …
Tourist: Thank you very much.
You: You're welcome. Enjoy your shopping!

2 Your conversation

Work in groups of three and make a similar conversation. Choose a place in your town, village or area: a nice cafe / an interesting museum / a big department store / a cheap supermarket / …

More ideas → p. 101

It takes about … minutes on foot / by tram / …
It's open from … to …
Thanks for your help.
You're welcome!
Have a nice day.

→ I can help tourists. ✔

Tips for tourists to Ireland

1 A visit to Carlingford

Conor and his mum took Moritz to Carlingford, an old town by the sea. Read the brochure. What special things can you see and do there?

If you visit Carlingford, you'll see the real Ireland. If you go to the harbour, you can visit the old castle. And you can eat great fish and oysters in the harbour! If you come here in August, you should go to the Oyster Festival.

Carlingford also has a surprise: a Leprechaun Cavern! If you go there, you'll hear about the Carlingford leprechauns. You can do a tour and go down into the magic cavern.

Every year in Carlingford there's a leprechaun hunt. If it's nice weather, you'll have a great day out. You probably won't see a real leprechaun if you go on the hunt. But if you're lucky, you might find one of the hundred leprechaun statues and €500. So if you want to have a fun day, visit Carlingford!

2 NOW YOU

Say what tourists can do if they come to your area.

If you come to ..., you can see/eat/...

If you visit ..., you'll ...

If it's nice/bad weather, you should ...

LOOK AT LANGUAGE: *if*-sentences, type 1: results

If-sentences tell us what can or will happen as a result of something else. An *if*-sentence has two parts: an *if*-clause and a main clause.

a **Read the explanation. Copy the table and complete it with four more examples from the text.**

if-clause	main clause
if + simple present	*will/can/might*
*If you **visit** Carlingford,*	*you'll **see** the real Ireland.*
...	...

b **What do you notice about the order of the two clauses in this example?**
You probably won't see a real leprechaun if you go there.

c **We can also use *if*-clauses to give instructions. Complete the examples.**

if-clause	main clause
if + simple present	*should* or imperative
*If you **come** here in August,*	...
*If you **want** to have a fun day,*	...

LF 11-12 → p. 140

 WB 1-3, pp. 49-50

3 How to catch a leprechaun

a Conor is telling Moritz about leprechauns. Complete their conversation with the correct form of the verbs.

Conor: If you catch a leprechaun, people say you (1 get) … three wishes. But be careful. If you (2 not watch) … him, he'll disappear!
Moritz: Ha! But how do you catch a leprechaun?
Conor: If you leave out some chocolate coins with gold paper, he (3 come) … to get the coins. Leprechauns love gold.
Moritz: What about food? What food do leprechauns like?
Conor: If you (4 make) … a good Irish dinner with meat, potatoes and soda bread, they'll smell it and come to get some. Or if you leave out some beer, a leprechaun (5 appear) … very quickly!

Fast Finishers 12 → p. 107

b Do you believe in leprechauns or magic? Why (not)?

LOOK AT LANGUAGE: *if*-sentences, type 0: facts and rules

a Some if-sentences are about facts and rules. Match the two clauses.

1	If people eat bad oysters,	a	it becomes green.
2	If you mix yellow and blue,	b	they get hungry.
3	If people don't eat,	c	they get sick.

b Complete the explanation. What tense is in the main clause?

if + simple present	…

c Complete these sentences.

1 If it rains, … 2 If people don't get enough sleep, … 3 If people are happy, …

LF 12b → p. 141

4 How to make soda bread at home

a Partner B: Look at page 95.
Partner A: First read what you need for soda bread.

If you want to make Irish food at home, try soda bread – it's easy! You need:
- 500g flour (if you like brown bread, you can use wholemeal flour)
- 2 teaspoons of baking soda and 1 teaspoon of salt
- about 400ml buttermilk (and maybe a little milk)

b Put the recipe in the right order. You and your partner have different sentences. Look at the sentences below. First read out sentence c.

a Put some flour on it. Make a deep cross in it with a knife.
b Bake for 40–45 minutes at 200°C. The bread is ready if it sounds 'empty'.
c *Mix the flour, the baking soda and the salt in a big bowl.*
d Mix everything together. Fast Finishers 13 → p. 107

→ I can give instructions and express rules. ✔

Understanding body language

1 Body, face and hands

a Look at the drawings: match them with what they mean.

1 I feel confident.
2 I need to think.
3 I agree.
4 I feel upset.
5 I don't want to wait. / I'm impatient.

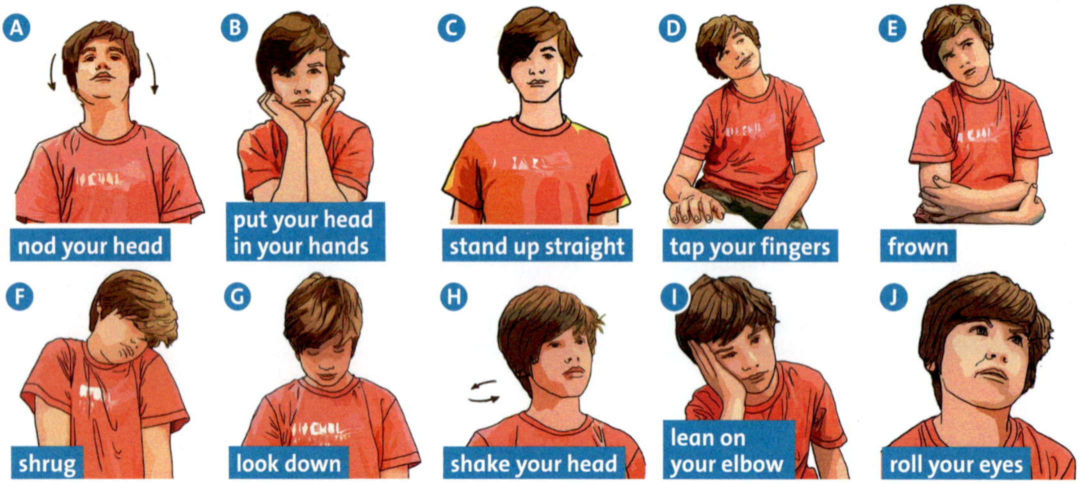

6 I'm bored.
7 I disagree. / I don't understand.
8 I don't care.
9 I'm annoyed.
10 I feel sad/ lonely/ unsure.

b Choose a picture and do the body language.
Your partner says what you mean and thinks of a situation you could be in.
You're tapping your fingers because you're impatient. You're waiting in a fast food restaurant.

2 Different language, different body language?

2.7 a Listen to two students. How do they answer these questions?

1 Do you feel different when you speak English or another language? How?
2 Is your voice different? How?
3 Do you use different body language? How?

b Think about the questions for you. Then discuss them in class.

3 VIEWING Yu Ming

Watch the first part of a short film (until 1.13) without the sound.
Look at Yu Ming's body and his face. What can you say about his job and how he feels about it? How do you know? Look at 1 again for help.

Step by step: understanding body language
- Look at people's faces.
- Look at their body movements.
- Look at their hands.

SF 11 → p. 157

 WB 1-2, p. 51

→ I can use and understand body language. ✔

Yu Ming is ainm dom (My name is Yu Ming)

1 From China to Dublin SF 19 → p. 165

a Watch the film about Yu Ming (until 3:40). Find out:

- where he goes and what he does there
- what he does then
- what his body language shows about his feelings

b Watch the next scenes (until 8:15).

1. Sum up the problem in the hostel and in the restaurant.
2. Describe how Yu Ming feels in these two situations.
3. Describe how he feels when he's in the street and in the park.

c Watch the scene in the pub (until 10:31).

1. What is the problem?
2. Who helps him and how?
3. Why does the barkeeper think old Paddy speaks Chinese?

d Describe the end of the film. How does Yu Ming feel? How do you feel? SF 12 → p. 158

2 The music

Watch the film again and listen to the music. Make notes about different scenes:

- Where is Yu Ming?
- What kind of music is it?
- How does the music emphasize how Yu Ming feels?

ACROSS CULTURES

- What did you find out about the Irish language in the film? Who speaks it and where do people speak it?
- What about Germany? Do people speak different languages in different areas?

3 Your review

Write a short review of the film (7–10 sentences). Write:

- what the film is about
- what happens in the film
- what people can or might learn from the film
- your opinion of the film (give reasons)
- if you would recommend this film

More ideas → p. 102

In a film review we usually use the simple present to talk about what happens, for example *Yu Ming travels to Ireland.*
You can use *First*, *Then* and *At the end* to tell the story.

I can understand problems and feelings in a short film. ✔

It's a tech thing

ACROSS CULTURES

For much of its history, Ireland was a poor country where most people lived from farming.

- In 1973 Ireland joined the EEC (this later became the EU – the European Union).
- From the 1990s to 2008 Ireland's economy boomed. Many international technology companies moved to Ireland because it was an English-speaking EU country.
- In 2002 Ireland started using the euro.
- In 2008 the Irish economy crashed.
- Today Ireland has a strong economy again. It is one of the richest European states and has a high-tech profile.

What can you say about Germany and Europe/the EU?

1 CoderDojos

Conor goes to a CoderDojo in Dublin. Read the advert and find out:

- who can join
- how much it costs
- what you can do there
- if you need your own laptop

Join a Coder Dojo!

If you're 7–17, you can join one of our clubs! We have clubs in 60 countries. You can learn how to code, create apps and games and build websites. All you need is a laptop (but you can also borrow one in some clubs).

2.8 **2 Keela Donovan**

One of the girls in Conor's CoderDojo is Keela Donovan. Conor wrote an article about Keela for his school magazine. Read about her. Why does she like coding?

Keela Donovan, cool coder

by Conor O'Brien

Keela Donovan is really cool. If you look at her Facebook profile, you'll see that she's a CoderDojo coder and mentor, and an award winner of the *Irish Tech Projects* competition in Dublin. It also says that Keela was the *EU Digital teen of the Year* when she was fourteen – for helping teenagers in Europe with their computer skills. And Keela's profile picture is a photo of her with her dad because he was the one who helped her become a coder.

Keela started coding when she was eight years old. Her dad suggested going to a CoderDojo in Dublin.

After she had been to a few classes, Keela made her own website. Keela liked working with code because she enjoys being creative and making things. She continued going to classes and two years later, she developed an app which helps music fans to find out what concerts are on in their area and buy tickets. She has also developed an app to help teenagers to eat healthily. Keela loves using code to make apps which can help people with problems.

Keela isn't just an amazing coder. She helps other people to code – especially girls. When she was twelve, she set up a website to help coders in Europe develop their skills. Keela also started mentoring other girls at CoderDojo because she wants girls to get into coding and find out how great technology is. She thinks that girls need more help to get into the world of tech and science.

According to Keela, everyone can code – why don't you find a class?

3 Teens and technology

Read the text again and answer the questions.

1 What is Keela's opinion of girls and technology?
2 Do you think girls need special help with technology? Why (not)?
3 Why is it a good idea for kids to start coding when they are young?

4 WORDS Word patterns

a **Look at this sentence from the text. What verb form follows the verb *start*?**
Keela **started coding** when she was eight years old.

b **Find five more verbs with the same pattern in the second paragraph of the article.**

c **Discuss these questions.**
1 Do you enjoy using technology? What do you like (or hate) doing? Give examples.
2 Can you code? If yes: When and how did you start learning to code? If no: Can you imagine learning to code? Why (not)?

Wordbank 5 → p. 113

5 How important is technology?

a **Rank these statements from 1–5 (1 = I completely disagree, 5 = I completely agree).**
A I think all schools should have coding lessons on the timetable.
B All schools should have free Wi-Fi for students.
C Schools should have a room where all students can use computers in the breaks.
D Students should be allowed to use phones at schools.
E Teachers should use more technology in lessons.

b **Compare your ideas with a partner and then with your teacher.**

TF 4 → p. 125f.

I can understand and discuss an article. ✔

WB 1-2, p. 52

4 YOUR CHECK

You can find the answers for these tasks on page 253.

1 Check your vocabulary

a An Irish quiz: Write the correct thing, place or person.

1 People drink and listen to music here.
2 He's a small man who loves gold.
3 It's special bread you get in Ireland.
4 People were starving at this time.
5 It was a time of violence in Ireland.
6 It's another name for the Irish language.

b You're shopping for souvenirs. Complete the sentences with *one* or *ones*.

1 You can get this T-shirt in orange or pink. I'll buy the orange … for my big sister.
2 My little sister loves funny socks. I'll take these … for her.
3 Mum might like the blue gloves. But I think she'll love the green …
4 A book is a good present for Dad. I'll take this … for him.
5 Mmm, sweets. I'll buy these … for me!

c Match the pictures with the descriptions.

1 He's frowning.
2 He's shaking his head.
3 He's rolling his eyes.
4 He's nodding his head.
5 He's shrugging.

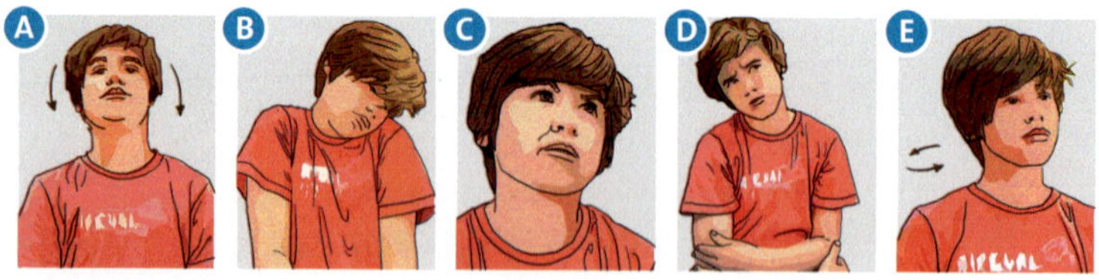

d Complete the sentences. (Think about the verb patterns of the word before the gap.)

code • develop • listen • see • use • work

1 Conor loves … computers.
2 He started … at CoderDojo when he was ten.
3 He's planning … an app.
4 He wants … for a technology company later.
5 In his free time he also enjoys … to music.
6 He's hoping … his favourite band.

2 Check your language

a Complete the sentences with the past perfect or the simple past.

Moritz (1 already / learn) … a lot about Ireland. But after he (2 see) … all the sights in Dublin, Moritz also (3 spend) … a few days in the west of Ireland. He (4 not want) … to go home because he (5 enjoy) … his visit so much!

b Match the correct sentence parts.

1	If you like food,	a	go to Connemara.
2	If you like music,	b	you might see one!
3	If you like boats,	c	try Irish stew.
4	If you like the country,	d	you'll like Irish pubs.
5	If you believe in leprechauns,	e	visit the Jeanie Johnston.

3 Check your speaking

Look at the map of Dublin on p. 64 again. Tell your partner where you are on the map. Then give him/her directions to a place. Don't say the name – your partner has to follow your directions and then say the place. Then swap roles.

4 Check your writing

You're in Ireland for three days. Write a tweet for every day (140 characters). You can tweet about the weather, the food, the sights, …

Present snapshots of Ireland

GET READY

Work in groups. You're going to present snapshots of Ireland. Each student should present one aspect of Ireland in a group presentation. Decide what to include. Think about:

- Irish history
- the Irish language
- music and Irish dancing
- Irish food
- technology in Ireland

You can also do some research and find out about: SF 4 → p. 149

- other cities in Ireland
- sport in Ireland
- Ireland in the Eurovision Song Contest
- Fungie, the Dingle Dolphin

First think about the topics. Then discuss with your group. Decide who is going to do which part of the prensentation.

I love music, so I'd like to do something about Irish musical instruments.

If you do that, I'll present something on Irish sport.

GO AHEAD

Prepare your presentation.

- First work individually: Find information, music, recipes, pictures, etc. Then make slides, a poster or a recording for your part of the presentation. You can also do a dance or sing!
- Now work as a group. Put your presentation together. Agree on the order and how you will hand over to the next person.
- Practise your presentation together. Check each other's body language (see p. 68). Every student should look confident and interested.

That was my part about music. Now Melina is going to talk about Irish sport.

FINISH

Give your group presentations. Film them and then give feedback to each group:

- What did you learn? What did you find interesting?
- Was the group's body language confident?
- Were the handovers good?

I learned a lot about popular sports in Ireland and about Irish music. If I go to Ireland, I'll go and listen to traditional music.
Group Two's presentation was quite confident. They stood up straight and didn't look down. The handovers were fine.

1 LISTENING At the tourist information centre

2.9

You're on holiday in Britain with your dad. Your dad asks about a museum at the tourist information centre. Listen and complete the notes in your exercise book.

The Roman Museum

Open: Wed.–Sun. from 10 – (1) ______

Late opening: Thurs. to (2) ______

Lots of (3) ______ *, some helmets and leather shoes.*

Website – yes or no: (4) ______

Tickets: adult tickets: (5) ______

Students: free if under (6) ______

2 SPEAKING In Ireland

a You're planning some trips for a holiday in Ireland. Partner B: Turn the book around. Partner A: Ask Partner B questions about the Giant's Causeway.

How old / the Giant's Causeway?
How / happen?
Where / get information?
When / it / open?
a cafe / there?

b Partner A: Read the webpage. Answer Partner B's questions about the Fungie boat tours.

Fungie boat tours

Come and see Fungie, the dolphin which lives in Dingle Harbour. Fungie came to Dingle in 1983 and he loves meeting people!

Our boats leave every day, all year round if the weather is good. The trips take about one hour.

Family and group tickets.
If you don't see Fungie, you don't pay!

Book online or call us on [redacted]

a Partner B: Read the webpage. Answer Partner A's questions about the Giant's Causeway.

Science says it happened naturally 60 million years ago. But an old story says a giant whose name was Finn McCool created these amazing rocks in Antrim, Northern Ireland. He took a piece of the coast and threw it into the sea to make a path.

The Visitor Centre is open from 09:00 to 17:00 in winter and from 09:00 to 21:00 in summer. Visit the tourist information centre or enjoy good food in the cafe.

Gifts and souvenirs for sale in the gift shop.

b Partner B: Ask Partner A questions about the Fungie boat tours.

Who or what / Fungie?
When / Fungie / come / Dingle?
boat trips / every day?
How long / boat trips / take?
How / book?

3 USE OF ENGLISH A Dublin hero

Complete the article. Choose the best word (A–D) for each sentence: *1 …, 2 …, …*

Read the sentence and the four words. Choose the best word and then read the sentence with the word again. Does it sound right?

When Jamie Harrington was 16, he (1) … a man's life. The man (2) … sitting on Ha'penny Bridge in Dublin and wanted (3) … jump into the river. Jamie sat down and (4) … the man if he was OK. After they (5) … talked for 45 minutes, the man agreed to go to hospital. Jamie said he helped the man (6) … he likes (7) … people. Jamie said: 'He just needed to talk and I was just being nice and that costs (8) … at all.'

1	A kept	B helped	C saved	D prayed
2	A is	B was	C have	D had
3	A for	B in	C by	D to
4	A asked	B told	C said	D explained
5	A has	B have	C had	D hadn't
6	A because	B but	C so	D and
7	A help	B helping	C talk	D talking
8	A something	B anything	C nothing	D everything

4 VOCABULARY Directions

a Write the directions for the pictures.

1 
2 
3 
4 
5 
6 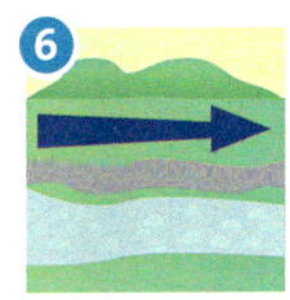

b Ask your partner for directions to a place near your school. Ask politely and say thanks.

5 WRITING A story

a Choose 4–6 of the things, places and people in the picture. Write a story which has all your words in it. Remember to use linking words.

b Read your story and check it.

c Swap stories and read your partner's story.

Unit 5 It's my life

In this unit you will

- talk about family and friends.
- describe interests, sports, games and online activities.
- discuss online bullying.
- give advice.
- use strategies to understand and learn words.

➔ At the end of the unit you'll make webpages for an online teen magazine.

1 Riku's friends

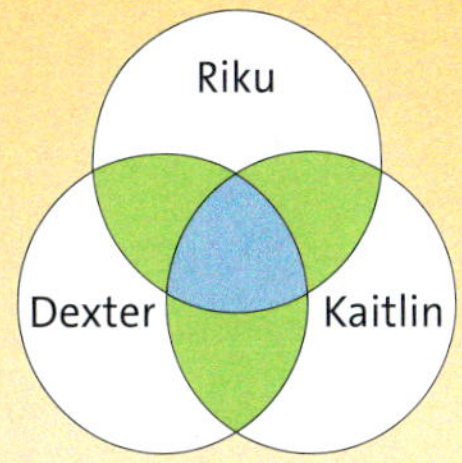

a Copy the diagram. Then look at the map and the three online friends. Write their home towns and interests in the circles. Write the interests that they have in common in the blue and green areas.

SF 18 → p. 164

2.10 b Listen to Riku's introduction on his website. Complete the diagram with more information.

c Make a diagram like the one in a for you and two other students. First talk together about your interests and find out what you have in common.

I like cooking. What about you? – Me too! / I prefer biking. Wordbank 6 → p. 114

2 Happy moments

a Close your eyes and think of a happy moment in your life. Then open your eyes. Tell your partner where you were, who you were with and when it happened.

b Take a big piece of paper. Write *Happiness is …* at the top. Then write as many things as you can on the poster. Think of your interests and activities you do with friends, online friends and family.

c WALK AROUND Put your posters on the walls or the desks. Find out what activities and interests are most common.

3 Offline and online friendship

Do you have online friends? How is your friendship the same or different to your friendship with real-life friends? In which way are they important to you?

I can tell my online friends things that I can't tell my real friends. I go swimming and biking with my real friends. You can't do that online! More ideas → p. 103

➔ I can talk about what makes me happy. ✔

WB 1, p. 55

Video stars

1 Videos

Do you watch videos on the internet? If **yes**: What types of videos do you like watching (pranks, gameplay videos, music videos, beauty videos, tech or film reviews, ...)? Why do you like them? If **no**: Why not?

2 Where the heck is Matt?

Read about Matt Harding, one of the first video stars. Copy and complete his profile. Fast Finishers 14 → p. 108

name	Matt Harding
channel	...
video star since	...
type of videos	...
sponsor	...
subscribers	...
total views	...

It all started with *Me at the Zoo*, YouTube's first video which Jawed Karim, one of the site's founders, uploaded in April 2005. **1 ■■■**. Since then millions of people have been entertaining the world with their videos.

One of the first video stars was American Matt Harding who has been uploading funny dance videos to the internet since 2003. Before he started travelling and making videos, Matt worked in a video game shop, for a video game magazine and also designed video games in Los Angeles.

In 2003 after he'd travelled around the world on a trip with a friend, Matt uploaded his first video to his travel blog. **2 ■■■**. In each country, he was doing a silly dance: for example, with a giraffe in Kenya, in a market in Beijing, on Hollywood Boulevard in Los Angeles, on a train in Siberia and even on top of Kilimanjaro. **3 ■■■**. But not many people saw the video until a fan uploaded it to the new site YouTube in 2005. The video got over a million views and Matt became a video star.

In May 2006 Matt uploaded a new dance video to his video channel *Where the heck is Matt?* This second video again showed him dancing in different places – even underwater! The video was much better quality because Matt had found a sponsor (a chewing gum company) who paid for the trip. **4 ■■■**.

However, after this, Matt changed how he made videos. **5 ■■■**. He also invited other people to present their own traditional dances. Secondly, to pay for his trips he used crowdfunding and not advertising. Today Matt has nearly 140,000 subscribers on his video channel and over 112 million views. But recently he has been spending more time with his family at home in Seattle and he hasn't been making dance videos.

Many fans subscribe to today's top video stars who have millions of followers on different social media sites. **6 ■■■**. This means that the most popular earn millions of dollars every year in advertising.

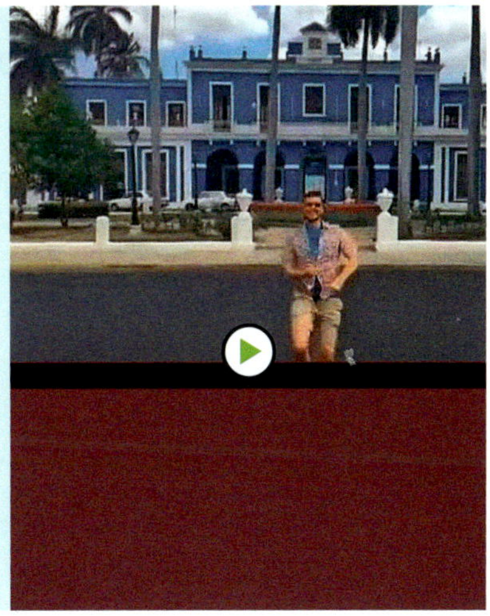

3 Missing information

Read the missing sentences a–f. Then read the article again and put the sentences in the correct place (1–6 ■■■): *1d, 2 …*

Look at the sentences before and after the gap to help you.

a This sponsored video went viral and got nearly 20 million views.
b This first video showed him in many different countries.
c Firstly, he invited other people to dance with him.
d He talked about elephants at the zoo.
e The silly dance made people smile.
f Some post a video or even several videos a day.

4 WORDS Word building: compound nouns

Gameplay **and** ***social media*** **are compound nouns: two different words which together have a new meaning: Match words from the boxes to make compound nouns.**

home • chewing • crowd • head • skate • web

board • gum • funding • phones • site • town

Compound nouns can be one word, two words or even have a hyphen (for example, *self-defence, T-shirt*). Learn the spelling or check in a dictionary. SF 2 → p. 147

5 Videos and memes

a **Watch Matt's videos online. What do you think of them? Why do you think they are so popular?**

b **Choose one or two of the pictures on these pages. Write a caption for the picture. Then compare your captions.**
I like this caption because …

6 NOW YOU

Choose task 1 OR task 2.

1 Make a profile of your favourite video star. You can use the profile headings in 2 and add other information.
2 Imagine somebody wants to be your sponsor for an online video: choose a type of video and then write a description of what you would like to do in your video. Explain why. More ideas → p. 103

Social media and other interests

1 Pets on social media

a These two pets are Riku's favourite animals on social media. Imagine they can talk: what might they say in these pictures?

b Now read about them. Why do you think they are popular? Do you think it's OK to use animals like this? Why (not)?

How long have you been using social media? Have you seen photos of Angry Cat? Her owners have been posting pictures of her on social media for years. She looks really angry – look at her eyes! However, Angry Cat's real name is Lucy and her owners say she isn't angry at all.

Since 2016, Pete the Pug's owners have been taking photos and videos of him in cute hats and clothes. You can often find him with celebrities on social media. But Pete hasn't been getting all the attention since last year: his sister, Penny the Pug, has been sharing his channel.

2 NOW YOU

What have you been doing since last weekend?

I've been ...

- doing sport / homework / ...
- listening to [singer / band]
- hanging out with friends / ...

Wordbank 6 → p. 114

I haven't been doing anything special.

LOOK AT LANGUAGE: the present perfect progressive

a Look at the examples of the present perfect progressive in blue in 1. We use this tense to talk about something that started in the past and has continued until now.
Complete the rule.
We make the present perfect progressive with ... + ... +-*ing*-form.

b We use *for* and *since* with the present perfect progressive to answer *How long ...?* Find an example of *for* and *since* in 1. Then choose the right word in the explanations.
We use *for* / *since* with a starting point.
We use *for* / *since* to talk about a length of time.

LF 13, 14 → p. 141

3 Lindsey Stirling

a Read about one of Kaitlin's favourite musicians. Complete the information with the present perfect progressive and **for** or **since**.

Lindsey Stirling

She (1 play) … the violin (2) … she was five and she (3 dance) … (4) … a long time too. (5) … 2007 Lindsey (6 upload) … videos of herself to her video channel where she mixes her love of violin and dance. Lindsey has her own music company and (7 fund) … her own music (8) … she started her music career. Her fans (9 support) … her (10) … years: her videos have over 2 billion views!

b Who's your favourite musician, singer or band? How long have they been performing? How long have you been listening to them or following them on social media?

4 LISTENING Questions & answers with Kaitlin

2.11 a Riku recorded an interview with Kaitlin for his site. Listen. Are the sentences true or false? Correct the false ones.

1 Kaitlin has been listening to music since she was very young.
2 She's been playing the violin for six years.
3 She's been following Lindsey since 2015.
4 She's been going to concerts since last year.
5 She's been following some new bands for a few months.

2.11 b Write the questions for Kaitlin's interview. Use *How long …?* and the present perfect progressive. Then listen to the interview again and check.

1 *How long have you been listening to music?*

5 Q&A with you

a Choose an activity from your happiness poster on p. 77.
What activity do you like doing?
How long have you been doing it?
Why do you like it?

b DOUBLE CIRCLE Ask and answer your questions in a. Then students in the outside circle move to the left.

c Tell the class what you found out in b.

d Imagine you have your own website. Write an 'About' part for your site.
Fast Finishers 15 → p. 108

I can talk about my interests. ✔

WB 1-2, p. 58

Explaining games

1 Games

Riku, Kaitlin and Dexter all love video games. What type of games do you prefer: video games, board games, card games, puzzles, …? Why? Who do you play them with?

Wordbank 7 → p. 115

2 A board game

a Partner B: Look at page 96.
Partner A: Look at the instructions for a board game. Match them with the correct pictures.

Aim of the game: to get all your tokens home

1 The game is for two to four players.
2 You need a board, a dice and tokens.
3 Each player has four tokens – green, red, yellow or blue.
4 First roll the dice. You need a six to start moving.
5 Next move your token along the squares on the board.
6 If another player's token is already on a square where you want to go, you can take it off and send it back to the starting point.
7 Get your token safely home.
8 The person with all four tokens on the home squares wins the game.

b MEDIATION You want to play the game with a German friend whose English isn't very good. Explain in German how to play the game. Does your partner know what the game is?

SF 16 → p. 161

3 Your game

a Choose a game that you enjoy playing. It can be any kind of game.
First think and make notes:

- What is the aim of the game?
- What equipment do you need?
- How do you play it? Think of 4–8 instructions. Wordbank 7 → p. 115 SF 7 → p. 152

b Explain to your partner in English the aim of the game (but don't say the name). Then explain how to play your game. You can draw diagrams or pictures too. Your partner can ask questions if he or she doesn't understand.

> The aim of the game is to …
> You need …
> First … Next …
> You can …

c Can your partner guess your game? If not, give your partner three choices.

I can give instructions for a game. ✔

Understanding opinions

1 Parents

You're going to watch a film that shows the relationship between a father and his son. Think about what parents and teenagers often have different opinions about. Then discuss.

2 VIEWING Coach, part 1

Watch the first situation from the film Coach (until 6:24). David lives with his mum, but today he's on a special trip with his dad. Complete the information.

1 David and his father are driving to … because …
2 David gets … from his dad.
3 Unfortunately there's a problem with …
4 … offers to help them because …
5 The father says no, but then changes his mind because …
6 On the coach …

SF 19 → p. 165

3 Opinions

a Watch the video again. Describe …

Remember to pay attention to body language.

1 how the father behaves towards his son.
2 how David reacts and talks to his father. What do you think is his opinion of his father?
3 how David and his dad are feeling when they sing together.
4 what David and his father think about being on the coach.

SF 12 → p. 158

b Explain what helped you in a (dialogue, body language, how they talk, …).

c Who says these things? What is the person talking about? What feelings are they expressing?

1 Lame! 2 Turn it down! 3 Sweet!
4 So it's car over me?

4 VIEWING Coach, part 2

a When they stop for lunch, the British fans burn a French flag and David's dad is angry. Watch and then discuss what happens.

b Complete these sentences.

1 In David's shoes, I'd feel …
2 In his dad's shoes, I'd be …
3 At the end of the video I felt …

ACROSS CULTURES

What did you find out about British football fans in this film? Why do you think they behave like this? Do German fans behave like this too?

I can understand opinions in a film. ✔

If I were you

1 Advice for Riku

a Riku is talking to Dexter about a problem. Read the chat and find out the problem. Say if you think Dexter gives him good advice or not.

Surfboy	My parents always say 'You ought to switch off that computer and do something with your friends'. They don't understand that I have online friends.
DD	Well, if I were you, I'd talk to them and explain.
Surfboy	But I've told them, they don't listen. It would be nice if they had time for me. But they just work all the time.
DD	If I were you, I wouldn't worry. A lot of parents think computers are bad. I read an article about all the good effects of computers – I'll send it to you. Maybe if you showed it to your parents, they'd understand.
Surfboy	Probably not – but I can try. Thanks, Dexter.

b What advice would you give to Riku? *You ought to …*

2 Advice for Dexter

Dexter has got a problem. He forgot to save his homework on his computer. Give him some advice. Use the verbs in the box or your own ideas.

If I were you, *I'd …* / *I wouldn't …*

do • copy • explain • go • say • worry

LOOK AT LANGUAGE: *if*-sentences, type 2

a Find four *if*-sentences in 1. Then choose the correct explanation.
We use *if*-sentences type 2 when a situation or an event is *likely/unlikely* to happen.
You can use *If I were you, I'd / I wouldn't* to put yourself in somebody's shoes and give advice.

b Copy and complete the table with the clauses from the examples in a. Then complete the rule for the verb forms.

if-clause	main clause
If I were you,	*I'd talk to them.*
…	…
…	…
…	…
simple …	*… / … + infinitive*

LF 15 → p.143

3 Advice from Kaitlin

2.12 **a** Complete the chat. Then listen and check.

Remember: the *if*-clause can be first or second in the sentence.

Surfboy Hey Kaitlin, I need some advice. I want a new hairstyle – maybe like my favourite Japanese soccer player.

Kait123 If I (1 be) … you, I'd try out some styles on the internet before you go to the hairdresser's. But you (2 have to) … upload a photo of yourself if you wanted to do that. I can send you a link.

Surfboy So if I (3 upload) … a photo, I could see myself with different hairstyles?

Kait123 Yes, you (4 get) … an idea of what suits you if you did that – and you (5 not have) … a horrible surprise at the hairdresser's.

b Take turns to give advice. Use these ideas or your own ideas.

My friend looks sad all the time.
My dad has lost his job.
People at school laugh about my clothes.
I want to learn the violin.

If I were you, I'd talk to …
I'd tell …
I wouldn't worry …
I'd ask …

4 Advice from Riku

Riku is part of a group of young surfers who want to keep plastic out of the water around Seattle. Look at his notes for a talk at his school. Write what he said.

Plastic in the oceans

1 you / care about the environment – you / stop buying plastic bags
2 we / recycle plastic bags – it / help to keep plastic out of the oceans
3 we / not put plastic bags in the oceans – sea animals and birds / not eat them
4 sea animals and birds / not get plastic in their stomachs – not die
5 you / tell people about plastic bags – maybe they / not buy them
6 we / ban plastic bags in our state – that / really help

If you cared about the environment, you'd stop buying plastic bags.

5 GAME What would you do if …?

Read the rules and then play this game.

- First everybody writes three questions with *What would you do if …?* Write each question on a different piece of paper. For example: *What would you do if you could change one thing in the world? What would you do if you met your favourite singer?* More ideas → p. 103
- Put all your pieces of paper on the table so that you can't see the questions.
- The first student takes a question and reads it out to the group.
- Then he or she answers the question. *If I could change one thing in the world, I'd …*

If you can't answer the question (or don't want to answer it), say *I don't know*.

→ I can give advice and talk about unlikely situations. ✔

Understanding and learning words

1 Understanding new words: sports

Riku is writing about skateboarding on his website. Look at the tips, then say what the blue words are in German. Explain which tip or tips helped you.

These can help you understand words:
- pictures and headings
- the words before/after a new word
- international words
- similar words in German or other languages you know
- words from the same word family
- word building rules (prefixes, suffixes, compounds, etc.)

SF 2 → p. 147

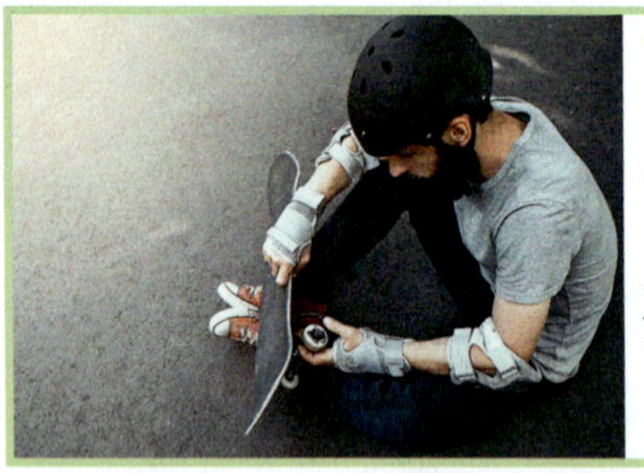

Skateboarding: the equipment

If you want to skateboard safely, you need the right equipment. First you need a good board with sandpaper material on the top. A good solid helmet is important to stop you from getting a concussion if you fall and hit your head. You'll also need good shoes which protect your ankles, wrist guards to protect your hands and elbow pads.

2 Using an online dictionary

Read the tips in the box. Use an online dictionary to check the words in different colours. SF 3 → p. 148

You can use a dictionary to check
- the meaning of the word
- the spelling
- what type of word it is (noun, verb, ...)
- the pronunciation
- if it is American (US) or British English

The history of skateboarding

The first skateboards in the 1950s were ordinary boards with roller-skate wheels on them. Surfers in California used them when there were no waves and called it 'sidewalk surfing'. In the 1970s companies made better boards and people started to do new tricks – like the ollie (when you jump into the air on your board). In the 1980s street skating and skateboarding with parkour became popular. And for the 2020 Olympics, skateboarding finally became an Olympic sport.

3 Learning vocabulary

Discuss how you learn vocabulary. What problems do you have when you learn vocabulary? How can you get better at learning words?

Five good reasons to use a vocabulary app. You can ...
- practise words using vocabulary cards.
- listen to the pronunciation.
- revise vocabulary in a game.
- see your learning statistics.
- learn on the go.

Step by step: understanding and learning words

- If you don't understand a word, use a strategy.
- If that doesn't work, use a dictionary.
- If you'd like to get better at learning words, try using a vocabulary app.

SF 1-3 → pp. 146-148

A letter to me

1 Dexter's letter

a Look at this letter from Dexter to himself. Answer these questions:

1 Address
- Where does Dexter write his address?
- What is different from a German address? (postcode, ...)

2 Start of letter
- How does Dexter start the letter?
- How else can you start a letter (or email?)

3 End of letter
- How does Dexter end the letter?
- How else can you end a letter?

b Now read the letter.
Why is Dexter writing it? What topics does he write about?

33 Main Street
London NW4 6JZ

12 July, 20

Dear Me

How are you? It's nearly the end of another school year and I'd like to tell you about some of the great things from this year and some of the not so good things.

Let's start with the not so good things :
First, school: you didn't get very good grades in science this year. But you know that if you worked harder, you'd do better.
You've been playing a lot of video games and not getting enough sleep. So you've been tired in lessons sometimes. You've forgotten your homework sometimes too.

And now the good things :
You were in the school football team again this year and the team has won nearly all their matches!
You've been working hard in English. Your spelling is much better.
You've been learning to cook at school. Yum!

In the summer, you ought to chill out with your friends. And in the next school year you ought to enjoy school, but work hard too.

Love
Me

2 Your letter

a Write a letter to yourself.
Write about the good and not so good things this year and tell yourself what you ought to do in the summer and in the next school year. SF 10 → p. 156

> **Remember:** start and end the letter in the right way.

b CHECK Read your letter again.
Check your spelling in a dictionary and make sure you have used the right verb forms. Put your letter in My file.
Read it again next year.

I can write a letter. ✔

Girl Online *(by Zoe Sugg)*

1 The book

a Look at the photo of the author, famous fashion blogger Zoella (Zoe Sugg), when she presented her book *Girl Online* in London. How is she feeling at the book presentation? What do you think she writes about in the book? What type of problems do you think the girl in the story might have?

2.13 b Listen to an online audio review of the book. What happened to Penny Porter, the girl in the book? How do you think she feels?

2 Penny's problem

2.14 Read part of the book: Penny's description of her problem and her last blog post. Copy the chart and make notes:

Fast Finishers 16 → p. 108

Setting	
Characters	
Problem	
Solution	

My email notification goes off again. Five more messages telling me that total strangers have written about me on Twitter. I click on one and see the word 'hate' and quickly click out again.

I sit on my bed, looking at my phone in terror. I imagine people all over the world reading about me, posting horrible messages about me. People I don't know. People who've never even met me. But they know who I am. They know my name. And they know my blog. What if they find out where I live? What if they come to this house? What am I going to do? I have to go back to school tomorrow. How will I face everyone? [...]

I have nowhere I can feel safe now. My readers will all hate me. Everyone will hate me. Tears are pouring down my face. I've never felt so scared or so completely alone. There's pressure in my head.
I can't see. I can't breathe. [...]

* * * * *

2.15

4 January

From Fairy Tale to Horror Story

Hello,

As most of you probably know by now, in the last couple of days, I had A LOT of online attention.

A lot of very negative attention.

For the last couple of days, total strangers have been posting lies and negative messages about me all over the internet. And celebrity websites have been writing articles about me without even checking the facts.

These people don't know me.

None of you know me. None of you know the truth about what really happened to me.

But all of you think you have the right to post an opinion or call me names.

I didn't know Brooklyn Boy's identity. I knew he was called Noah and I knew he liked music, but I didn't know he had a record deal and I definitely didn't know he was in a relationship with someone else.

And then someone found out about this blog and told everybody my identity.

For so long this blog has been my safe place – the place where I could talk about my feelings. But in the last couple of days I've seen how shallow the online world can be. It's a world where people think it's OK to hide behind their screens and their usernames and say horrible things about a person they don't even know. [...]

So to finish my last blog post on this site, I've just got one more thing to say.

Every time you post something online you have a choice.

You can make it something that adds to the happiness levels in the world – or you can make it something that takes away from them.

So, next time you want to post a comment or share a link, ask yourself: is this going to add to the happiness in the world?

And if the answer's no, then please delete.

There's enough sadness in the world already. I won't post on here any more.

But to everyone who added to my happiness while I did, thank you so much.

Penny Porter aka Girl Online xxx

3 The problem and the solution

a Read the problem and the blog post again. In the post how does Penny describe the people who hated her and the things that they did? Find the lines which say this.

b Describe Penny and how she feels in this situation. The words in the box can help you. Explain why you think this.

angry • brave • clever • horrible • lame • sad • silly • strong • stupid • weak

c Look at the comments on Penny's last blog post. Then write your comment.

Don't give in to haters and online bullies!
Your post made me feel bad about when I've judged people and I didn't know all the facts.
Good post – but why are you closing your blog? Why don't you fight these bullies?

d What can you do to protect yourself from online bullies? Brainstorm ideas. Then discuss with the class. You can make a poster for your classroom with the best ideas. TF 5 → p. 127

I can understand a problem and its solution in a story. ✔

You can find the answers for these tasks on page 254.

1 Check your vocabulary

a **Make compound words. Write if they are one word (1) or two words (2).**

1	board	a	park
2	foot	b	code
3	skate	c	game
4	hair	d	ball
5	post	e	walk
6	side	f	style

b **Complete the words to make phrases.**

I (1) p_ _ _ed a video last week and it went (2) v _ _ _l. People (3) s_ _ _ed links to my site all over the world! Now thousands of people have (4) s_ _ _ _ _ _ _ _d to my channel. I'm always on my computer after school. I use it to check (5) f_ _ _s for school work. But I always (6) s_ _ _ _h off my computer early, so that I can sleep.

c **Choose the correct word. You can use an online dictionary for help.**

1 I never *change / turn* my mind.

2 Don't *tell / call* people names!

3 HEY, *COOL / CHILL* OUT!

4 Please *present / give* me some advice.

5 Don't *give in / take in* to bullies.

2 Check your language

a **Complete the information on the band's website with the present perfect progressive, and *for* or *since*.**

The four of us (1 hang out) ... together (2) ... we were small. Josie (3 live) ... next to Sami (4) ... years and Ian and Ethan (5 write) ... music together (6) ... they left school. We (7 work) ... really hard on our first album (8) ... a year now. But we (9 not work) ... all the time! (10 you all / have) ... fun?

b **Complete the comments by fans.**

1 Well done, guys! If you (not work) ... so hard, you wouldn't be so successful.
2 I love your sound! I (buy) ... tickets if you went on tour!
3 Hey, if you (need) ... another singer, I'd join your band!

3 Check your speaking

Take turns to give advice. Use *You ought to* ...

1 I'm always late for school.
2 I always forget English vocabulary.
3 Somebody is posting horrible comments about me.
4 My parents don't listen to me.
5 I have problems with English pronunciation.
6 I want to be happy.

4 Check your writing

Write a short social media update about what you've been doing since last month (60–80 words).

Hi everybody!
Sorry for not posting for a long time! I've been very busy. Last week ...

Make webpages for a teen magazine

GET READY

Work in groups. You're going to make some webpages for a teen magazine.
First decide on a good name for your magazine.
Then decide what you would like to write.
Your pages can include:

- interviews with students in your group or articles about their interests, hobbies or sports
- news about video stars and celebrities
- problem letters and advice
- game reviews with instructions how to play a game
- music reviews of your favourite song or singer
- memes with photos and captions
- positive slogans with advice for life.

You've been training for swimming competitions for years – you ought to write something about your training.

If I were you, I'd do some memes with your pets – they're really cute!

GO AHEAD

Prepare your pages.
Write your reviews, articles, letters, etc. Remember to:

- give your pages or articles interesting headings
- take photos or find photos
- use dictionaries to find new words and check the spelling (see p. 86)

When you've finished your work, ask another student in your group to check it.

FINISH

Put your pages together for your online magazine.
Make a home page for your magazine which says what's in the magazine.
Put your magazine pages online (or print copies if that's not possible).
Read the other groups' magazines and give feedback.

Group 3's magazine was really cool / interesting / a bit short / ...
We loved the rabbit memes and ...
We missed ...
We think the design of the magazine pages was great / unclear / ...
It would be even better if the home page was clearer / ...

Unit 1

2 VIEWING **The most famous school** Unit 1 | p. 9 Ex. 2

a Fara, James and Theo have won scholarships to Eton, a famous boarding school.
Partner B:
Watch the video and make notes.
What do you find out about:
breakfast • uniforms • Eton language • sports

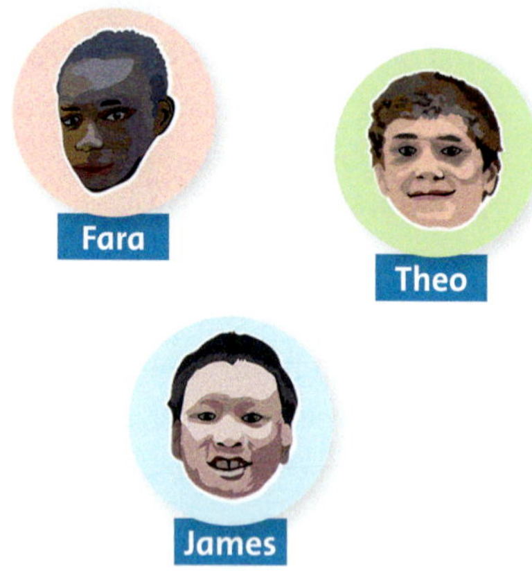

b Tell Partner A what you found out.

c Watch the video again. Then talk to your partner.
What do James and Fara think about Eton?
What do you think about Eton?
Would you like to go to a boarding school?
Why (not)?

Unit 2

2 **Another evening out** Unit 2 | p. 35 Ex. 2

a Partner B: Answer Partner A's questions about the Monster Truck Show.

b Partner B: Ask Partner A questions about his / her event. Find out:

- what the event is
- where it is
- if it's OK for wheelchairs
- when it starts
- how much it costs
- what you mustn't bring

Unit 3

3 **The end of the story** Unit 3 | p. 48 Ex. 3a

a **Partner A & B:**

Look at the pictures and read the newspaper article.

- Tell the story with your partner. Use the tips in the box.
- Write the story (in about 8–10 sentences). Use the tips in the box to help you. Start like this:
  Butcher knelt down and looked into the hole again. ...
  More ideas → p. 100
- Look at page 48 again.

Writing a story
- Describe the setting and characters.
- Describe what happens. Use adjectives and adverbs to make the story more interesting.
- Describe the feelings of the characters.
- Write what people say and think.
- Use linking words.

Treasure in a field

Farm worker Mr Gordon Butcher and his boss Mr Sydney Ford have got £1,000 each after they found Roman silver in a field. Usually the person who finds treasure gets a lot of money – for this treasure probably half a million or a million pounds. But because Mr Ford didn't tell the police when the two men found it, they couldn't get the money.

2 William and Kate Unit 3 | p. 53 Ex. 2

a Partner B: Read about William and Kate. Make notes on the main points.

Prince William is the first son of Charles, Prince of Wales, and Diana, Princess of Wales, and Britain's future king. William worked as a helicopter pilot in the Royal Air Force for five years and then as an ambulance pilot for two and a half years. Now, in his role as a member of the royal family, William supports charities that help young people to learn skills and become confident adults. William especially supports programmes for homeless young people and programmes which work to stop online bullying.

William married Catherine Middleton (Kate) in 2011 at Westminster Abbey in London. They met when they were both students of art history at university in Scotland. It was the first time somebody who wasn't 'royal' married a future king. Kate does charity work with young people, especially children with mental health problems and children whose parents use drugs.

William and Kate live in a large apartment with twenty-two rooms at Kensington Palace, but they also have a home in Norfolk in the east of England which was a wedding present from the Queen. Together they have three children: son George, daughter Charlotte and son Louis.

b Listen to Partner A. Then tell your partner about William and Kate in German. Use your notes.

c What is similar about the two brothers' lives? What is different? Discuss.

2 You're in Dublin Unit 4 | p. 64 Ex. 2

a Partner B: Give Partner A directions.

1 You're at the National Library.

2 You're at the Famine Memorial.

b Now ask for directions from your partner. Follow the directions on the map.

1 You're at the Post Museum and you want to go to the Jeanie Johnston.

2 You're at the Jeanie Johnston and you want to go to Trinity College.

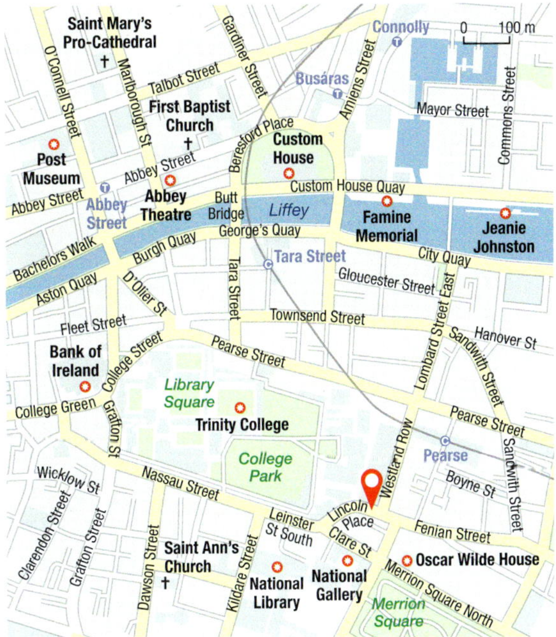

4 How to make soda bread at home Unit 4 | p. 67 Ex. 4

a Partner B: First read what you need for soda bread.

If you want to make Irish food at home, try soda bread – it's easy!

You need:

- 500g flour (if you like brown bread, you can use wholemeal flour)
- 2 teaspoons of baking soda and 1 teaspoon of salt
- about 400ml buttermilk (and maybe a little milk)

b Together put the recipe in the right order. You and your partner have different sentences. Look at the sentences below.

Partner A starts. Listen to your partner's sentence and then read out the next correct one.

e Put the bread on a baking sheet and put it in the oven.

f Then add the buttermilk. Add a little milk if you like softer bread.

g Let it cool a little – and then eat! The bread tastes best if you eat it warm from the oven.

h Knead the bread for about a minute and make a ball.

Fast Finishers 13 → p. 107

Unit 5

2 A board game Unit 5 | p. 82 Ex. 2

a Partner B: Look at the instructions for a video game. Match the instructions with the correct pictures.

Aim of the game: to fill lines with blocks and score points.

1 Look at the different blocks (there are 7 different types).
2 Start the game so that the blocks drop into the field.
3 The 'ghost' piece shows you where the block will fall.
4 You can move the blocks left and right to change where the block will fall.
5 You can turn the blocks to fit into a specific place.
6 You can make the blocks fall faster.
7 Fill the lines with the blocks.
8 You can play the game as a single player or as a multiplayer game.

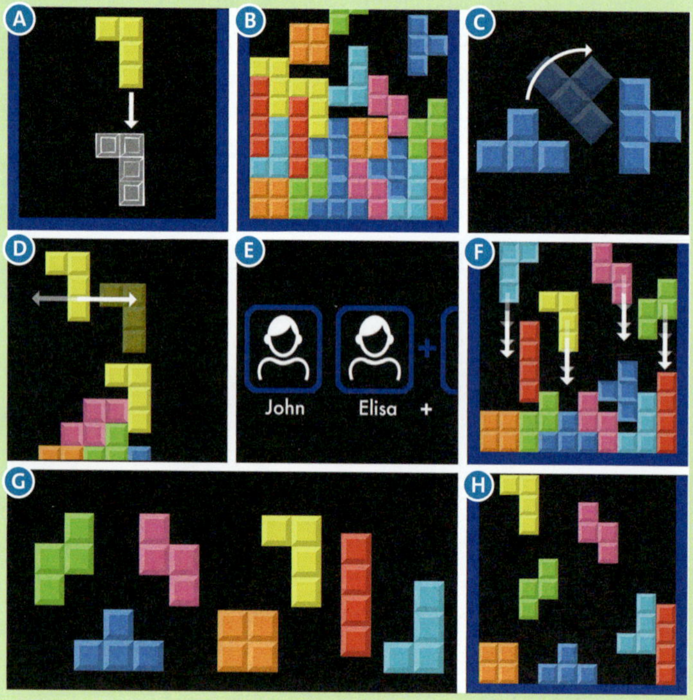

b MEDIATION You want to play the game with a German friend whose English isn't very good. Explain in German how to play the game. Does your partner know what the game is?

Unit 1

3 What do you think? Unit 1 | p. 11 Ex. 3

1

✔ She was right because ...
- she didn't want her parents to know she is homesick.
- she was thinking about her parents.
- she didn't want to worry her parents.

✘ She was wrong because ...
- she told lies.
- a lie is always a lie.
- it's not right to tell lies.

2

She doesn't want her friends to ...
- be worried about her.
- laugh about her.
- feel sorry for her.
- know how she feels.

3

✔ I think Ella's day sounds great.
I'd like to do lots of activities / have cake in the afternoon / be with my friends all day.

✘ I think Ella's day sounds horrible / hard / ...
I don't want to spend all my day with the same people / in one place.
I don't like lots of rules.

My day is longer / shorter / more fun / ... than Ella's day.
I get up earlier / later and go to bed earlier / later.
I do more homework / not as much homework.

5 Great people and places Unit 1 | p. 13 Ex. 5a

a Think of two great people and one great place and why you like them.

He / She is an amazing coach / neighbour / friend / ...	who	always makes me feel good / makes me laugh. listens to me / helps me with problems / gives me good advice. makes the best food / tells great stories / helps me with homework. is very kind / special ...
He / She is an amazing actor / singer / ...	who	is just the best! makes great films / always wins the ball / scores goals / makes great music /... works hard / trains hard / ... is also kind / helps other people / gives money to ...
... is the place	where	I was born / my best friend lives / my grandparents live. we go on holiday every year. I learned to swim / I met my best friend / ... somebody told me an important secret.

Unit 2

2 What happens next? Unit 2 | p. 30 Ex. 2b

b Discuss what you think happens next.

I think the car takes Sarah and Danny ...

I don't agree. I think the car takes them to ...

Maybe, but then Danny and Sarah get scared. They go home / call Sarah's mom / ...

No, I don't think they do that. I think they fight / help / use / hurt / ...

Or maybe they ...

After that they call the police / run away / ...

In the end ...

3 Your script Unit 2 | p. 31 Ex. 3b

b Write a simple script for the scene. Include everything in the box and complete this dialogue.

Sarah: Hi, ...
Mom: ...
Sarah: Could I please borrow ...?
Mom: What happened to ...?
Sarah: It ... I have an invitation to ...
Mom: It's dangerous downtown. Why don't you ...?
Sarah: Please ...
Mom: I use my car for ... If there's ...
Sarah: But you're a ...

a character description (what a person looks like / is like)
b character name
c description of setting (the place)
d dialogue
e instructions (how people do or say things)
f time of day

5 Instructions and rules Unit 2 | p. 33 Ex. 5c

c Do your parents have rules? What mustn't you do at home? Tell your partner.

I mustn't
- wear shoes in our flat.
- leave dirty clothes on my bedroom floor.
- have my phone at the dinner table.
- put my feet on the table.
- use bad language.
- shout at my brother/sister.
- eat too many sweets.
- leave food when we eat.
- play computer/video games after 8 o'clock.
- be noisy when my little brother/sister is sleeping.
- have my phone in my room when I sleep.
- go to bed late on school nights.
- do my homework in the morning.

2 Paragraph headings Unit 2 | p. 36 Ex. 2a

a Read the article. Think of headings for paragraphs 1–6. Choose from these ideas.

– Help from others
– Future dreams
– Not much free time
– Help from Grandma
– Not always the boss
– Long days
– The start of a business
– Decide your own future
– Look good and feel good
– Tips from great people
– Wear a bow tie!
– Family is important

Unit 3

3 The end of the story Unit 3 | p. 48 Ex. 3a

Write the story (in about 8–10 sentences). Use the tips in the box and the story words to help you.
Start like this:

Butcher knelt down and looked into the hole again. ...

things	verbs	adjectives	adverbs
dish	clean	beautiful	carefully
hole	dig	clean	cleverly
money	hide	deep	excitedly
museum	hold	dirty	happily
police	keep	excited	hard
spade	kneel	nervous	
spoon	pick up	silver	
visitor	sell	surprised	
	show	worried	
	think		

4 What happened to Charlie? Unit 3 | p. 55 Ex. 4

Look at the picture and read the end of the story again.
Continue the story: write a paragraph about what happened to Charlie.
Put your writing in My file.

Freddie	ran as fast as he could. got to Charlie. got Charlie out of the water. ran to the house for help. fell into the water. carried Charlie back to the house.

Charlie	couldn't get air. got his head over the water. was lucky. made Freddie fall into the water. became ill later.

4 b Saint Patrick and the snakes Unit 4 | p. 63 Ex. 4

Look at the cartoon. Match the sentence parts to make a story.

1 The snakes had really annoyed Saint Patrick,
2 After they had been in the car for ten minutes,
3 One snake wanted to go to the bathroom
4 One snake said he felt sick because
5 Another snake asked 'How much further?',
6 Saint Patrick hadn't thought it would be so hard

a he had eaten too many frogs.
b to drive the snakes out of Ireland.
c because he had forgotten to go before.
d the snakes started to get bored.
e so he decided to drive them out of Ireland.
f although they had only been in the car a short time.

2 Your conversation Unit 4 | p. 65 Ex. 2

Work in groups of three and make a similar conversation.
Choose a place in your town, village or area: a nice cafe / an interesting museum / a big department store / a supermarket / ...

Use the dialogue.

Tourist: Excuse me. Do you speak English?
You: ... Can I help you?
Tourist: Is there a cafe/supermarket/ ... near here?
You: Erm ... Opa/Mama/ ..., sie/er fragt nach ...
Opa/...: ...
You: There's a good/nice/cheap/... one in ... Street / next to ... / ...
Tourist: Great! Do you know how long it's open?
You: Let me just ask my grandad / ...
Opa/...: ...
You: It's open ...
Tourist: Good. Can you tell me the way to ...?
You: Wo ist ...?
Opa/...: ...
You: ...
Tourist: Thanks for ...
You: You're welcome. Enjoy ...

5 Your review Unit 4 | p. 69 Ex. 3

Write a review of the film. Write:

what the film is about

This film is about	a Chinese boy in Ireland. learning a new language. problems when you're in a different country. different cultures. following a dream. getting away from a boring life.

what happens in the film

First But Then At the end	Yu Ming gets a job in a pub. he talks to an older man in a pub. Yu Ming lives in China. he travels to the west of Ireland. Yu Ming travels to Dublin. he has problems when he talks to people because they can't understand him.

what people can or might learn from the film

I think people can learn about	Ireland and the Irish. the Irish language. how to behave with / help people from different countries. how to live in a different country.

your opinion of the film (give reasons)

I liked this film I didn't like this film	because	it shows how a person feels when ... it was interesting/funny/... I'm interested in Ireland. it had nice pictures of Ireland. it had good music. it was too long/slow/... there was no action. the story wasn't interesting. it's a sad/... story.

if you would recommend this film

I'd recommend this film I wouldn't recommend this film	to people who like / are interested in films with a happy ending / ...	because ...

Unit 5

3 Offline and online friendship Unit 5 | p. 77 Ex. 3

Do you have online friends? How is your friendship the same or different to your friendship with real-life friends? In which way are they important to you?

online friends

- It's easier to find people with the same interests or problems.
- My friends come from all over the world.
- I can tell them things I can't tell real friends.
- They can give me advice from a different view of life.
- I can talk to them when my real friends are busy.
- I never feel lonely.
- You don't know if online friends tell the truth.
- I can unfriend online friends when I don't want to be their friend.

real friends

- They know me better.
- They know my family.
- We live in the same place and know the same people.
- We have the same type of life.
- I can do outdoor activities with them.
- I can hang out with them at their home.
- I can go to different places with them.
- They will always be there for me.

6 NOW YOU Unit 5 | p. 79 Ex. 6

Imagine somebody wants to sponsor you to make an online video:
Describe what you would like to do in the video and why.

I'd like to	make a music video	because	it's really cute.
	make a beauty video		I'm really good at playing video games.
	make a comedy video		I like changing how I look.
	make a video about my pet		I'm a really good singer
	make a prank video		I like making people laugh.
	make a gameplay video		I love it when people are surprised.

In my video I'll be in my bathroom / my living room / my garden / outside in town / …
I'll be with my brother / my best friend / my dog / …

4 GAME What would you do if …? Unit 5 | p. 85 Ex. 5

First everybody writes three questions with *What would you do if …?*
Write each question on a different piece of paper. For example: *What would you do if you met your favourite singer?*

What would you do if …

- you didn't have to go to school?
- you could travel to any country in the world?
- you found a lot of money?
- there was an earthquake?
- you were a superhero?
- you went to Mars?

Unit 1

1 Your writing Unit 1 | p.10 after Ex. 2c

Read this fun article and check your writing. Is the information true for you?

What does your writing say about you?

- Do you have **heavy writing** – do you put the pen hard on the paper? Then you have strong feelings.
- If your writing goes **to the right**: you're very friendly.
- If it goes **to the left**: you like to be alone. You're independent and maybe shy.
- If you write with **big letters**: you like to have lots of attention[1] and you're often bored. You're creative.
- **Small** letters: you know what you want in life.

2 Read for fun Unit 1 | p.17 after Ex. 3

The London dragon boat[2] festival

Every year in June there are dragon boat races[3] on the River Thames in London. Dragon boat racing is a very old sport that started in China 2,500 years ago and is now popular in countries all over the world. Dragon boats are very long, thin[4] boats which can move very fast. Twenty people sit in the boats and work as a team. At the festival there is also Chinese lion dancing, music, karate shows and a food festival.

3 Sweets Unit 1 | p.19 after Ex. 2

Sweets in Britain have funny names. Can you match the sweets and the names?

1 *Jelly babies* (people usually eat the head first)
2 *Gobstoppers* (balls in different colours: 'gob' means 'mouth', but it isn't a nice word)
3 *Love hearts* (they have messages[5] on them)
4 *Rock* (a long stick you buy by the sea)
5 *Flying saucers*[6] (another name for UFOs)
6 *Wine*[7] *gums* (they don't have wine in them!)

D

E

A

B

C

F

Lösung zu Fast finishers 3: 1D • 2E • 3C • 4F • 5A • 6B

[1]**attention** [əˈtenʃn] *Aufmerksamkeit* [2]**dragon boat** [ˈdræɡən bəʊt] *Drachenboot* [3]**race** [reɪs] *(Wett-)Rennen*
[4]**thin** [θɪn] *schlank, dünn* [5]**message** [ˈmesɪdʒ] *Botschaft (Mitteilung)* [6]**saucer** [ˈsɔːsə] *Untertasse*
[7]**wine** [waɪn] *Wein*

Unit 2

4 Read for fun Unit 2 | p. 25 after Ex. 1

Elvis Aaron Presley

Nickname[1]: *the King of Rock and Roll* or just *the King*
Born: 8 January 1935 in Mississippi
Died: 16 August 1977 (age 42) at his home Graceland in Memphis (after a heart attack[2] from overeating and drug use)
Music: had his first number 1 in 1955; sold over 1 billion[3] records[4]
Favourite clothes: white jumpsuits
Favourite food: grilled peanut butter and banana sandwiches
Home: Graceland, now a museum (His favourite room was 'the Jungle[5] Room' with green carpet on the floor and ceiling[6] and a waterfall on one wall.)
Likes: fast cars, giving presents

5 Student and teacher jokes Unit 2 | p. 29 after Ex. 4b

Match sentences a–g with the correct speech bubbles.

a We'll have the other half this afternoon.
b I couldn't give you a worse grade.
c You can't sleep in my class.
d What do you call a teacher without students?
e I know I can't. It's too loud.
f We'll only have half a day of school this morning.
g Why did I get zero for the test?
h Happy.

6 Sloppy Joes recipe Unit 2 | p. 34 after Ex. 3c

Put the recipe in the right order. *1 g, ...*

a Add one can of tomato soup to the beef.
b After cooking add salt and pepper.
c Add 500g of minced beef[7] (or minced chicken or a vegetarian alternative) and fry for 6 minutes.
d Then add two big spoons of vinegar[8] to the sauce.
e Put the beef (or the alternative) and the sauce on the bun – and enjoy!
f Cook everything for 10 minutes.
g Chop[9] one onion and fry it in oil.
h Put 6 burger buns in the oven just before you want to eat.

Lösung zu Fast finishers 5: 1c • 2e • 3g • 4b • 5d • 6h • 7f • 8a | **Lösung zu Fast finishers 6:** g • c • a • d • f • b • h • e

[1]**nickname** [ˈnɪkneɪm] *Spitzname* [2]**heart attack** [ˈhɑːt əˌtæk] *Herzinfarkt* [3]**billion** [ˈbɪliən] *Milliarde*
[4]**record** [ˈrekɔːd] *Schallplatte* [5]**jungle** [ˈdʒʌŋɡl] *Dschungel* [6]**ceiling** [ˈsiːlɪŋ] *(Zimmer-)Decke*
[7]**minced beef** [mɪnst ˈbiːf] *Rinderhackfleisch* [8]**vinegar** [ˈvɪnɪɡə] *Essig* [9](to) **chop** [tʃɒp] *klein schneiden*

Unit 3

7 What am I? Unit 3 | p. 45 after Ex. 4b

Read the descriptions and say what the thing is.

1 I'm very strong and can break ships. But I'm made of water and scared of the sun. What am I?
2 I'm made of linen or cotton[1] and I go with you to school and work. I have two arms, but no hands. What am I?
3 I'm made of metal or paper. People need me, but they always give me away. What am I?
4 I'm made of glass. When you see me, you see yourself! What am I?
5 I'm made of paper. I have cities with no people, forests with no trees and seas with no water. What am I?
6 I have five fingers, but no arms. I'm made of leather or wool. What am I?

8 Read for fun Unit 3 | p. 47 after Ex. 3a

'Cosplay' or 'costume play' is a big hobby in many countries. People wear costumes from characters in films, video games and comics and play that character. They don't just wear the costume, they walk and talk like the character. Cosplay fans go to special competitions to show their costumes and meet other fans.

People spend a lot of time sewing their costumes and they need to be very creative. It can sometimes take 700 hours to make a costume. Often fans need special hair and make-up, weapons and bags – or even dress their pets!

9 Cat small talk Unit 3 | p. 51 after Ex. 3

Complete the speech bubbles.

Lösung zu Fast finishers 7: 1 ice • **2** a shirt • **3** money • **4** a mirror • **5** a map • **6** a glove

[1]**cotton** ['kɒtn] *Baumwolle*

Unit 4

10 Saint Patrick's Day tongue-twister[1] Unit 4 | p. 63 after Ex. 3b

Say this tongue-twister five times.

I wish to wash my Irish wristwatch.[2]

11 Irish signs Unit 4 | p. 64 after Ex. 2b

Look at the Irish signs. What do they mean?

1 

2 

3 

4 

5 

6 

12 What's your leprechaun name? Unit 4 | p. 67 after Ex. 3a

Take the first letter of your first name.

A	Angry	J	Juicy	S	Sloppy
B	Big ears	K	Karate	T	Thunder
C	Curly	L	Lucky	U	Untidy
D	Dublin	M	Magic	V	Vampire
E	Exciting	N	Nobody	W	Waterfall
F	Friendly	O	Oyster	X	Xtra-nice
G	Gold	P	Potato	Y	Yellow
H	Happy	Q	Quiet	Z	Zero
I	Irish	R	Royal		

Take the month you were born.

January	McFrog	July	McSweet
February	O'Candy	August	O'Heart
March	McShamrock	September	McCastle
April	O'Happy	October	O'Strange
May	McNoodles	November	McMuffin
June	O'Strawberry	December	O'Wish

If you don't like your leprechaun name, think of a new one!

13 Read for fun Unit 4 | p. 67 after Ex. 4b

THE BLARNEY STONE

In Blarney Castle in the south of Ireland, there's a very special stone which is over 300 years old. It's called the Blarney Stone and if you kiss it, you'll get the 'gift of the gab' – the power to talk cleverly about any subject at all. Many famous politicians, writers and actors have kissed the Blarney Stone.

The stone is on a wall at the top of the castle. To get there you have to climb the castle's steps. Then you have to lean back and hold on very carefully. If you don't like high places, then you shouldn't try it!

Lösung zu Fast Finishers 11: **1** ladies/gentlemen • **2** airport • **3** cafe • **4** police • **5** Welcome! • **6** open

[1] **tongue-twister** [ˈtʌŋ twɪstə] *Zungenbrecher* [2] **wristwatch** [ˈrɪstwɒtʃ] *Armbanduhr*

Unit 5

14 Read for fun   Unit 5 | p. 79 after Ex. 2

Top 5 most popular type of online videos

All the most-viewed online videos are music videos. But what do you think the most popular non-music videos are? You might be surprised ...

5 Comedy videos
These are clips from comedy TV shows as well as[1] silly videos people make at home.

4 Gameplay videos
These videos where people play games are very popular. The video star with the most views is a gamer.

3 Vlogs
These are basically[2] video blogs about people's lives.

2 How-to tutorials[3]
These can be about all sorts of topics: how to put on make-up, how to troubleshoot[4] problems on your computer or how to learn a technical skill.

1 And number one is ... **product reviews**! For example, tech reviews and film reviews.

15 Fun photos   Unit 5 | p. 81 after Ex. 5d

Write captions for these photos.

16 Knock, knock!   Unit 5 | p. 88 after Ex. 2

People love these jokes in Britain! Look at the first joke. Then match the last lines in the box to the other jokes. Do you think they're funny? Which one is your favourite?

1 Just in time for dinner.
2 You're welcome!
3 Abby birthday!

A	B	C	D
Knock, knock. *Who's there?* *Barbie.* *Barbie who?* *Barbie Q chicken!*	*Knock, knock.* *Who's there?* *Tank.* *Tank who?* ...	*Knock, knock.* *Who's there?* *Abby.* *Abby who?* ...	*Knock, knock.* *Who's there?* *Justin.* *Justin who?* ...

Lösung zu Fast finishers 16: B 2 • C 3 • D 1

[1] **... as well as ...** *sowohl ... als auch ...* [2] **basically** [ˈbeɪsɪkli] *im Prinzip, grundsätzlich* [3] **tutorial** [tjuːˈtɔːriəl] *Anleitung*
[4] (to) **troubleshoot** [ˈtrʌblʃuːt] *Fehler beheben, Probleme lösen*

Wordbank 1: Describing people

Unit 1 | p. 13 Ex. 4

He or she has ...

Skills and activities: He or she ...
- is good at maths / swimming / basketball / ...
- plays tennis / does self-defence / speaks Chinese / ...

Personality: He or she is ...
- friendly/funny/independent/kind/mean/polite/quiet/shy/unfriendly/...

confident

lazy

rude

violent

Likes & hates: He or she ...
- likes animals / playing computer games / shopping / ...
- hates/dislikes spiders / running / ...

Wordbank 2: Chores

Unit 2 | p.32 Ex. 2

Food and meals

- go shopping
- cook dinner / help with the cooking
- set/clear the table
- wash the dishes / do the washing-up
- dry the dishes
- load/empty the dishwasher

My room

- tidy my room
- pick up my clothes from the floor
- put my dirty clothes in the washing basket
- put dirty cups/ glasses/plates in the kitchen

Washing

- do the washing
- hang out the washing
- put the washing in the dryer
- fold the clothes
- do the ironing / iron clothes
- put clean clothes away (in the cupboard/ wardrobe)

Cleaning

- clean the bathroom / the floor / the windows
- vacuum the carpets/ floors
- sweep the floor
- dust the shelves

Family and pets

- babysit my sister/brother/...
- look after / play with / feed my pet(s)
- clean out my rabbit's/hamster's/ ... cage

Outside

- cut the grass
- sweep up leaves
- shovel snow
- take out the dog
- water the plants

Recycling

- Take out the recycling.
- Put bottles in the bottle bank.
- Put paper in the paper container.

Wordbank 3: History of Britain

[1]**sword** [sɔːd] *Schwert* [2]**armour** [ˈɑːmə] *Rüstung* [3]**spear** [spɪə] *Speer* [4]**warrior** [ˈwɒriə] *Krieger/in*

Wordbank 4: Museums and other sights

Unit 3 | p. 46 Ex. 1a

At the art museum: drawings / photos / pictures / …

paintings

sculptures

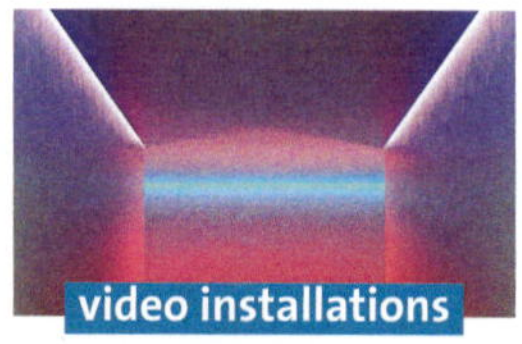
video installations

At the natural history museum: animals / …

stuffed animals

animal skulls

dinosaurs

wildlife photos

At the zoo: bear / bird / elephant / fox / lion / spider / …

monkey

hippopotamus

rhino

peacock

reptiles

crocodile

insects

butterfly

At the aquarium
fish / dolphin / shark / …

starfish

jellyfish

octopus

seahorse

At the city museum
clothes / stones / weapons / …

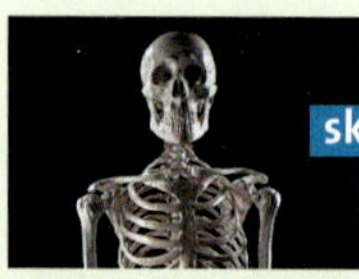
skeletons

jewellery

pottery

At the open-air museum
old houses / farm buildings / farm objects / furniture / …

a windmill

a watermill

tools

At the science museum: experiments / machines / models / planes / trains / …

interactive exhibits

robots

spacecraft

simulators

Wordbank 5: Technology

being creative

- make / build / create / develop an app, a game, ...
- set up a website / ...
- code

a tech company

set up a blog

technology (tech)

using hardware

- devices / equipment
- keyboard
- mouse

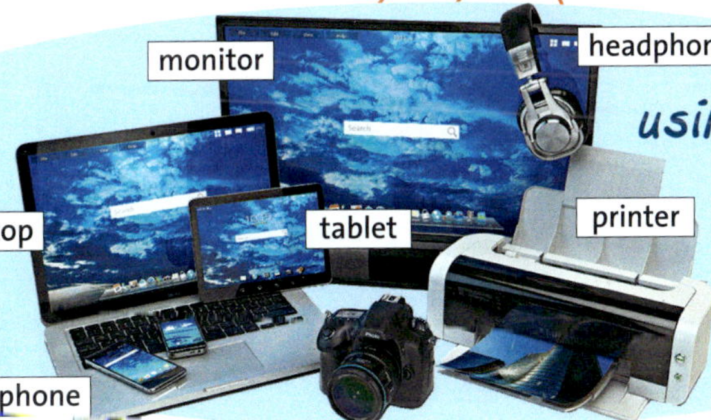

digital photo camera

using a computer

- access / upload / download / back up / save files
- download / open an attachment
- install a programme

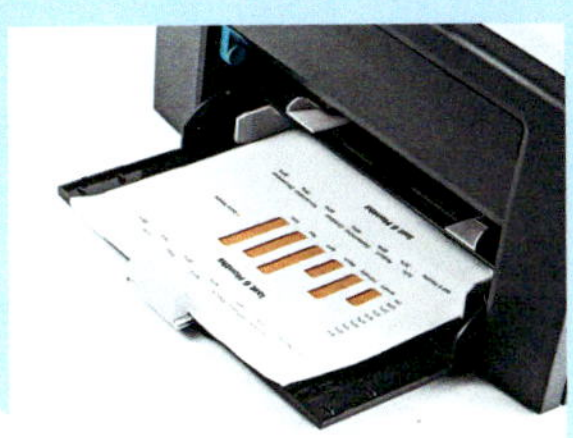

print out copies / pictures

using the internet

- chat
- go online
- surf the web
- search for information
- use social media

browse websites

Wordbank 6: Interests and activities

Unit 5 | p. 77 Ex. 1c

I love ...

biking / bird watching / playing cards / chilling out / cooking / going to church / doing self-defence / doing sports / having a picnic / making models / mountain sports / relaxing / playing the guitar, the piano, the violin / taking care of my pet / watching sports events / ...

doing acrobatics on horseback

doing archery

collecting stamps

knitting

crocheting[1]

doing nail art

doing parkour

playing the drums

helping to protect the environment

doing martial arts[2]

kayaking

photography / taking photos

looking at the stars (astronomy)[3]

being a lifesaver

trainspotting

working out / going to the gym

[1] **crocheting** ['krəʊʃeɪɪŋ] *Häkeln* [2] **martial arts** *(pl)* [mɑːʃl 'ɑːts] *Kampfsport*
[3] **astronomy** [ə'strɒnəmi] *Astronomie, Sternkunde*

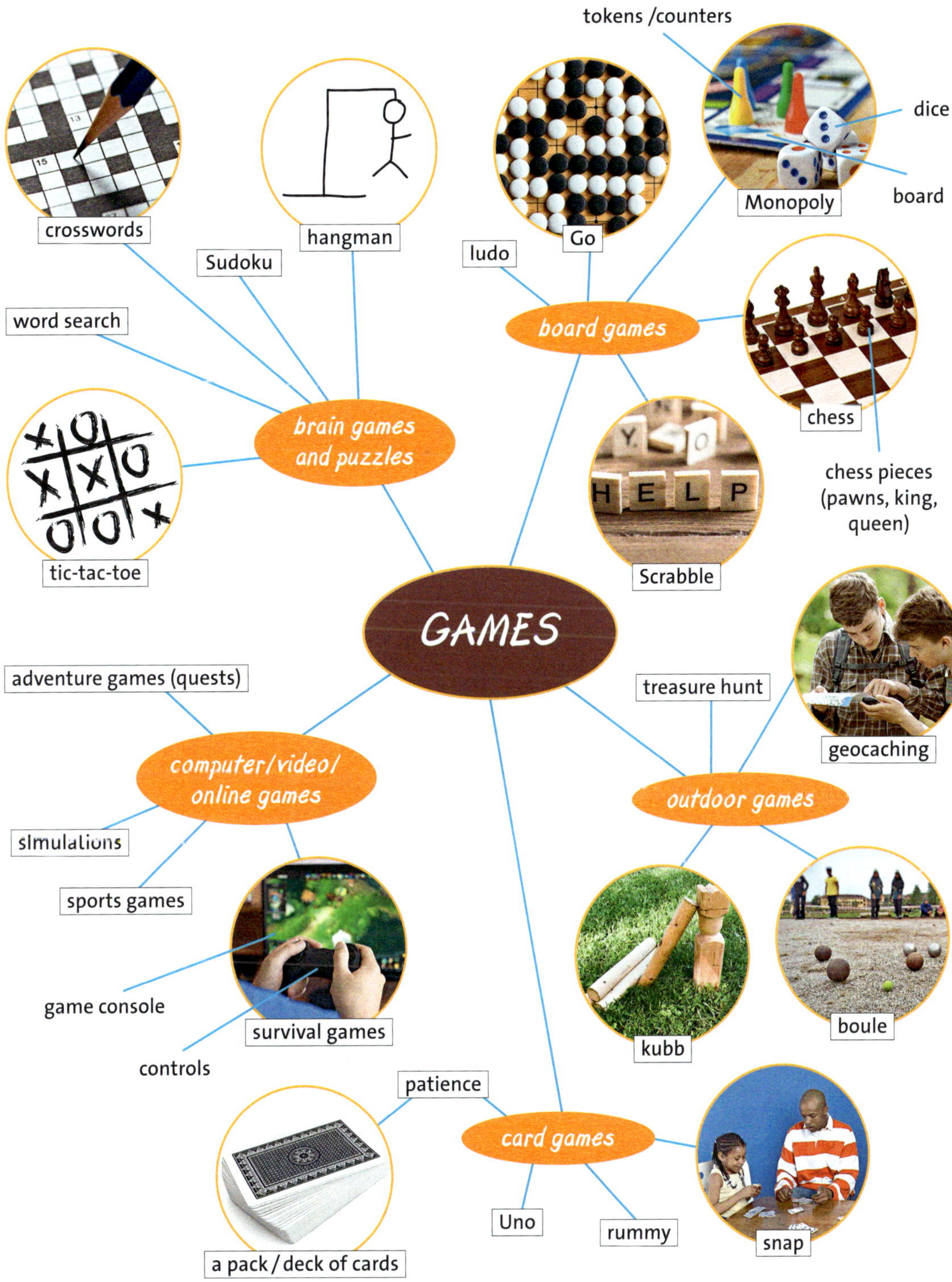

What you do

attack / build / catch (enemies) / collect (resources) / complete / conquer / create / fight / make / move (a token) / put down (a card) / roll (a dice / two dice) / score (points) / take turns / think / turn over (a card) / win / write

TF1 STORY A school trip

Rick Riordan has written five books about Percy Jackson. This story is from his first book *Percy Jackson and the lightning[1] thief[2].* Percy and his class are on a school trip when something strange happens to him.

1 Percy Jackson

a **What do you know about the Percy Jackson books or films? What type of stories are they?**

b **Read the first paragraph. Explain what a troubled kid is and describe the sort of problems Percy might have.**

My name is Percy Jackson. Until a few months ago, I was a boarding student at Yancy Academy, a private school for troubled kids in upstate New York. Am I a troubled kid? Yeah. You could say that.

Things really started going bad last May, when our sixth-grade class took a trip to Manhattan – twenty-eight kids and two teachers on a yellow school bus, going to the Metropolitan Museum of Art to look at ancient Greek and Roman stuff[3]. I know – it sounds terrible. But Mr. Brunner, our Latin teacher, was leading[4] this trip. Mr. Brunner was this middle-aged guy in a motorized wheelchair. He had thin hair and an untidy beard and an old jacket which always smelled like coffee. He told stories and jokes and let us play games in class. He also had this awesome collection of Roman weapons, so he was the only teacher whose class didn't put me to sleep.

I hoped the trip would be okay. At least, I hoped I wouldn't get in trouble. I was wrong. [...]

Mr. Brunner led the museum tour. He showed us a tall stone column[5] with a big sphinx on the top, and started telling us about it. Everybody around me was talking and every time I told them to shut up[6], the other teacher, Mrs. Dodds, gave me the evil eye[7].

Mrs. Dodds was this little math teacher who always wore a black leather jacket, even though she was fifty years old. She looked mean[8] enough to ride a Harley right into your locker. She had come to Yancy halfway through the year, when our last math teacher became ill. [...]

Nancy Bobofit said something about the naked guy on the column, and I turned around and said,

'Shut up!'

Mr. Brunner stopped his story.

'Mr. Jackson,' he said, 'did you have a comment?'

My face was totally red. I said, 'No, sir.'

Mr. Brunner pointed to one of the pictures on the column. 'Maybe you'll tell us what this picture shows?'

I actually recognized[9] it. 'That's Kronos eating his kids, right?'

Behind me, Nancy Bobofit said to a friend, 'Like we're going to use this in real life. Like it's going to say on our job applications, "Please explain why Kronos ate his kids." '

'And why, Mr. Jackson,' Brunner said, 'does this matter[10] in real life?'

I said, 'I don't know, sir.'

'I see.' Mr. Brunner looked disappointed. [...]

'Well, it's time for lunch.'

The class walked off. My best friend Grover and I were going to follow when Mr. Brunner said, 'Mr. Jackson.' I told Grover to keep going. Then I turned toward Mr. Brunner. 'Sir?'

'What you learn from me,' he said, 'is very important. I will accept only the best from you, Percy Jackson.'

I was angry, this guy pushed[11] me so hard. He wanted me to be as good as everybody else, but I have dyslexia[12] and attention deficit disorder[13]. I just couldn't learn all those names and facts. I said something about trying harder. Mr. Brunner told me to go outside and eat my lunch.

The class was on the front steps of the museum. [...]

I wanted to eat my sandwich, but Nancy Bobofit appeared in front of me and dropped her half-eaten lunch in Grover's lap.

---

[1] **lightning** ['laɪtnɪŋ] *Blitz(e)* [2] **thief,** *pl* **thieves** ['θi:f, θi:vz] *Dieb/in* [3] **stuff** [stʌf] *Zeug* [4] (to) **lead, led, led** [li:d, led] *leiten*
[5] **column** ['kɒləm] *Säule* [6] (to) **shut up, shut, shut** [ʃʌt 'ʌp] *den Mund halten* [7] (to) **give sb. the evil eye** *jn. böse anschauen*
[8] **mean** [mi:n] *gemein, fies* [9] (to) **recognize** ['rekəgnaɪz] *(wieder)erkennen* [10] (to) **matter** ['mætə] *wichtig sein*
[11] (to) **push sb.** [pʊʃ] *jn. (an)treiben* [12] **dyslexia** [dɪs'leksiə] *Legasthenie*
[13] **attention deficit disorder (ADD)** *Aufmerksamkeitsdefizit-Syndrom*

'Oops.' She smiled at me. I tried to stay cool. I don't remember touching her, but suddenly Nancy was sitting on her butt[1] in the fountain[2].

Mrs. Dodds appeared next to us. [...]

'Come with me,' she said. 'Now.'

I turned to look at her, but she wasn't there. She was standing at the museum entrance[3]. How did she get there so fast?

I have moments like that a lot, when my brain falls asleep or something. The school counselor[4] told me this was part of the attention deficit disorder. I wasn't so sure.

I went after Mrs. Dodds. Halfway up the steps, I looked back at Grover. He was looking between me and Mr. Brunner. But Mr. Brunner was reading his book. I looked back up. Mrs. Dodds was now inside the building.

I followed her into the museum. Except for us, the gallery was empty. Mrs. Dodds was making this weird[5] noise, like an animal.

'You've been giving us problems, honey,' she said.

I did the safe thing. I said, 'Yes, ma'am.'

The look in her eyes was terrible. She's a teacher, I thought nervously. She isn't going to hurt me.

Thunder shook the building.

'It's time to die,' she hissed[6]. Her eyes were red. Her fingers turned into claws. Her jacket became large, leathery[7] wings[8]. She wasn't human.

Then things got even stranger. Mr. Brunner came into the gallery with a pen in his hand.

'Percy!' he shouted, and threw the pen to me. I caught the pen, but when it hit my hand, it wasn't a pen. It was a sword. My hands were shaking so bad I nearly dropped it.

Mrs Dodds said, 'Die, honey!' And she flew straight at me. I used the sword. It hit her shoulder and passed through her body like she was made of water. Hisss! Mrs. Dodds exploded into yellow powder[9].

I was alone. There was a pen in my hand and Mr. Brunner wasn't there. Nobody was there but me. My hands were still shaking. I went back outside. [...]

Mr. Brunner was sitting under his red umbrella, reading his book. I went over to him and he looked up.

'Sir,' I said, 'where's Mrs. Dodds?'

He looked at me. 'Who?'

'The other teacher. Mrs. Dodds.'

He frowned. 'Percy, there is no Mrs. Dodds on this trip. There has never been a Mrs. Dodds at Yancy Academy. Are you feeling all right?' ◇

2 What happened?

a **Read the text and answer the questions.**

1 What did Percy's teacher Mrs Dodds try to do?
2 What happened to her?
3 What did Mr Brunner say?

b **Choose one of the situations in a. Act out the scene and freeze.**

3 People in the story

a **Read the text again. What are the people in the story like? Make a mind map or a list with adjectives and phrases for Percy, Mr Brunner and Mrs Dodds.**

Percy
- was a boarding student at Yancy Academy
- is a troubled kid
...

b **Compare your mind maps or lists. If you already knew the Percy Jackson films or books, tell your partner more about Percy. (Use your notes from 1.)**

c **Choose one of the characters. Use your list or mind map to make a fact file about the character and add more details about him or her. Use your imagination and be creative! You can also draw a picture.**

[1]**butt** *(AE, infml)* [bʌt] *Hintern* [2]**fountain** [ˈfaʊntən] *(Spring-)Brunnen* [3]**entrance** [ˈentrəns] *Eingang* [4]**school counsellor,** *AE* **counselor** [ˈkaʊnsələ] *Schulpsychologe/-psychologin* [5]**weird** [wɪəd] *seltsam* [6]**(to) hiss** [hɪs] *zischen* [7]**leathery** [ˈleðəri] *ledrig, ledern* [8]**wing** [wɪŋ] *Flügel* [9]**powder** [ˈpaʊdə] *Pulver*

TF2 POEM The Ant-Eater

Unit 2

2.16
2.17
2.18

1 A boy called Roy

Read or listen to the poem. What happened to Roy?

This poem is by Roald Dahl (1916–1990), a very famous British writer from Wales. He wrote many funny poems, stories and novels for children and some scary stories for adults.

Some wealthy[1] folks from U.S.A.,
Who lived near San Francisco Bay,
Possessed[2] an only child called Roy,
A plump and unattractive boy –
Half-baked, half-witted[3] and half-boiled,
But worst of all, most dreadfully[4] spoiled.
Whatever Roy desired[5] each day,
His father bought him right away –
Toy motor-cars, electric trains,
The latest model aeroplanes,
A colour television-set,
A saxophone, a clarinet,
Expensive teddy-bears that talked,
And animals that walked and squawked[6].
That house contained[7] sufficient[8] toys
To thrill a half a million boys.
(As well as this, young Roy would choose,
Two pairs a week of brand-new shoes.)
And now he stood there shouting, "What
"On earth is there I haven't got?
"How hard to think of something new!
"The choices are extremely few!"
Then added, as he scratched his ear,
"Hold it! I've got a good idea!
"I think the next thing I must get
"Should be a most peculiar[9] pet –
"The kind that no one else has got –
"A giant ANT-EATER! Why not?"
As soon as father heard the news,
He quickly wrote to all the zoos.
"Dear Sirs," he said, "My dear keepers,
"Do any of you have ant-eaters?"
They answered by return of mail.
"Our ant-eaters are not for sale."
Undaunted[10], Roy's fond[11] parent hurled
More messages across the world.
He said, "I'll pay you through the nose
"If you can get me one of those."
At last he found an Indian gent
(He lived near Delhi, in a tent),
Who said that he would sacrifice[12]
His pet for an enormous price
(The price demanded[13], if you please,
Was fifty thousand gold rupees).
The ant-eater arrived half-dead.
It looked at Roy and softly said,
"I'm famished. Do you think you could
"Please give me just a little food?
"A crust of bread, a bit of meat?
"I haven't had anything to eat
"In all the time I was at sea,
"For nobody looked after me."
Roy shouted, "No! No bread or meat!
"Go find some ants! They're what you eat!"
The starving creature crawled[14] away.
It searched[15] the garden night and day,
It hunted every inch of ground,
But not one single ant it found.
"Please give me food!" the creature cried.

[1] **wealthy** [ˈwelθi] *reich* [2] (to) **possess** [pəˈzes] *besitzen* [3] **half-witted** [hɑːf ˈwɪtɪd] *schwachsinnig* [4] **dreadful** [ˈdredfl] *schrecklich* [5] (to) **desire** [dɪˈzaɪə] *wünschen, begehren* [6] (to) **squawk** [kwɔːk] *krähen, gackern* [7] (to) **contain** [kənˈteɪn] *enthalten* [8] **sufficient** [səˈfɪʃnt] *ausreichend, genügend* [9] **peculiar** [pɪˈkjuːliə] *sonderbar, eigenartig* [10] **undaunted** [ʌnˈdɔːntɪd] *unverzagt, nicht entmutigt* [11] **fond** [fɒnd] *liebevoll* [12] **sacrifice** [ˈsækrɪfaɪs] *opfern* [13] (to) **demand** [dɪˈmɑːnd] *fordern* [14] (to) **crawl** [krɔːl] *kriechen* [15] (to) **search** [sɜːtʃ] *(etwas / nach etwas) suchen*

"Go find an ant!" the boy replied.
By chance, upon[1] that very day,
Roy's father's sister came to stay –
A foul old hag of eighty-three
Whose name, it seems, was Dorothy.
She said to Roy, "Come let us sit
"Out in the sun and talk a bit,"
Roy said, "I don't believe you've met
"My new and most unusual pet?"
He pointed down among[2] the stones
Where something lay[3], all skin[4] and bones.
"Ant-eater!" he yelled[5]. "Don't lie there yawning[6]!
"This is my ant! Come say good-morning!"
(Some people in the U.S.A.
Have trouble with the words they say.
However hard they try, they can't
Pronounce simple words like AUNT.
Instead of[7] AUNT, they call it ANT,
Instead of CAN'T, they call it KANT.)
Roy yelled, "Come here, you so-and-so!
"My ant would like to say hello!"
Slowly, the creature raised[8] its head.
"D'you mean that that's an *ant*?" it said.
"Of course!" cried Roy. "Ant Dorothy!
"This ant is over eighty-three."
The creature smiled. Its tummy rumbled.
It licked its starving lips and mumbled[9],
"A giant ant! By gosh[10], a winner!
"At last I'll get a decent[11] dinner!
"No matter[12] if it's eighty-three.
"If that's an ant, then it's for me!"
Then, taking very careful aim[13],
It pounced upon the startled[14] dame.
It grabbed[15] her firmly by the hair
And ate her up right then and there,
Murmuring as it chewed the feet,
"The largest ant I'll ever eat."
Meanwhile, our hero Roy had sped
In terror to the potting-shed[16].
And tried to make himself obscure
Behind a pile of horse-manure[17].
But ant-eater came sneaking in
(Already it was much less thin)
And said to Roy, "You little squirt[18],
"I think I'll have you for
dessert."

2 Roy and the ant-eater

a Describe Roy. Use words from the poem.

b Explain what lines 39–52 say about the ant-eater.

c Explain why Roy wanted an ant-eater and describe how he looked after it when it arrived.

3 The ant-eater and Aunt Dorothy

a What mistake did the ant-eater make? Why?

b What is the message of this poem?

4 WORDS

Match the words from the poem with the words in the box.

1 spoiled (line 6)
2 famished (l. 47) / starving (l. 55)
3 creature (l. 55)
4 foul old hag (l. 63)
5 its tummy rumbled (l. 85)
6 pounced upon (l. 92)

a terrible old woman
b animal
c its stomach made a noise
d gets everything he wants
e jumped on
f very hungry

---

[1] **upon** *(that day)* [əˈpɒn] *an (dem Tag)* [2] **among** [əˈmʌŋ] *inmitten, zwischen* [3] (to) **lie, lay, lain** [laɪ, leɪ, leɪn] *liegen* [4] **skin** [skɪn] *Haut* [5] (to) **yell** *[jel]* *schreien* [6] (to) **yawn** [jɔːn] *gähnen* [7] **instead of** [ɪnˈsted əv] *anstatt, anstelle von* [8] (to) **raise** [reɪz] *(an)heben* [9] (to) **mumble** [ˈmʌmbl] *murmeln, brummeln* [10] **(By) gosh!** [gɒʃ] *Mensch!* [11] **decent** [ˈdiːsnt] *anständig, ordentlich* [12] **no matter** [ˈmætə] *ganz egal* [13] (to) **take aim** *zielen* [14] **startled** [ˈstɑːtld] *erschrocken* [15] (to) **grab** [græb] *packen, sich etwas schnappen* [16] **potting-shed** [ˈpɒtɪŋ ʃed] *Gartenschuppen* [17] **manure** [məˈnjʊə] *Dung, Mist* [18] **squirt** [skwɜːt] *Angeber, Wicht*

TF3 COMIC The Bridge of Swords

Unit 3

1 The knight[3] and the dragon[4]

a Before you read the story, look at the pictures on this page.
Partner A: Describe Sir Lancelot.
Partner B: Describe the dragon.
Listen. Can you add anything to your partner's description?

b Read the story. Why is it called *The Bridge of Swords*?

This is part of a Cornelsen comic story by Doris Ertel-Zellner, Reinhold Zellner and Bernd Kissel. It tells a story about Sir Lancelot, one of King Arthur's Knights of the Round Table. In the story, the evil Red Knight has taken Queen Guinevere, the wife[1] of King Arthur, to his fortress[2].

[1] **wife,** *pl* **wives** [waɪf, waɪvz] *Ehefrau* [2] **fortress** [ˈfɔːtrəs] *Festung* [3] **knight** [naɪt] *Ritter* [4] **dragon** [ˈdrægən] *Drache*
[5] (to) **rescue** *[jel]* *retten* [6] (to) **fear** [fɪə] *befürchten*

[1]**armour** [ˈɑːmə] *Rüstung* [2]**leader** [ˈliːdə] *Anführer/in, Leiter/in* [3]**crystal clear** [ˈkrɪstl klɪə] *glasklar, kristallklar*

[1]**fear** [fɪə] *Angst*

[1](to) **choke** [tʃəʊk] *keine Luft mehr bekommen, ersticken* [2](to) **pant** [pænt] *keuchen, hecheln* [3]**beyond** [bɪˈjɒnd] *jenseits, außerhalb* [4]**caretaker** [ˈkeəteɪkə] *Aufseher, Verwalter* [5]**spell** [spel] *Zauberspruch*
[6](to) **destroy** [dɪˈstrɔɪ] *zerstören, vernichten*

2 Write the story

a Write the events in the right order in your exercise book. Leave space between the events.

- a They go into the Forest of Fear.
- b Sir Lancelot goes to rescue Queen Guinevere with his two squires[1] and his dog.
- c They rescue the caretaker of the Red Knight.
- d The caretaker takes them to the Bridge of Swords.
- e His squire saves him.
- f He meets a dragon.

b Add more details to each event.

3 The bridge

a Write a speech bubble for Sir Lancelot in the last picture.

b How does Sir Lancelot get across the bridge? Think of ideas, share them with a partner and then tell the class your best idea.

c Sir Lancelot rescues Guinevere. What does she say? Draw a picture with speech bubbles or write their conversation.

[1]**squire** [ˈskwaɪə] *Knappe; Gutsherr*

Scary fairies

1 Describe them

a What do you think of when you hear the word 'fairy'? Describe what you think a fairy looks like. Are fairies good or bad?

b Look at the pictures of four Irish 'fairies' and describe them.

A legend is a very old, traditional story about a person or a place. People tell legends as if they are true stories – they may be true, but often they are not.

A

B

C

D

2 Irish legends

a Make groups of four. Each of you should read about a different fairy on p. 126. Then tell your group about your fairy.

b Are the descriptions in the legends similar to your descriptions from 1b? Tell the class.

3 A fairy meeting

a Which of the fairies would you least[1] like to meet? Tell your partner and explain why.

b Imagine an interview with one of the fairies in the article. Write five questions you would like to ask on a piece of paper. Leave space for answers between each question.

c Swap your paper with another student and answer his or her questions.

d Put your interviews on the walls. Walk around and read them.

4 What do you think?

a Legends aren't real stories and probably the creatures[2] in them never existed. Do you enjoy reading stories like this? Why (not)? Tell the class.

b Do you know any legends from your area? Present them to the class.

[1]**least** [liːst] *am wenigsten* [2]**creature** [ˈkriːtʃə] *Geschöpf, (Lebe-)Wesen*

2.19

Scary fairies

The Irish enjoy telling stories and legends about scary fairies that you might meet in Ireland.

1 If you go to County Sligo or County Down, you might see the **Dullahan** (the Irish say: DOO-luhhahn). The Dullahan is an Irish headless horseman[1]. On dark and stormy nights, he rides through the countryside[2] on a wild black horse which breathes fire from its nostrils[3]. The horseman carries a whip in one hand. In the other hand he carries his head which he uses like a lamp to see across the fields. If he stops riding and his head calls out a name, that person will die. The only thing that can stop the rider is something made of gold.

2 The **banshee**[4] is a ghost who wails. Banshees may appear as beautiful young women in a long white or silver dress. Or they may be ugly[5] old witches[6] with long wild hair. All banshees have red eyes from crying. If she wails outside a house three times, one person in that house or family will die. She does not cause[7] death, but warns a family that it will happen. And if anybody sees her, she'll disappear in a white cloud. According to[8] legend, the banshee only wails for families which have 'O' or 'Mc' in their last name (for example, O'Brien or McKenzie).

3 The **Dearg-due** (DAH-ruhg DU-ah) is a mythical[9] female vampire who drinks the blood of men. According to the story, a beautiful young woman had fallen in love with a poor man, but her father forced[10] her to marry a rich old man. Her husband was very cruel[11] to her, so she decided to kill herself. After her husband and father had buried[12] her, she rose[13] from her grave and killed them. The story says that one night every year she rises from her grave and looks for young men. Many people say that the Irishman Bram Stoker wrote the story of *Dracula* after he had heard the story of the Dearg-due.

4 A **changeling**[14] is a fairy baby which the fairies have left in place of a human baby. Changelings look like humans, but they are unfriendly, greedy babies. They eat and eat, but they are never full. A changeling might also have dark eyes and look very old and wise. They love making people sad. If you have a changeling in the house, it will take all the happiness out of your home. However, if you treat[15] it well and it grows into a healthy, beautiful child, the fairies might come and take it back and give you your own child.

[1] **horseman** [ˈhɔːsmən] *Reiter* [2] **countryside** [kʌntrisaɪd] *Land(schaft); Natur* [3] **nostril** [ˈnɒstrəl] *Nasenloch, (Pferd) Nüster* [4] **banshee** [bænˈʃiː] *Todesfee (irische Mythologie)* [5] **ugly** [ˈʌgli] *hässlich* [6] **witch** [wɪtʃ] *Hexe* [7] (to) **cause** [kɔːz] *bewirken, verursachen* [8] **according to** [əˈkɔːdɪŋ tə] *laut ...; ... zufolge* [9] **mythical** [ˈmɪθɪkl] *mythisch, legendär* [10] (to) **force sb to do sth.** [fɔːs] *jn. zwingen, etwas zu tun* [11] **cruel** [kruːəl] *grausam* [12] (to) **bury** [ˈberi] *beerdigen, begraben* [13] (to) **rise, rose, risen** [raɪz, rəʊz, ˈrɪzən] *sich erheben, auferstehen* [14] **changeling** [ˈtʃeɪndʒlɪŋ] *Wechselbalg (vertauschtes Kind)* [15] (to) **treat** [triːt] *behandeln*

TF5 SONG Mama said

2.20

1 Family and friends

Close your book and listen to the song. What does the singer say about his parents and friends?

This song is by Lukas Graham, a Danish band that sings in English. The father of lead singer Lukas Graham Forchhammer was Irish, but he grew up in a free community[1] in Copenhagen. In this song he sings about his childhood[2] and his life now.

[…]
Remember asking both my mom and dad
Why we never travelled to exotic lands
We only ever really visit friends
Nothing to tell when the summer ends
We never really went buying clothes
Folks[3] were passing[4] on the stuff in plenty loads[5]
New shoes once a year and then
Out to play ball so we could ruin them

CHORUS
When mama said that it was okay
Mama said that it was quite alright
Our kind of people had a bed for the night
And it was okay

Mama told us we were good kids
And daddy told us never listen to the ones
Pointing nasty[6] fingers and making fun[7]
'Cause we were good kids

Don't get me wrong I didn't have it bad
I got enough loving from my mom and dad
But I don't think they really understood
When I said that I wanted a deal in Hollywood
I told them I'd be singing on TV
The other kids were calling me a wannabe[8]
The older kids they started bugging[9] me
But now they're all standing right in front of me

I know which place I'm from, I know my home
When I'm in doubt[10] and struggling[11]
That's where I go
An old friend can give advice
When new friends only know a half story
That's why I always keep them tight[12]
And why I'm okay,
I said, I'm okay. […]

2 Lukas' childhood

2.20

a **Listen to the song again and read the words. Complete the fact file[13] about Lukas when he was a child.**

In his childhood
Never went ...
Never bought ... (got them from ...)
Got new shoes ...
His dream was ... and ...
Other kids ...

b **What did Lukas' mum and dad say to him and his sisters? What do you think of this explanation and advice?**

3 Lukas now

Answer the questions.

1 When Lukas has a problem now, where does he go?
2 Who is most important to him: old friends or new friends? Why?
3 What does he mean when he says he's 'okay'? Why does he feel like that?

[1] **community** [kəˈmjuːnəti] *Gemeinschaft, Gemeinde* [2] **childhood** [ˈtʃaɪldhʊd] *Kindheit* [3] **folks** [fəʊks] *Leute*
[4] (to) **pass sth. on** *etwas weitergeben, weiterreichen* [5] **in plenty loads** [ˈplenti] *etwa: massenhaft* [6] **nasty** [ˈnɑːsti] *gemein, fies*
[7] (to) **make fun** (of sb.) *sich lustig machen (über jn.)* [8] **wannabe** [ˈwɒnəbi] *Möchtegern* [9] (to) **bug** [bʌg] *ärgern, nerven*
[10] (to) **be in doubt** [daʊt] *zweifeln, Zweifel hegen/haben* [11] (to) **struggle** [ˈstrʌgl] *kämpfen, sich abmühen*
[12] **tight** [taɪt] *eng, fest* [13] **fact file** [ˈfækt faɪl] *Informationsbogen, Steckbrief*

LF 1 Relative clauses 128
LF 2 Revision: The simple present and the present progressive 129
LF 3 Contact clauses 130
LF 4 Adverbs of manner 131
LF 5 must – (to) have to 132

Revision: the past tenses
LF 6 The simple past 134
LF 7 The past progressive 134
LF 8 The present perfect 135
LF 9 Question tags 137
LF 10 The past perfect 139
LF 11 Revision: The *will*-future 140
LF 12 *If*-sentences (1) 140
LF 13 The present perfect progressive 141
LF 14 The present perfect and the present perfect progressive 143
LF 15 *If*-sentences (2) 143

Grammatical terms 144

LF 1 Relativsätze — Relative clauses

a Gebrauch

Unit 1 pp. 12–13

Relativsätze erläutern **ein Nomen.**
Man verwendet sie, um deutlich zu machen, **über wen oder was man spricht**. Ohne den Relativsatz bliebe unklar, wer oder was gemeint ist.

Beachte:
- Englische Relativsätze haben – wie alle Nebensätze – die **Wortstellung S – V – O.**
- Vor dieser Art von Relativsätzen steht im Englischen kein Komma.

Use

What's the name of the **man** **who wrote** ***Romeo and Juliet***?
Wie heißt der ***Mann****, der* **Romeo und Julia** *geschrieben hat?*

The drama club needs a **leaflet** **which tells people about their new play.**
Die Theater-AG braucht ein ***Faltblatt****, das den Leuten von ihrem neuen Stück berichtet.*

Ella is the **student** **who shares a room with Roxy.**
... ***Schülerin****, die ein Zimmer mit Roxy teilt.*

b Die Relativpronomen *who, which, that*

Unit 1 pp. 12–13

Du verwendest:
- ***who*** für **Personen**
- ***which*** für **Dinge**
- ***that*** für **Dinge und Personen**

The relative pronouns *who, which, that*

Tara is the **girl** **who** has curly brown hair.

Hockey is a **sport** **which** you play with sticks.
Everyone wants to live in a **country** **that** is safe.
There's the Russian **boy** **that** is in your year.

c Das Relativpronomen *whose*

Unit 1 pp. 12–13

Du verwendest ***whose*** (deren, dessen) für Personen (und Dinge), um auszudrücken, dass jemand oder etwas zusammengehört. Auf ***whose*** folgt immer ein **Nomen.**

The relative pronoun *whose*

Tara is the **girl** **whose hair** is brown and curly.
... ***Mädchen****, dessen Haare braun und lockig sind.*

⚠ – Fragewort ***whose*** (wessen)
– Relativpronomen ***whose*** (deren, dessen)

– Relativpronomen ***who*** + Kurzform von ***is***

Whose baby is this? *(Wessen Baby ...?)*
That's the baby **whose** mother is in hospital. *(..., dessen Mutter ...)*
The woman **who's** in hospital is my aunt. *(..., die im Krankenhaus ist, ...)*

d Das Relativpronomen *where*

Unit 1 pp. 12–13

Du verwendest ***where*** in Relativsätzen, die sich auf **Ortsbezeichnungen** *(place, house, room, shop, town, ...)* beziehen.

The relative pronoun *where*

We have **a shop at our school where** you can buy snacks. *(..., wo man Snacks kaufen kann.)*
I need **a room for myself where** I can be alone. *(..., in dem ich allein sein kann.)*

LF 2 Wiederholung: Einfache Form und Verlaufsform der Gegenwart

Revision: Simple present and present progressive

Unit 1 p. 13

Mit dem deutschen Satz „**Sam und Mike spielen Hockey**" kann man zwei verschiedene Dinge ausdrücken:
– dass Hockey ihr **Hobby** ist
oder

Sam and Mike **play** hockey every Saturday afternoon.

– dass sie **gerade dabei** sind, Hockey zu spielen.

Look, Sam and Mike **are playing** hockey.

Im Englischen musst du entweder das ***simple present*** oder das ***present progressive*** verwenden, je nachdem, was du sagen willst:

- Du verwendest das ***simple present*** für alles, was **regelmäßig** stattfindet (also für Gewohnheiten, Hobbys, routinemäßige Handlungen), und für **Dauerzustände** (also für alles, was immer so ist).
  Signalwörter: *always, usually, often, sometimes, never, every day, on Fridays, ...*

Do you sometimes **make** dinner? –
No, I **don't**. Mum usually **cooks** the meals.

My sister **doesn't like** takeaways.

We all **love** Mexican food.

- Du verwendest das ***present progressive*** für alles, was gerade **im Gang** (also noch nicht abgeschlossen) ist.
  Signalwörter: *now, at the moment, today, ...*

Are you **doing** your homework? –
No, **I'm not**. **I'm looking** at a cook book at the moment. **I'm planning** to make a cake.

LF 3 Relativsätze ohne Relativpronomen — Contact clauses

Unit 1
pp. 16–17

Die Relativpronomen ***who***, ***which*** und ***that*** sind entweder **Subjekt** oder **Objekt** des Relativsatzes.

- Wenn das Relativpronomen **direkt vor dem Verb** steht, ist es **Subjekt** des Relativsatzes.
- Wenn ein **Nomen oder Pronomen zwischen dem Relativpronomen und dem Verb** steht, dann ist das Relativpronomen **Objekt** des Relativsatzes.

Wenn das Relativpronomen **Objekt des Relativsatzes** ist, dann wird es oft **weggelassen**. (Im Deutschen ist das nicht möglich.)
Relativsätze ohne Relativpronomen werden ***contact clauses*** genannt.

S V
The Halls live in a flat **that is** too expensive.

O S V
They need a flat **that they can afford**.

O S V
They need a flat **that they can afford**.
They need a flat **they can afford**.
... Wohnung, die sie sich leisten können.

O S V
Ava has an uncle **who she has** never **met**.
Ava has an uncle **she has** never **met**.
... Onkel, den sie noch nie getroffen hat.

S V
Ava has an uncle **who lives** in the USA.
... Onkel, der in den USA lebt.

⚠ Vorsicht:
Wenn das **Relativpronomen direkt vor dem Verb** steht, dann ist es **Subjekt** und **darf nicht weggelassen werden**.

BY THE WAY Anders als im Deutschen steht eine zum Verb gehörende **Präposition** in der Regel hinter dem Verb (und einem Objekt) – also an der gleichen Stelle wie im Hauptsatz. Auch in diesen Fällen wird das Relativpronomen meist weggelassen.

Roxy is the girl (**that**) **I share a room with**.
... das Mädchen, ***mit*** *dem ich ein Zimmer teile.*

The cafe (**that**) **we often go to** is called *The Happy Chipper*.
Das Café, ***zu*** *dem wir oft gehen, ...*

LF4 Adverbien der Art und Weise — Adverbs of manner

a Gebrauch

Unit 2 pp. 28–29

Adjektive beziehen sich auf ein **Nomen**. Man verwendet sie, um Personen oder Dinge näher zu beschreiben. Sie drücken aus, **wie etwas oder jemand ist**.

Adverbien der Art und Weise beziehen sich auf ein **Verb**. Man verwendet sie, um Handlungen oder Vorgänge näher zu beschreiben. Sie drücken aus, **wie jemand etwas tut** oder **wie etwas geschieht**.

⚠ Im Deutschen können Adverbien der Art und Weise zwischen Verb und Objekt stehen.
Englische Adverbien der Art und Weise **dürfen nicht zwischen Verb und Objekt** stehen! Sie stehen gewöhnlich am Ende des Satzes (1), manchmal aber auch direkt vor dem Verb (2) oder am Satzanfang (3).

Use

Healthy food is important for everyone.
***Gesundes Essen** ...*

It's important to **eat healthily**.
..., sich gesund zu ernähren.

*Die Polizistin **öffnete** vorsichtig **die Kiste**.*

1 The police officer **opened the box** carefully.
2 He quickly answered the letter.
3 Quietly she opened the door.

b Formen

Unit 2 pp. 28–29

- Die meisten Adverbien der Art und Weise sind **aus Adjektiven abgeleitet**. Sie werden gebildet, indem *-ly* an das Adjektiv angehängt wird.

⚠ Beachte die folgenden **Besonderheiten bei der Schreibung** der Adverbien:
- *-le* wird zu *-ly*:
  terrible → terribly
- *-y + -ly* wird zu *-ily*:
  happy → happily

- **Unregelmäßige Formen**:
  - Das Adverb zu *good* heißt *well*.
  - Bei *fast* und *hard* haben Adjektiv und Adverb dieselbe Form.

Forms

adjective	adverb	adjective	adverb
bad	bad**ly**	quick	quick**ly**
clear	clear**ly**	quiet	quiet**ly**
loud	loud**ly**	slow	slow**ly**

adjective		adverb
comfortable	→	comfortably
horrible	→	horribly
crazy	→	crazily
tidy	→	tidily

a good fighter	he/she fights well
a fast car	he/she drives fast
hard work	he/she works hard

c Adverb oder Adjektiv nach bestimmten Verben?

Du weißt jetzt, dass **Adverbien der Art und Weise** beschreiben, wie (auf welche Art und Weise) eine **Tätigkeit** ausgeführt wird.

Adverb or adjective after certain verbs?

Always **behave kindly** to other people.
Work hard and learn to **think quickly**.

Einige Verben beschreiben aber nicht Tätigkeiten, sondern **Zustände** oder **Eigenschaften** („wie jemand oder etwas **ist**"). Nach solchen Verben stehen **Adjektive**.

Tätigkeit:	Zustand/Eigenschaft:
Verb + **Adverb**	**Verb** + **Adjektiv**
She **shouted angrily** at me.	She **felt/got angry**.
Sie schrie mich wütend an.	*Sie fühlte sich / wurde wütend.*
He **reacted nervously**.	He **looked/seemed nervous**.
Er reagierte nervös.	*Er sah nervös aus / schien nervös zu sein.*

Zu diesen Verben gehören auch ***smell*** (riechen), ***sound*** (klingen), ***taste*** (schmecken) sowie ***become*** (werden) und ***stay*** (bleiben).

The soup **smelled nice**, but it **tasted horrible**.
The song **sounds beautiful**, doesn't it?
The class **became quiet**.

LF 5 „müssen": *must* – *(to) have to*

"müssen": must – (to) have to

a Unit 2 pp. 32–33

Wenn man sagen will, dass etwas **notwendig ist** oder **getan werden muss**, verwendet man ***must*** oder ***(to) have to***.

- ***must*** wird verwendet bei Befehlen oder wenn man seine innere Überzeugung ausdrückt.
- Mit ***(to) have to*** berichtet man, was von anderen angeordnet wurde.

Weil ***must*** nur als **Gegenwartsform** benutzt werden kann, muss man Formen von ***(to) have to*** verwenden, wenn man über die **Vergangenheit** oder die **Zukunft** spricht.

When I was a little boy, I always **had to** empty the dishwasher.
Als ich ein kleiner Junge war, musste ich immer den Geschirrspüler ausräumen.

Teacher: You **will have to** work harder this year, Ava.
Du wirst dieses Jahr härter arbeiten müssen, Ava.

BY THE WAY Auch mit ***(to) need to*** kann man zum Ausdruck bringen, dass jemand etwas tun muss.

You **need to** be very fit if you want to run a marathon.
Man muss sehr fit sein, wenn man einen Marathon laufen will.

b Verneinte Aussagesätze

Unit 2
pp. 32–33

Um zu sagen, dass jemand etwas **nicht tun muss** oder **nicht tun musste**, verwendet man ***don't/doesn't have to*** bzw. ***didn't have to***.

⚠ Vorsicht:
mustn't bedeutet „nicht dürfen" und wird für Verbote verwendet.

BY THE WAY Auch mit ***don't/doesn't/didn't need to*** kann man zum Ausdruck bringen, dass jemand etwas nicht tun muss. Außerdem gibt es noch das Hilfsverb ***needn't*** mit derselben Bedeutung.

Negative statements

Ava has to tidy her room, but she **doesn't have to** help in the kitchen.
..., aber sie muss nicht in der Küche helfen.

We **didn't have to** wait long.
Wir mussten nicht lange warten.

You **mustn't** feed the pigeons.
Du darfst die Tauben nicht füttern.
Bread is bad for them.

You { **don't have to** / **don't need to** / **needn't** } help me.
Du musst mir nicht helfen. / Du brauchst mir nicht zu helfen.

c Fragen

Unit 2
pp. 32–33

Fragen danach, ob jemand etwas **tun muss** oder **tun musste**, bildet man mit ***Do/Does ... have to ...?*** bzw. ***Did ... have to ...?***

Fragewörter *(what/where/when/why/...)* stehen wie im Deutschen am Satzanfang.

Questions

Does your sister **have to** help at home?
Muss deine Schwester zu Hause helfen?

Did you **have to** wait long?
Musstest du / Musstet ihr lange warten?

What do you **have to** do at home?
Was musst du zu Hause machen?

LF 6-8 Wiederholung: Die Zeitformen der Vergangenheit — Revision: The past tenses

LF 6 Die einfache Form der Vergangenheit — The simple past

a Gebrauch

Unit 3 pp. 46–47

Du verwendest das ***simple past*** für **abgeschlossene Handlungen in der Vergangenheit**. Es sagt aus, **wann etwas geschehen ist** oder **wann jemand etwas getan hat**.
Meist steht das *simple past* mit Zeitbestimmungen wie *in 2014, last weekend, thirty years ago*.

Use

The Jorvik Viking Centre **opened** in 1984.
Over thirty years ago they **discovered** lots of things like dishes, shoes and bones.
They even **found** a Viking sock.

b Form

Unit 3 pp. 46–47

- Bei **regelmäßigen Verben** bildest du das *simple past* aus dem Infinitiv des Verbs und der Endung ***-ed***. Es gibt nur eine Form.
- Einige Verben haben **unregelmäßige Formen** im *simple past*. Auf den Seiten 244f. findest du eine Liste der unregelmäßigen Verben aus *Go Ahead 7*.
- **Verneinte Aussagesätze** bildest du mit *didn't* + Infinitiv des Verbs.
- **Fragen** bildest du mit *did* + Infinitiv.

Form

I/You
He/She/It } watch**ed** TV last night.
We/You/They

(to) drive	– **drove**	(to) go	– **went**
(to) know	– **knew**	(to) meet	– **met**
(to) send	– **sent**	(to) take	– **took**

I **didn't spend** too many hours on the computer last weekend.

What did you **do** last night?
Did you **watch** TV?

LF 7 Die Verlaufsform der Vergangenheit — The past progressive

a Gebrauch

Unit 3 pp. 46–47

Mit dem ***past progressive*** drückst du aus, dass zu einer **bestimmten Zeit in der Vergangenheit** etwas **gerade im Gang** und **noch nicht abgeschlossen** war.

Use

Police officer: Mr Clarke, what **were you doing** between 8 and 10 o'clock yesterday morning?
Mr Clarke: I **was working** in the garden.

Lucy lost her mobile while she **was taking** the dog for a walk.
Lucy verlor ihr Handy, während sie den Hund ausführte.

Das *past progressive* wird oft verwendet, wenn man sagen will, **was gerade vor sich ging**, als etwas anderes geschah. (Die andere Handlung steht im *simple past* – hier: *phoned*).

Lucy **was taking** the dog for a walk when Rosie phoned.
Lucy führte gerade den Hund aus, als Rosie anrief.

b **Form**

Unit 3 pp. 46–47

- Das *past progressive* wird mit *was/were* und der *-ing*-Form des Verbs gebildet.

Form

I **was working**.
You **were working**.
He/She/It **was working**.
We/You/They **were working**.

- Bei **Fragen** im *past progressive* rückt *was/were* vor das Subjekt des Satzes.
- **Verneinte Aussagesätze** im *past progressive* bildest du mit *wasn't/weren't* und der *-ing*-Form des Verbs.

Rosie: **What were** you **doing** this morning? I tried to ring you, but you didn't answer. **Were** you **having** a shower?
Lucy: No, I **wasn't having** a shower. I was out. I had to take our dog for a walk.

LF 8 Das *present perfect* — The present perfect

a **Gebrauch**

Unit 3 pp. 46–47

Mit dem ***present perfect*** drückt man aus, dass **jemand irgendwann etwas getan hat** oder dass **irgendwann etwas geschehen ist**. Der genaue Zeitpunkt des Geschehens ist unwichtig und wird nicht genannt.

Use

Over 18 million people **have** already **visited** the Jorvik Viking Centre.
Über 18 Millionen Menschen haben schon das Jorvik Viking Centre besucht.

Oft hat die Handlung **Auswirkungen** auf die Gegenwart oder die Zukunft: Das Museum wurde modernisiert, sodass man nun neue Sehenswürdigkeiten betrachten kann.

We **have** just **modernized** our museum so you can see lots of new sights now.

Beachte:
Im Deutschen sind Perfekt und Präteritum oft austauschbar. Im Englischen musst du aufpassen, wenn du über die Vergangenheit sprichst!

- John möchte wissen, **ob** (nicht wann!) Paul schon einmal in York gewesen ist. → *present perfect*
- Paul bejaht die Frage. → *present perfect* Dann fügt er hinzu, **wann** er in York war: *I went there ... last October.* → *simple past*

John: **Have** you ever **been** to York?
Warst du schon mal in York? / Bist du schon mal in York gewesen?
Paul: Yes, I **have**. I **went** there with my parents last October.
Ja. Ich bin letzten Oktober mit meiner Familie dort hingefahren.

b Form

Unit 3
pp. 46–47

- Das *present perfect* wird mit *have/has* und der 3. Form des Verbs gebildet. Die 3. Form heißt **Partizip Perfekt *(past participle)***.

  Bei **regelmäßigen Verben** wird das *past participle* mit Infinitiv + *-ed* gebildet.

  Unregelmäßige Verben haben eigene *past participle*-Formen. Auf den Seiten 244f. findest du eine Liste der unregelmäßigen Verben aus *Go Ahead 7*.

- **Verneinte Aussagesätze** werden mit *have not (haven't)* bzw. *has not (hasn't)* und dem *past participle* gebildet.
- In **Fragen** sind Subjekt und *have/has* vertauscht. **Fragewörter** stehen wie im Deutschen am Satzanfang.

Form

I/You	**have visited**	York.
He/She/It	**has visited**	York.
We/You/They	**have visited**	York.

Short forms:

I'**ve**/You'**ve**	**visited**	...
He'**s**/She'**s**/It'**s**	**visited**	...
We'**ve**/You'**ve**/They'**ve**	**visited**	...

infinitive	simple past	past participle
(to) be	was/were	**been**
(to) drive	drove	**driven**
(to) make	made	**made**
(to) take	took	**taken**

We **haven't been** to York yet.
Wir waren noch nicht in York. / Wir sind noch nicht in York gewesen.

Have you ever **visited** the Jorvik Viking Centre?
Hast du jemals das Jorvik Viking Centre besucht?

Where have you **been**?
Wo warst du? / Wo bist du gewesen?

c **Das *present perfect* mit *already, just, never, yet* usw.**

Unit 3
pp. 46–47

Das *present perfect* wird oft mit den folgenden **unbestimmten Zeitangaben** verwendet:

- *already* schon, bereits
- *just* gerade (eben), soeben
- *recently* kürzlich, in letzter Zeit
- *never* (noch) nie
- *not ... yet* noch nicht
- *ever?* jemals? schon mal?
- *yet?* schon?

The present perfect with *already, just, never, yet*, etc.

Have you **been** to England **recently**?
– Yes, we **have**. We**'ve** **just** **come** back.

Can I borrow your Harry Potter book? – I'm sorry, but I **haven't** **finished** it **yet**.

Have you **seen** the Jorvik Viking Centre **yet**?
– No, I **haven't**. What is it? I**'ve** **never** **heard** of it.

LF 9 Frageanhängsel

Question tags

a **Gebrauch**

Unit 3
pp. 50–51

In der gesprochenen Sprache werden oft sogenannte **Frageanhängsel** an Aussagesätze angehängt, um den Gesprächsfluss aufrechtzuerhalten.
Im Deutschen verwenden wir z.B. „nicht wahr?", „nicht?", „oder?", „gell?".

Use

Asha is talking to her grandparents about her project, **isn't she?**
Asha spricht gerade mit ihren Großeltern über ihr Projekt, nicht wahr?

Her grandparents don't live in York, **do they?**
Ihre Großeltern leben nicht in York, oder?

Her Grandad came to England in 1955, **didn't he?**
Ihr Großvater kam 1955 nach England, nicht?

Wenn man vom Gesprächspartner eine **Bestätigung** seiner Aussage erwartet, geht die **Stimme** am Ende des Satzes **nach unten**.

Wenn man **nicht sicher** ist und nachfragen möchte oder wenn man **überrascht** ist, geht die **Stimme** am Satzende **nach oben**.

It's cold in here, **isn't it?**
– Yes, it is. I'll close the window.
Es ist kalt hier, nicht wahr? – ...

The film starts at 8, **doesn't it?**
– No, it doesn't. It starts at 8:45.
Der Film fängt um 8 an, oder? – ...

You don't really speak Japanese, **do you?**
Du sprichst doch nicht wirklich Japanisch, oder?

b Form

Unit 3 pp. 50–51

Englische Frageanhängsel bestehen aus **Hilfsverb + Personalpronomen**.

- Wenn der **Aussagesatz** bejaht ist, ist das **Frageanhängsel** verneint.
- Wenn der **Aussagesatz** verneint ist, ist das **Frageanhängsel** bejaht.

Beachte:

- Wenn der **Aussagesatz ein Hilfsverb enthält**, dann benutzt man dieses Hilfsverb auch im Frageanhängsel.

  Ausnahme: *I am ..., aren't I?*

- Wenn der **Aussagesatz kein Hilfsverb enthält**, dann steht im Frageanhängsel ***don't, doesn't*** oder ***didn't***.

Form

She's German, **isn't she**?
He's not from here, **is he**?

They **live** in Bradford, **don't they**?
Lewis **can** skype with his grandparents, **can't he**?

Lewis **doesn't** see his grandparents very often, **does he**?
He **can't** visit them very often, **can he**?

The bus stop **is** near here, **isn't it**?
You **don't** know when the bus comes, **do you**? We **can** go by bike, **can't we**?
We **will** be back before 8 o'clock, **won't we**?
You**'ve** got a new bike, **haven't you**?
I**'m** late, **aren't I**?

They **miss** India, **don't they**?
Your grandma **lives** in Berlin, **doesn't she**?
Asha's mum **grew** up in England, **didn't she**?

Auf Aussagen mit Frageanhängseln kann man mit **Zustimmung** oder mit **Widerspruch** reagieren.

⚠ Im Deutschen widerspricht man einer verneinten Aussage meist mit **„Doch!"**.
Im Englischen verwendet man das Hilfsverb aus dem Aussagesatz: *You **don't** ..., do you? – Oh yes, I **do**!*

Bejahte Aussage	**You live in London, don't you?** *Du lebst in London, nicht?*	
Zustimmung	**Yes, I do. / Yes, that's right.**	*Ja./Stimmt.*
Widerspruch	**No, I don't.** (I live in ...)	*Nein. (Ich lebe in ...)*
Verneinte Aussage	**You don't speak German, do you?** *Du sprichst kein Deutsch, nicht wahr?*	
Zustimmung	**No, I don't. / That's right.**	*Nein./Stimmt.*
Widerspruch	**I do! / Oh yes, I do!**	*Doch!*

LF 10 Das Plusquamperfekt — The past perfect

a Gebrauch

Unit 4
pp. 62–63

Um zu sagen, dass eine Handlung **vor einer anderen Handlung** oder **vor einem bestimmten Zeitpunkt in der Vergangenheit** stattfand, wird das *past perfect* verwendet.

Wie du weißt, drückt das ***simple past*** aus, dass etwas **zu einem bestimmten Zeitpunkt in der Vergangenheit** stattfand:
In den 40er-Jahren des 19. Jahrhunderts gab es eine Hungersnot in Irland.

Vorher war bereits etwas anderes geschehen: Viele Menschen hatten Irland verlassen. Was vorher geschehen war, steht im *past perfect*.

Beachte den Unterschied:
Der erste Satz sagt aus, dass John bereits gegangen war, als Katie ankam.
Der zweite sagt aus, dass John die Party verließ, als Katie eintraf.

Use

Even **before the Great Famine**, many people had left Ireland.
Schon vor der Großen Hungersnot hatten viele Menschen Irland verlassen.

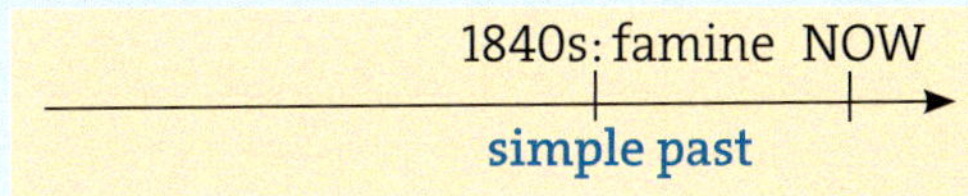

There was a famine in Ireland **in the 1840s**.

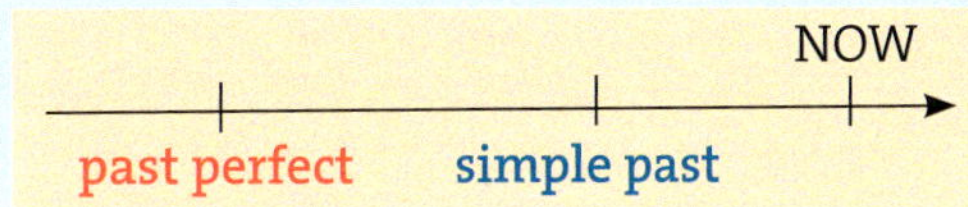

Many people had left the country before there was a famine in Ireland.

John had left the party when Katie arrived.
John hatte die Party (schon) verlassen, ...
John left the party when Katie arrived.
John verließ die Party, ...

b Form

Unit 4
pp. 62–63

- Das *past perfect* besteht aus *had* und dem Partizip Perfekt *(past participle)*.
  Bei **regelmäßigen Verben** wird das *past participle* mit Infinitiv + *-ed* gebildet.
  Die *past participle*-Formen der **unregelmäßigen Verben** stehen auf den Seiten 244f.
- **Beachte:**
  Im Deutschen verwendet man „war" oder „hatte". Im Englischen steht immer ***had***.
- **Verneinte Aussagesätze** werden mit *had not (hadn't)* und dem *past participle* gebildet.
- In **Fragen** sind Subjekt und *had* vertauscht. **Fragewörter** stehen am Satzanfang.

Form

I/You
He/She/It } had work**ed** in the garden.
We/You/They

I/You
He/She/It } had **left** Ireland.
We/You/They

Many people had **died**, and many people had **left** the country.
... ***waren*** *gestorben* ... ***hatten*** *verlassen*

People were angry because the British government hadn't **helped** them.

Had many people **left** before the famine?
How many people had **left** the country?

LF 11 Wiederholung: Das Futur mit *will* — Revision: The *will*-future

a Gebrauch

Unit 4 p. 66

Das Futur mit *will* wird hauptsächlich verwendet, um zu sagen, was in **Zukunft** geschehen wird. Oft geht es um **Vermutungen** oder um Dinge, die wir nicht beeinflussen können.
Das Futur mit *will* steht häufig mit *I think, I'm sure* oder den Wörtern *probably* oder *definitely*.

Use

I'm sure we**'ll enjoy** our trip to Carlingford.

b Form

Unit 4 p. 66

- Das *will-future* wird mit *will* und dem Infinitiv des Verbs gebildet.
  Es gibt nur eine Form für alle Personen.
  Die Kurzform von *will* ist *'ll*.
- **Verneinte Aussagesätze** werden mit *will not* (Kurzform: *won't*) und dem Infinitiv des Verbs gebildet.
- Bei **Fragen** steht *will* vor dem Subjekt. **Fragewörter** stehen wie im Deutschen am Satzanfang.

Form

I/You
He/She/It
We/You/They } **will have** a great day. / **'ll have** a great day.

I/You
He/She/It
We/You/They } **will not see** a leprechaun. / **won't see** a leprechaun.

Will { I/you, he/she/it, we/you/they } **have** a fun day?

When **will** we **be** back?

LF 12 *if*-Sätze (I) — *if*-sentences (I)

a *if*-Sätze, Typ 1

Unit 4 pp. 66–67

if*-Sätze** bestehen aus zwei Teilen: einem **Nebensatz**, der mit ***if eingeleitet wird, und einem **Hauptsatz**.

***if*-Sätze vom Typ 1** sind **„Was ist, wenn …"-Sätze**. Sie werden auch **Bedingungssätze** genannt: Der Nebensatz mit *if* nennt eine Bedingung („Wenn …"). Im Hauptsatz steht, was unter dieser Bedingung geschieht („dann …").

Beachte:

- Wenn der Satz mit dem Hauptsatz beginnt, steht vor dem Nebensatz mit *if* kein Komma.
- Nicht verwechseln: ***if*** = „wenn, falls"
  when = „wenn, sobald"

***if*-sentences, type 1**

If you visit Carlingford, you'll see the real Ireland.

Bedingung („wenn")	**If you visit Carlingford, …** *Wenn Sie Carlingford besuchen, …*
Folge („dann")	**… you'll see the real Ireland.** *… werden Sie das wahre Irland sehen.*

You'll see the real Ireland **if** you visit Carlingford.

If I see him, I'll tell him.
(Es ist nicht sicher, ob ich ihn sehe.)
When I see him, I'll tell him.
(Ich weiß bereits, dass ich ihn sehe.)

Bei *if*-Sätzen vom Typ 1 steht im **Nebensatz** das *simple present*.

Im **Hauptsatz** steht
- das *will-future* (1, 2)
- ein Modalverb + Infinitiv (3–5) oder
- eine Befehlsform (Imperativ) (6).

⚠ Vorsicht: Im Nebensatz darf **nicht das *will-future*** stehen!

	if-clause	main clause	
simple present	If you visit Carlingford,	(1) you'll hear about the leprechauns. (2) you'll have a great day out.	*will*-future
		(3) you can go to the old castle. (4) you might find one of the statues. (5) you should go to the Oyster Festival.	*can/might/should* + infinitive
		(6) go on a tour and visit the magic cavern.	imperative

b *if*-Sätze, Typ 0

Unit 4 p. 67

Manche *if*-Sätze beschreiben **Tatsachen** oder **Regeln**, die **immer gelten** („was unter bestimmten Bedingungen immer geschieht"). Solche *if*-Sätze werden als Typ 0 bezeichnet.

In diesen allgemeingültigen *if*-Sätzen steht sowohl im Nebensatz als auch im Hauptsatz das *simple present*.

if-sentences, type 0

If it is very cold, water turns to ice.

If people don't get enough sleep, they get ill.

If you mix red and yellow, you get orange.

LF 13 Das *present perfect progressive* — The present perfect progressive

a Gebrauch

Unit 5 pp. 80–81

Das ***present perfect progressive*** wird verwendet, wenn etwas **in der Vergangenheit begann** und **bis in die Gegenwart andauert**. Dabei wird die **Dauer** des Vorgangs besonders hervorgehoben.

Beachte:
Im **Deutschen** benutzen wir in solchen Fällen meist das **Präsens**. Im Englischen steht das ***present perfect progressive***.

Use

They have been watching TV all afternoon.
Sie sehen schon den ganzen Nachmittag fern.

They have been watching a lot of TV recently.
Sie sehen in letzter Zeit viel fern. /
Sie haben in letzter Zeit viel ferngesehen.

b **Form**

Unit 5 pp. 80–81

- Das *present perfect progressive* wird mit *have been / has been* und der *-ing*-Form des Verbs gebildet.

Form

I/You	**have been watching**	TV.
He/She/It	**has been watching**	TV.
We/You/They	**have been watching**	TV.

Short forms:

I**'ve**/You**'ve**	**been watching**	...
He**'s**/She**'s**/It**'s**	**been watching**	...
We**'ve**/You**'ve**/ They**'ve**	**been watching**	...

- **Verneinte Aussagesätze** werden mit *have not been (haven't been)* bzw. *has not been (hasn't been)* und der *-ing*-Form gebildet.

My brother thinks he **hasn't been getting** enough attention recently.
Mein Bruder glaubt, dass er in letzter Zeit nicht genug Aufmerksamkeit bekommt / bekommen hat.

- In **Fragen** sind Subjekt und *have/has* vertauscht.
  Fragewörter stehen wie im Deutschen am Satzanfang.

Have you **been waiting** long?
Wartest du schon lange?
How long have you **been standing** here?
Wie lange stehst du hier schon?

c **Deutsch „seit" – *since* und *for***

Unit 5 pp. 80–81

Im Deutschen verwenden wir das Wort „seit", um zu sagen, **seit wann** oder **wie lange** etwas schon andauert.

Im Englischen musst du zwischen *since* und *for* unterscheiden:

- Mit *since* gibt man einen **Zeitpunkt** an *(since 2 o'clock; since 2014; since May)*. *since* + **Zeitpunkt** drückt aus, **wann etwas begonnen hat** – die Kinder haben um zwei Uhr begonnen zu spielen.
- Mit *for* gibt man einen **Zeitraum** an *(for three hours; for years; for a long time)*. *for* + **Zeitraum** drückt aus, **wie lange etwas bereits andauert** – die Kinder spielen schon drei Stunden.

German "seit" – *since* and *for*

It's five o'clock now.
The children have been playing tennis **since two o'clock**.
(starting point: two o'clock)
*Die Kinder spielen **seit zwei Uhr** Tennis.*

since + Zeitpunkt

The children have been playing tennis **for three hours**. *(how long: three hours)*
*Die Kinder spielen **seit drei Stunden** Tennis.*

for + Zeitraum

LF 14 Das *present perfect* und das *present perfect progressive*

The present perfect and the present perfect progressive

Unit 5
pp. 80–81

- Das *present perfect progressive* wird verwendet, wenn es darum geht, dass eine **Tätigkeit noch andauert**: Katie ist immer noch dabei, Fotos zu machen.
- Das *present perfect* wird verwendet, wenn es um das **Ergebnis** oder um die **Auswirkungen** auf Gegenwart oder Zukunft geht: Katie hat jetzt schon viele Fotos. (Zum *present perfect* siehe LF 8, S. 135f.)

⚠ Vorsicht bei **Zustandsverben**: Sie stehen **nicht im *present perfect progressive***!
Du musst das *present perfect* verwenden, auch wenn der Zustand noch andauert.
Zustandsverben sind Verben, mit denen man über **Zustände** (z.B. *be, have, cost, seem, sound*), **Gedanken** (z.B. *believe, know, understand*) oder **Gefühle** (z.B. *like, love, hate*) spricht.
Beachte auch in diesen Fällen:
Präsens im Deutschen – *present perfect* im Englischen!

Katie **has been taking** photos all morning.
Katie macht schon den ganzen Morgen Fotos.

Katie **has taken** lots of photos since breakfast.
Katie hat seit dem Frühstück viele Fotos gemacht.

We**'ve been** here all day. Can't we go home now?
*Wir **sind** jetzt (schon) den ganzen Tag hier. ...*

He**'s known** her for years.
*Er **kennt** sie (schon) seit Jahren.*

They**'ve had** that dog since Christmas.
*Sie **haben** diesen Hund seit Weihnachten.*

Never: He ~~knows her for years~~.
They ~~have that dog since Christmas~~.

LF 15 *if*-Sätze (II)

if-sentences (II)

a *if*-Sätze, Typ 2

Unit 5
pp. 84-85

***if*-Sätze vom Typ 2** sind **„Was wäre, wenn ...“-Sätze**. Der Nebensatz mit *if* nennt eine Bedingung, und im Hauptsatz steht, was unter dieser Bedingung geschehen würde oder geschehen könnte.

Bei diesen *if*-Sätzen hält es der Sprecher/ die Sprecherin für **unwahrscheinlich**, dass die Bedingung erfüllt wird (Satz 1), oder die Bedingung ist **nicht erfüllbar** (Satz 2).
Es handelt sich nur um **Annahmen**.

if-sentences, type 2

Bedingung („wenn“)	**If I were you**, ... *Wenn ich du wäre, ...*
Folge („dann“)	... **I'd** (= I would) **talk to them**. *... würde ich mit ihnen reden.*

(1) It would be nice **if** my parents had more time for me.
Es wäre schön, wenn meine Eltern mehr Zeit für mich hätten.
(Aber ich halte das für unwahrscheinlich.)

(2) **If** I were you, I wouldn't worry.
Wenn ich du wäre, würde ich mir keine Sorgen machen.
(Aber ich bin natürlich nicht du.)

Bei *if*-Sätzen vom Typ 2 steht im **Nebensatz** das ***simple past***. Im **Hauptsatz** steht meist das **Modalverb *would* + Infinitiv** (1).
Im Hauptsatz kann auch stehen:
- das **Modalverb *could* + Infinitiv** (2)
- das **Modalverb *might* + Infinitiv** (3).

⚠ Vorsicht: Im Nebensatz darf **nicht *would*** stehen!

	if-clause	main clause	
simple past	**If** you **showed** the article to your parents,	(1) they'**d** (= they **would**) **understand** you better. *würden sie dich besser verstehen.*	*would* + infinitive
		(2) they **could understand** you better. *könnten sie dich besser verstehen.*	*could* + infinitive
		(3) they **might understand** you better. *könnten sie dich vielleicht besser verstehen.*	*might* + infinitive

Beachte die Redewendung ***If I were you, ...*** Oft werden **Ratschläge** mit dieser Wendung eingeleitet.

If I were you, I'd try out some styles first before I went to the hairdresser's.
Wenn ich du wäre, würde ich ... / Ich an deiner Stelle würde ...

b *if*-Sätze, Typ 1 und 2 im Vergleich

Unit 5 pp. 84-85

- **Typ 1:** Der Sprecher / Die Sprecherin hält es für **wahrscheinlich**, dass es aufhört zu regnen.
- **Typ 2:** Der Sprecher / Die Sprecherin hält es für **unwahrscheinlich**, dass es aufhört zu regnen.

(Zu *if*-Sätzen vom Typ 1 siehe LF 12, S. 140f.)

Comparison of *if*-sentences 1 and 2

If the rain **stops**, we **can have** a picnic.
(I think it might stop.)

If the rain **stopped**, we **could have** a picnic.
(But I don't think it will stop.)

Grammatische Fachbegriffe (Grammatical terms)

adjective ['ædʒɪktɪv]	Adjektiv, Eigenschaftswort	*bad, careful, tidy, good, ...*
adverb of frequency [ˌædvɜːb əv 'friːkwənsi]	Häufigkeitsadverb	*always, usually, often, sometimes, never*
adverb of manner [ˌædvɜːb əv 'mænə]	Adverb der Art und Weise	*badly, carefully, tidily, well, ...*
adverbial phrase [ædvɜːbiəl freɪz]	adverbiale Bestimmung	*at school, in town, on Saturday, at the weekend, ...*
article ['ɑːtɪkl]	Artikel	*the, a*
comparative [kəm'pærətɪv]	Komparativ	*younger, more famous*
comparison [kəm'pærɪsn]	Steigerung	*old – older – oldest*
contact clause ['kɒntækt klɔːz]	Relativsatz ohne Relativpronomen	*We need a flat* ***we can afford***.
future ['fjuːtʃə]	Zukunft, Futur	

going to-future ['gəʊɪŋ tʊ fjuːtʃə]	Futur mit *going to*	*I'm **going to stay** at home tomorrow.*
if-clause ['ɪf klɔːz]	Nebensatz mit *if*	*If the rain stops, ...*
if-sentence ['ɪf sentəns]	*if*-Satz, Bedingungssatz	*If the rain stops, we'll have a picnic.*
imperative [ɪm'perətɪv]	Befehlsform, Imperativ	*go, sing, don't play*
infinitive [ɪn'fɪnətɪv]	Grundform des Verbs, Infinitiv	*open, see, read*
irregular verb [ɪˌregjʊlə 'vɜːb]	unregelmäßiges Verb	*go – went – gone*
main clause ['meɪn klɔːz]	Hauptsatz	*We'll have a picnic.*
modal verb [ˌməʊdl 'vɜːb]	Hilfsverb	*can, must*
negative statement [ˌnegətɪv 'steɪtmənt]	verneinte Aussage	*I don't like chemistry.*
noun [naʊn]	Nomen, Hauptwort, Substantiv	*Jalen, girl, brother, time, ...*
object ['ɒbdʒɪkt]	Objekt	*Ben has **an idea**.*
past participle [ˌpɑːst 'pɑːtɪsɪpl]	Partizip Perfekt, 3. Form des Verbs	*happened, eaten, gone, ...*
past perfect [ˌpɑːst 'pɜːfɪkt]	Vorvergangenheit, Plusquamperfekt	*John **had** already **left** the party.*
past progressive [ˌpɑːst prə'gresɪv]	Verlaufsform der Vergangenheit	*We **were having** breakfast.*
personal pronoun [ˌpɜːsənl 'prəʊnaʊn]	Personalpronomen (persönliches Fürwort)	*I, you, he, she, it, we, they; me, you, him, her, it, us, them*
plural ['plʊərəl]	Plural, Mehrzahl	*teachers, babies, men*
positive ['pɒsətɪv]	Positiv	*old, young, famous*
positive statement [ˌpɒsətɪv 'steɪtmənt]	bejahte Aussage	*I like animals.*
possessive adjective [pəˌzesɪv 'ædʒɪktɪv]	Possessivbegleiter	*my, your, his/her/its, our, your, their*
possessive pronoun [pəˌzesɪv 'prəʊnaʊn]	Possessivpronomen	*mine, yours, his/hers/its, ours, yours, theirs*
present perfect [ˌpreznt 'pɜːfɪkt]	*present perfect*	*I **have visited** Hollywood.*
present perfect progressive [ˌpreznt pɜːfɪkt prə'gresɪv]	Verlaufsform des *present perfect*	*Olivia **has been working** all morning.*
present progressive [ˌpreznt prə'gresɪv]	Verlaufsform der Gegenwart	*I'**m playing** computer games.*
question ['kwestʃn]	Frage(satz)	*What did you do yesterday?*
question tag ['kwestʃn tæg]	Frageanhängsel	*You live in Munich, **don't you?***
question word ['kwestʃn wɜːd]	Fragewort	*what?, when?, where?, how?*
relative clause [ˌrelətɪv 'klɔːz]	Relativsatz	*I have an aunt **who lives in Italy**.*
relative pronoun [ˌrelətɪv 'prəʊnaʊn]	Relativpronomen	*who, which, that, whose, where*
short answer ['ʃɔːt ɑːnsə]	Kurzantwort	*Yes, I am. / No, I don't. / ...*
simple past [ˌsɪmpl 'pɑːst]	einfache Form der Vergangenheit	*Kinga **flew** to Poland last summer.*
simple present [ˌsɪmpl 'preznt]	einfache Form der Gegenwart	*Ben **plays** football every Saturday.*
subject ['sʌbdʒɪkt]	Subjekt	***My mum** is working.*
superlative [suː'pɜːlətɪv]	Superlativ	*youngest, the most famous*
will-future ['wɪl fjuːtʃə]	Futur mit *will*	*I'm sure you **will like** Plymouth.*
yes/no question [jes'nəʊ kwestʃən]	Entscheidungsfrage	*Are you 12? Do I look OK?*

SF1 Learning words ... 146
SF2 Understanding new words ... 147
SF3 Using an online dictionary ... 148
SF4 Doing (internet) research ... 149
SF5 Listening ... 150
SF6 Reading a text ... 151
SF7 Marking up a text and note-taking ... 152
SF8 Filling in forms ... 153
SF9 How to write good texts ... 154
SF10 Writing an email / a letter ... 156
SF11 Being polite ... 157
SF12 Expressing opinions and feelings ... 158
SF13 Giving a talk ... 159
SF14 Paraphrasing ... 160
SF15 Describing pictures ... 160
SF16 Mediation ... 161
SF17 Doing better in tests ... 162
SF18 Working with charts and diagrams ... 164
SF19 Viewing ... 165

SF1 Learning words

Unit 2 p. 37, **Unit 3** pp. 45, 48, **Unit 5** p. 86

Wie und wo lerne ich Vokabeln?

1 Führe dein Vokabelheft, deine Vokabelkartei oder Computer-Vokabelliste aus Klasse 6 weiter. Du lernst neue Vokabeln am besten an einem ruhigen und aufgeräumten Platz, an dem du nicht abgelenkt wirst. Wiederholen kannst du sie immer und überall – beim Warten, im Bus, im Bett, ... Für unterwegs kannst du sie dir aufs Handy sprechen oder per Vokabeltrainer-App üben. Je öfter du die Vokabeln wiederholst, desto besser wirst du sie dir merken können.

2 Du merkst dir neue Wörter noch besser, wenn du ...

a sie unter **Oberbegriffen** sortierst und diese z. B. auf **Karteikarten** sammelst. Auf eine Seite schreibst du den Oberbegriff, auf die andere die passenden Wörter dazu.

business

sell
CEO

Falls dir Abbildungen helfen, kannst du welche hinzufügen. Sammle Wörter, die zu einem Wortfeld gehören, auch einmal in einem ***word web*** (Wortnetz), das du immer wieder passend ergänzt.

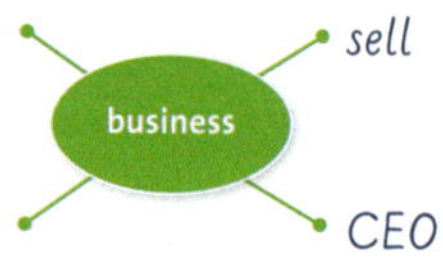

b **Gegensatzpaare** sammelst, z. B. auf der letzten Seite deines Vokabelheftes.

healthy ◄► sick
ever ◄► never
(to) agree ◄► (to) disagree

c **Synonyme** (Wörter mit der gleichen Bedeutung) sammelst und ähnliche Bedeutungen notierst.

in my opinion ►► in my view
suprised ►► puzzled
(to) need to do sth. ►► must do sth.

3 Tipps zum Lernen von Vokabeln

Lerne und wiederhole regelmäßig. Versuche, jeden Tag 10 Minuten Vokabeln zu lernen.

Lerne mit jemandem zusammen. Es macht mehr Spaß und ihr könnt euch gegenseitig abfragen.

Lerne Wörter nicht als Einzelwörter, sondern präge sie dir mit einer Phrase oder einem Beispielsatz ein.

Verteile Klebezettel mit Problemwörtern im Haus (am Kleiderschrank, Kühlschrank etc.).

SF 2 Understanding new words

Unit 1 pp. 15, 21, **Unit 2** p. 27, **Unit 5** pp. 79, 86

Wie kann ich meinen Wortschatz erweitern?

So kannst du neue Wörter verstehen und deinen Wortschatz vergrößern:

1 Bilder und Überschriften
Bilder zeigen dir oft Dinge, deren englische Bezeichnungen du im Text noch nicht kennst.

2 Erschließen aus dem Kontext
Manchmal hilft dir der Kontext, also die Wörter oder die Sätze vor und nach dem neuen Wort.

3 Internationalismen
Viele englische Wörter sind international gebräuchlich. Du verstehst sie problemlos, z. B. *computer, laptop, sneakers, sound, clip, ...*

4 Ähnlichkeiten zum Deutschen
Manche Wörter sind deutschen Wörtern in Schrift und Klang ähnlich, sodass du sie leicht erschließen kannst, z. B. *material* – Material, *battery* – Batterie, *carnival* – Karneval.

5 Wortfamilien und Wortbildungsgesetze

a Zu einem Wort gehören immer mehrere Wörter der gleichen Wortfamilie, die du einfach verstehst: Kennst du das Verb *play*, verstehst du auch *player*. Manchmal sind sogar die Formen gleich: *cold* bedeutet „kalt“, *a cold* ist eine Erkältung.

b Manche Wörter sind aus mehreren Teilwörtern (meist zweien) zusammengesetzt *(compound nouns)*. Du kennst *business* und *woman* und kannst dir daher *businesswoman* erschließen.

c Oft werden Wörter mit Hilfe verschiedener Vor- oder Nachsilben gebildet:

Präfixe (Vorsilben)		
un-	Aus einem positiven Adjektiv wird ein negatives.	*fortunately* → *unfortunately*
super-	Ein Nomen oder Adjektiv wird verstärkt.	*hero* → *superhero* *cool* → *supercool*
Suffixe (Nachsilben)		
-ful	Aus einem Nomen wird ein Adjektiv.	*colour* → *coulourful* *hope* → *hopeful*
-less	Mit *-less* verkehrt man Adjektive in ihr Gegenteil. Es bedeutet „ohne“. Es kann auch aus einem Nomen ein Adjektiv machen.	*hopeful* → *hopeless* *thankful* → *thankless* *bone* → *boneless*
-y	Aus einem Nomen wird ein Adjektiv.	*health* → *healthy* *sport* → *sporty*
-ing	Aus einem Verb wird ein Nomen.	*begin* → *beginning* *sew* → *sewing*
-er	Aus einem Tätigkeitsverb wird eine Person.	*call* → *caller* *code* → *coder*

SF3 Using an online dictionary

Unit 1 p.21, Unit 2 p.27, Unit 5 p.86

Online-Wörterbücher und Wörterbuch- bzw. Vokabeltrainer-Apps auf Tablets und Smartphones bieten eine schnelle und komfortable Art des Nachschlagens.

1 Wie benutze ich ein Online-Wörterbuch?

a Suchfeldeingabe
Gib das Wort in das Suchfeld ein und beachte die richtige Schreibweise. Wähle die Suchrichtung:
Deutsch – Englisch oder Englisch-Deutsch. Dann erhältst du die Bedeutung(en) des Wortes.

Deutsch ↔ Englisch
parkour

b Aussprache anhören
Durch einen Klick auf das Lautsprechersymbol [🔊] kannst du dir das Wort anhören. Manchmal gibt es regionale Varianten, d.h. Wörter werden z.B. im britischen Englisch anders ausgesprochen als im amerikanischen Englisch.

guard *noun*
BrE /gɑːd/ 🔊; NAmE /gɑːrd/ 🔊

Quelle: Oxford Advanced Learners Dictionary © Oxford University Press

c Wortart wählen
Manchmal kann das gleiche Wort ein Substantiv, ein Adjektiv oder ein Verb sein. *guard* z.B. kann als Nomen und als Verb verwendet werden. In unserem Kontext wird es in Verbindung mit *wrist* (Handgelenk) gebraucht und als Nomen benutzt.

You'll also need good shoes which protect your ankles, wrist guards to protect your hands and elbow pads.

d Unterschiedliche Bedeutungen beachten
Oft sind mehrere Beispiele (auch ganze Sätze) angegeben, die dir Informationen geben, wie das Wort verwendet werden kann. Wähle das Beispiel, das dem Satz in deinem Text am nächsten kommt. Achte dabei auf den Inhalt: Da es hier um die Ausrüstung beim Skateboarden geht, ist die dritte Bedeutung richtig.

A guard stood in front of the building. *Eine **Wache** stand vor dem Gebäude.*
The building is under guard. *Das Gebäude steht unter **Bewachung**.*
Wear a protective guard for safety reasons. *Trage aus Sicherheitsgründen einen **Schutz**/eine **Schutzvorrichtung**.*

2 Vokabeltrainer-Apps

Vokabeltrainer-Apps bieten neben den Informationen Bedeutung, Wortart, Aussprache und Verwendung über zusätzliche Vorteile:
- Du kannst deinen eigenen Wortschatz eingeben und gezielt üben – auch unterwegs.
- Wortschatz kannst du als Karteikarten anzeigen und vorlesen lassen.
- Es gibt zusätzlich verschiedene spielerische Möglichkeiten des Wiederholens und Übens.
- Dein Lernfortschritt wird in Statistiken dokumentiert.

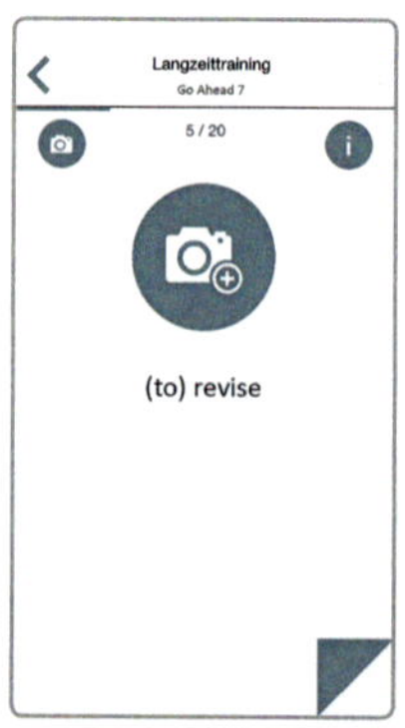

SF4 Doing internet research

Unit 3 p. 52, Unit 4 p. 73

Im Internet kannst du dir schnell und einfach Informationen aus aller Welt besorgen.
Aber Vorsicht!

- Nicht alles, was du im Netz findest, ist wichtig und richtig.
- Verliere nicht den Überblick bei der Fülle an Informationen, die es gibt.
- Benutze auch andere Quellen, wie Bücher (auch aus der Bücherei), Zeitungen und Magazine.

Wie gehe ich vor?

1 Suchen

- Behalte dein Thema genau im Blick und formuliere passende Suchbegriffe. Welche Stichwörter gehören zum Thema?
- Gib nicht nur einen Suchbegriff ein, sondern zwei oder mehrere. Du suchst z.B. Informationen zu *Mo Bridges*. Wenn du nur *Mo* eingibst, wirst du zunächst wenig Passendes finden. Wenn du aber *Moziah + Bridges + bow ties* eingibst, dann hast du bessere Ergebnisse.

2 Auswählen

Sortiere das Ergebnis der Suchmaschine gut aus und beschäftige dich nur mit den Seiten und Links, die wirklich zu deinem Thema und deiner Aufgabe passen.

Dann prüfe:

a Von wem stammt die Seite? Wie verlässlich ist die Information? Ist es z.B. ein Online-Lexikon oder ein Chat-Forum? Achte auf die Endung der URL, sie kann dir wichtige Hinweise geben:

- *.com* bedeutet, es ist eine kommerzielle Webseite, die auch Werbung enthalten kann
- *.gov* weist auf eine offizielle Webseite der Regierung hin
- *.uk* bedeutet, es ist eine britische Seite
- Vorsicht auch bei Wikipedia. Das Onlinelexikon ist von freiwilligen Helfern geschrieben und kann Fehler enthalten.

b Passen die Informationen wirklich zu deinem Thema? Überfliege die Seite und achte auf Überschriften und Bilder.

3 Sichern

Setze *bookmarks*, um die ausgewählten Seiten später schnell wieder aufzurufen. Mache dir Notizen oder drucke wichtige Seiten sofort aus und markiere wichtige Textstellen.

- Wenn du Inhalte einer Webseite verwendest, nenne immer den Autor oder Urheber der Seite, das Datum des Downloads und den Pfad.
- Schreibe die Texte nicht wörtlich ab – gib die Inhalte in deinen eigenen Worten wieder. Ordne deine Ergebnisse mit Überschriften oder sortiere sie in einer Mindmap.

SF5 Listening

Unit 1 p.14, Unit 2 p.35, Unit 3 p.43

Es gibt in der Begegnung mit dem Englischen viele Situationen, in denen es darauf ankommt zu verstehen, was gesagt wurde, z.B. am Flughafen, in Gesprächen, Filmen oder Videos.

Wie kann ich Hörverstehensaufgaben am besten bewältigen?

1 Vor dem Hören

Lies dir die Aufgabenstellung genau durch und überlege, was du tun sollst. Wenn du etwas nicht verstehst, frage nach. Schaue dir auch das Beispiel an. Es kann dir helfen.
Finde die Schlüsselwörter in der Aufgabenstellung. Diese zeigen dir, worauf du beim Hören achten musst. Du kannst sie auch herausschreiben.
Mache dir keine Sorgen, wenn du nicht alles verstehst.
Du brauchst nicht jedes Wort zu kennen, um die Aufgaben zu lösen.

2 Beim Hören

Versuche, zunächst grob zu verstehen, worum es in dem Text geht *(listening for gist)*.
Konzentriere dich auf die Schlüsselwörter aus der Aufgabenstellung.
Achte auf den Kontext. Manchmal gibt der Text weitere Informationen, die verdeutlichen, was gemeint ist. So kannst du Wörter erschließen, die du nicht kennst.
Mache dir kurze Notizen auf einem Notizzettel oder mit Bleistift auf deinem Aufgabenblatt.
Bleib ruhig, wenn du beim ersten Mal nicht alles verstehst.
Du hörst den Text meist zweimal.

3 Nach dem Hören

Vervollständige deine Notizen sofort. Auch was du nicht geschafft hast aufzuschreiben, ist wahrscheinlich noch in deinem Gedächtnis.
Lies noch einmal genau durch, was du geschrieben hast. Passen deine Antworten zu den Fragen?
Konzentriere dich beim zweiten Hören auf das, was du beim ersten Mal nicht verstanden hast.

Es gibt zahlreiche Möglichkeiten zum Üben des Hörverständnisses. Wähle etwas aus, was dir gefällt – z.B. deine Lieblingslieder oder deine Lieblingsbücher als Hörbuch.

Schau dir deine Lieblingsfilme oder -serien auf Englisch an. Blende Untertitel ein, falls du Probleme beim Verstehen hast. Blende sie aus, wenn du dich sicherer fühlst oder eine Episode schon mehrfach gesehen hast.

Bei Telefonnummern wird zweimal die gleiche Zahl *double*[1], dreimal die gleiche Zahl *triple*[2] ausgesprochen. Die Zahl 0 ist im britischen Englisch *oh*, im Amerikanischen *zero*. Bei E-Mail-Adressen gilt: „@" wird *at* und „." wird *dot* ausgesprochen.

Ein paar Minuten pro Tag können viel bewirken. Je mehr du übst, desto sicherer wirst du.

SF 6 Reading a text

Unit 2 p. 27, Unit 4 pp. 60–61

Du begegnest z.B. im Internet oder auf Reisen häufig englischen Texten. Wenn du effektive Lesestrategien entwickelst, wirst du sicherer mit Texten umgehen können. Je mehr englische Texte du liest, desto größer wird dein Wortschatz und desto schneller und besser verstehst du Texte.

Lesestrategien

1 Reading for gist
Darunter versteht man, die Kerngedanken eines Textes allgemein zu verstehen. Man muss dazu nicht jedes Detail verstehen oder jedes unbekannte Wort nachschlagen.

2 Reading for detail
Hier geht es darum, ganz genaue, spezifische Informationen in einem Text zu finden. Einzelne Wörter können grundlegend für das Verständnis des Textes sein.

3 Skimming
Mit *Skimming* verschaffst du dir schnell einen **Überblick** darüber, worum es in einem Text geht, z.B. eine Zeitungsseite oder eine Website.
Achte dabei vor allem auf Überschriften (auch Untertitel und Zwischenüberschriften), Bilder, Bildunterschriften oder fett gedruckte Wörter. Dabei ist es nicht wichtig, dass du jedes einzelne Wort liest und alle Details verstehst.

4 Scanning
Beim *Scanning* durchsuchst du einen Text gezielt nach **bestimmten Informationen**, z.B. Öffnungszeiten, Preise oder Abfahrtszeiten. Überlege dir passende Schlüsselbegriffe. Möchtest du zum Beispiel wissen, ob etwas für Kinder geeignet ist, suchst du gezielt nach den Wörtern *children* oder *kids*. Lies nicht Zeile für Zeile, sondern diagonal. Überfliege dabei den Text auf der Suche nach den Schlüsselwörtern.

Wie verbessere ich meine Lesefähigkeit?

Schaue dir vor dem Lesen die Aufgaben zum Text an. Überlege dir, was du tun sollst und welche Leseweise gefordert ist.

Verschaffe dir beim ersten Lesen einen Überblick: Worum geht es inhaltlich? Bilder oder Überschriften geben dir wertvolle Hinweise.

Lies nicht Wort für Wort, sondern vollständige Sätze und versuche, den Sinn zu erfassen.

Sei aufmerksam und konzentriert beim Lesen. Lass dich nicht von unbekannten Vokabeln entmutigen, sondern versuche, Zusammenhänge zu erschließen.

Nutze Pausen, um über das Gelesene nachzudenken und die Konzentration zu erhalten.

SF7 Marking up a text and note-taking

Unit 1 p. 13, **Unit 2** pp. 34, 37, **Unit 3** pp. 44, 52, **Unit 5** p. 82

Notizen, z. B. bei einem Telefonat oder Gespräch, sind gute Gedankenstützen. Sie helfen dir besonders, wenn du deine Notizen sinnvoll anlegst und optisch gut strukturierst.

1 Texte markieren

Wenn du Informationen aus einem Text verwenden möchtest, hebe die wichtigen Informationen hervor. Dadurch strukturierst du den Text optisch.

Du kannst die relevanten Stellen
- mit Textmarker hervorheben
- unterstreichen
- umkreisen
- mit Symbolen und Abkürzungen markieren (?, !, ☺, ☹, →)
- durch Notizen am Rand hervorheben.

Beispiel:
Für Gäste, die das Konzept des Potluck Dinners noch nicht kennen, gibt es einen Merkzettel, was man bei der Vorbereitung und der Auswahl der Gerichte bedenken sollte.

Tips for potluck guests

1) Be well prepared. Bring everything you need to serve your dish, like spoons. Remember to bring your own plates and cups. ☺
2) Bring food that you can eat off a plate. Don't bring anything that needs an extra bowl – your host will be grateful for your help to reduce the washing up! !
3) Avoid the dangerous triple "s": smelly, spicy, and strange. Don't put too much garlic in your dish. You should bring something that most people like to eat. ☹
4) How about vegetarians? Not everybody likes meat. Bring something fresh like a green salad or a vegetarian side dish. *veggies!*

2 Erstellen von Notizen

Notizen beim Zuhören oder Lesen helfen dir, dich später besser zu erinnern, wenn du etwas zusammenfassen, nacherzählen oder vortragen musst.
- Versuche, dich auf die Informationen zu konzentrieren, die für dich wichtig sind. Du musst nicht alles aufschreiben!
- Notiere nur die wichtigsten Wörter, die Schlüsselwörter *(key words)*. Das sind in der Regel Substantive oder Verben.
- Strukturiere schon beim Schreiben die Notizen optisch mit Überschriften und Absätzen. Du kannst beispielsweise *wh*-Fragewörter *(what, where, when, who, why)* als Zwischenüberschriften verwenden.
- Verwende Ziffern statt Zahlenwörter (12 statt twelfth).
- Benutze Abkürzungen („Aug“ statt „August“, „&“ statt „and“, „/“ statt „or“) und Symbole (z. B. ✗ für „nein“ oder „falsch“, ✓ für „ja“ oder „richtig“, „...“ für Lücken).

The First Baptist Church of Memphis
POTLUCK DINNER

when?	*Sunday, Aug 12, after church*
what to bring?	*mac & cheese* ✗ *enchiladas* ✗ *hot dishes* ✗ *taco salad* ✓ *dessert / cake* ✓
why?	*choir from Germany is visiting Memphis ...*

SF 8 Filling in forms

Unit 1 p. 15

Das Ausfüllen von Formularen (online oder per Hand) ist eine wichtige Fähigkeit im Alltag.

1 Allgemeine Tipps

- Lies vor dem Ausfüllen alles aufmerksam durch und mache dir überall klar, was verlangt ist.
- Achte auf saubere Schrift. Überprüfe am Ende, ob du alles vollständig ausgefüllt hast.

2 Korrektes Ausfüllen von Formularen

- Zutreffende Felder werden meist mit Häkchen *(tick ✔)* markiert. Andere Varianten des Markierens sind das Ankreuzen *(put a cross ✘)*, das Einkreisen von Zutreffendem *(circle)* oder das Durchstreichen von Nichtzutreffendem *(delete as appropriate)*. Bei Formularen am Computer kannst du oft per Drop-down-Menü die zutreffende Antwort (durch Aufklappen und Anklicken) wählen.
- Datumsangaben:

  Im **britischen** Englisch ist das Datumsformat genauso wie im Deutschen, getrennt durch Schrägstriche. Der 12. August 2025 wird so geschrieben: 12/08/2025.

  Im **amerikanischen** Englisch gilt dagegen das Format Monat/Tag/Jahr, getrennt durch Schrägstriche. Der 12. August 2025 wird 08/12/2025 geschrieben.

  Manchmal gibt es das Format dd/mm/yyyy. Dann gibst du Tag und Monat mit zwei Stellen und das Jahr vierstellig an.

3 Wichtige Ausdrücke

- Mit *last name* (oder *surname / family name*) ist der Nachname gemeint; mit *first name* (*forename*) der Vorname.
- DOB bedeutet date of birth, also das Geburtsdatum.
- *gender* bezeichnet das Geschlecht – *male* (Abkürzung *m*) bedeutet männlich, *female* (Abkürzung *f*) steht für weiblich, *unspecified* für Menschen, die sich keinem Geschlecht zuordnen wollen.
- *contact information*: *mobile* meint die Handynummer; *landline* das Festnetz.
- Der Ausdruck *required field* bedeutet, dass du in dieses Feld zwingend etwas hineinschreiben musst.
- *parent/guardian*: *parents* sind Elternteile, ein *guardian* ist ein Erziehungsberechtigter oder Vormund.

Application for the trip of the drama club to the Royal Theatre

Last name: Miller

First name: Roxy

DOB: 15/02/20[redacted]

Gender: m ☐ f ☑ unspecified ☐

Contact information (required fields):

Mobile:

Name and mobile/landline of parent or guardian:

Name: Harold Miller

Mobile:

Landline:

Information on allergies (please specify): N/A

Signature: R. Miller

- Wenn Zusatzinformationen verlangt werden *(please specify)*, mache präzise, knappe Angaben.
- In Felder, die nicht zutreffen, kann man *N/A* hineinschreiben (*not applicable* = nicht zutreffend), z. B. wenn man keine Allergien hat.
- *signature* ist die eigene Unterschrift.

SF 9 How to write good texts

Unit 2 p. 31, **Unit 3** p. 48

Beachte die folgenden vier Schritte, um deinen Schreibprozess zu strukturieren und lebendigere Texte zu schreiben. Sie sind auch gut bei der Planung von Projekten oder Präsentationen.

1 Sammle Ideen für deinen Text

Sammle zuerst alles, was dir zum Thema einfällt. Deine Ideen kannst du z.B so sammeln und ordnen:

- **Listen:** Schreibe zunächst alle Ideen zu deinem Thema auf, jeweils in einer neuen Zeile. Dann streiche durch, was du nicht verwenden willst. Nimm Farben oder Symbole, um sie zu gruppieren (→ SF 7).
- **Fragen:** Stelle *(wh-)*Fragen und notiere Antworten dazu *(who, where, when, why, what, how?)*
- **Mindmaps:** Schreibe das Thema in die Mitte und deine Gedanken außen herum (s. Abb. **A**).
- **Haftnotizen:** Sammle deine Ideen auf Klebezetteln, die du leicht ändern, ergänzen oder neu anordnen kannst (s. Abb. **B**).

A

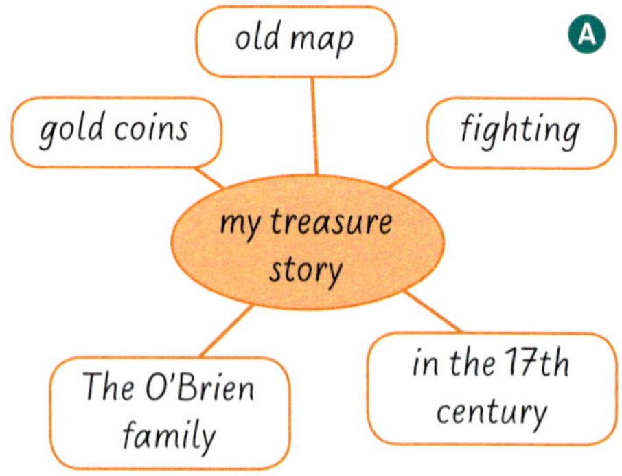

B

2 Entwirf und strukturiere deinen Text

Ordne deine Notizen in **Einleitung**, **Hauptteil** und **Schluss** *(beginning, main body, ending)*.
In der Einleitung führst du zum Thema hin und erklärst, worum es geht.
Im Hauptteil (unterteilt in Absätze) entwickelst du die Handlung logisch.
Im Schlussteil findest du ein interessantes Ende oder fasst das Geschehen zusammen. Ein **logischer Aufbau** hilft dabei, deinen Text leichter verständlich zu machen. Dazu gehören:

- Chronologie, d.h. sinnvoller zeitlicher Ablauf
- logische Zusammenhänge (Grund und Folge, Ursache und Wirkung)
- Entwicklung der Handlung (roter Faden, Aufbau von Spannung)

Neben Überlegungen zur Handlung solltest du dir auch Gedanken zum **Wortschatz** machen: Sammle lebendige Verben sowie treffende Substantive und abwechslungsreiche Adjektive und Adverbien zu deinem Themengebiet (z.B. für die Schatzsuche *to hide, to dig, to discover / a deep hole, a hidden treasure / fast, greedy*).
Schreibe zuerst einen Entwurf (s. Abb. **C**).

C

First draft: Treasure story

beginning:
two children discover map with an „x" on it, in their grandfather's old farm house → treasure?

main body:
ask grandpa about history of the house → flashback: house belonged to farmer's family, times of fighting, hide their money → children dig for hidden treasure → find it in garden → box with ancient gold coins

ending:
take coins to the police, now in a museum, get money

3 Schreibe deinen Text

Mithilfe der Notizen schreibst du nun deinen Text (Abb. D). Achte darauf, deinen Text interessant zu gestalten, und zwar durch

- adjectives, die die Personen, ihre Gefühle, Gegenstände oder Orte genauer beschreiben, z. B. *wooden, exciting, thrilling*.
- adverbs, die beschreiben, wie etwas geschieht, z. B. *really, carefully*.
- linking words (z. B. *and, but, so*), die Sätze miteinander verbinden.
- time words, die dir helfen, die zeitliche Abfolge des Geschehens zu verdeutlichen, z. B. *a hundred years ago, first, next month*.
- wörtliche Rede (Unterhaltungen zwischen Personen).
- inneren Monolog (Gedanken einer einzelnen Person)

4 Überprüfe und korrigiere deinen Text

Mache nach dem Schreiben eine kurze Pause. Dann fange an, den Text inhaltlich und sprachlich zu verbessern. Überprüfe, ob dein Text vollständig und verständlich ist. Hast du lebendig formuliert und typische Fehler (s. Abb. E) vermieden?

Beim Korrekturlesen empfehlen sich **mehrere Durchgänge**: Beim ersten Mal achtest du auf inhaltliche Logik und Verständlichkeit, dann auf lebendige Sprache und danach auf sprachliche und grammatikalische Fehler.

Überprüfe auch das **Layout** deines Textes: Benötigst du eine Überschrift? Hast du Abschnitte eingefügt? Hast du bei einem Brief an die richtigen Anrede-und Schlussformeln gedacht?

A Treasure in the Shed **D**

"What's this?", Emma asked, holding an old piece of paper in her hand. We were playing in the bedroom of the old farm house where our grandfather lived. "It looks like a map. There's an X on it." "Oh, that's really exciting! Let's go and ask Grandpa."

Grandpa told us the story of the old farm house. The O'Brien family had lived in this house some hundreds of years ago. They worked extremely hard and had enough money to lead a happy life. Then there was some fighting where they lived, so the O'Briens decided to go somewhere to hide until the war was over. But they never came back.

"No one really knows what happened to them - or their money", Grandpa finished the story.

What an exciting story. "Maybe this map shows where they hid their money? Let's go and find out!" Together we studied the map carefully. This looked like the house. And this could be the garden ...

Grandpa gave us some spades and we started digging. Finally, Emma hit something: It was a wooden box! Could the old story really be true? Grandpa opened the box. We could not believe our eyes: There were golden coins in it, shining and glittering. "We found the O'Brien family treasure!"

Typische Fehlerquellen **E**

- **Groß- und Kleinschreibung:** Im Englischen werden Eigennamen, Tage, Monate und Feiertage, Nationalitäten und Länder das Personalpronomen *I* und Anreden *(Mr, Mrs)* **immer groß** geschrieben.
- **Wörter mit „stummen" Buchstaben:** *climb, know.*
- **unregelmäßige Pluralformen:** z. B. *child-children, man-men, shelf-shelves.*
- gleicher Klang, aber unterschiedliche Schreibweisen und Bedeutungen: *to-two-too, then-than, there-their-they're, wear-where.*
- **Präpositionen:** *in the picture, by train, on the bus, on TV.*
- **unregelmäßige Verben** (siehe Liste auf Seite 244f.) – z. B. *say, said, said; go, went, gone.*
- Satzbau im Englischen stets nach dem Muster subject-verb-object, auch in Nebensätzen.

SF10 Writing an email / a letter

Unit 1 p. 10, **Unit 3** p. 57, **Unit 5** p. 87

Mit Briefen oder E-Mails kann man mit Menschen auf der ganzen Welt verbunden sein. Daher ist es wichtig, schriftlich miteinander kommunizieren zu können.

E-Mail-Adresse und Betreff

Hier steht die E-Mail-Adresse des Empfängers.

Hier kannst du weitere Empfänger eintragen.

Hier schreibst du stichwortartig, worum es in deiner E-Mail geht.

Hier schreibst du deinen Text.

Aufbau von einem Brief oder einer E-Mail

1 Einleitung: Persönliche Anrede

Schreibst du an einen Freund oder eine Freundin, beginne immer mit einer persönlichen Anrede, z. B. *Dear Olivia* oder *Hi, Ben!*
Schreiben an Organisationen oder Firmen beginnst du mit *Dear Mr … / Dear Mrs … / Dear Ms …*
Wenn du den Namen nicht kennst, schreibst du *Dear Sir or Madam.*
Sage, warum du schreibst und worauf du dich beziehst. In einem persönlichen Schreiben frage, wie es ihm oder ihr geht. Hier kannst du dich auch für die letzte Nachricht bedanken oder dich entschuldigen, falls du länger nicht geschrieben hast.

2 Mittelteil: Erzähle, was passiert ist

Hier schreibst du dem Empfänger Wichtiges, nimmst Stellung oder beantwortest Fragen.
In einem persönlichen Schreiben frage deinen Freund oder deine Freundin, was ihm oder ihr passiert ist.

3 Schluss: Persönlicher Gruß

Beende deinen Brief mit einem freundlichen Gruß (z. B. *Best wishes, Love, Lots of love, All the best, …*) und deinem Namen.
Briefe oder E-Mails an Organisationen beendest du mit *Best regards* oder förmlicher mit *Yours sincerely* (BE) bzw. *Sincerely* (AE) und deinem Namen. In englischen Briefen schreibst du die Adresse rechts oben und darunter das Datum.

Dear Riya
Thanks for your message! I miss you and all our friends from home.
I'm sending you a letter because we can only use Wi-Fi sometimes in my boarding house. I'm writing this at night with a torch!
You asked if the school is like Hogwarts. Well, we don't play Quidditch, but we do some sports that I've never done before – like lacrosse. It's a strange sport which you play with nets on sticks! The school food is good too, but it doesn't appear by magic – and I miss my dad's curries, and takeaway pizza ☺.
I've made lots of friends here. Roxy, the girl who shares my room, is showing me the school. It's nice to have a roommate, but I miss my own room at home where I can read and be alone. I miss my mum and dad too. Maybe everybody is homesick in the beginning and then it goes away.
Say hi to everyone at school from me! But don't say I'm homesick – that's our secret. Ok?
Love Ella xx

33 Main Street
London NW4 6JZ

12 July, 20

SF11 Being polite

Unit 1 pp. 14, 19, Unit 3 p. 51, Unit 4 pp. 64, 68

Im Umgang miteinander ist es stets wichtig, höflich zu sein. Hierzu kommt es auf nonverbale Signale ebenso an wie auf das, wie man etwas sagt.

1 Körpersprache

- Schaue deinem Gegenüber in die Augen und halte Blickkontakt.
- Ein offenes, freundliches Lächeln öffnet dir viele Türen!
- Lege die Arme locker zusammen, statt sie zu verschränken.
- Wende deinen Körper deinem Gesprächspartner zu.

2 Höflichkeit

Formuliere Fragen und Bitten zurückhaltend und höflich. Sage *Please* und *Excuse me*. Formulierungen wie *I want* ... sind unhöflich. Bedanke dich stets für geleistete Hilfe *(Thank you)*.

Excuse me, I have a problem.
Could you please tell me ...
I would like to know where ...
Sorry, I don't understand this sign.

Thanks. / Thank you for your help.

Zeige Interesse an Deinem Gegenüber.
Dazu gehört auch **Smalltalk** – zum Beispiel, sich nach dem Befinden des anderen zu erkundigen, über unverfängliche Kleinigkeiten zu sprechen (z. B. das Wetter) oder ein nettes Kompliment zu machen.
Vergiss nicht, dich freundlich zu verabschieden.

Goodbye. Have a good day!

Wenn man etwas nicht verstanden hat, kann man seinen Gesprächspartner bitten, das Gesagte zu wiederholen:

I'm (really) sorry, I didn't get that.
Can you repeat that, please?
Sorry, can you say that again?

In manchen Situationen kommt es auf die Schreibweise eines Wortes an. Dann kann es hilfreich sein, wenn es buchstabiert wird:

Oh, that is a hard / unusual name / word.
I've never heard that before.
Can you spell that, please?

Zur Sicherheit kann man durch Nachfragen noch einmal überprüfen, ob man etwas richtig verstanden oder notiert hat:

I'm not sure I understood it correctly.
Can I read it back to you?
Did you say it starts at 8 pm?
Do you mean the big building with the glass front?

SF 12 Expressing opinions and feelings

Unit 3 p. 49, Unit 4 p. 69, Unit 5 p. 83

In vielen Situationen tauschst du dich mit anderen über deine Ideen und Meinungen aus. Dabei musst du sowohl deinen eigenen Standpunkt begründen als auch auf andere angemessen eingehen.

Die eigene Meinung ausdrücken

Wenn du im Rahmen einer Diskussion in der Klasse, in einer Präsentation oder in einem schriftlichen Kommentar deine eigene Meinung darstellst, ist es wichtig, dass du dich zum einen höflich, zum anderen klar und präzise äußerst, und deine Ansicht auch begründest.

1 Stelle dar, was du denkst

Sage zu Beginn einer Diskussion oder eines Textes klar, was genau du zu einer Frage oder einem Thema denkst. Lege dir nützliche Wörter und höfliche Redewendungen zurecht:

(Personally,) I am sure that / believe / feel / find / think ...
In my opinion, / view, ...
If you ask me ...

2 Begründe deine Meinung

Nenne Gründe und Argumente, die deinen Standpunkt unterstützen.

Firstly, ... / Secondly, ... / Thirdly, ...
Let's not forget that ...

3 Drücke deine Gefühle aus

In manchen Situationen kann es deine Position verstärken, wenn du deine persönlichen Empfindungen wiedergibst.

I was (really) angry / surprised / worried / ...
I felt upset.
I felt that ... was clever / hard / unfair / ...
I can't / couldn't believe that ...

4 Fasse das Gesagte zusammen

Am Schluss fasse deine Argumente prägnant zusammen. Nenne den Aspekt, der dir am Wichtigsten ist.

To sum up, ...

5 In einer Diskussion angemessen reagieren

In Diskussionen geht es nicht nur um die eigene Meinung, sondern um den Austausch von Gedanken und Ideen. Daher musst du auch auf das eingehen, was andere gesagt haben und ihre Meinungen respektieren. Bleibe beim Thema. Sei auch bei Meinungsverschiedenheiten sachlich und höflich.

Wenn du der Meinung eines anderen zustimmst, kannst du diese Redewendungen verwenden:

I think so too.
I agree with you.
Maybe you're right.
That's true.
You've got a good point there.
That's just what I think too.

Wenn du anderer Meinung bist, sind diese Redewendungen hilfreich:

I'm not so / quite sure here.
I don't agree with you about ...
I'm not sure that's true.
Well, it's not as simple as that.
You may be right there, but ...
I can't believe ...

SF 13 Giving a talk

Das Vorbereiten einer Präsentation

Sammeln

Nutze verschiedene Medien, um Informationen zu sammeln: Internet, Bücher, Zeitschriften, Zeitungen. Vorsicht: Nicht alles, was du findest, ist richtig und wichtig! Prüfe deine Informationen also sorgfältig (SF 4 → p. 149).

Aufschreiben

Du kannst die Informationen in einer *mind map*, als Stichpunkte oder in einer Tabelle zusammentragen.
Auch kleine Karteikarten bieten sich für deine Notizen an. Schreibe groß und deutlich nur die wichtigsten Stichworte, keine ganzen Sätze. Strukturiere deine Notizen genauso wie deine Präsentation. Hebe die wichtigsten Begriffe mit verschiedenen Farben hervor.
Notiere kurz, wann du welches Medium einsetzt.

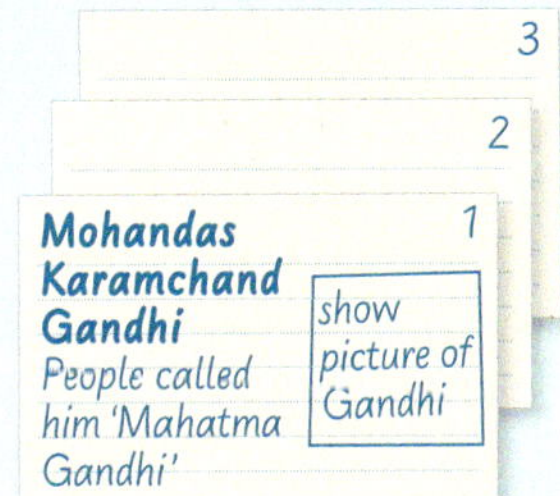

Ordnen

So baust du deinen Vortrag auf:
- **Einleitung:** Nenne das Thema.
- **Hauptteil:** Nenne deine Hauptpunkte. Erzähle dann mehr zu jedem Punkt. Binde deine Bilder ein.
- **Abschluss:** Betone den wichtigsten Punkt noch einmal und bedanke dich fürs Zuhören. Erkundige dich, ob es Fragen gibt.

Hello everyone. Today I'm going to talk about ...

First, I'd like to tell you ... Look at this picture.

To sum up, I think ... Thank you for listening. Do you have any questions?

Veranschaulichen

Veranschauliche deinen Vortrag mit Bildern oder Gegenständen. Achte darauf, dass die Verwendung der Bilder erlaubt ist, nutze daher z. B. *creative commons*-Bilder.

Bei einer Präsentation am Computer:
- Wähle ein einfaches Folienlayout.
- Verwende eine Schriftgröße von mindestens 16 pt.
- Beschränke dich auf wenig Text.
- Wähle nur ein Bild pro Folie.

Auch interessante Zitate oder Sprüche machen dein Referat interessant!

You can see ... in this picture / on this map.

Üben

Übe deinen Vortrag mehrmals vor dem Spiegel oder mit einem Partner / einer Partnerin. Achte auf die Zeit.

Das Vortragen der Präsentation

- Bereite alles in Ruhe vor: hänge dein Plakat auf / schalte den Beamer an etc.
- Sprich langsam, laut und deutlich. Lies nicht von deinen (Computer-)Folien ab. Schau nicht nur auf deine Notizen, sondern schau auch deine Zuhörer/innen an und lächle.

SF14 Paraphrasing

Unit 1 p. 18

Es gibt immer wieder Situationen, in denen dir der genaue Begriff für etwas nicht einfällt. Dann musst du ihn umschreiben können.

Wie umschreibe ich etwas?

1 **Erkläre** das Wort, indem du einen passenden Oberbegriff *(umbrella word)* findest, z. B.:

Personen	person, man, woman, boy, girl, child, ...	*A boarder is a student who lives in a boarding school.*
Orte	place, building, room, area, country, region, ...	*A boarding house is the place where boarders live.*
Dinge	food, drink, game, musical instrument, sport, ...	*Lacrosse is a type of sport that you play with sticks and a ball.*

It's a type of ... / It's a person ... / It's a place ... / It's a thing ...

2 **Beschreibe** den Sachverhalt. Sage, wie etwas aussieht, wo man es findet oder was man damit tut, z. B. *Coding is when you write a computer program.*

SF15 Describing pictures

Unit 2 p. 36, Unit 3 p. 42

1 **Auf den ersten Blick**
Beschreibe die Situation:
This picture shows ...

2 **Was ist wo?**

- Sage dann, wen oder was du siehst und wo sich die Personen und Dinge im Bild oder Foto befinden.
  Beschreibe, was zu sehen ist:
  In the foreground / In the middle
  I can see a Roman queen ...
  ***In the background** there are ...*
  On the left / On the right
  I can see ...
  In front of the ...**, there are ...* ***Next to / Behind / Between ... ***At the bottom / At the top ...***

3 **Schau genau!**
Beschreibe die Personen genauer, z. B. Alter, Haare, Kleidung. Bei Gegenständen sind Farbe, Form und Größe interessant.

4 **Wer macht was?**
Was tun die Personen gerade? Verwende dafür das *present progressive*.

5 **Was denkst du?**
Vermute, woher sich die Personen kennen, was vielleicht vorher passiert ist oder was gleich geschehen könnte. Vielleicht kannst du auch erkennen, wie sich die Personen fühlen.
I think ... / Maybe ... They look very ...

SF 16 Mediation

Unit 1 p. 19, **Unit 3** p. 53, **Unit 4** p. 65, **Unit 5** p. 82

Situationen, in denen du zwischen zwei Sprachen vermitteln musst oder dir fremdsprachige Inhalte erschließt (z. B. eine Speisekarte), nennt man Mediation. Dabei überträgst du nur die wichtigsten Informationen von der einen in die andere Sprache. Mediation ist keine wörtliche Übersetzung.

Wann ist Mediation nötig?

Englisch → Deutsch

- Du möchtest jemandem z. B. englische Spielregeln oder einen englischen Artikel auf Deutsch erläutern.
- Du bist mit deiner Familie in England. Dein kleiner Bruder will z. B. Süßigkeiten kaufen oder wissen, was in einer Broschüre oder auf einem Schild steht.

Deutsch → Englisch

- Jemand spricht dich auf der Straße auf Englisch an, weil er/sie einen bestimmten Ort sucht.
- Ein Austauschschüler / eine Austauschschülerin besucht dich und spricht nicht sehr gut Deutsch.

Was muss ich beachten?

1 Keine Panik vor unbekannten Wörtern
Bei einer Mediation musst du nicht jedes Wort verstehen. Es genügt, wenn du die zentrale Aussage wiedergeben kannst.

2 Gib nur die wichtigsten Informationen weiter
Gib nur das Wesentliche wieder und vergiss dabei bedeutungstragende Wörter (z. B. „fast" oder „mindestens") nicht. Lasse unwichtige Wörter und Satzteile weg.

3 Sage es anders
Wenn du ein Wort nicht kennst, versuche es durch ein anderes mit ähnlicher Bedeutung zu ersetzen oder es zu umschreiben. Beispiele:

außer dienstags → *but not on Tuesdays*
Mindestalter 14 Jahre → *you must be 14 or older*
ermäßigte Eintrittskarten → *cheaper tickets*

4 Sage es kurz
Bilde kurze und einfache Sätze, um Fehler zu vermeiden.

5 Achte in Gesprächen auf die Pronomen und die Satzstellung
Denke daran, dass die Wortstellung in englischen Sätzen oft anders ist als im Deutschen.
Und überlege immer, an wen du dich gerade wendest und passe die Pronomen entsprechend an (siehe Beispiel am Foto).

6 Nützliche Ausdrücke
Mit diesen Wendungen kannst du deine Mediation einleiten:
He/She asks/says/thinks/would like to ...
Here it says that we should/mustn't/...

SF 17 Doing better in tests

Revision 1 pp. 40–41, **Revision 2** pp. 74–75

Wie kann ich meine Leistungen verbessern?

Mit diesen Tipps kannst du häufige Fehler vermeiden und bessere Ergebnisse in Tests erzielen.

1 Lerne aus deinen Fehlern: Führe ein Fehlerprotokoll

Ein Fehlerprotokoll *(error log)* kann dir helfen, deine typischen Fehler zu erkennen. Lege eine Übersicht an, in der du notierst, welche Fehler du gemacht hast und wie sie verbessert werden müssen – als handgeschriebene Liste, Notizbuch, Schnellhefter, Karteikasten oder Computerdatei. Ergänze sie, wenn du eine korrigierte Arbeit zurückbekommst und nutze diese Kategorien:

GR = *grammar*: Grammatikfehler, z. B. falsche Verbform (~~sayed~~ statt *said*), falsche Präposition (*in* statt *on*) etc. Hier kann dir oft das Language File ab S. 128 helfen.

SP = *spelling*: Falsche Schreibweise, z. B. *He ~~new~~ I would like it* statt *He knew*.

WW = *wrong word*: Du verwechselst Wörter und ihre Bedeutungen bzw. kannst sie nicht korrekt anwenden. Wiederhole die Vokabeln mithilfe des *Vocabulary* ab S. 166.

FF = *false friend*: Leider gibt es einige Wörter, die im Deutschen und Englischen ähnlich klingen oder aussehen, aber eine andere Bedeutung haben (z. B. *rock* = Fels, Rock = *skirt*).

WO = *word order*: Fehler bei der Wortstellung (*Yesterday ~~read I~~* ... statt *Yesterday I read*).

sentence with error (fehlerhafter Satz)	correct sentence (korrigierter Satz)	type of error (Art des Fehlers)	notes (Hinweise, Tipps und Notizen)
I became a great DVD for Christmas.	I got a great DVD for Christmas.	false friend (FF)	to become = werden to get = bekommen
My father new I would like it.	My father knew I would like it.	spelling (SP)	klingt gleich, hat andere Bedeutung
My brohter also liked it.	My brother also liked it.	spelling (SP)	Buchstaben vertauscht
I saw it in the internet.	I saw it on the internet.	Grammar (GR)	falsche Präposition
It gives many great films at the moment.	There are many great films at the moment.	wrong word (WW)	Es gibt = There is / there are!
My dad sayed he wanted to see you.	My dad said he wanted to see you.	Grammar (GR)	(to) say, said, said – s. Liste *irregular verbs* (S. 244 f.)
If it rains tomorrow, can we go to the cinema.	If it rains tomorrow, we can go to the cinema.	Word order (WO)	Wenn ein Nebensatz vorausgeht, ändert sich die Wortstellung *subject – verb* des Hauptsatzes nicht.

2 Tipps für Tests

- Konzentriere dich. Es geht nicht um Tempo, sondern um gute Ergebnisse!
- Wiederhole auch bekannten Wortschatz regelmäßig. Lerne neue Wendungen im Zusammenhang, statt nur Einzelwörter (z. B. *I look forward to Christmas.*)
- Wenn du etwas nicht verstehst, schlage im *Language file* oder deinen Unterlagen nach und frage deine Lehrkraft oder deine Mitschüler/innen.

3 Prüfungsvorbereitung

- Beginne rechtzeitig mit deiner Vorbereitung. Verschaffe dir zunächst einen Überblick über den Prüfungsstoff und teile ihn in überschaubare Abschnitte ein. Hake Erledigtes ab.
- Lerne, deine typischen Fehler zu vermeiden – mit Hilfe deines *error logs*.
- Informiere dich über die üblichen Aufgabenstellungen.

4 Während der Prüfung

- Bleibe stets konzentriert und optimistisch. Lass dich nicht nervös machen.
- Lies dir die Arbeitsanweisungen genau durch. Markiere Wichtiges (→ SF 7).
- Wenn du fertig bist, überprüfe, ob du alle geforderten Punkte abhaken kannst.
- Teile dir die Zeit gut ein. Oft hilft es, mit etwas Leichtem zu beginnen. Wenn du bei einer Aufgabe nicht weiterkommst, lege sie beiseite und schaue sie später wieder an. Gehe am Ende noch einmal in Ruhe deine Antworten durch und korrigiere sie.

5 Hinweise zum Jahrgangsstufentest (Beginn von Klasse 7)

Die folgende Übersicht zeigt dir, welche Aufgabenformen möglich sind.

skill	mögliche Aufgabenformen	Erklärung
Listening (→ SF 5)	matching	Ordne vorgegebene Überschriften zu.
	multiple choice (→ Revision 1, Ex 1 p. 40)	Wähle aus mehreren Alternativen die richtige aus.
	note-taking (filling in grids) (→ Revision 2, Ex. 1 p. 74)	Ergänze eine Tabelle oder einen Notizzettel stichwortartig.
Writing (→ SF 9 + 10)	email / letter (→ Unit 5, Ex. 2 p. 87)	Schreibe ca. sechzig Wörter zu einem Thema und behandle dabei drei inhaltliche Aspekte.
Reading (→ SF 6)	true / false / not in the text	Wähle eine der Möglichkeiten aus.
	multiple choice	Wähle aus mehreren Alternativen die richtige aus.
	short answer questions	Gib eine stichwortartige Antwort.
	matching people and statements	Ordne verschiedene Aussagen den Personen zu.
	matching statements and signs	Ordne die richtigen Bedeutungen den Schildern zu.
Use of English	matching statements with gaps in the text (→ Revision 1, Ex. 3 p. 41)	Ordne mehreren Lücken im Text die passende Aussage zu.
	matching questions and answers	Ordne mehreren Fragen die passende Antwort zu.
	mixed grammar with multiple choice (→ Revision 2, Ex. 3 p. 75)	Ordne in einem Lückentext das passende Wort zu.
	open mixed grammar (→ Your check 1, Ex. 1b p. 22)	Finde in einem Lückentext das passende Wort selbst.

SF18 Working with graphs and diagrams

Unit 1 p. 10, **Unit 2** p. 25, **Unit 5** p. 77

Tabellen und Diagramme können dabei helfen, Information darzustellen, zu veranschaulichen, zu vergleichen und sie leichter zu verstehen.

Arten von Diagrammen

<table>
<tr><th>Englisch</th><th>Deutsch</th><th>verwendet für ...</th><th>Beispiel</th></tr>
<tr><td>table / chart</td><td>Tabelle</td><td>eine kurze Übersicht über alle vorliegenden Daten</td><td><table><tr><th></th><th>COLUMN TITLE 1</th><th>COLUMN TITLE 2</th><th>COLUMN TITLE 3</th><th>COLUMN TITLE 4</th></tr><tr><td>First Row</td><td>140 598</td><td>148 564</td><td>153 264</td><td>201 700</td></tr><tr><td>Second Row</td><td>240 452</td><td>248 698</td><td>249 364</td><td>289 560</td></tr><tr><td>Third Row</td><td>278 564</td><td>283 478</td><td>285 421</td><td>295 120</td></tr><tr><td>Fourth Row</td><td>360 455</td><td>364 458</td><td>368 897</td><td>375 562</td></tr><tr><td>Fifth Row</td><td>420 451</td><td>422 659</td><td>435 985</td><td>482 597</td></tr><tr><td>**TOTAL**</td><td>**1 440 520**</td><td>**1 467 857**</td><td>**1 492 931**</td><td>**1 644 539**</td></tr></table></td></tr>
<tr><td>line graph</td><td>Linien- oder Kurvendiagramm</td><td>einen zeitlichen Verlauf oder eine Entwicklung bzw. einen Trend</td><td></td></tr>
<tr><td>bar graph</td><td>Balken- oder Säulendiagramm</td><td>eine Rangfolge oder direkte Vergleiche</td><td>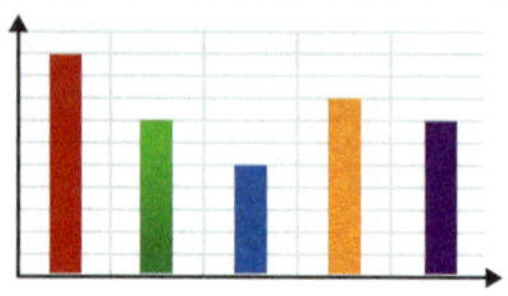</td></tr>
<tr><td>Venn diagram</td><td>Venn- oder Mengen-diagramm</td><td>die Darstellung von Beziehungen zwischen zwei oder mehr Mengen und hervorzuheben, worin sie sich unterscheiden und wo sie Gemeinsamkeiten besitzen.</td><td></td></tr>
<tr><td>pie chart</td><td>Tortendiagramm / Kreisdiagramm</td><td>den Vergleich von Anteilen einzelner Teile im Vergleich zum Ganzen, oft in Prozent angegeben</td><td>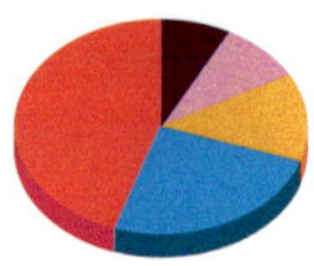</td></tr>
<tr><td>infographic</td><td>Infografik / Piktogramm</td><td>bildliche Veranschaulichung von Zahlen mit Hilfe von Symbolen</td><td></td></tr>
</table>

Wie gewinnst du Informationen aus Grafiken und Tabellen?

Schritt 1: Schau dir zuerst die Überschrift, die Erklärungen und Beschriftungen an. Sie geben dir Hinweise auf den Inhalt.

Schritt 2: Schau dir danach die Einheiten der Zahlenangaben auf den beiden Achsen an. Möglich sind Größen- oder Mengenangaben, Jahreszahlen oder Prozentsätze.

Wortschatz zum Beschreiben von Diagrammen

The line graph is about ...
The horizontal axis shows ...
There are more than ...
One quarter / 25 per cent of the ...
The number grows / drops / does not change.

SF 19 Viewing

Unit 1 pp. 9, 17, **Unit 2** pp. 30, 37, **Unit 3** pp. 44, 52, **Unit 4** pp. 59, 69, **Unit 5** p. 83

Bei Aufgaben zum *Viewing* verstehst du manches übers Sehen, manches übers Hören.

1 Vor dem Sehen *(pre-viewing)*

- Überlege, was du schon weißt: Welche **Art** von Film wirst du sehen – eine Dokumentation (z.B. Unit 1, S. 9), einen Kurzfilm (z.B. Unit 2, S. 30), einen Cartoon (z.B. Unit 3, S. 44)?
- Was verraten dir der **Titel** des Filmes oder die Überschrift über das Thema? Was weißt du bereits darüber? Welche Vokabeln aus diesem Themenbereich kennst du? Sind Bilder dabei, die dir einen ersten Eindruck verschaffen?
- Schaue dir die **Aufgabenstellungen** an und stelle sicher, dass du verstehst, was verlangt ist. Du musst nie jedes einzelne Detail oder Wort eines Filmes verstehen, sondern immer nur bestimmte Aspekte. Die Arbeitsanweisungen zeigen dir, worauf du dich konzentrieren musst.

2 Während des Sehens *(while-viewing)*

Versuche beim ersten Sehen die Gesamtzusammenhänge zu verstehen *(global understanding)* und wichtige Dinge von weniger wichtigen zu unterscheiden. Die *wh*-Fragen *(who? what? where? when?)* geben dir einen Überblick über den Handlungsverlauf *(plot)*, die Figuren *(characters)*, den Schauplatz *(setting)* und die Zeit der Handlung *(time)*.

Erst beim zweiten Anschauen geht es um detailliertes Verstehen. Vieles kannst du aus den Bildern oder dem Handlungsverlauf erschließen (Abb. 1).

Geräusche und Musik sind wichtige stilistische Mittel: Veränderungen in der Lautstärke oder der Geschwindigkeit kündigen oft eine Entwicklung in der Handlung an. Musik drückt häufig Gefühle aus bzw. verstärkt sie.

- Achte auf die Körpersprache der Personen (Abb. 2), ihren Gesichtsausdruck und den Klang der Stimmen. Häufig werden Gefühle ohne Sprache ausgedrückt. Oft sieht man dann eine Nahaufnahme des Gesichts *(close-up)*.

3 Nach dem Sehen *(post-viewing)*

- Ergänze deine Notizen und markiere Wichtiges.
- Vergleiche deine Erwartungen vor dem Sehen mit der tatsächlichen Handlung: Was hast du richtig vorhergesehen, was hat dich überrascht?

> – The film tells the story of ... It is set in ... (time/place).
> – The music in this scene is dramatic/sad/... . I think it shows that ...
> – The body language in the scene helped me to understand ...
> – I liked / didn't like the film because ...

Das **Vocabulary (S.166–193)** enthält alle neuen Wörter und Wendungen des Buches, die du lernen musst. Sie stehen in der Reihenfolge, in der sie im Buch zum ersten Mal vorkommen.

Hier siehst du, wie das Vocabulary aufgebaut ist:

Dies ist das Gegenteil-Zeichen: **king** ◄► **queen** bedeutet: „**king** ist das Gegenteil von **queen**"

Diese Zahl gibt die **Seite** an, auf der die Wörter zum ersten Mal vorkommen. p. 26 = Seite 26

p. 26	**king** [kɪŋ]	König	**king** ◄► **queen** **man** ◄► **woman**
	(to) **change (into)** [tʃeɪndʒ]	(sich) (ver)ändern (zu/in); wechseln; (sich) verwandeln (in), werden (zu); sich umziehen	*verb:* (to) **change** – *noun:* **change** = Veränderung, Wechsel, Verwandlung (to) **change** (Verb) = **1.** (sich) (ver)ändern; wechseln; (sich) verwandeln **2.** umsteigen

(to) **change**

„ändern"	They had to **change** their plans.	Sie mussten ihre Pläne ändern.
„sich verändern"	He **has changed** a lot recently.	Er hat sich ... sehr verändert.
„wechseln"	American kids **change** rooms between classes. Can you **change** your clothes before we go?	... wechseln das Klassenzimmer ... deine Kleidung wechseln
„sich umziehen"	Give me five minutes. I'd like to **change** first.	Ich möchte mich erst umziehen.

Die orangen Kästen solltest du dir immer besonders gut ansehen. Dort stehen wichtige Hinweise zu den neuen Wörtern.

mask [mɑːsk]	Maske	At carnival people wear **masks**. 
claw [klɔː]		Look at the **claws** on that bird's foot!
so (that)		⚠ **so** = **1.** (*auch* so that) = sodass; **2. so** big/cold/... = so groß/kalt/... **3.** also, daher
emergency [iˈmɜːdʒənsi]		In an **emergency** you should call the police.
weapon [ˈwepən]		
quick [kwɪk]		►► **fast** **quick/fast** ◄► **slow**
accountant [əˈkaʊntənt]	Buchhalter/in	Did someone take money from the company? We're still waiting for the **accountant**'s report.
		Jack married his boyfriend Alex. They're **gay**.
		Our children **behaved** very well when we took them to the restaurant. ⚠ *English:* He's **behaving** strangely. *German:* Er **benimmt sich** seltsam.
peace [piːs]		Will there ever be **peace** everywhere in the world?
bracelet [ˈbreɪslət]		**bracelets** 

Dies ist das Zeichen für ein Synonym: ►► **fast** bedeutet: „**fast** ist ein Synonym von **quick**"

Die Lautschrift zeigt dir, wie ein Wort ausgesprochen wird. Eine Übersicht über die Lautschriftzeichen findest du auf Seite 242.

Das rote **Warnschild mit Ausrufezeichen** bedeutet: Vorsicht, hier kannst du leicht Fehler machen!

Im **Vocabulary** werden folgende Abkürzungen und Symbole verwendet:
p. = *page* (Seite) • *sb.* = *somebody* (jemand) • *AE* = *American English* • *BE* = *British English*
sth. = *something* (etwas) • *pl* = *plural* (Mehrzahl) • *no pl* = es gibt das Wort nicht in der Mehrzahl

Tipps zum Wörterlernen findest du im **Skills file 1** auf der Seite 146.

Wenn du nachschlagen möchtest, was ein englisches Wort bedeutet oder wie man es ausspricht, dann solltest du das **English – German dictionary** auf den Seiten 194–218 verwenden.

Und wenn du vergessen hast, wie etwas auf Englisch heißt, dann kann dir das **German – English dictionary** auf den Seiten 219–241 helfen.

Unit 1

Away at school

pp. 8/9	**conversation** [kɒnvə'seɪʃn]	Gespräch	►► **a talk between people; a chat**
	(to) **fill** sth. **in** [fɪl 'ɪn]	etwas ausfüllen; etwas einsetzen	⚠ (to) **fill in** = **1.** ausfüllen – (to) **fill in** a form **2.** einsetzen – (to) **fill in** your name / the right word / the missing information (to) **fill** = füllen
	form [fɔːm]	Formular	If you'd like to work in our shop, please fill in this **form**.
	boarding school ['bɔːdɪŋ skuːl]	Internat	Harry and Ron became friends ... while they went to a famous **boarding school**.
	boarder ['bɔːdə]	Internatsschüler/in	... while they were **boarders** at a famous school.
	choir ['kwaɪə]	Chor	a **choir** 
	(to) **code** [kəʊd]	kodieren, programmieren *(Computer)*	*verb:* (to) **code** – *noun* (person who codes): **coder** ['kəʊdə] (Kodierer/in, Programmierer/in)
	(to) **fence** [fens]	fechten *(Sport)*	**fencing** 
	(to) **knit** [nɪt]	stricken	⚠ Der erste Buchstabe von „(to) **knit**" wird nicht ausgesprochen: [nɪt]! (vgl. (to) **know**, (to) **knock**)
	orchestra ['ɔːkɪstrə]	Orchester	⚠ Betonung auf der 1. Silbe: orchestra ['ɔːkɪstrə]
	self-defence [self dɪ'fens]	Selbstverteidigung	**defence** = Verteidigung
	sign language ['saɪn læŋgwɪdʒ]	Zeichensprache, Gebärdensprache	
	roommate ['ruːmmeɪt]	Zimmergenosse/-genossin	**classmates** = students in the same class **roommates** = people who share the same room
	facilities *(pl)* [fə'sɪlətiz]	Einrichtungen, Geräte	The **facilities** at the first hotel were much better than they are here!
	tennis court ['tenɪs kɔːt]	Tennisplatz	
	Wi-Fi ['waɪ faɪ]	WLAN, kabellose Datenübertragung	
	chapel ['tʃæpl]	Kapelle *(kleiner kirchlicher Raum)*	a small church or a room, for example in a boarding school, used as a church
	examination [ɪgzæmɪ'neɪʃn] *(infml auch:* **exam** [ɪg'zæm])	Prüfung	⚠ (to) **take/do an exam** = eine Prüfung machen

Text 1

p. 10	**culture** ['kʌltʃə]	Kultur	⚠ Betonung auf der 1. Silbe: culture ['kʌltʃə]
	phone call *(oft auch kurz:* **call**) ['fəʊn kɔːl]	(Telefon-)Anruf	There was a **phone call** / **call** from your friend. = Your friend phoned.
	(to) **make friends**	Freunde finden	

nut [nʌt]	Nuss	**nuts** 
(to) **be/feel homesick** ['həʊmsɪk]	Heimweh haben	
if [ɪf]	ob	⚠ **if** = **1.** *wenn, falls*: We'll come to your party **if** we're free. **2.** *ob*: I don't know **if** I can come.
sports **that** I've never done before	Sportarten, die ich noch nie gemacht habe	⚠ Kein Komma im Englischen: *English:* **sports that** I don't play *German:* **Sportarten, die** ich nicht mache
net [net]	Netz *(Sport)*	
stick [stɪk]	Stock; Schläger *(Sport)*	
(to) **appear** [ə'pɪə]	auftauchen, erscheinen	A funny picture **appeared** on the screen. *(erscheinen)* (to) **appear to be/do** sth. = etwas zu sein/zu tun scheinen: He **appeared to be** very sad.
magic ['mædʒɪk]	Zauberei, Magie	**by magic** = durch Zauberei *noun:* **magic** – *adjective:* **magic** = magisch
(to) **show** [ʃəʊ], **showed** [ʃəʊn], **shown**	zeigen	

verbs with two objects:

verb		person	thing
(to) **buy**	Please buy	**me**	a pony!
(to) **cook**	I'll cook	**you**	lasagne.
(to) **give**	I can give	**you**	my pen.
(to) **make**	She made	**me**	a toy car.
(to) **offer**	He offered	**us**	a nice room.
(to) **show**	Please show	**me**	your new bike.
(to) **describe**	—	—	—
(to) **explain**	—	—	—
(to) **say**	—	—	—

	thing	person
Please buy	a pony	**for** me!
I'll cook	lasagne	**for** you.
I can give	it	**to** you.
She made	a toy car	**for** me.
He offered	it	**to** us.
Please show	it	**to** me.
Please describe	the photo	**to** the class.
She explained	the game	**to** her friends.
Who said	this	**to** you?

my own room [əʊn]	mein/ein eigenes Zimmer	Do you share a room with your sister? Or do you have your **own** room?
beginning [bɪ'gɪnɪŋ]	Anfang	**beginning** ◄► **end** ⚠ **in the beginning** = am Anfang
Say hi to everyone.	Grüß/t alle.	
secret ['siːkrət]	Geheimnis; geheim	This is a **secret** message. *(geheim)* It's our **secret**. *(Geheimnis)* Don't tell anyone!
p. 11 **loud** [laʊd]	laut	You should speak **in a loud voice** if you want us all to hear you. ⚠ **in a loud voice** = mit lauter Stimme
light [laɪt]	Licht	At boarding school **lights** out (= Licht aus) is at ten pm. That's terrible!
lie [laɪ]	Lüge	Jo didn't tell the truth. She ... ... **lied to** us. (... *uns angelogen)* = **told** us **lies**. *German:* **„lügen"** = (to) **lie** *oder* (to) **tell a lie/tell lies**
(to) **keep** [kiːp], **kept, kept** [kept]	halten; behalten	(to) **keep** sth. **secret** = etwas geheim halten
She didn't **want her friends to** know ...	Sie wollte nicht, dass ihre Freunde/Freundinnen ... wussten.	⚠ *English:* I **want you to help** your sister. *German:* Ich **möchte, dass du** ... hilfst.

	(to) **compare (to/with)** [kəm'peə]	vergleichen (mit)	Work with a partner and **compare** your texts.
	(to) **discuss** sth. [dɪ'skʌs]	über etwas diskutieren; etwas besprechen	Mum and I **discussed** the problems I'm having in maths. She helped a lot!
	advantage [əd'vɑːntɪdʒ]	Vorteil	Rafael has an **advantage** in Spanish class: he speaks Spanish at home.
	disadvantage [dɪsəd'vɑːntɪdʒ]	Nachteil	I have never played that card game, so I am **at a disadvantage**. *(im Nachteil)*

Introduction 1

p. 12	**a film which has ...**	ein Film, der ... hat	songs **which** I sing every day the cat **which** ate my sandwich ⚠ Das Relativpronomen **which** benutzt du nur für Dinge und Tiere.
	a girl whose name ... [huːz]	ein Mädchen, dessen Namen ...	
	a girl **who ...**	ein Mädchen, das ...	I know a girl **who** has six cats.
	(to) **belong** [bɪ'lɒŋ]	(hin)gehören	This book **belongs** on that shelf. *(hingehören)* This bag **belongs to** Jill. (= This is Jill's bag.)
p. 13	**enemy** ['enəmi]	Feind/in	**friend ◄► enemy**
	(to) **marry** ['mæri]	heiraten	Jack **married** Alex in May. = They **married** in May.
	(to) **kill** [kɪl]	töten	

Skills training

p. 14	**each other** [iːtʃ 'ʌðə]	einander, sich (gegenseitig)	⚠ **each** = jeder/jede/jedes (einzelne) **Each** student can ask one question. **each other** • They played **against each other**. Sie spielten gegeneinander. • They talked **to each other**. Sie redeten miteinander. • Alex and Stan like **each other**. Alex und Stan mögen sich.
	boyfriend ['bɔɪfrend]	(fester) Freund	
	girlfriend ['gɜːlfrend]	(feste) Freundin	
	(to) **get** sth.	etwas verstehen, mitbekommen	Sorry, could you please repeat that? I didn't **get** it. ⚠ (to) **get** = **1.** verstehen, mitbekommen; **2.** holen/besorgen; bekommen; **3.** (**to** a place) = (an einen Ort) gelangen, (hin)kommen (nach); **4.** (wet/old/...) = werden
p. 15	**application** [æplɪ'keɪʃn]	Antrag; Bewerbung	**application form** = Antragsformular; Bewerbungsformular
	capital (letter) ['kæpɪtl]	Großbuchstabe	⚠ **capital** = **1.** (= capital city) Hauptstadt; **2.** (= capital letter) Großbuchstabe
	date of birth [bɜːθ]	Geburtsdatum	**birth** = Geburt
	gender ['dʒendə]	Geschlecht *(als soziales Merkmal)*	

male [meɪl]	männlich; Mann	**man** ◄► **woman** **male** ◄► **female**
female ['fiːmeɪl]	weiblich; Frau	
unspecified [ʌn'spesɪfaɪd]	nicht angegeben, keine Angabe *(Formular)*	
guardian ['gɑːdiən]	Vormund	
(to) **join a club** [dʒɔɪn]	in einen Klub eintreten	We moved to London last year, so I had to **join** a new football club.
(to) **look forward to** sth. ['fɔːwəd] (to) **look forward to doing** sth.	sich auf etwas freuen sich darauf freuen, etwas zu tun	⚠ *English:* We **look forward to hearing** from you. *German:* Wir **freuen uns darauf,** von Ihnen **zu hören**.
signature ['sɪgnətʃə]	Unterschrift	
full [fʊl]	vollständig; voll	Please write your **full** name. Tell me the **full** story. My wardrobe is **full of** nice clothes. *(voll mit/von, voller)*
address [ə'dres]	Adresse	What's your **address**? – 11 Greatfield Street. ⚠ Beachte die Schreibweise: **address**
careful ['keəfl]	aufmerksam; sorgfältig	Read the text **carefully**. *(aufmerksam)* This text needs **careful** checking. *(sorgfältige Überprüfung)* ⚠ **careful** = **1.** vorsichtig; **2.** aufmerksam; **3.** sorgfältig
instruction [ɪn'strʌkʃn]	Anweisung	Before you use this machine, please read the **instructions** carefully.
(to) **follow** ['fɒləʊ]	(be)folgen; verfolgen	Always **follow** the rules, please. *(befolgen)* Someone was **following** me on my way home. *(folgen, verfolgen)*

Introduction 2

p. 16 **immigrant** ['ɪmɪgrənt]	Einwanderer, Einwanderin	⚠ Betonung auf der 1. Silbe: immigrant ['ɪmɪgrənt]
Caribbean [kærɪ'biːən]	Karibik; karibisch	⚠ Beachte die Schreibweise und die Betonung: **Caribbean** [kærɪ'biːən]
refugee [refju'dʒiː]	Flüchtling	My friend wasn't born here. He came here as a **refugee** some years ago because there were terrible problems in his home country.
one third	ein Drittel	1/2 = a/one **half** (*pl.* **halves**) 1/3 = a/one **third** 1/4 = a/one **quarter**; a/one **fourth** *(AE)* 1/5 = a/one **fifth** 1/6 = a/one **sixth** ...
first language [fɜːst 'læŋgwɪdʒ]	Muttersprache	Mark's English is very good, but his **first language** is German.
government ['gʌvənmənt]	Regierung	
lorry ['lɒri]	Lastwagen, LKW	a big **lorry** 
(to) **freeze** [friːz], **froze** [frəʊz], **frozen** ['frəʊzn]	(ge)frieren; erstarren	Rivers and lakes sometimes **freeze** in winter. Suddenly the lights went out, and I **froze**.
channel ['tʃænl]	Kanal	**the (English) Channel** = der Ärmelkanal
tunnel ['tʌnl]	Tunnel	⚠ Aussprache: **tunnel** ['tʌnl]

Study skills

p. 18	(to) **paraphrase** ['pærəfreɪz]	umschreiben, mit anderen Worten sagen	When you **paraphrase**, you make the words simpler and easier to understand.
	useful ['juːsfl]	nützlich, hilfreich	Here are some **useful** tips for your exam.
	phrase [freɪz]	Ausdruck, (Rede-)Wendung	A **phrase** is a group of words which has a special meaning, for example "Just a minute".
	(to) **add** [æd]	hinzufügen, addieren	When you **add** blue to yellow, you get green.

Skills training

p. 19	**dummy** ['dʌmi]	Schnuller	The baby is holding a **dummy**. 
	polite [pə'laɪt]	höflich	

Text 2

p. 20	**description** [dɪ'skrɪpʃn]	Beschreibung	*noun:* **description** – *verb:* (to) **describe**
	independent (of/from) [ɪndɪ'pendənt]	unabhängig (von)	
	notebook ['nəʊtbʊk]	Notizbuch	
	bully ['bʊli]	Mobber/in, Tyrann/in	*noun:* **bully** – *verb:* (to) **bully** = tyrannisieren, mobben
	junior high (school) *(AE)* [dʒuːniə 'haɪ skuːl]	*Schule für Kinder zwischen 12 und 14*	
	mirror ['mɪrə]	Spiegel	
	argument ['ɑːgjumənt]	Streit; Argument	**argument** • I'd like to think about my **arguments** before we discuss this. *(Argument)* • I had an **argument** with my sister. We shouted a lot. *(Streit)*
		⚠	Betonung auf der 1. Silbe: argument ['ɑːgjumənt]
	inside out [ɪnsaɪd 'aʊt]	verkehrt herum, auf links *(Kleidung)*	You're wearing your T-shirt **inside out**. (to) **turn** your T-shirt **inside out** = dein T-Shirt auf links ziehen
	detention [dɪ'tenʃn]	Nachsitzen	I was late three times this week, so I had **detention** on Friday.
	vocabulary [və'kæbjələri] (*infml auch:* **vocab** ['vəʊkæb])	Vokabeln; Vokabelverzeichnis; Wortschatz	Reading English books is good for your **vocabulary**. *(Wortschatz)* At the back of your book you'll find the **vocabulary** pages. *(Vokabeln, Vokabelverzeichnis)*
	(to) **copy** ['kɒpi]	kopieren, abschreiben	*verb:* (to) **copy** – *noun:* **copy** = Kopie; Exemplar
	gobbledygook *(infml)* ['gɒbldiguːk]	Kauderwelsch	
	normal ['nɔːml]	normal ⚠	Betonung auf der 1. Silbe: normal ['nɔːml]
	police *(pl)* [pə'liːs]	Polizei	**police** ist immer Plural: Where **are** the police? We have to call **them**. Wo **ist** die Polizei? Wir müssen **sie** rufen.

(to) **be gone** [gɒn]	weg sein	I don't know where the dog is. He was here two minutes ago and now he's **gone**.
(to) **plug** sth. **in** [plʌg 'ɪn]	etwas einstecken, anschließen	*verb:* (to) **plug in** – *noun:* **plug** = Stecker
p. 21 **(to) ring** [rɪŋ], **rang** [ræŋ], **rung** [rʌŋ]	läuten, klingeln	Your mobile is **ringing**, ...
(to) **answer the phone** ['ɑːnsə]	ans Telefon gehen	... don't you want to **answer** it? *English*: (to) **answer the phone** *German*: **ans Telefon gehen** *English*: (to) **answer the door** *German*: **aufmachen, zur/an die Tür gehen** 
(to) **notice** ['nəʊtɪs]	(be)merken	We all **noticed** that Jill looked very sad. I didn't **notice** him because I was playing a video game.
as [æz], [əz]	wie; als, während	My dog watched me **as** I ate my sandwich. *(als/während)* **As** I was saying, it's not easy. *(wie)* **as** = **1.** wie *(Konjunktion)*; **2.** als, während *(Konjunktion)*; **3.** als *(Präposition)*: **as** a singer/teacher; **4.** wie *(Präposition)*: **as** good as new *(so gut wie neu)*
ordinary ['ɔːdnri]	normal, gewöhnlich	This isn't an **ordinary** day. It's a special day: my birthday! ►► **= normal, usual**
extraordinary [ɪk'strɔːdnri]	außergewöhnlich	**ordinary** ◄► **extraordinary** Das -a- in diesem Wort sprichst du nicht: [ɪk'strɔːdnri]
line [laɪn]	Telefonanschluss; Telefonleitung	The **line went dead**. = Die (Telefon-)Leitung war tot. *(= Der andere Teilnehmer hatte aufgelegt.)*
caller ['kɔːlə]	Anrufer/in	*verb:* (to) **call** – *noun* (what you do when you call sb.): a **(phone) call** – *noun* (person who calls)*:* **caller**
(to) **crack** [kræk]	lösen *(z. B. Problem)*, knacken *(z. B. Code)*	They couldn't **crack** the enemy's secret code.
of course [əv 'kɔːs]	natürlich, selbstverständlich	Where's my phone? ... Oh, **of course**! In my bag.
trick [trɪk]	List, Streich	(to) **play a trick on sb.** = jm. einen Streich spielen

Your task

p. 23 (to) **prepare (for)** [prɪ'peə]	vorbereiten; sich vorbereiten (auf)	Let's **prepare** food for the party. *(vorbereiten)* I must **prepare for** the maths test tomorrow. *(mich vorbereiten auf)*
slide [slaɪd]	Dia(-); Folie *(bei Präsentation m. Computerprogramm)*	
(to) **introduce** sb. **to** sb./sth. [ˌɪntrə'djuːs]	jm. jn./etwas vorstellen, jn. mit jm./etwas bekanntmachen	We haven't met. Let me **introduce** myself. Can you **introduce** me **to** your sister, John? *verb:* (to) **introduce** – *noun:* **introduction** [ˌɪntrə'dʌkʃn] = Einleitung; Vorstellung *(Bekanntmachen)*

Unit 2

Jesse's world

pp. 24/25	**daily** ['deɪli]	täglich	a **daily** event or something that happens **daily** = it happens every day
	(to) **exchange** [ɪks'tʃeɪndʒ]	austauschen	*verb:* (to) **exchange** – *noun:* **exchange** = (Aus-)Tausch, Schüleraustausch
	chore [tʃɔː]	(Haus-)Arbeit, *(lästige)* Pflicht	(to) **do chores** = (Haus-)Arbeiten erledigen
	(to) **take notes** [teɪk 'nəʊts]	(sich) Notizen machen *(beim Lesen oder Zuhören)* ⚠	**note** = Notiz; kurzer Brief (to) **take notes** verwendet man, wenn man sich beim Lesen oder Zuhören Notizen macht. (to) **make notes** sagt man, wenn man eigene Ideen aufschreibt als Vorbereitung auf z. B. einen Vortrag oder eine Präsentation.
	scene [siːn]	Szene	
	script [skrɪpt]	Drehbuch	
	(to) **relax** [rɪ'læks]	sich entspannen ⚠	*English:* I'm **relaxing**. *German:* Ich **entspanne mich**.
	(to) **concentrate (on)** ['kɒnsntreɪt]	sich konzentrieren (auf) ⚠	*English:* I can't **concentrate on** the test. *German:* Ich kann **mich** nicht **auf** den Test **konzentrieren**. *verb:* (to) **concentrate** ['kɒnsntreɪt] – *noun:* **concentration** [kɒnsn'treɪʃn] = Konzentration
	weekday ['wiːkdeɪ]	Werktag, Wochentag	Monday to Friday are **weekdays**.
	(to) **text** sb. [tekst]	jm. eine SMS schicken	**Text** me when you're back from London, OK? ⚠ **text** = **1.** Text; **2.** SMS; **3.** (to) **text** sb. = jm. eine SMS schicken
	(to) **play sport(s)**	Sport treiben	

Text 1

p. 26	**hero** ['hɪərəʊ], *pl* **heroes**	Held/in	She was a real **hero** (= she was very brave): she saved the dog from the river.
	suit [suːt]	(Herren-)Anzug; (Damen-)Kostüm	**suits** 
	evil ['iːvl]	böse; *(das)* Böse	He's an **evil** man. *(adjective)* They fight against **evil**. *(noun)*
	power ['paʊə]	Kraft, Macht	Who has the **power** to fight evil?
	(to) **catch** [kætʃ], **caught**, **caught** [kɔːt]	(ein)fangen; erwischen; nehmen *(z. B. Zug, Bus)*	The police **caught** the burglars. *(fangen)* I'd like to **catch** the train at 12:55. *(nehmen)*
	scarf [skɑːf], *pl* **scarves** [skɑːvz]	Schal	two **scarves** 
	(to) **escape (from)** [ɪ'skeɪp]	entkommen (aus), fliehen (vor/aus)	We **escaped** before the hurricane hit our town. *verb:* (to) **escape** – *noun:* **escape** = Flucht
	prince [prɪns]	Prinz	

king [kɪŋ]	König	**king ◄► queen** **man ◄► woman**
well [wel]	gut *(Adverb)*	Your English is very **good**. = You speak English very **well**.
(to) **change (into)** [tʃeɪndʒ]	(sich) (ver)ändern (zu/in); wechseln; (sich) verwandeln (in), werden (zu); sich umziehen	*verb:* (to) **change** – *noun:* **change** = Veränderung, Wechsel, Verwandlung (to) **change** (Verb) = **1.** (sich) (ver)ändern; wechseln; (sich) verwandeln **2.** umsteigen

(to) **change**

„ändern“	They had to **change** their plans.	Sie mussten ihre Pläne ändern.
„sich verändern“	He **has changed** a lot recently.	Er hat sich ... sehr verändert.
„wechseln“	American kids **change** rooms between classes. Can you **change** your clothes before we go?	... wechseln das Klassenzimmer ... deine Kleidung wechseln
„sich umziehen“	Give me five minutes. I'd like to **change** first.	Ich möchte mich erst umziehen.

mask [mɑːsk]	Maske	At carnival people wear **masks**. 
claw [klɔː]	Kralle; Klaue	Look at the **claws** on that bird's foot!
so (that)	sodass	⚠ **so** = **1.** (*auch* so that) = sodass; **2. so** big/cold/... = so groß/kalt/... **3.** also, daher
emergency [iˈmɜːdʒənsi]	Notfall	In an **emergency** you should call the police.
weapon [ˈwepən]	Waffe	
quick [kwɪk]	schnell	**►► fast** **quick/fast ◄► slow**
accountant [əˈkaʊntənt]	Buchhalter/in	Did someone take money from the company? We're still waiting for the **accountant**'s report.
gay [geɪ]	schwul	Jack married his boyfriend Alex. They're **gay**.
(to) **behave** [bɪˈheɪv]	sich benehmen; sich verhalten	Our children **behaved** very well when we took them to the restaurant. ⚠ *English:* He's **behaving** strangely. *German:* Er **benimmt sich** seltsam.
peace [piːs]	Frieden	Will there ever be **peace** everywhere in the world?
bracelet [ˈbreɪslət]	Armband	**bracelets** 
lasso [læˈsuː], *pl* **lassos** *or* **lassoes**	Lasso	⚠ Aussprache: **lasso** [læˈsuː]
truth [truːθ]	Wahrheit	(to) **tell the truth ◄►** (to) **tell lies** *noun:* **truth** – *adjective:* **true**
p. 27 (to) **scan (a text for)** [skæn]	(einen Text) überfliegen (nach), absuchen (nach)	(to) read a text quickly, looking only for important information
paragraph [ˈpærəgrɑːf]	(Text-)Abschnitt	Each **paragraph** in your text should start on a new line.
(to) **jump** [dʒʌmp]	springen	They're **jumping** into the water. 

Introduction 1

p. 28	(to) **fit** [fɪt]	passen (zu)	⚠ **fit** = **1.** fit *(adjective)*; **2.** (to) **fit** = passen (zu) *(verb)*
	comfortable ['kʌmftəbl]	bequem, gemütlich	When you play sport, you should wear **comfortable** clothes.
	(to) **train** [treɪn]	trainieren; ausbilden	The police **train** dogs to find drugs. *(ausbilden)* The team is **training** for the next competition. *(trainieren)* ⚠ **train** = **1.** Zug; **2.** (to) **train** = trainieren; ausbilden
	(to) train **hard** [hɑːd]	hart trainieren	We must work **hard** at school. ⚠ *adjective:* **hard** = hart, schwer: It's hard **work**. *adverb:* **hard** = hart: We work **hard**.
	(to) **mime** [maɪm]	vorspielen, pantomimisch darstellen	

Skills training

p. 30	**thunder** ['θʌndə]	Donner *(bei Gewitter)*	
	setting ['setɪŋ]	Schauplatz *(z. B. Film/ Geschichte)*	The **setting** of the film is a small village in France.
	(to) **be down (by) ... %**	um ... % gesunken sein	Good news! Crime is **down by** 10% in our town.
	(to) **steal** [stiːl], **stole** [stəʊl], **stolen** ['stəʊlən]	stehlen, rauben	I'm always careful, I didn't lose my phone. I'm sure someone **stole** it from me.
	character ['kærəktə]	Charakter; Figur *(aus einer Geschichte)*	It's a nice old town. It has **character**. *(Charakter)* Two **characters** in this story are really evil. *(Figur in einer Geschichte)* ⚠ Betonung auf der 1. Silbe: **char**acter ['kærəktə]
	plot [plɒt]	Handlung(sverlauf) *(z. B. Film/Geschichte)*	the story that a play, book, film tells us
	Next ... [nekst]	Als Nächstes ...	**Next** I'd like to look at some photos with you. ⚠ **next** = **1.** der/die/das nächste; **2.** als Nächstes
	(to) **get in(to) a car** (to) **get out of a car**	in ein Auto einsteigen aus einem Auto aussteigen	***German* „einsteigen" – „aussteigen"** • You **get on a bus/plane/train**. You **get off a bus/plane/train**. • You **get in(to) a car/taxi**. You **get out of a car/taxi**.
	typical (of) ['tɪpɪkl]	typisch (für)	⚠ That's **typical of** him. = Das ist **typisch für** ihn.
p. 31	**dialogue** ['daɪəlɒg]	Dialog	⚠ Betonung auf der 1. Silbe: **di**alogue ['daɪəlɒg]
	soundtrack ['saʊndtræk]	Filmmusik; Tonspur	
	Oh my god! [gɒd]	Oh mein Gott!	**god** = Gott
	the only student ['əʊnli]	der einzige Schüler / die einzige Schülerin	Lilly is **the only** English student at our school. *(der/ die einzige)* Don't be scared, it's **only** a little mouse! *(nur)* ⚠ **only** = **1.** nur, bloß; erst; **2.** (der/die/das) einzige
	actually ['æktʃuəli]	eigentlich; tatsächlich	More work? Well, **actually**, I'm quite hungry!
	hopeful ['həʊpfl]	zuversichtlich, hoffnungsvoll	*adjective:* **hopeful** – *verb:* (to) **hope** – *noun:* **hope** = Hoffnung

Introduction 2

p. 32	**gross** *(infml)* [grəʊs]	widerlich	Strawberries with ketchup? Ugh, how **gross**!
	dirty ['dɜːti]	schmutzig	**dirty ◄► clean**

	twins *(pl)* [twɪnz]	Zwillinge	**twin brother/sister** = Zwillingsbruder/-schwester
	(to) **vacuum** ['vækjuəm]	Staub saugen	*verb:* (to) **vacuum** – *noun:* **vacuum cleaner** ['vækjuəm kliːnə] = Staubsauger
	because of [bɪ'kɒz əv]	wegen	We went home **because of** the rain. (= ... **because** it was raining.)
	(to) **set the table** [set], **set, set**	den Tisch decken	(to) **set, set, set** = stellen, legen, setzen
	(to) **load the dishwasher** [ləʊd]	die Spülmaschine einräumen	
	trash *(AE)* [træʃ]	Abfall, Müll	*BE* = rubbish
p. 33	**comment** ['kɒment]	Kommentar	*noun:* **comment** – *verb:* (to) **comment on** sth. = etwas kommentieren
	(to) **cut** [kʌt], **cut, cut**	schneiden; *(Rasen)* mähen	We can play football in the garden, but we should **cut** the grass first.
	mustn't do ['mʌsnt]	nicht tun dürfen	⚠ you **mustn't** = **du darfst nicht** you **needn't** / you don't have to = **du brauchst nicht**

Study skills

p. 34	**potluck (dinner)** *(AE)* [pɒt'lʌk, pɒtlʌk 'dɪnə]	*(Abend-)Essen, zu dem jeder etwas mitbringt*	We had a **potluck dinner** with some friends. Everyone brought something different.
	macaroni [mækə'rəʊni]	Makkaroni	
	sloppy ['slɒpi]	schlabberig; nachlässig, schludrig	I can't read your text. Your writing is too **sloppy**.
	(to) **listen for** sth.	auf etwas horchen, *(beim Zuhören)* auf etwas achten	Please **listen to** this text. *(zuhören, sich den Text anhören)* Please **listen** only **for** the information you need. *(beim Zuhören achten auf ...)*

Skills training

p. 35	**(to) ask for** sth.	um etwas bitten, nach etwas fragen	

verbs + for:

(to) **ask for** sth.	**um** etwas **bitten**
(to) **listen for** sth.	*(beim Zuhören)* **auf** etwas **achten**
(to) **look for** sth.	**nach** etwas **suchen**
(to) **prepare for** sth.	**sich auf** etwas **vorbereiten**
(to) **scan a text for** sth.	**einen Text überfliegen auf der Suche nach** etwas
(to) **wait for** sth.	**auf** etwas **warten**

voice message ['vɔɪs mesɪdʒ]	Sprachnachricht	
concert ['kɒnsət]	Konzert	⚠ Betonung auf der 1. Silbe: concert ['kɒnsət]
hall [hɔːl]	Halle, Saal	**hall** = **1.** Halle, Saal: Our town has a new concert **hall**. **2.** Flur, Diele: We opened the door and went into the **hall**.
accessible (to) [ək'sesəbl]	erreichbar (für), zugänglich (für)	**wheelchair accessible** = **accessible to** people in wheelchairs = rollstuhlgerecht (mit dem Rollstuhl zu erreichen)
glass [glɑːs]	Glas	Can I have **a glass of** orange juice, please? *(ein Glas Orangensaft)* There's too much rubbish. Using **glass** bottles helps.
truck [trʌk]	Last(kraft)wagen, LKW	►► **lorry**
guest [gest]	Gast	someone who visits someone else

Text 2

p. 36	**bow tie** [bəʊ 'taɪ]	Fliege *(Krawatte)*	**bow** = Schleife
	style [staɪl]	Stil; Art	
	creative [kri'eɪtɪv]	kreativ	⚠ Betonung auf der 2. Silbe: cre<u>a</u>tive [kri'eɪtɪv]
	sporty ['spɔːti]	sportlich	a **sporty** person = a person who likes sport and is good at it
	heading ['hedɪŋ]	Überschrift	
	(to) **express** [ɪk'spres]	ausdrücken, zum Ausdruck bringen	(to) **express yourself** = sich zum Ausdruck bringen *verb:* (to) **express** – *noun:* **expression** [ɪk'spreʃn] = Ausdruck
	(to) **make** sb. **do** sth.	jn. dazu bringen, etwas zu tun	You can give people good advice, but you can't **make** them **do** what you want.
	(to) **sew** [səʊ], **sewed** [səʊd], **sewn** [səʊn]	nähen	⚠ Aussprache: **sew** [səʊ]
	sewing machine ['səʊɪŋ məʃiːn]	Nähmaschine	I make my own clothes with my **sewing machine**. 
	material [mə'tɪəriəl]	Stoff; Material	This is nice **material** for a dress. *(Stoff)* Let's look for **material** for our presentation. *(Material)*
	(to) **start a business**	ein Geschäft aufmachen, einen Betrieb gründen/eröffnen	
	CEO [siː iː'əʊ] **(Chief Executive Officer** [tʃiːf ɪgzekjətɪv 'ɒfɪsə]**)**	Geschäftsführer/in	►► **the boss of a company**
	customer ['kʌstəmə]	Kunde, Kundin	"Do you need any help?" the shop assistant asked the **customer**.
	successful [sək'sesfl]	erfolgreich	Mo had a good business idea which was very **successful**.
	profit ['prɒfɪt]	Gewinn *(Profit)*	(to) **make a profit** = Gewinn/Profit machen ⚠ Betonung auf der 1. Silbe: <u>pro</u>fit ['prɒfɪt]
	advice *(no pl)* [əd'vaɪs]	Rat, Ratschlag, Ratschläge	⚠ **advice** ist unzählbar! *German:* Er gab mir **einen Rat**. *English:* He gave me **some advice**.
	president ['prezɪdənt]	Präsident/in	⚠ Betonung auf der 1. Silbe: <u>pre</u>sident ['prezɪdənt]
	future ['fjuːtʃə]	Zukunft; zukünftige(r, s)	I'll be more careful in the **future**. *(noun)* What are your **future** plans? *(adjective)* ⚠ Betonung auf der 1. Silbe: <u>fu</u>ture ['fjuːtʃə]
	fashion ['fæʃn]	Mode	I'd like to learn to sew and **design** and make my own **fashion**.
	(to) **design** [dɪ'zaɪn]	entwerfen, gestalten	
	at any age / at the age of ...	in jedem Alter / im Alter von ... Jahren	You can play this game **at any age**. I learned to drive **at the age of** 18.
	(to) **find out (about** sth.**)**	herausfinden; sich (über etwas) informieren	Let's **find out** when the concert starts. **Find out about** the fencing club at our school and give a short talk about it.
p. 37	(to) **tie** [taɪ]	binden, schnüren	When it's hot, I always **tie** my hair back. Can you **tie** a tie?
	article ['ɑːtɪkl]	Artikel	⚠ Betonung auf der 1. Silbe: <u>ar</u>ticle ['ɑːtɪkl]

Your task

p. 39	**vote** [vəʊt]	Abstimmung, Votum	(to) **have a vote (on sth.)** = abstimmen (über etwas) *noun:* **vote** – *verb:* (to) **vote (on sth.)** = wählen; abstimmen (über etwas)

Unit 3

People of Britain

pp. 42/43	(to) **link (to/with)** [lɪŋk]	verbinden (mit)	*verb:* (to) **link** – *noun:* **link** = Verbindung; Link
	capsule ['kæpsjuːl]	Kapsel	
	ancient ['eɪnʃənt]	(ur)alt, historisch	►► **very old** Mr Ford is **ancient**! He must be over 90!
	Briton ['brɪtn]	Brite/Britin	
	Roman ['rəʊmən]	Römer/in; römisch	
	Viking ['vaɪkɪŋ]	Wikinger/in	⚠ Aussprache: ['vaɪkɪŋ]
	the Angles ['æŋglz]	die Angeln *(germanisches Volk)*	
	Saxon ['sæksn]	Sachse/Sächsin; sächsisch	
	Norman ['nɔːmən]	Normanne/Normannin; normannisch	
	about [ə'baʊt]	ungefähr	We get up at **about** 8.30 on Sundays. ⚠ **about** = **1.** ungefähr; **2.** von, über *(Präposition)*
	750 BC [biː 'siː]	750 v. Chr.	750 **BC** = 750 years before Christ [kraɪst] was born
	400 AD [eɪ 'diː]	400 n. Chr.	400 **AD** = 400 years after Christ was born
	tribe [traɪb]	(Volks-)Stamm	
	land [lænd]	Land *(Grund und Boden)*	*noun:* **land** – *verb:* (to) **land** = landen ⚠ *German:* **„Land"**: *(Staat)* = **country** *(Grund und Boden)* = **land**
	(to) **settle** ['setl]	sich niederlassen, sich ansiedeln	They **settled** there. = Sie **ließen sich** dort nieder. *verb:* (to) **settle** – *noun:* **settler** ['setlə] = Siedler/in
	(to) **conquer** ['kɒŋkə]	erobern	
	castle ['kɑːsl]	Burg	a Scottish **castle** 
	(to) **divide (up) (into)** [dɪ'vaɪd]	auf-/einteilen (in)	The teacher **divided** the class **into** groups of four.

Text 1

p. 44	**empire** ['empaɪə]	Imperium, Reich	
	temple ['templ]	Tempel	
	bath [bɑːθ]	Bad; Badewanne	⚠ *English:* **have a bath** *or* **take a bath** *German:* **baden, ein Bad nehmen** *(in der Badewanne)*
	(to) **invade** [ɪn'veɪd]	einmarschieren (in), eindringen (in)	The Romans **invaded** Britain. = Die Römer **marschierten in** Großbritannien ein.

	precious metal [preʃəs 'metl]	Edelmetall	Betonung auf der 1. Silbe: <u>**me**</u>tal ['metl] **precious** = wertvoll **metal** = Metall
	(to) **trade** [treɪd]	handeln, Handel (be)treiben	*verb* (to) **trade** – *noun:* **trade** = Handel
	army ['ɑːmi]	Armee	Betonung auf der 1. Silbe: <u>**ar**</u>my ['ɑːmi]
	emperor ['empərə]	Kaiser	a man = **emperor** a woman = **empress** ['emprəs]
p. 45	**daughter** ['dɔːtə]	Tochter	Do they have children? – Yes, they have one **daughter**, Jane.
	fine [faɪn]	fein *(z. B. Stoff)*; dünn *(z. B. Haar)*	
	wool [wʊl]	Wolle	Scottish kilts are often made of **wool**.
	linen ['lɪnɪn]	Leinen; Wäsche	This is nice material. Is it **linen**?
	husband ['hʌzbənd]	Ehemann	Zoe married Carl, so he is now her **husband**.
	soldier ['səʊldʒə]	Soldat/in	**soldiers** 
	side [saɪd]	Seite *(z. B. Straßenseite)*	How can I get to the other **side** of the river? *German:* **„Seite"**: What **page** are we on? *(Buch-/Heftseite)* the other **side** of the street *(Straßenseite)*
	bone [bəʊn]	Knochen	**boneless** = knochenlos
	(to) **create** [kri'eɪt]	(er)schaffen, erstellen	Jonathan **created** a special smoothie for his mum.
	object ['ɒbdʒɪkt]	Objekt, Gegenstand	Betonung auf der 1. Silbe: <u>**ob**</u>ject ['ɒbdʒɪkt]
	knife [naɪf], *pl* **knives** [naɪvz]	Messer	Aussprache – das „k" wird nicht gesprochen: **knife** [naɪf] 
	silver ['sɪlvə]	Silber	a **silver** heart 
	leather ['leðə]	Leder	
	son [sʌn]	Sohn	A prince is a king's or queen's **son**. **brother** ◄► **sister** **son** ◄► **daughter**
	axe [æks]	Axt, Beil	an **axe** 

Introduction 1

p. 46	**kind (of)** [kaɪnd]	Art, Sorte	What **kind of** shoes do you usually wear?
	(to) dig [dɪg], **dug, dug** [dʌg]	graben	He's **digging** a hole in the sand. 
	earth [ɜːθ]	Erde	
	(to) **discover** [dɪ'skʌvə]	entdecken	

	dish [dɪʃ]	Schüssel, Schale	a lasagne **dish** *(Schüssel)* Haggis is a Scottish **dish**. *(Gericht)* **dish** = **1.** Gericht; **2.** Schüssel, Schale; **3. dishes** *(pl)* = Abwasch
	sock [sɒk]	Socke	
	(to) **complete** [kəm'pliːt]	vervollständigen	*verb:* (to) **complete** – *adjective:* **complete** = vollständig, komplett
	specific [spə'sɪfɪk]	bestimmte(r, s), spezielle(r, s); genau, präzise	She gave us very **specific** instructions. *(genau, präzise)* Any **specific** time when you need the car back? *(bestimmte/r)*
p. 47	**beard** [bɪəd]	Bart	This man has a white **beard**. 
	exact [ɪg'zækt]	genau, exakt	*adjective:* **exact** information *adverb:* **exactly** the same colour
	fantasy ['fæntəsi]	Fantasie; Fantasy *(Literatur-, Filmgattung)*	

Skills training

p. 48	(to) **kneel** [niːl], **knelt, knelt** [nelt]	knien	Der erste Buchstabe von „(to) **kneel**" wird nicht ausgesprochen: [niːl]! (vgl. (to) **know**, (to) **knock**, (to) **knit**, **knife**)
	plough [plaʊ]	Pflug	*noun:* **plough** – *verb:* (to) **plough**
	he had dug ...	er hatte ... gegraben	He came back to where **he had dug** the hole earlier.
	(to) **touch** [tʌtʃ]	anfassen, berühren	In a museum you mustn't **touch** anything.
	(to) **scrape** [skreɪp]	kratzen, schaben	
	a bit [bɪt]	ein bisschen	5 o'clock in the morning? That's **a bit** early for me. This is the hardest **bit** of the task. **bit** = Teil, Stück(chen)
	(to) **lean** [liːn]	lehnen	He's **leaning forward** to look at his computer screen. 
	forward ['fɔːwəd]	vorwärts, nach vorne	one step **forward** ◄► one step **back**
	way [weɪ]	Weg; Art und Weise	**way** = **1.** Weg: You're in the **way**. Please get out of the **way**. **2.** Art und Weise: Look, this is the **way** you do it.
	although [ɔːl'ðəʊ] *(kurz auch:* **though** [ðəʊ])	obwohl	We stayed up and watched the late film **although** we were really tired. *(oder:* ..., **though** we were really tired.)
	(to) **explode** [ɪk'spləʊd]	explodieren	*verb:* (to) **explode** – *noun:* **explosion** [ɪk'spləʊʒn] = Explosion
	soft [sɒft]	weich; *(Stimme)* leise	This is my favourite pullover because it is so **soft**. *(weich)* "I'm not sure," she said in a **soft** voice. *(leise)*
	spade [speɪd]	Spaten, Schaufel	a **spade**  = shovel

	deep [diːp]	tief	a **deep** voice ◄► a **high** voice in a deep voice = mit tiefer Stimme
	(to) **throw** [θrəʊ], **threw** [θruː], **thrown** [θrəʊn]	werfen	You **throw** the ball, and I'll try to catch it.
	at last [ət ˈlɑːst]	schließlich, endlich	We stood at the bus stop for nearly an hour when the bus came **at last**.
	round [raʊnd]	rund	A ball is **round**. *(rund)* Let's play a **round** of golf. *(Runde)* They sailed **round** the world. *(um ... (herum))* *adjective:* **round** – *noun:* **round** = Runde – *preposition:* **round** = um ... herum = **around**
	plate [pleɪt]	Teller	Who can wash these **plates**? 
	(to) **turn** sth. **(over)** [tɜːn]	etwas umdrehen	I **turned** the piece of paper **over** and read the text on the back. (to) **turn** = (sich) umdrehen He **turned** and walked away.
	excitement [ɪkˈsaɪtmənt]	Aufregung, Spannung	**noun: excitement** – *adjectives:* **exciting** = aufregend; **excited** = aufgeregt
	(to) **boil** [bɔɪl]	kochen *(in Wasser)*; sieden	Excitement was **boiling up**. = Aufregung kochte (in ihm) hoch / machte sich breit. ⚠ *German* **„kochen"**: Let's **cook** omelettes. *(Mahlzeit zubereiten)* Let's **boil** some eggs. *(in Wasser kochen)* The water is **boiling**. *(sieden)*
	(to) **hide** [haɪd], **hid** [hɪd], **hidden** [ˈhɪdn]	verstecken; sich verstecken	Let's **hide** in the wardrobe. I **hid** some money in an old book.
p. 49	**upset** [ʌpˈset]	aufgebracht, verärgert	I felt **upset for** him. = Er tat mir leid. *adjective:* **upset** = aufgebracht, verärgert *verb:* (to) **upset** sb., **upset**, **upset** = jn. aufregen, ärgern, erschüttern
	greedy [ˈɡriːdi]	gierig, habgierig	What? You ate all the cake? You're so **greedy**!
	century [ˈsentʃəri]	Jahrhundert	There are one hundred years in a **century**.

Introduction 2

p. 50	**factory** [ˈfæktri]	Fabrik	a **factory** 
p. 51	**stranger** [ˈstreɪndʒə]	Fremde/r	*adjective:* **strange** = seltsam, sonderbar – *noun:* **stranger** = Fremde/r
	on time	pünktlich	Our train arrived **on time**.

Study skills

p. 52	**death** [deθ]	Tod	**date of death** = Todesdatum **date of birth** ◄► **date of death** *noun:* **death** – *verb:* (to) **die** – *adjective:* **dead**
	structure [ˈstrʌktʃə]	Struktur	*noun:* **structure** – *verb:* (to) **structure** sth. = etwas strukturieren, aufbauen
	(to) **sum** sth. **up** [sʌm ˈʌp]	etwas zusammenfassen	To **sum up**, ... = Um (es) zusammenzufassen, ... / Zusammenfassend kann man sagen, ...

	(to) **point** sth. **out** [pɔɪnt ˈaʊt]	auf etwas hinweisen, aufmerksam machen	Mr Jones **pointed out** that profits were down by 8%.
	confident [ˈkɒnfɪdənt]	(selbst)sicher; zuversichtlich	He's very shy. He'd like to become more **confident**. The interview went very well. I'm **confident** I'll get the job.
	source [sɔːs]	Quelle *(z. B. Website, Text)*	Where did you find this information? You always have to write down your **source** or **sources**.
	fact [fækt]	Tatsache	Many people believe this is a very old building, but the **fact** is, it's only 50 years old.
	(to) **highlight** [ˈhaɪlaɪt]	hervorheben, unterstreichen	*verb:* (to) **highlight** – *noun:* **highlight** = Höhepunkt; Schlaglicht
	main [meɪn]	Haupt-, wichtigste(r, s)	the **main** thing/problem/point = the most important thing/problem/point

Skills training

p. 53	**royal** [ˈrɔɪəl]	königlich	
	symbol (of) [ˈsɪmbl]	Symbol (für)	⚠ A heart is a **symbol of** love. (Symbol für ...) Betonung auf der 1. Silbe: **sym**bol [ˈsɪmbl]

Text 2

p. 54	**flyer** [ˈflaɪə]	Flieger/in	►► **someone who flies**
	visit [ˈvɪzɪt]	Besuch	*noun:* **visit** – *verb:* (to) **visit** a person who visits somebody = a **visitor** [ˈvɪzɪtə]
	rug [rʌg]	Teppich, Läufer	►► **a small carpet**  a colourful **rug**
	ground [graʊnd]	(Erd-)Boden	Don't sit on the **ground**. It's too cold.
	(to) **spin** [spɪn], **spun, spun** [spʌn]	(sich) drehen	►► **(to) turn** The wheel was **spinning** fast.
	(to) **arrive** [əˈraɪv]	ankommen	The party was over when we **arrived**. **arrive ◄► leave**
	a few [fjuː]	ein paar, einige	You're hungry? There are still **a few** apples in the kitchen.
	(to) **nod (your head)** [nɒd]	(mit dem Kopf) nicken	(to) **nod to** sb. = jm. zunicken *verb:* (to) **nod (your head)** – *noun:* **nod (of your head)** = Kopfnicken
	disappointed (with) [dɪsəˈpɔɪntɪd]	enttäuscht (von)	The zoo was closed! We were very **disappointed**. *(enttäuscht)* The show was boring – very **disappointing**. *(enttäuschend)* ⚠ (to) **disappoint** sb. = jn. enttäuschen
	duck [dʌk]	Ente	**ducks** 
	towards [təˈwɔːdz]; **toward** [təˈwɔːd] *(AE)*	nach, auf ... zu, in Richtung (von)	Nick was running **towards** me. He seemed very excited.

	I didn't know **what to say.**	Ich wusste nicht, was ich sagen sollte.	I was so surprised! I didn't know ... **... what to do / what to say.** **... how to answer.** **... where to go.**
	(to) **continue** [kən'tɪnjuː]	fortfahren, weitermachen; (sich) fortsetzen, weitergehen	The show will **continue** in 20 minutes. Let's stop now and **continue** tomorrow. "Let me tell you something else ...", she **continued**.
p. 55	**light** [laɪt]	leicht; hell	**light** = **1.** leicht; **2.** hell; **3.** Licht, Lampe
	rude [ruːd]	unhöflich, frech	**polite ◄► rude** I didn't buy anything because the shop assistant was very **rude**.
	distance ['dɪstəns]	Distanz, Entfernung	**in the distance** = in der Ferne
	halfway [hɑːf'weɪ]	auf halbem Wege, halb(wegs)	You want to go back? Now? We're more than **halfway** there already!
	below [bɪ'ləʊ]	unter(halb von); unten	Write your name **below** all the other names on the list, please. *(unter)* Look at the pictures **below**. *(unten)*
	hardly ['hɑːdli]	kaum	It's so dark in here, I can **hardly** see you. It's an easy task, **hardly any** work. *(kaum Arbeit)* *adjective:* **hard** = hart, schwer: It's **hard** work. *adverbs:* **1. hard** = hart: We work **hard**. **2. hardly** = kaum: They **hardly** work.

Your task

p. 57	**caption** ['kæpʃn]	Bildunterschrift	
	entry ['entri]	Eintritt, Zutritt; (Tagebuch-) Eintrag	**Entry** is free on Mondays. / "No **entry**!" a dictionary **entry**, a diary **entry**
	interest (in) ['ɪntrəst]	Interesse (an)	*noun:* **interest (in)** – *adjective:* **interesting** = interessant
	(to) **decorate** ['dekəreɪt]	dekorieren, schmucken	Betonung auf der 1. Silbe: decorate ['dekəreɪt]

Unit 4

Irish stories

pp. 58/59	**similar (to** sb./sth.**)** ['sɪmələ]	(jm./einer Sache) ähnlich	Your new bike is **similar to** mine.
	snapshot ['snæpʃɒt]	Schnappschuss	a photo that you take quickly; a bit of information
	pub [pʌb]	Kneipe	
	Gaelic ['geɪlɪk]	Gälisch *(Sprache)*	a language which many people in Ireland still speak
	dock [dɒk]	Hafen, Dock	
	stew [stjuː]	Eintopf(gericht)	a meal of meat and vegetables cooked together
	St = Saint [seɪnt]	St = Sankt	
	statue ['stætʃuː]	Statue	This is a famous **statue**. 
	monument ['mɒnjumənt]	Monument, Denkmal	Betonung auf der 1. Silbe: monument ['mɒnjumənt]

	musician [mju'zɪʃn]	Musiker/in	What's your job? – I'm a **musician**. I play the cello in an orchestra.
	famine ['fæmɪn]	Hungersnot	
	memorial (to sb./sth.**)** [mə'mɔːriəl]	Denkmal (für jn./etwas), Gedenkstätte	This is a **memorial to** people who died while trying to save others.

Text 1

p. 60	(to) **skim a text** [skɪm]	einen Text überfliegen *(um den Inhalt grob zu erfassen)*	(to) read a text quickly to find the main idea(s)
	population [pɒpju'leɪʃn]	Bevölkerung, Einwohner(zahl)	One fifth of this country's **population** are over 50.
	(to) **choose to do** sth.	sich entscheiden, beschließen etwas zu tun	I asked him many questions, but he **chose not to answer** any of them.
	(to) **starve** [stɑːv]	verhungern	(to) die because you don't have enough to eat
	disease [dɪ'ziːz]	Krankheit	⚠ • **disease** wird für ansteckende oder sehr ernsthafte Erkrankungen verwendet: She has a blood **disease**. Thousands of trees died from **disease**. • Das allgemeinere Wort für „Krankheit" ist **illness**: After a week of **illness**, she went back to school.
	crowded ['kraʊdɪd]	überfüllt, voll *(von Menschen)*	**Crowds** of people were in the shops. = The shops were very **crowded**. *adjective:* **crowded** – *noun:* **crowd** = (Menschen-)Menge
	deck [dek]	Deck	Let's go **on deck**. *(an Deck gehen)*
	bucket ['bʌkɪt]	Eimer	a **bucket** and a spade 
	(to) **spread** (sth.) [spred], **spread, spread**	(etwas) verbreiten *(Virus, Krankheit)*; sich ausbreiten	The disease is **spreading**. *(breitet sich aus)* Some animals can **spread** disease. *(verbreiten)*
	coffin ['kɒfɪn]	Sarg	a **coffin** made of wood 
	shark [ʃɑːk]	Hai	
p. 61	(to) **manage (to do** sth.**)** ['mænɪdʒ]	(es) schaffen (etwas zu tun)	It was hard work, but we **managed to** finish on time.

verbs + infinitive with "to"

They	**chose**	**to leave** the country.
We	**decided**	**not to go** to Spain.
Don't	**forget**	**to buy** some milk!
This list can	**help**	you **to remember** everything.
I	**hope**	**to be** back at 7:30.
I won't	**manage**	**to write** a letter in French.
I'm	**planning**	**to go** to Scotland in June.
Please	**remember**	**to buy** some juice!
Can you	**try**	**to be** more careful?
I really	**want**	**to buy** a new bike.

captain ['kæptɪn]	Kapitän/in	

	(to) **make sure that ...**	sicherstellen, dass ...; dafür sorgen, dass ...	**Make sure** that you turn off the lights when you leave the room.
	owner ['əʊnə]	Besitzer/in	*noun:* **owner** – *verb:* (to) **own** sth. = etwas besitzen – *adjective:* your **own** room = dein eigenes Zimmer
	root [ruːt]	Wurzel	This tree has very deep **roots**. I'm American, but my family has Irish **roots**.
	(to) **be called** [kɔːld]	heißen	Our dog **is called** Fido. *(heißt)* a dog **called** Fido *(namens, mit Namen)*
	emigration [emɪ'greɪʃn]	Auswanderung	(to) **emigrate** ['emɪgreɪt] *auswandern* **emigration** [emɪ'greɪʃn] **emigrant** ['emɪgrənt] *Auswanderer/-in* (to) **immigrate** ['ɪmɪgreɪt] *einwandern* **immigration** [ɪmɪ'greɪʃn] *Einwanderung* **immigrant** ['ɪmɪgrənt]
	pattern ['pætn]	*(wiederkehrendes)* Muster, Schema	

Introduction 1

p. 62	**southern** ['sʌðən]	südlich, Süd-	⚠ Aussprache: **south** [saʊθ] – **southern** ['sʌðən] 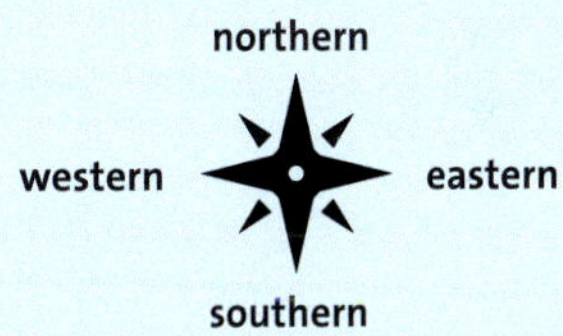
	violence ['vaɪələns]	Gewalt; Gewalttätigkeit	*noun:* **violence** – *adjective:* **violent** ['vaɪələnt] = gewalttätig; gewaltsam
	Catholic ['kæθlɪk]	Katholik/in; katholisch	⚠ Betonung auf der 1. Silbe: **Catholic** ['kæθlɪk]
	independence (from) [ɪndɪ'pendəns]	Unabhängigkeit (von)	*noun:* **independence** – *adjective:* **independent** = unabhängig
	Protestant ['prɒtɪstənt]	Protestant/in; protestantisch, evangelisch	⚠ Betonung auf der 1. Silbe: **Protestant** ['prɒtɪstənt]
	pleased [pliːzd]	froh, erfreut, zufrieden	**Pleased to meet you.** = Freut mich, Sie kennenzulernen.
p. 63	**slave** [sleɪv]	Sklave, Sklavin	
	(to) **pray** [preɪ]	beten	*verb:* (to) **pray** – *noun:* **prayer** [preə] = Gebet
	(to) **study** ['stʌdi]	studieren; lernen *(z. B. für Prüfungen)*	She wants to **study** history at university. I'll stay at home this afternoon and **study** for tomorrow's test.
	priest [priːst]	Priester/in	
	shamrock ['ʃæmrɒk]	Kleeblatt	
	holy ['həʊli]	heilig	For many people Jerusalem is a **holy** city.
	national day [næʃnəl 'deɪ]	Nationalfeiertag	
	tradition [trə'dɪʃn]	Tradition	⚠ Betonung auf der 2. Silbe: tradition [trə'dɪʃn] *noun:* **tradition** – *adjective:* **traditional** = traditionell
	snake [sneɪk]	Schlange	a green **snake** 
	(to) **attack** [ə'tæk]	angreifen	*verb:* (to) **attack** – *noun:* **attack** = Angriff

	(to) **drive** [draɪv], **drove** [drəʊv], **driven** ['drɪvn]	(an)treiben *(Tiere)* ⚠	(to) **drive** = **1.** fahren *(mit dem Auto)*; **2.** (an)treiben *(Tiere)* You **drive** a car, but you **ride** your bike.
	scientist ['saɪəntɪst]	(Natur-)Wissenschaftler/in	I love science. I want to become a **scientist**.
	background ['bækgraʊnd]	Hintergrund	There are two boys in the **foreground**. In the **background** you can see a lake. **background** ◄► **foreground** ['fɔːgraʊnd] = Vordergrund

Skills training

p. 65	**bank** [bæŋk]	Bank *(Geldinstitut)*	
	the nearest ... ['nɪərəst]	der/die/das nächstgelegene ... ⚠	**nearest** = nächstgelegen *(räumlich)*: The **nearest** shop is just round the corner. **next** = nächstfolgend *(Reihenfolge)*: We have to get off at the **next** stop.
	the nearest **one**	der/die/das Nächstgelegene	

one/ones

Wenn du ein schon einmal genanntes **Nomen** nicht wiederholen willst, kannst du **one** (Singular) bzw. **ones** (Plural) verwenden:

I have three **cats**, two black **ones** and a white **one**.
Ich habe drei Katzen, zwei schwarze und eine weiße.

Could you give me a **pen**, please? – Which **one**? This **one**? – No, the blue **one**, please.
Kannst du mir bitte einen Stift geben? – Welchen? Diesen? – Nein, den blauen, bitte.

Introduction 2

p. 66	**oyster** ['ɔɪstə]	Auster	an **oyster**
	surprise [sə'praɪz]	Überraschung	*noun:* **surprise** – *verb:* (to) **surprise** = überraschen
	cavern ['kævən]	Höhle	►► **a big cave**
	hunt [hʌnt]	Jagd	*noun:* **hunt** – *verb:* (to) **hunt** = jagen
	you **might** find ... [maɪt]	du könntest ... finden, vielleicht findest du ...	That **might** be true, but I'm not sure. You **might** hate school, but you learn a lot there.
p. 67	**coin** [kɔɪn]	Münze	I need a one-euro **coin** for this locker.
	beer [bɪə]	Bier	Let's go to the pub and have a **beer**.
	flour ['flaʊə]	Mehl	You need eggs, **flour** and sugar to make this cake.
	wholemeal ['həʊlmiːl]	Vollkorn-	White bread is boring. I only eat **wholemeal** bread.
	teaspoon ['tiːspuːn]	Teelöffel	**spoon** = Löffel **teaspoon** = Teelöffel **tablespoon** = Esslöffel **fork** = Gabel **knife**, *pl* **knives** = Messer

	baking soda ['beɪkɪŋ səʊdə]	Back-Natron, Backsoda	
	buttermilk ['bʌtəmɪlk]	Buttermilch	
	a little ['lɪtl]	ein wenig, ein bisschen	►► **a bit**
	cross [krɒs]	Kreuz	*noun:* **cross** – *verb:* (to) **cross** = kreuzen, überqueren
	(to) **bake** [beɪk]	backen	Put the cake in the oven and **bake** it for 45 minutes.

	bowl [bəʊl]	Schüssel, Schale	a salad **bowl** made of wood 
	baking sheet ['beɪkɪŋ ʃiːt]	Backblech	
	(to) **cool** [kuːl]	(ab)kühlen	*verb:* (to) **cool** – *adjective:* **cool** = kühl; „cool"
	(to) **knead** [niːd]	kneten	⚠ Der erste Buchstabe von „(to) **knead**" wird nicht ausgesprochen: [niːd]! (vgl. (to) **know**, (to) **knock**, (to) **knit**, (to) **kneel**)

Study skills

p. 68	**impatient** [ɪm'peɪʃnt]	ungeduldig	**impatient** ◄► **patient** ['peɪʃnt] = geduldig
	(to) **stand up (straight)**	(gerade) stehen; sich (gerade) hinstellen	**Stand up straight** when you give your presentation.
	(to) **tap** sth. [tæp]	(leise) klopfen, tippen an etwas	**tap your fingers** = mit den Fingern klopfen
	(to) **frown** [fraʊn]	die Stirn runzeln	*verb:* (to) **frown** – *noun:* **frown** = das/ein Stirnrunzeln
	(to) **shrug (your shoulders)** [ʃrʌg]	mit den Achseln/Schultern zucken	*verb:* (to) **shrug (your shoulders)** – *noun:* **shrug** = das/ein Achselzucken
	elbow ['elbəʊ]	Ellbogen	
	(to) **roll** [rəʊl]	rollen; (sich) verdrehen *(Augen)*	**roll your eyes** = die Augen verdrehen
	I don't care. [keə]	Es ist mir egal.	⚠ Who **cares**? = Wen interessiert das? / Was soll's? / Na und? I **care** about you. = Du bist mir nicht egal. / Du liegst mir am Herzen.
	(to) **annoy sb.** [ə'nɔɪ]	jn. ärgern	It **annoys** me that the trains are always late. = I find it very **annoying** that ... *(ärgerlich)*
	lonely ['ləʊnli]	einsam	I have my own flat and I'm often alone, but I never feel **lonely**.
	unsure [ʌn'ʃʊə]	unsicher	⚠ **sure** ◄► **unsure** **friendly** ◄► **unfriendly** **safe** ◄► **unsafe** but **patient** ◄► **impatient**
	movement ['muːvmənt]	Bewegung	*verb:* (to) **move** – *noun:* **movement**

Skills training

p. 69	**hostel** ['hɒstl]	Wohnheim; Hostel *(günstige Unterkunft für Reisende)*	
	(to) **emphasize** ['emfəsaɪz]	betonen, deutlich machen	Let me **emphasize** (= make it very clear) again how important good work at school is.
	review [rɪ'vjuː]	Besprechung, Rezension, Kritik	*noun:* **review** – *verb:* (to) **review** = besprechen, rezensieren; überprüfen
	(to) **recommend** sth. **(to sb.)** [rekə'mend]	(jm.) etwas empfehlen	I can **recommend** the music store on 3rd Street. They have great stuff!

Text 2

p. 70	**tech** *(infml)* [tek]	Technik	►► **technology**

farming ['fɑːmɪŋ]	Landwirtschaft	They are **farmers**. They have a **farm**. They live from **farming**.
European Union (EU) [jʊərəpiːən 'juːniən], [iː 'juː]	Europäische Union (EU)	
economy [ɪ'kɒnəmi]	(Volks-)Wirtschaft	*noun:* **economy** – *adjective:* **economic** [iːkə'nɒmɪk] = wirtschaftlich, Wirtschafts-
(to) **crash** [kræʃ]	abstürzen (lassen), zusammenbrechen	⚠ **crash** = **1.** abstürzen (lassen), zusammenbrechen; **2.** krachen; einen Unfall haben, zusammenstoßen (mit) *verb:* (to) **crash** – *noun:* **crash** = Zusammenstoß, Unfall; Zusammensturz, Absturz
profile ['prəʊfaɪl]	Profil; Beschreibung, Portrait	⚠ Betonung auf der 1. Silbe: profile ['prəʊfaɪl]
mentor ['mentɔ]	Mentor/in *(Ratgeber/in)*	*noun:* **mentor** – *verb:* (to) **mentor** = betreuen als Mentor/in
award [ə'wɔːd]	Preis *(Auszeichnung)*	**award-winning** = preisgekrönt **award-winner** = Preisträger/in
digital ['dɪdʒɪtl]	digital	⚠ Betonung auf der 1. Silbe: digital ['dɪdʒɪtl]
skill [skɪl]	Fähigkeit, Fertigkeit	Her computer **skills** are amazing.
(to) **suggest** [sə'dʒest]	vorschlagen	⚠ Tom **suggested (that) we go** to the cinema. Tom **suggested going** to the cinema.
p. 71 (to) **develop** [dɪ'veləp]	entwickeln; sich entwickeln	She **developed** new apps. (entwickeln) Her business has **developed** well. (sich entwickeln)
especially [ɪ'speʃəli]	insbesondere	I love team sports, **especially** football.
(to) **set** sth. **up**	etwas einrichten, aufbauen	I'd like to **set up** my own business.
according to ... [ə'kɔːdɪŋ tə]	laut ...; ... zufolge	**According to** my mum, I was the prettiest baby in the world.
(to) **imagine** sth. [ɪ'mædʒɪn]	sich etwas vorstellen	

verbs + *-ing*-form

Alex	**enjoys**	**making** things.	I	**remember**	**seeing** her in 1995.
I'll	**continue**	**learning** Chinese.	Her dad	**suggested**	**going** to a CoderDojo.
We	**hate**	**walking** in the rain.	Keela	**started**	**mentoring** people.
She	**likes/loves**	**coding**.	Please	**stop**	**making** so much noise!
Can you	**imagine**	**being** a musician?			

(to) **be allowed to do** sth. [ə'laʊd]	etwas tun dürfen	**Are** you **allowed** to use dictionaries in your English tests? – No, dictionaries **are not allowed**. *(... sind nicht erlaubt)*

Your task

p. 73 **dolphin** ['dɒlfɪn]	Delfin	
handover ['hændəʊvə]	Übergabe	

Unit 5

It's my life

pp. 76/77	**strategy** ['strætədʒi]	Strategie	⚠ Betonung auf der 1. Silbe: **stra**tegy ['strætədʒi]
	webpage ['webpeɪdʒ]	Webseite	"Click here for a list of all the **webpages** on our website."
	happiness ['hæpinəs]	Glück, Zufriedenheit	*adjective:* **happy** – *noun:* **happiness**
	skate park ['skeɪt pɑːk]	Skatepark	*verb:* (to) **skateboard**, *kurz auch:* (to) **skate**
	(to) **prefer** sth. **to** sth. [prɪ'fɜː]	etwas einer Sache vorziehen, etwas lieber tun/haben als etwas	I **prefer** juice **to** cola. (= I like juice more than cola.) What about a nice sandwich? – Well, **I'd prefer** a fruit salad. (Ich würde ... vorziehen.) ⚠ *simple past* und *-ing-form* mit **-rr-**: **preferred, preferring**
	biking ['baɪkɪŋ]	*(das)* Radfahren	►► **riding a bike**
	friendship ['frendʃɪp]	Freundschaft	Sue is my best friend. My **friendship** with Sue is very important to me.

Text 1

p. 78	**What/Where/... the heck is ...?** *(infml)* [hek]	Was/Wo/... ist denn nur/bloß ...?	Lynn? **Who the heck** is Lynn? – She's the girl I met at the skating rink!
	sponsor ['spɒnsə]	Sponsor/in *(Geldgeber/in)*	*noun:* **sponsor** – *verb:* (to) **sponsor** = sponsern
	subscriber [səb'skraɪbə]	Abonnent/in	*noun (person):* **subscriber** – *verb:* (to) **subscribe to** sth. = etwas abonnieren
	total ['təʊtl]	Gesamt-; total	*adjective:* **total:** The **total** profit this year was £ 100,000. – *noun:* **total** = Gesamtmenge, Gesamtzahl: I had to pay a **total** of £ 53 for all the articles.
	view [vjuː]	Aufruf *(eines Videos im Internet)*; (An-)Blick, (Aus-)Sicht	From our hotel room we had a great **view** of the sea. *noun:* **view** – *verb:* (to) **view** = anschauen
	site [saɪt]	*(kurz für)* Website; Stelle, Platz, Stätte	the **site** of the accident *(Unfallstelle)* a tourist **site** *(touristischer Ort)*
	founder ['faʊndə]	Gründer/in	*noun (person):* **founder** – *verb:* (to) **found** = gründen ⚠ (to) **found** = gründen: They **founded** a club. **found** = *simple past des Verbs* **find**: I **found** money in the street.
	since then [sɪns 'ðen]	seitdem	They emigrated to Ireland in 2012 and have lived in Dublin **since then**.
	(to) **entertain** sb. [entə'teɪn]	jn. unterhalten	
	silly ['sɪli]	dumm, blöd; albern	I felt really **silly** when I fell into the river.
	giraffe [dʒə'rɑːf], *pl* **giraffe** *or* **giraffes**	Giraffe	
	underwater [ʌndə'wɔːtə]	unter Wasser, Unterwasser-	We stayed **underwater** for some time and took photos of the dolphins with an **underwater** camera.
	quality ['kwɒləti]	Qualität, Qualitäts-; Eigenschaft	More expensive clothes are often **better quality**. *(... sind von besserer Qualität.)*

	chewing gum ['tʃuːɪŋ gʌm]	Kaugummi	(to) **chew** = kauen **gum** = Gummi; Zahnfleisch
p. 79	**however** [haʊ'evə]	allerdings, jedoch	Sophie wanted to stay up late. **However**, she fell asleep at 8 pm.
	Firstly ['fɜːstli], ... **/Secondly** ['sekəndli], ... **/Thirdly, ...** ['θɜːdli]	Erstens ... / Zweitens ... / Drittens ...	There's a lot of shopping to do: **firstly**, we need something to eat. **Secondly**, we have to get some juice. And **thirdly**, ...
	crowdfunding ['kraʊdfʌndɪŋ]	Crowdfunding *(Schwarmfinanzierung)*	**funding** = Finanzierung, *(finanzielle)* Mittel (to) **fund** = finanzieren
	advertising ['ædvətaɪzɪŋ]	Werbung, Reklame	*noun:* **advertising** – *verb:* (to) **advertise** (sth.) ['ædvətaɪz] = Werbung machen (für etwas)
	social media *(pl)* [səʊʃl 'miːdiə]	soziale Medien ⚠	**on social media** = **in** den sozialen Medien
	social ['səʊʃl]	sozial	
	(to) **earn** [ɜːn]	verdienen *(Geld)* ⚠	*German:* **„Geld verdienen"**: **1.** *(Gehalt bekommen)* (to) **earn money** **2.** *(Profit machen)* (to) **make money**
	(to) **go viral** ['vaɪrəl]	sich *(im Internet)* rasend schnell verbreiten *(viral = wie ein Virus)*	**viral** = Virus-, viral
	elephant ['elɪfənt]	Elefant	an **elephant** 
	several ['sevrəl]	mehrere, einige	We have **several** bikes for under £400 in our shop.
	hyphen ['haɪfn]	Bindestrich, Trennstrich	
	meme [miːm]	Internet-Mem, Internetphänomen	an idea, picture, video, website etc. which people get to know through the internet

Introduction 1

p. 80	**pug** [pʌg]	Mops *(Hund)*	
	cute [kjuːt]	niedlich, süß	
	attention [ə'tenʃn]	Aufmerksamkeit	(to) **pay attention (to)** = achten (auf), aufpassen (auf)
	length [leŋθ]	Länge; Dauer	*noun:* **length** – *adjective:* **long**
p. 81	**violin** [vaɪə'lɪn]	Geige, Violine	
	career [kə'rɪə]	Karriere; (schulischer/beruflicher) Werdegang	
	billion ['bɪliən]	Milliarde	►► **one thousand million (1,000,000,000)**

Skills training

p. 82	**ludo** ['luːdəʊ]	Mensch ärgere dich nicht *(Spiel)*	
	aim [eɪm]	Ziel	*noun:* **aim** – *verb:* (to) **aim at** sth. = zielen auf etwas
	token ['təʊkən]	Spielfigur; Chip (Wertmarke); (Geschenk-)Gutschein	
	dice [daɪs], *pl* **dice**	Würfel	**two dice** 
	square [skweə]	Kästchen, Spielfeld; Platz *(in der Stadt)*	Move your token on three **squares**. There's a statue in the **square** (in our town).
	block [blɒk]	Block; Klotz	

	single ['sɪŋgl]	Einzel-, einzelne(r, s)	A **single** room in a hotel is a room for only one person.
	multiplayer [mʌlti'pleɪə]	Mehrspieler-	
p. 83	**unfortunately** [ʌn'fɔːtʃənətli]	unglücklicherweise, leider	**unfortunately ◄► fortunately** ['fɔːtʃənətli] = zum Glück, glücklicherweise
	(to) **offer** ['ɒfə]	bieten, anbieten	Mr Taylor **offered** them a good deal. = He made them a good **offer** *(Angebot)*.
	(to) **change your mind**	seine Meinung ändern	Daniel had wanted to go out, but then he **changed his mind** and stayed at home.
	(to) **react (to)** [ri'ækt]	reagieren (auf)	How do you **react to** a very sad film? Do you cry?
	What do they think of/ about ...?	Was halten sie von ...? / Wie denken sie über ...?	Tell me what you **think of** this film. Do you like it?
	lame [leɪm]	lahm, langweilig	**►► boring, not at all interesting**
	(to) **turn** sth. **down**	etwas leise(r) stellen, herunterregeln	Your music is too loud. Please **turn** it **down**.
	in sb.'s shoes	an jds. Stelle	You really have a big problem! I wouldn't know what to do if I were **in your shoes**.
	like this [laɪk 'ðɪs]	so, auf diese Art	Look, it's easy if you do it **like this**. **1.** something **like this** *(so etwas)* **2.** it's always **like this** *(so)*

Introduction 2

p. 84	(to) **switch** sth. **on/off** [swɪtʃ 'ɒn], [swɪtʃ 'ɒf]	etwas einschalten / ausschalten	*verb:* (to) **switch** sth. **on/off** – *noun:* **switch** = Schalter 
	you **ought to** switch off ... ['ɔːt tə]	du solltest ... ausschalten	**►►** you **should**
	effect [ɪ'fekt]	(Aus-)Wirkung, Einfluss, Effekt	*noun:* **effect** – *adjective:* **effective** [ɪ'fektɪv] = effektiv
	likely ['laɪkli]	wahrscheinlich	**likely ◄► unlikely** [ʌn'laɪkli] to **be likely to do** sth. = wahrscheinlich etwas tun (werden) "Take a raincoat – **it's likely to** rain," they said.
p. 85	**hairstyle** ['heəstaɪl]	Frisur	
	(to) **suit** (sb.) [suːt]	geeignet sein für, passen (zu); jm. stehen *(Frisur, Kleidung)*	Does this hairstyle **suit** me? *(Steht mir ...?)* Would 6 o'clock **suit** you? *(... dir passen?)*
	plastic ['plæstɪk]	Plastik, Kunststoff	
	environment [ɪn'vaɪrənmənt]	Umwelt; Umfeld, Umgebung	Cycling is good for the **environment**. *(Umwelt)* working/learning **environment** *(-Umfeld, -Umgebung)* *noun:* **environment** – *adjective:* **environmental** [ɪnvaɪrən'mentl] = Umwelt-
	(to) **recycle** [riː'saɪkl]	recyceln, wiederverwerten	*verb:* (to) **recycle** – *noun:* **recycling** = Recycling
	(to) **ban** [bæn]	verbieten	Junk food is **banned** at our school. *(ist verboten)* *verb:* (to) **ban** – *noun:* **ban (on)** = Verbot (von)

Study skills

p. 86	**etc.** *(aus dem Lateinischen)* [et'setərə]	usw. (und so weiter)	
	(to) **protect (from/against)** [prə'tekt]	(be)schützen (vor)	An umbrella **protects** you **from** the rain.
	meaning ['mi:nɪŋ]	Bedeutung	*noun:* **meaning** – *verb:* (to) **mean** = bedeuten; meinen, sagen wollen
	pronunciation [prənʌnsi'eɪʃn]	Aussprache	*noun:* **pronunciation** – *verb:* (to) **pronounce** [prə'naʊns] = aussprechen
	(to) **revise** [rɪ'vaɪz]	*(Lernstoff)* wiederholen	*verb:* (to) **revise** – *noun:* **revision** [rɪ'vɪʒn] = Wiederholung (von Lernstoff)
	statistics *(pl)* [stə'tɪstɪks]	Statistik(en)	The **statistics show** that ... = die Statistik zeigt / die Statistiken zeigen, dass ...
	on the go	unterwegs	I'm hungry. I only had a quick snack **on the go** this afternoon.

Skills training

p. 87	**postcode** ['pəʊstkəʊd]	Postleitzahl	
	yum *(infml)* [jʌm]	lecker	
	(to) **chill out** *(infml)* [tʃɪl 'aʊt]	sich entspannen, abhängen	**Chilling out on the beach**

Text 2

p. 88	**solution (to a problem)** [sə'lu:ʃn]	Lösung (eines Problems) ⚠	the **solution to** this problem = die Lösung für dieses Problem / dieses Problems
	notification [nəʊtɪfɪ'keɪʃn]	Benachrichtigung, Mitteilung	
	(to) **go off**	klingeln *(Wecker)*; losgehen *(Alarm, Waffe)*	It was 6 o'clock, and the alarm on my phone **went off**.
	(to) **click (on)** [klɪk]	klicken (auf)	Strange things happened when I **clicked** on that link, so I quickly **clicked** out again.
	terror ['terə]	(panische) Angst	We heard an explosion, and we all ran away in **terror**.
	all over the world	überall auf der Welt, auf der ganzen Welt	**all over** the world / the country = everywhere in the world / the country
	nowhere ['nəʊweə]	nirgendwo(hin)	**everywhere** ◄► **nowhere** ►► **not ... anywhere**
	tear [tɪə]	Träne	**Tears** came to my eyes. = I started crying.
	(to) **pour** [pɔ:]	strömen; gießen, schütten	I **poured** sauce over my potatoes. *(gießen)* Tears **poured** down her face. *(strömen)*
	pressure ['preʃə]	Druck	(to) **put pressure on** sb. = jn. unter Druck setzen
	(to) **breathe (in/out)** [bri:ð]	(ein-/aus-)atmen	When you're underwater, you can't **breathe**.
p. 89	**fairy tale** ['feəri teɪl]	Märchen	**fairy** = Fee, Elfe **tale** = Erzählung, Geschichte (= story)

a couple (of) ['kʌpl]	ein paar; ein Paar	(= some, several:) We ate **a couple of** sandwiches. (= two people who are together:) They're a nice **couple**.
negative ['negətɪv]	negativ	**negative ◄► positive** ['pɒzətɪv]
none [nʌn]	keine(r, s)	**None** of my friends has ever tried German fruit tea.
right	Recht	Hey, stop that! Who gave you the **right** to read my mails? *(das Recht, ... zu lesen)*
(to) **call** sb. **names**	jn. beschimpfen	He was really angry. Mike had **called him names** in front of the whole class.
identity [aɪ'dentəti]	Identität	My first language is part of my **identity**. *(Meine Muttersprache ist Teil meiner Identität.)*
record deal ['rekɔːd diːl]	Plattenvertrag	**record** = Schallplatte **deal** = Geschäft; Vereinbarung
relationship [rɪ'leɪʃnʃɪp]	Beziehung, Verhältnis	(to) **be in a relationship with** sb. = mit jm. eine Beziehung haben
shallow ['ʃæləʊ]	flach, seicht; oberflächlich	**deep ◄► shallow** The sea is very **shallow** here, so it's safe for children to play. 
choice [tʃɔɪs]	(Aus-)Wahl	*verb:* you can **choose** – *noun:* you have the **choice**
(to) **delete** [dɪ'liːt]	löschen	I **deleted** the message **from** my phone. *(... die Nachricht auf/von meinem Telefon ...)*
sadness ['sædnəs]	Traurigkeit	**happiness ◄► sadness** *adjective:* **sad** – *noun:* **sadness**
not (...) any more [eni 'mɔː]	nicht mehr	This bag is very old. I do**n't** use it **any more**.
aka (= also known as)	alias, auch bekannt als	
weak [wiːk]	schwach	**weak ◄► strong**
(to) **give in (to** sb./sth.**)**	(jm./einer Sache) nachgeben	It's often hard, but I never **give in** to bullies.
(to) **judge** [dʒʌdʒ]	(be)urteilen	*verb:* (to) **judge** – *noun:* **judge** = Richter/in

irregular verbs							
(to) **choose**	**chose**	**chosen**	*(aus)wählen*	(to) **stand**	**stood**	**stood**	*(auf)stehen*
(to) **hit**	**hit**	**hit**	*schlagen, treffen*	(to) **swim**	**swam**	**swum**	*schwimmen*
(to) **know**	**knew**	**known**	*kennen; wissen*	(to) **think**	**thought**	**thought**	*denken*
(to) **leave**	**left**	**left**	*verlassen; abfahren*	(to) **understand**	**understood**	**understood**	*verstehen*
(to) **read**	**read**	**read**	*lesen*	(to) **wear**	**wore**	**worn**	*tragen (Kleidung)*
(to) **sit**	**sat**	**sat**	*sitzen*	(to) **write**	**wrote**	**written**	*schreiben*

► Unregelmäßige Verben S. 244f.

Das **DICTIONARY** besteht aus **zwei alphabetischen Wörterlisten**:
English – German (S. 194–218) und **German – English** (S. 219–241).

Im **English – German dictionary** kannst du nachschlagen, wenn du wissen möchtest, was ein englisches Wort bedeutet, wie man es ausspricht oder wie es geschrieben wird.

Im **Dictionary** werden folgende **Abkürzungen** und **Symbole** verwendet:
pl = plural (Mehrzahl) • *AE = American English* • *BE = British English* • *infml = informal* (umgangssprachlich)
sb. = somebody • *sth. = something* • *jn.* = jemanden • *jm.* = jemandem
° Mit diesem Kringel sind Wörter markiert, die nicht zum Lernwortschatz gehören.

Die **Fundstellenangaben** zeigen, wo ein Wort zum ersten Mal vorkommt.
Die Ziffern in Klammern bezeichnen Seitenzahlen:
5 = *Go Ahead 5* • 6 = *Go Ahead 6* • 7:1 (18) = *Go Ahead 7*, Unit 1, Seite 18

Tipps zur Arbeit mit einem Wörterbuch findest du im Skills file 3 auf Seite 148.

A

a [ə] ein, eine 5 **My dad is a teacher.** Mein Papa ist Lehrer (von Beruf). 5 **three times a week** dreimal pro Woche 6

about [ə'baʊt]:
1. ungefähr 7: 3 (42/43)
2. über 5
about the story über die Geschichte 5 **ask about sth.** wegen etwas (an)fragen 5 **It isn't only about playing games.** Es geht nicht nur darum, Spiele zu spielen. 5 **the good/bad thing about bikes** das Gute/Schlechte an Fahrrädern 5 **What about you?** Und du? / Was ist mit dir? 5

accessible (to) [ək'sesəbl] erreichbar (für), zugänglich (für) 7: 2 (35) **wheelchair accessible** rollstuhlgerecht *(mit dem Rollstuhl zu erreichen)* 7: 2 (35)

accident ['æksɪdənt] Unfall 5

according to [ə'kɔːdɪŋ tə] laut, zufolge 7: 4 (71)

accountant [ə'kaʊntənt] Buchhalter/in 7: 2 (26)

ache [eɪk] Schmerz(en) 6

across [ə'krɒs] über *(quer über)* 6

act [ækt] aufführen, spielen 5 **°act out** vorspielen, aufführen

action ['ækʃn] Aktion, Handlung; Action *(spannende Filmhandlung)* 7: 2 (39)

activity [æk'tɪvəti] Aktivität, Tätigkeit 5 **after-school activities** AGs *(freiwillige Veranstaltungen in der Schule nach Unterrichtsschluss)* 6

actor ['æktə] Schauspieler/in 6

actually ['æktʃuəli] eigentlich; tatsächlich 7: 2 (31)

AD [eɪ 'diː]: **400 AD** 400 n. Chr. 7: 3 (42/43)

add [æd] hinzufügen, addieren 7: 1 (18)

address [ə'dres] Adresse 7: 1 (15)

adult ['ædʌlt] Erwachsene/r 5

advantage [əd'vɑːntɪdʒ] Vorteil 7: 1 (11)

°advert ['ædvɜːt] Anzeige, Werbung

advertise (sth.) ['ædvətaɪz] Werbung machen (für etwas) 7: 5 (79)

advertising ['ædvətaɪzɪŋ] Werbung, Reklame 7: 5 (79)

advice [əd'vaɪs] *(no pl)* Rat, Ratschlag, Ratschläge 7: 2 (36)

afford sth./to do sth. [ə'fɔːd] sich etwas leisten können / sich leisten können, etwas zu tun 6

after [ɑːftə] nach *(zeitlich)* 5

afternoon [ɑːftə'nuːn] Nachmittag 5

after-school activities [ɑːftə skuːl æk'tɪvətiz] AGs *(freiwillige Veranstaltungen in der Schule nach Unterrichtsschluss)* 6

again [ə'gen] wieder, noch einmal 5

against [ə'genst] gegen 6

age [eɪdʒ] Alter 5 **at any age** in jedem Alter 7: 2 (36) **at the age of 12** im Alter von 12 (Jahren) 5

ago [ə'gəʊ]: **many years ago** vor vielen Jahren 6

agree [ə'griː]: **agree (with sb./sth.)** jm. zustimmen; mit etwas einverstanden sein 6 **°agree on** sich einigen auf

ahead [ə'hed]: **Go ahead.** Nur zu! / Dann mal los! 5

aim [eɪm]:
1. Ziel 7: 5 (82)
2. aim at sth. zielen auf etwas 7: 5 (82)

air [eə] Luft 5

°air force ['eə fɔːs] Luftwaffe

airport ['eəpɔːt] Flughafen 6

aka (= also known as) [eɪ keɪ 'eɪ] alias, auch bekannt als 7: 5 (89)

album ['ælbəm] Album 5

all [ɔːl] alle(s) 5 **all over the world** überall auf der Welt, auf der ganzen Welt 7: 5 (88) **all year** das ganze Jahr (über) 5 **(not) at all** überhaupt (nicht) 6

allowed [ə'laʊd] erlaubt 7: 4 (71) **be allowed to do sth.** etwas tun dürfen 7: 4 (71)

alone [ə'ləʊn] allein 6

along the path [ə'lɒŋ] den Weg entlang 6

alphabet ['ælfəbet] Alphabet 5

already [ɔːl'redi] schon 6

also ['ɔːlsəʊ] auch 5

°alternative [ɔːl'tɜːnətɪv] Alternative; alternativ

although [ɔːl'ðəʊ] obwohl 7: 3 (48)

always ['ɔːlweɪz] immer 5

am [æm]: **I'm (= I am)** ich bin 5

am [eɪ'em]: **9 am** 9 Uhr morgens/vormittags 6

amazing [ə'meɪzɪŋ] erstaunlich; großartig 6

°ambulance ['æmbjələns] Krankenwagen

°ambulance pilot ['æmbjələns paɪlət] Rettungspilot

an [ən] ein, eine 5

ancient ['eɪnʃənt] (ur)alt, historisch 7: 3 (42/43)

and [ænd], [ənd] und 5

Angles ['æŋglz] Angeln *(germanisches Volk)* 7: 3 (42/43)

angry ['æŋgri] wütend 5

animal ['ænɪml] Tier 5

°ankle ['æŋkl] Knöchel, Fußgelenk

annoy sb. [ə'nɔɪ] jn. ärgern 7: 4 (68)

annoyed [ə'nɔɪd] verärgert, ärgerlich 7: 4 (68)

annoying [ə'nɔɪɪŋ] ärgerlich 7: 4 (68)

another [ə'nʌðə] ein/e andere/r/s; noch ein/e 6
answer ['ɑːnsə]:
1. **answer (to)** Antwort (auf) 5
2. (be)antworten 5
answer the door aufmachen, zur/an die Tür gehen 7: 1 (21) **answer the phone** ans Telefon gehen 7: 1 (21)
any ['eni]: **Are there any ...?** Gibt es (irgendwelche) ...? 5 **not (...) any more** nicht mehr 7: 5 (89) **there aren't any ...** es gibt keine ... 5
anybody ['enibɒdi] irgendjemand; jede/r (beliebige) 6 **not (...) anybody** niemand 6
anyone ['eniwʌn] irgendjemand; jede/r (beliebige) 6 **not (...) anyone** niemand 6
anything ['eniθɪŋ] *(in Fragen)* irgendetwas 6 **anything else** sonst noch etwas 6 **not (...) anything** nichts 6
anywhere [eniweə] irgendwo(hin); überall 6 **anywhere else** irgendwo anders, sonst irgendwo 6 **not (...) anywhere** nirgends 6
apartment [ə'pɑːtmənt] *(AE)* Wohnung 5
app [æp] App 5
appear [ə'pɪə] auftauchen, erscheinen 7: 1 (10) **appear to be/do** zu sein/zu tun scheinen 7: 1 (10)
apple ['æpl] Apfel 5
application [æplɪ'keɪʃn] Antrag; Bewerbung 7: 1 (15)
application form [æplɪ'keɪʃn fɔːm] Bewerbungsformular, Antragsformular 7: 1 (15)
April ['eɪprəl] April 5
aquarium [ə'kweəriəm] Aquarium 5
Arabic ['ærəbɪk] arabisch; Arabisch 6
are [ɑː] bist, sind, seid 5 **The shirts are £6.** Die Hemden kosten 6 Pfund. 5 **they are** sie sind 5
area ['eəriə] Gegend, Bereich 5
°**argue (about)** ['ɑːgjuː] argumentieren; streiten (über/wegen)
argument ['ɑːgjumənt]:
1. Argument 7: 1 (20)
2. Streit 7: 1 (20)
get into an argument with sb. in Streit geraten mit jm. 7: 1 (20)
arm [ɑːm] Arm 6
army ['ɑːmi] Armee 7: 3 (44)
around [ə'raʊnd]: **around ...** um (... herum) 5 **go around and around** sich (immer wieder) drehen 6 **turn around** (sich) umdrehen 5 **walk around** umhergehen 6
arrival [ə'raɪvl] Ankunft 6
arrive [ə'raɪv] ankommen 7: 3 (54)
°**arrow** ['ærəʊ] Pfeil
art [ɑːt] Kunst 5
article ['ɑːtɪkl] Artikel 7: 2 (37)
artist ['ɑːtɪst] Künstler/in 6
as [æz], [əz] wie; als, während 7: 1 (21) **as a singer** als Sänger/in 6 **as good as** genauso gut wie 6 **not as good as** nicht so gut wie 6
ask [ɑːsk] fragen 5 **ask for sth.** um etwas bitten, nach etwas fragen 7: 2 (35) **ask sb. to do sth.** jn. bitten, etwas zu tun 5
°**aspect** ['æspekt] Aspekt
assembly [ə'sembli] Schulversammlung 5
assistant [ə'sɪstənt]:
1. **(= shop assistant)** Verkäufer/in 5
°2. Assistent/in
at [æt], [ət] an; in; bei; auf 5 **at 7 o'clock** um 7 Uhr 5 **at any age** in jedem Alter 7: 2 (36) **at Ben's house** bei Ben zu Hause, bei Ben daheim 5 **at home** zu Hause, daheim 5 **at night** nachts, in der Nacht 5 **at school** in der Schule 5 **at the cinema** im Kino 5 **at work** bei der Arbeit, am Arbeitsplatz 5 **(not) at all** überhaupt (nicht) 6 **be good at sth.** etwas gut können; gut in etwas sein 5 °**at least** wenigstens, zumindest
ate [eɪt], [et] *siehe* **eat**
Atlantic Ocean [ətlæntɪk 'əʊʃn] atlantischer Ozean, Atlantik 6
attack [ə'tæk]:
1. angreifen 7: 4 (63)
2. Angriff 7: 4 (63)
attention [ə'tenʃn] Aufmerksamkeit 7: 5 (80) **pay attention (to)** achten (auf), aufpassen (auf) 7: 5 (80)
°**audio** ['ɔːdiəʊ] Audio-, Ton-
August ['ɔːgəst] August 5
aunt [ɑːnt] Tante 5
avocado [ævə'kɑːdəʊ] Avocado 6
award [ə'wɔːd] Preis *(Auszeichnung)* 7: 4 (70)
award-winner [ə'wɔːd wɪnə] Preisträger/in 7: 4 (70)
award-winning [ə'wɔːd wɪnɪŋ] preisgekrönt 7: 4 (70)
away [ə'weɪ] weg, fort 5
awesome ['ɔːsəm] *(AE, infml)* klasse, stark, großartig 6
axe [æks] Axt, Beil 7: 3 (45)

B

baby ['beɪbi] Baby 5
back [bæk]:
1. zurück 5
2. Rücken; Rückseite, hinterer Teil 5
at the back hinten 5
background ['bækgraʊnd] Hintergrund 7: 4 (63)
backpack ['bækpæk] Rucksack 6
bacon ['beɪkən] Speck 5
bad [bæd] schlecht; schlimm 5
badminton ['bædmɪntən] Badminton, Federball 5
bag [bæg] Tasche 5
baggage ['bægɪdʒ] *(AE)* Gepäck 6
baggy ['bægi] weit (geschnitten), sackig *(Kleidung)* 6
bagpipes *(pl)* ['bægpaɪps] Dudelsack 6
bake [beɪk] backen 7: 4 (67)
baking sheet ['beɪkɪŋ ʃiːt] Backblech 7: 4 (67)
baking soda ['beɪkɪŋ səʊdə] Back-Natron, Backsoda 7: 4 (67)
balcony ['bælkəni] Balkon 5
bald [bɔːld] kahl, glatzköpfig 6
ball [bɔːl] Ball 5
balloon [bə'luːn] Ballon 5
ban [bæn]:
1. verbieten 7: 5 (85)
be banned verboten sein/werden 7: 5 (85)
2. **ban (on)** Verbot (von) 7: 5 (85)
banana [bə'nɑːnə] Banane 5
band [bænd] Band, Musikgruppe 5
bank [bæŋk] Bank *(Geldinstitut)* 7: 4 (65)
bar [bɑː] Bar 7: 4 (58/59)
barbecue ['bɑːbɪkjuː] Grillfest, Grillen 5
bark (at sb.) [bɑːk] (jn. an)bellen 6
barkeeper ['bɑːkiːpə] *(AE)* Barkeeper 7: 4 (69)
°**basically** ['beɪsɪkli] im Prinzip, grundsätzlich
basketball ['bɑːskɪtbɔːl] Basketball 5
bat [bæt] Fledermaus 6
bath [bɑːθ] Bad; Badewanne 7: 3 (44) **have/take a bath** baden, ein Bad nehmen *(in der Badewanne)* 7: 3 (44)
bathroom ['bɑːθruːm] Bad(ezimmer) 5
Bavaria [bə'veəriə] Bayern 6
BC [biː 'siː]: **750 BC** 750 v. Chr. 7: 3 (42/43)
be [biː], **was/were, been** sein 5

beach [biːtʃ] Strand 5 **on the beach** am Strand 5
bear [beə] Bär 6
beard [bɪəd] Bart 7: 3 (47)
beat [biːt], **beat, beaten** schlagen, besiegen 6
beaten ['biːtn] *siehe* **beat**
beautiful ['bjuːtɪfl] wunderschön 6
°**beauty** ['bjuːti] Schönheit
became [bɪ'keɪm] *siehe* **become**
because [bɪ'kɒz] weil 5
because of [bɪ'kɒz əv] wegen 7: 2 (32)
become [bɪ'kʌm], **became, become** werden 5
bed [bed] Bett 5 **go to bed** ins Bett gehen 5
bedroom ['bedruːm] Schlafzimmer 5
bedtime ['bedtaɪm] Schlafenszeit 7: 1 (11)
beef [biːf] Rindfleisch 6
been [biːn] *siehe* **be**
beer [bɪə] Bier 7: 4 (67)
beetroot ['biːtruːt] Rote Beete 6
before [bɪ'fɔː]:
1. bevor; vor *(zeitlich)* 5
2. zuvor; vorher 6
beginning [bɪ'gɪnɪŋ] Anfang 7: 1 (10)
behave [bɪ'heɪv] sich benehmen; sich verhalten 7: 2 (26)
behind [bɪ'haɪnd] hinter 5
°**Beijing** [beɪ'dʒɪŋ] Peking
believe (in) [bɪ'liːv] glauben (an) 6
bell [bel] Glocke 6
belong [bɪ'lɒŋ] (hin)gehören 7: 1 (12)
below [bɪ'ləʊ] unter(halb von); unten 7: 3 (55)
best [best] beste(r, s); am besten 5 **Best wishes** Viele Grüße ... *(Briefschluss)* 5 **like sth. best** etwas am liebsten mögen 5
better ['betə] besser 6 **do better** besser abschneiden 7: 1 (22) **like sth. better** etwas lieber mögen 7: 1 (22)
between [bɪ'twiːn] zwischen 5
big [bɪg]:
1. groß 5
2. schwer, dick *(Person)* 6
big wheel [bɪg 'wiːl] Riesenrad 6
bike [baɪk] Fahrrad 5
biking ['baɪkɪŋ] *(das)* Radfahren 7: 5 (76/77)
billion ['bɪliən] Milliarde 7: 5 (81)
bin [bɪn] (Müll-)Eimer 5
bird [bɜːd] Vogel 5
birth [bɜːθ] Geburt 7: 1 (15) **date of birth** Geburtsdatum 7: 1 (15)
birthday ['bɜːθdeɪ] Geburtstag 5 **Happy birthday.** Herzlichen Glückwunsch zum Geburtstag. 5
biscuit ['bɪskɪt] Keks, Plätzchen 5
bit [bɪt] Teil, Stück(chen) 7: 3 (48) **a bit** ein bisschen 7: 3 (48)
black [blæk] schwarz 5
blazer ['bleɪzə] Blazer *(Jackett, oft Teil der Schuluniform)* 5
blew [bluː] *siehe* **blow**
block [blɒk] Block; Klotz 7: 5 (82)
blog [blɒg] Blog *(Internet-Tagebuch)* 6
blond [blɒnd] blond 6
blow [bləʊ], **blew, blown** blasen; wehen 5
blown [bləʊn] *siehe* **blow**
blue [bluː] blau 5
board [bɔːd]:
1. Tafel 5
2. Brett 6
board [bɔːd] an Bord gehen 6
board game ['bɔːd geɪm] Brettspiel 7: 5 (82)
boarder ['bɔːdə] Internatsschüler/in 7: 1 (8/9)
boarding card ['bɔːdɪŋ kɑːd] Bordkarte 6
boarding house ['bɔːdɪŋ haʊs] Wohngebäude eines Internats 7: 1 (8/9)
boarding school ['bɔːdɪŋ skuːl] Internat 7: 1 (8/9)
boat [bəʊt] Boot; Schiff 5
body ['bɒdi] Körper 6
body language ['bɒdi læŋgwɪdʒ] Körpersprache 7: 2 (30)
boil [bɔɪl] kochen *(in Wasser)*; sieden 7: 3 (48)
boiled [bɔɪld] gekocht 6
bone [bəʊn] Knochen 7: 3 (45)
boneless ['bəʊnləs] knochenlos 7: 3 (45)
book [bʊk] Buch 5
°**bookmark** ['bʊkmɑːk] markieren; zu den Lesezeichen hinzufügen *(Computer)*
boom [buːm] boomen *(Wirtschaft, Geschäft)* 7: 4 (70)
boot [buːt] Stiefel 6
bored [bɔːd] gelangweilt 5 **I'm bored** mir ist langweilig 5
boring ['bɔːrɪŋ] langweilig 5
born [bɔːn]: **he was born** er wurde geboren 5
borrow ['bɒrəʊ] (aus)leihen, sich borgen 5
boss [bɒs] Boss, Chef/in 7: 2 (36)
both [bəʊθ] beide 6
bottle ['bɒtl] Flasche 6 **message in a bottle** Flaschenpost 6
bottom ['bɒtəm] unteres Ende 6
bought [bɔːt] *siehe* **buy**
boulevard ['buːləvɑːd] *(AE)* Boulevard, Prachtstraße 6
bow [bəʊ] Schleife 7: 2 (36)
bow tie [bəʊ 'taɪ] Fliege *(Krawatte)* 7: 2 (36)
bowl [bəʊl] Schüssel, Schale 7: 4 (67)
bowling ['bəʊlɪŋ] Bowling, Kegeln 5
box [bɒks] Kasten, Kiste, Kästchen 5
boy [bɔɪ] Junge, Bub 5
boyfriend ['bɔɪfrend] (fester) Freund 7: 1 (14)
bracelet ['breɪslət] Armband 7: 2 (26)
braces *(pl)* ['breɪsɪz] Zahnspange, Zahnklammer 6
°**bracket** ['brækɪt] Klammer
°**brainstorm** ['breɪnstɔː] Ideen (ungeordnet) sammeln
brave [breɪv] mutig 6
bread [bred] Brot 5
break [breɪk] Pause 5 **take a break** Pause machen, abschalten 7: 4 (58/59)
break [breɪk], **broke, broken** (zer) brechen; kaputtgehen; kaputtmachen 5
breakfast ['brekfəst] Frühstück 5 **have breakfast** frühstücken 5
breathe (in/out) [briːð] (ein-/aus-)atmen 7: 5 (88)
bridge [brɪdʒ] Brücke 6
bring [brɪŋ], **brought, brought** bringen, mitbringen 5
Britain ['brɪtn] Großbritannien 5
British ['brɪtɪʃ] britisch 5
Briton ['brɪtn] Brite/Britin 7: 3 (42/43)
°**brochure** ['brəʊʃə] Broschüre, Prospekt
broke [brəʊk] *siehe* **break**
broken ['brəʊkən] *siehe* **break** **be broken** zerbrochen, kaputt, sein 6
brother ['brʌðə] Bruder 5
brought [brɔːt] *siehe* **bring**
brown [braʊn] braun 5
bucket ['bʌkɪt] Eimer 7: 4 (60)
buffet ['bʊfeɪ] Büfett 6
build [bɪld], **built, built** bauen 6
builder ['bɪldə] Bauarbeiter/in 6
building ['bɪldɪŋ] Gebäude 6
built [bɪlt] *siehe* **build**
bully ['bʊli]:
1. Mobber/in, Tyrann/in 7: 1 (20)
2. tyrannisieren, mobben 7: 1 (20)

°**bun** [bʌn] weiches Brötchen *(z. B. für Hamburger)*
burger ['bɜːgə] Hamburger *(Frikadelle)* 5
burglar ['bɜːglə] Einbrecher/in 5
burn [bɜːn], **burnt, burnt** brennen, verbrennen 6
burnt [bɜːnt] *siehe* **burn**
bus [bʌs] Bus 5 **by bus** mit dem Bus 5 **on the bus** im Bus 5
bus stop ['bʌs stɒp] Bushaltestelle 6
business ['bɪznəs] Geschäft, Betrieb 6 **start a business** ein Geschäft aufmachen, einen Betrieb gründen/eröffnen 7: 2 (36)
businessman, *pl* **businessmen** ['bɪznəsmən], ['bɪznəsmɪn] Geschäftsmann 6
businesswoman, *pl* **businesswomen** ['bɪznəswʊmən], ['bɪznəswɪmɪn] Geschäftsfrau 6
busy ['bɪzi]:
1. hektisch, belebt 6
2. (viel)beschäftigt 6
be busy beschäftigt sein 6
but [bʌt], [bət] aber 5
butter ['bʌtə] Butter 5
buttermilk ['bʌtəmɪlk] Buttermilch 7: 4 (67)
buy [baɪ], **bought, bought** kaufen 5
by [baɪ]: **by bike/car/...** mit dem Fahrrad/Auto/... 5 **by the sea** am Meer 6 **step by step** Schritt für Schritt 7: 1 (18) °**by Roald Dahl** von Roald Dahl
Bye. [baɪ] Tschüs. 5

C

cab [kæb] *(AE)* Taxi 6
cafe ['kæfeɪ] Café 5
cage [keɪdʒ] Käfig 5
cake [keɪk] Kuchen, Torte 5
°**Caledonia** [kælɪ'dəʊniə] Kaledonien *(lateinisch-keltische Bezeichnung für Schottland)*
calendar ['kælɪndə] Kalender 6
California [kælə'fɔːniə] Kalifornien 6
call [kɔːl]:
1. nennen; rufen; anrufen 6
call sb. names jn. beschimpfen 7: 5 (89) **be called** heißen 7: 4 (61)
2. **(= phone call)** Telefonanruf 7: 1 (10)
caller ['kɔːlə] Anrufer/in 7: 1 (21)
came [keɪm] *siehe* **come**
camera ['kæmərə] Fotoapparat; Kamera 6
camp [kæmp] (Zelt-)Lager 6
camping ['kæmpɪŋ] Camping 5 **go camping** campen/zelten gehen 5
can [kæn], [kən] können 5 **it can't (= cannot) play** es kann nicht spielen 5
candle ['kændl] Kerze 5
candy ['kændi] *(AE)* Süßigkeit(en), Bonbon 6
canteen [kæn'tiːn] Kantine, (Schul-)Mensa 5
cape [keɪp] Cape *(Umhang)* 7: 2 (26)
capital (city) ['kæpɪtl] Hauptstadt 6
capital (letter) ['kæpɪtl] Großbuchstabe 7: 1 (15)
capsule ['kæpsjuːl] Kapsel 7: 3 (42/43)
captain ['kæptɪn] Kapitän/in 7: 4 (61)
caption ['kæpʃn] Bildunterschrift 7: 3 (57)
car [kɑː] Auto 5
car park ['kɑː pɑːk] Parkplatz 6
card [kɑːd] Karte 5
care [keə]: **care about sth.** etwas wichtig nehmen 7: 4 (68) **I care about you.** Du bist mir nicht egal. / Du liegst mir am Herzen. 7: 4 (68) **I don't care.** Es ist mir egal. 7: 4 (68) **Who cares?** Wen interessiert das? / Was soll's? / Na und? 7: 4 (68)
career [kə'rɪə] Karriere; (schulischer/beruflicher) Werdegang 7: 5 (81)
careful ['keəfl]:
1. vorsichtig 5
2. aufmerksam; sorgfältig 7: 1 (15)
Caribbean [kærɪ'biːən] Karibik; karibisch 7: 1 (16)
carnival ['kɑːnɪvl] Karneval 6
carpet ['kɑːpɪt] Teppich 5
carrot ['kærət] Möhre, Karotte 6
carry ['kæri] tragen; befördern, transportieren 5
°**cartoon** [kɑː'tuːn] Comic
castle ['kɑːsl] Burg 7: 3 (42/43)
cat [kæt] Katze 5
catch [kætʃ], **caught, caught** (ein)fangen; erwischen; nehmen *(z. B. Zug, Bus)* 7: 2 (26)
cathedral [kə'θiːdrəl] Kathedrale, Dom 6
Catholic ['kæθlɪk] Katholik/in; katholisch 7: 4 (62)
caught [kɔːt] *siehe* **catch**
cave [keɪv] Höhle 6
cavern ['kævən] Höhle 7: 4 (66)
°**ceiling** ['siːlɪŋ] (Zimmer-)Decke
celebrate ['selɪbreɪt] feiern 5
celebrity [sə'lebrəti] Prominente/r, Promi 7: 5 (80)
cellar ['selə] Keller 6
°**Celsius** ['selsiəs]: **°C = degree(s) Celsius** Grad Celsius
cent [sent] Cent 5
centre ['sentə] Zentrum 5
century ['sentʃəri] Jahrhundert 7: 3 (48)
CEO (Chief Executive Officer) [siː iː'əʊ], [tʃiːf ɪgzekjətɪv 'ɒfɪsə] Geschäftsführer/in 7: 2 (36)
chair [tʃeə] Stuhl 5
championship ['tʃæmpiənʃɪp] Meisterschaft 5
chance [tʃɑːns] Chance, Gelegenheit 6
change [tʃeɪndʒ]:
1. umsteigen 6
2. **change (into)** (sich) (ver)ändern (zu/in); wechseln; (sich) verwandeln (in), werden (zu); sich umziehen 7: 2 (26)
change your mind seine Meinung ändern 7: 5 (83)
3. Veränderung; Wechsel; Verwandlung 7: 2 (26)
channel ['tʃænl] Kanal 7: 1 (16) **the (English) Channel** der Ärmelkanal 7: 1 (16)
chapel ['tʃæpl] Kapelle *(kleiner kirchlicher Raum)* 7: 1 (8/9)
character ['kærəktə]:
1. Charakter; Figur *(aus einer Geschichte)* 7: 2 (30)
°2. Buchstabe, (Schrift-)Zeichen
charge (a mobile phone) [tʃɑːdʒ] (ein Mobiltelefon) aufladen 6
charity ['tʃærəti] wohltätige Organisation 6
chart [tʃɑːt] Diagramm; Tabelle 6
pie chart Tortendiagramm 6
chat [tʃæt]:
1. **chat (with)** chatten (mit); sich unterhalten (mit) 6
2. Unterhaltung, Chat 6
chat show ['tʃæt ʃəʊ] Talkshow 6
cheap [tʃiːp] billig, preiswert 5
check [tʃek]:
1. (über)prüfen, kontrollieren 5
2. Check, Kontrolle 5
cheer [tʃɪə] jubeln, *(Sportler/innen)* anfeuern 6
cheerleader ['tʃɪəliːdə] Cheerleader *(Stimmungsanheizer/in bei Sportereignissen)* 6
cheerleading ['tʃɪəliːdɪŋ] Cheerleading *(Anfeuern der Mannschaften bei Sportereignissen)* 6
cheese [tʃiːz] Käse 5
chess [tʃes] Schach 5

chest of drawers, *pl* **chests of drawers** [tʃest əv 'drɔːz] Kommode 5
chew [tʃuː] kauen 7: 5 (78)
chewing gum ['tʃuːɪŋ gʌm] Kaugummi 7: 5 (78)
chicken ['tʃɪkɪn] Huhn; (Brat-)Hähnchen 5
child, *pl* **children** [tʃaɪld], ['tʃɪldrən] Kind 5
chill out [tʃɪl 'aʊt] *(infml)* sich entspannen, abhängen 7: 5 (87)
chips *(pl)* [tʃɪps] Pommes frites 5
chocolate ['tʃɒklət] Schokolade 5 **hot chocolate** Kakao, heiße (Trink-)Schokolade 5
choice [tʃɔɪs] (Aus-)Wahl 7: 5 (89)
choir ['kwaɪə] Chor 7: 1 (8/9)
choose [tʃuːz], **chose, chosen** (aus)wählen 5 **choose to do sth.** sich entscheiden, beschließen etwas zu tun 7: 4 (60)
°**chop** [tʃɒp] klein schneiden
chore [tʃɔː] (Haus-)Arbeit, *(lästige)* Pflicht 7: 2 (24/25) **do chores** (Haus-)Arbeiten erledigen 7: 2 (24/25)
chose [tʃəʊz] *siehe* **choose**
chosen ['tʃəʊzn] *siehe* **choose**
2. *siehe* **choose**
Christmas ['krɪsməs] Weihnachten 6
church [tʃɜːtʃ] Kirche 5
°**Church of England** [tʃɜːtʃ əv 'ɪŋglənd] Anglikanische (Staats-) Kirche Englands
cinema ['sɪnəmə] Kino 5 **at the cinema** im Kino 5
circle ['sɜːkl] Kreis 6
city ['sɪti] (Groß-)Stadt 5
class [klɑːs] Klasse; Unterricht; Kurs 5
class teacher ['klɑːs tiːtʃə] Klassenlehrer/in 5
classmate ['klɑːsmeɪt] Mitschüler/in 5
classroom ['klɑːsruːm] Klassenraum 5
claw [klɔː] Kralle; Klaue 7: 2 (26)
clean [kliːn]:
1. sauber 6
2. sauber machen, putzen 6
cleaner ['kliːnə] Reinigungskraft 6
cleaning ['kliːnɪŋ]: **do the cleaning** putzen 6
clear [klɪə] klar, deutlich 6
clearly ['klɪəli]: **speak clearly** deutlich sprechen 6
clever ['klevə] schlau, klug 6
click (on) [klɪk] klicken (auf) 7: 5 (88)
clock [klɒk] (Wand-, Stand-, Turm-)Uhr 5
close [kləʊz] schließen, zumachen 5
closed [kləʊzd] geschlossen 5
clothes *(pl)* [kləʊðz] Kleidung(sstücke) 5
club [klʌb] Klub, Verein 5 **join a club** in einen Klub eintreten 7: 1 (15) **school club** AG 5
coach [kəʊtʃ]:
1. (Reise-)Bus 5
2. Trainer/in 6
coast [kəʊst] Küste 6
code [kəʊd]:
1. kodieren, programmieren *(Computer)* 7: 1 (8/9)
2. Code 7: 1 (20)
coder ['kəʊdə] Kodierer/in, Programmierer/in 7: 1 (8/9)
coffin ['kɒfɪn] Sarg 7: 4 (60)
coin [kɔɪn] Münze 7: 4 (67)
cola ['kəʊlə] Cola 5
cold [kəʊld]:
1. kalt 5
be cold frieren 6
2. Kälte 6
3. Erkältung 6
have a cold erkältet sein 6
collage ['kɒlɑːʒ] Collage 5
°**collect** [kə'lekt] (ein)sammeln
college ['kɒlɪdʒ] Hochschule 5
colour ['kʌlə] Farbe 5 **What colour is ...?** Welche Farbe hat ...? 5
come [kʌm], **came, come** (mit) kommen 5
°**comedy** ['kɒmədi] Comedyshow; Komödie
comfortable ['kʌmftəbl] bequem, gemütlich 7: 2 (28)
comic ['kɒmɪk] Comic 5
comment ['kɒment]:
1. Kommentar 7: 2 (33)
2. **comment on sth.** etwas kommentieren 7: 2 (33)
°**common** ['kɒmən] häufig, weit verbreitet, gewöhnlich **have sth. in common** etwas gemeinsam haben
community college [kə'mjuːnəti kɒlɪdʒ] weiterführende Schule *(BE)* 5
company ['kʌmpəni] Firma, Gesellschaft 6
compare (to/with) [kəm'peə] vergleichen (mit) 7: 1 (11)
competition [kɒmpə'tɪʃn] Wettbewerb 5
complete [kəm'pliːt]:
1. vervollständigen 7: 3 (46)
2. vollständig, komplett 7: 3 (46)
computer [kəm'pjuːtə] Computer 5
concentrate (on) ['kɒnsntreɪt] sich konzentrieren (auf) 7: 2 (24/25)
concentration [kɒnsn'treɪʃn] Konzentration 7: 2 (24/25)
concert ['kɒnsət] Konzert 7: 2 (35)
°**concussion** [kən'kʌʃn] Gehirnerschütterung
confident ['kɒnfɪdənt] (selbst) sicher; zuversichtlich 7: 3 (52)
conquer ['kɒŋkə] erobern 7: 3 (42/43)
console [kən'səʊl]: **games console** Spielekonsole 6
°**consonant** ['kɒnsənənt] Konsonant
contact ['kɒntækt]:
1. Kontakt 6
2. **contact sb.** Kontakt aufnehmen mit jm., sich in Verbindung setzen mit jm. 6
continue [kən'tɪnjuː] fortfahren, weitermachen; (sich) fortsetzen, weitergehen 7: 3 (54)
conversation [kɒnvə'seɪʃn] Gespräch 7: 1 (8/9)
cook [kʊk]:
1. Koch, Köchin 6
2. kochen, *(Essen)* zubereiten 6
cool [kuːl]:
1. cool 5
2. kühl 6
3. (ab)kühlen 7: 4 (67)
copy ['kɒpi]:
1. Kopie; Exemplar 7: 1 (20)
2. kopieren, abschreiben 7: 1 (20)
cornflakes *(pl)* ['kɔːnfleɪks] Cornflakes 5
°**correct** [kə'rekt]:
1. korrekt
2. korrigieren
cost [kɒst], **cost, cost** kosten 6
costume ['kɒstjuːm] Kostüm, Verkleidung 6
°**cotton** ['kɒtn] Baumwolle
cough [kʌf]:
1. husten 6
2. (der) Husten 6
could [kʊd]:
1. **she could** sie konnte 5
2. **I could** ich könnte 5
count [kaʊnt] zählen 6 **count on sb.** sich auf jn. verlassen 6
country ['kʌntri] Land 5
°**county (Co.)** ['kaʊnti] Grafschaft, Bezirk
couple ['kʌpl] Paar 7: 5 (89)
a couple (of) ein paar; ein Paar 7: 5 (89)

course ['kɔːs]:
1. main course Hauptgericht 6
°**2.** Kurs(us)
cousin ['kʌzn] Cousin/e 5
cover ['kʌvə]:
1. bedecken 6
°**2.** Umschlag, Titelseite
°**inside cover** Umschlaginnenseite *(Buch)*
crab [kræb] Krebs 5 **hermit crab** Einsiedlerkrebs 5
crack [kræk] lösen *(z. B. Problem)*, knacken *(z. B. Code)* 7: 1 (21)
crash [kræʃ]:
1. Zusammenstoß, Unfall; Zusammensturz, Absturz 7: 4 (70)
2. abstürzen (lassen), zusammenbrechen 7: 4 (70)
crash (into) krachen; einen Unfall haben, zusammenstoßen (mit) 5
3. Crash! Krach! *(z. B. in Comics)* 5
crazy ['kreɪzi] verrückt 6
cream [kriːm] Sahne; Creme 6
create [kri'eɪt] (er)schaffen, erstellen 7: 3 (45)
creative [kri'eɪtɪv] kreativ 7: 2 (36)
°**creative commons** *(pl)* [krieɪtɪv 'kɒmənz] Creative Commons *(schöpferisches Gemeingut: gemeinnützige Organisation, die das einfache Verbreiten von Nutzungsrechten zum Ziel hat)*
crime [kraɪm] Verbrechen; Kriminalität 6
crime film ['kraɪm fɪlm] Krimi 6
crisps *(pl)* [krɪsps] (Kartoffel-)Chips 5
cross [krɒs]:
1. Kreuz 7: 4 (67)
2. kreuzen, überqueren 7: 4 (67)
crowd [kraʊd] (Menschen-)Menge 7: 4 (60)
crowded ['kraʊdɪd] überfüllt, voll *(von Menschen)* 7: 4 (60)
crowdfunding ['kraʊdfʌndɪŋ] Crowdfunding *(Schwarmfinanzierung)* 7: 5 (79)
cry [kraɪ] weinen 6
culture ['kʌltʃə] Kultur 7: 1 (10)
cup [kʌp] Tasse 5 **a cup of ...** eine Tasse ... 5
cupboard ['kʌbəd] Schrank *(z. B. Küchenschrank)* 5
curly ['kɜːli] lockig 6
curry ['kʌri] Curry 6
curtain ['kɜːtn] Vorhang, Gardine 5
customer ['kʌstəmə] Kunde, Kundin 7: 2 (36)
cut [kʌt], **cut, cut** schneiden; *(Rasen)* mähen 7: 2 (33)
cute [kjuːt] niedlich, süß 7: 5 (80)

D

dad [dæd] Papa, Vati 5
daily ['deɪli] täglich 7: 2 (24/25)
dance [dɑːns] tanzen 5
dancing (das) Tanzen 5
dancer ['dɑːnsə] Tänzer/in 6
danger ['deɪndʒə] Gefahr 6
dangerous ['deɪndʒərəs] gefährlich 5
dark [dɑːk] dunkel 6
date [deɪt]:
1. Datum 5
2. Verabredung, Date *(auch die Person, mit der man ausgeht)* 6
date of birth [deɪt əv 'bɜːθ] Geburtsdatum 7: 1 (15)
daughter ['dɔːtə] Tochter 7: 3 (45)
day [deɪ] Tag 5 **one day** eines Tages 6
day out, *pl* **days out** [deɪ 'aʊt] (Tages-)Ausflug 6
dead [ded] tot 5 **The line went dead.** Die (Telefon-)Leitung war tot. 7: 1 (21)
deal [diːl] Geschäft; Vereinbarung 7: 5 (89)
Dear ... [dɪə] Liebe/r ... 5
death [deθ] Tod 7: 3 (52) **date of death** Todesdatum 7: 3 (52)
December [dɪ'sembə] Dezember 5
decide [dɪ'saɪd]: **decide (to do sth.)** beschließen, sich entscheiden (etwas zu tun) 6 °**decide on sth.** etwas beschließen, sich für etwas entscheiden
decision [dɪ'sɪʒn] Entscheidung 6
deck [dek] Deck 7: 4 (60) **on deck** an Deck 7: 4 (60)
decorate ['dekəreɪt] dekorieren, schmücken 7: 3 (57)
deep [diːp] tief 7: 3 (48)
deer, *pl* **deer** [dɪə] Reh; Hirsch 6
red deer Rotwild 6
defence [dɪ'fens] Verteidigung 7: 1 (8/9)
definitely ['defɪnətli] auf jeden Fall; ganz bestimmt 6
°**definition** [defɪ'nɪʃn] Definition
°**degree** [dɪ'griː]: **degree(s) Celsius** Grad Celsius
delayed [dɪ'leɪd] verspätet 6
delete [dɪ'liːt] löschen 7: 5 (89)
dentist ['dentɪst] Zahnarzt/-ärztin 6
department store [dɪ'pɑːtmənt stɔː] Kaufhaus 6
describe (sth. to sb.) [dɪ'skraɪb] (jm. etwas) beschreiben 5
description [dɪ'skrɪpʃn] Beschreibung 7: 1 (20)
desert ['dezət] Wüste 6
design [dɪ'zaɪn] entwerfen, gestalten 7: 2 (36)
desk [desk] Schreibtisch, Schülertisch 5
dessert [dɪ'zɜːt] Nachspeise, Dessert 5
detective [dɪ'tektɪv] Detektiv/in 6
detective series, *pl* **detective series** [dɪ'tektɪv sɪəriːz] Krimiserie 6
detention [dɪ'tenʃn] Nachsitzen 7: 1 (20)
develop [dɪ'veləp] entwickeln; sich entwickeln 7: 4 (71)
°**diagram** ['daɪəgræm] Diagramm
dialogue ['daɪəlɒg] Dialog 7: 2 (31)
°**diary** ['daɪəri] Tagebuch; Kalender
diary entry ['daɪəri entri] Tagebucheintrag 7: 3 (57)
dice, *pl* **dice** [daɪs] Würfel 7: 5 (82)
dictionary ['dɪkʃənri] Wörterbuch, *(alphabetisches)* Wörterverzeichnis 5
did [dɪd] *siehe* **do I didn't like ... (= did not)** ich mochte ... nicht 5
die [daɪ] sterben 5
difference ['dɪfrəns] Unterschied 5
different ['dɪfrənt] verschieden; anders 5
dig [dɪg], **dug, dug** graben 7: 3 (46)
he had dug ... er hatte ... gegraben 7: 3 (48)
digital ['dɪdʒɪtl] digital 7: 4 (70)
dining room ['daɪnɪŋ ruːm] Esszimmer 5
dinner ['dɪnə] Abendessen 5 **for dinner** zum Abendessen 5 **have dinner** (zu) Abend essen 5
°**direct** [də'rekt] direkt, unmittelbar
direction [də'rekʃn] Richtung 6
directions *(pl)* [də'rekʃnz] Wegbeschreibung(en) 5 **ask for directions** nach dem Weg fragen 5 **give directions** den Weg beschreiben 5
director [də'rektə] Regisseur/in 6
dirty ['dɜːti] schmutzig 7: 2 (32)
disadvantage [dɪsəd'vɑːntɪdʒ] Nachteil 7: 1 (11) **at a disadvantage** im Nachteil 7: 1 (11)
disagree [dɪsə'griː] nicht zustimmen, widersprechen 6
disappear [dɪsə'pɪə] verschwinden 5
disappoint sb. [dɪsə'pɔɪnt] jn. enttäuschen 7: 3 (54)
disappointed (with) [dɪsə'pɔɪntɪd] enttäuscht (von) 7: 3 (54)
disappointing [dɪsə'pɔɪntɪŋ] enttäuschend 7: 3 (54)

disco ['dɪskəʊ] Disco 5
discover [dɪ'skʌvə] entdecken 7: 3 (46)
discuss sth. [dɪ'skʌs] über etwas diskutieren; etwas besprechen 7: 1 (11)
disease [dɪ'ziːz] Krankheit 7: 4 (60)
dish [dɪʃ]:
1. Schüssel, Schale 7: 3 (46)
2. Gericht *(Mahlzeit)* 6
side dish Beilage 6
dishes *(pl)* ['dɪʃɪz] Abwasch 6
dishwasher ['dɪʃwɒʃə] Geschirrspülmaschine 6 **load the dishwasher** die Spülmaschine einräumen 7: 2 (32)
distance ['dɪstəns] Distanz, Entfernung 7: 3 (55) **in the distance** in der Ferne 7: 3 (55)
dive [daɪv] einen Kopfsprung machen, *(ins Wasser)* springen 5
divide (up) (into) [dɪ'vaɪd] auf-/einteilen (in) 7: 3 (42/43)
divorced [dɪ'vɔːst] geschieden 5
do [duː], **did, done** machen, tun 5 **do better** besser abschneiden 7: 1 (22) **do sport** Sport treiben 5 **do your homework** Hausaufgaben machen 5 **it doesn't help** es hilft nicht 5
dock [dɒk] Hafen, Dock 7: 4 (58/59)
doctor ['dɒktə] Arzt, Ärztin 6
documentary [dɒkju'mentri] Dokumentarfilm 6
dog [dɒg] Hund 5
dogs' home [dɒgz 'həʊm] Hundeheim 6
dollar ($) ['dɒlə] Dollar 7: 5 (79)
dolphin ['dɒlfɪn] Delfin 7: 4 (73)
done [dʌn] *siehe* **do**
door [dɔː] Tür 5 **answer the door** aufmachen, zur/an die Tür gehen 7: 1 (21)
down [daʊn] hinunter, herunter 5 **be down (by) ... %** um ... % gesunken sein 7: 2 (30)
download [daʊn'ləʊd] herunterladen 6
downstairs [daʊn'steəz] (nach) unten *(die Treppe hinunter)* 5
°**downtown** [daʊn'taʊn] *(AE)* im/ins Stadtzentrum
°**dragon boat** ['drægən bəʊt] Drachenboot
drama ['drɑːmə] Schauspiel, darstellende Kunst 5
drank [dræŋk] *siehe* **drink**
°**draw** [drɔː], **drew, drawn** zeichnen
drawing ['drɔːɪŋ] Zeichnung 5
dream [driːm] Traum(-) 5
dress [dres] Kleid 5
dress code ['dres kəʊd] Kleiderordnung, Dresscode 6
dressed [get 'drest]: **get dressed** sich anziehen 5
drink [drɪŋk]:
1. Getränk 5
2. drink, drank, drunk trinken 5
drive [draɪv] Zufahrt *(z. B. zu einer Garage)* 5
drive [draɪv], **drove, driven:**
1. *(mit dem Auto)* fahren 5
2. (an)treiben *(Tiere)* 7: 4 (63)
driven ['drɪvn] *siehe* **drive**
driver ['draɪvə] Fahrer/in 6
drop [drɒp]:
1. (sich) fallen lassen 6
2. fallen, sinken 7: 5 (82)
drove [drəʊv] *siehe* **drive**
drug [drʌg] Droge, Rauschgift 6
drunk [drʌŋk] *siehe* **drink**
duck [dʌk] Ente 7: 3 (54)
dug [dʌg] *siehe* **dig**
dummy ['dʌmi] Schnuller 7: 1 (19)
DVD [diːviː'diː] DVD 5

E

each [iːtʃ] jeder/jede/jedes (einzelne) 7: 1 (14)
each other [iːtʃ 'ʌðə] einander, sich (gegenseitig) 7: 1 (14)
ear [ɪə] Ohr 6
earache ['ɪəreɪk] Ohrenschmerzen 6
early ['ɜːli] früh 5
earn [ɜːn] verdienen *(Geld)* 7: 5 (79)
earth [ɜːθ] Erde 7: 3 (46)
earthquake ['ɜːθkweɪk] Erdbeben 6
east [iːst] Osten; östlich; Ost- 6
eastbound ['iːstbaʊnd] in Richtung Osten *(Zug, Bus)* 6
Easter ['iːstə] Ostern 6
eastern ['iːstən] östlich, Ost- 7: 4 (62)
easy ['iːzi] einfach, leicht 5
eat [iːt], **ate, eaten** essen; fressen 5
eaten ['iːtn] *siehe* **eat**
economic [iːkə'nɒmɪk] wirtschaftlich, Wirtschafts- 7: 4 (70)
economy [ɪ'kɒnəmi] (Volks-)Wirtschaft 7: 4 (70)
effect [ɪ'fekt] (Aus-)Wirkung, Einfluss, Effekt 7: 5 (84)
effective [ɪ'fektɪv] effektiv, wirksam 7: 5 (84)
e-friend ['iːfrend] E-Mail-Freund/in 6
egg [eg] Ei 5
eight [eɪt] acht 5
elbow ['elbəʊ] Ellbogen 7: 4 (68)
elephant ['elɪfənt] Elefant 7: 5 (79)
elevator ['elɪveɪtə] *(AE)* Lift *(Aufzug)* 6
eleven [ɪ'levən] elf 5
else [els]: **anything else** sonst noch etwas 6 **anywhere else** sonst irgendwo 6 **everybody/everyone else** alle anderen; jede/r andere 6
email ['iːmeɪl] E-Mail 5
embarrassed [ɪm'bærəst] verlegen 6
emergency [i'mɜːdʒənsi] Notfall 7: 2 (26)
emigrant ['emɪgrənt] Auswanderer, Auswanderin 7: 4 (61)
emigrate ['emɪgreɪt] auswandern, emigrieren 7: 4 (61)
emigration [emɪ'greɪʃn] Auswanderung 7: 4 (61)
emperor ['empərə] Kaiser 7: 3 (44)
emphasize ['emfəsaɪz] betonen, deutlich machen 7: 4 (69)
empire ['empaɪə] Imperium, Reich 7: 3 (44)
empress ['emprəs] Kaiserin 7: 3 (44)
empty ['empti]:
1. leer 6
2. leeren 6
end [end]:
1. Ende, Schluss 5
2. (be)enden 6
endless ['endləs] endlos 6
enemy ['enəmi] Feind/in 7: 1 (13)
engineer [endʒɪ'nɪə] Ingenieur/in; Techniker/in 6
English-speaking ['ɪŋglɪʃ spiːkɪŋ] englischsprachig 7: 4 (70)
enjoy [ɪn'dʒɔɪ] genießen 6 **enjoy doing sth.** genießen, etwas zu tun 6
enough [ɪ'nʌf] genug 6
entertain sb. [entə'teɪn] jn. unterhalten 7: 5 (78)
entry ['entri] Eintritt, Zutritt; (Tagebuch-)Eintrag 7: 3 (57)
envelope ['envələʊp] (Brief-)Umschlag 5
environment [ɪn'vaɪrənmənt] Umwelt; Umfeld, Umgebung 7: 5 (85)
environmental [ɪnvaɪrən'mentl] Umwelt- 7: 5 (85)
equipment [ɪ'kwɪpmənt] *(no pl)* Ausrüstung 6
escalator ['eskəleɪtə] Rolltreppe 6
escape [ɪ'skeɪp]:
1. Flucht 7: 2 (26)
2. escape (from) entkommen (aus), fliehen (vor/aus) 7: 2 (26)

especially [ɪ'speʃəli] insbesondere 7: 4 (71)
etc. [et'setərə] *(aus dem Lateinischen)* usw. (und so weiter) 7: 5 (86)
EU (= European Union) [iː 'juː] EU (Europäische Union) 7: 4 (70)
euro, *pl* **euros** ['jʊərəʊ] Euro 5
European Union [jʊərəpiːən 'juːniən] Europäische Union 7: 4 (70)
even ['iːvn] sogar, selbst 6 **not even** (noch) nicht einmal 6 **without even checking ...** ohne überhaupt zu checken ... 7: 5 (89)
evening ['iːvnɪŋ] Abend 5 **in the evening** abends, am Abend 5
event [ɪ'vent] Ereignis 5
ever ['evə] jemals, schon einmal 6
every ['evri] jede(r, s) 5
everybody ['evribɒdi] jeder; alle 5
everyone ['evriwʌn] jeder; alle 5
everything ['evriθɪŋ] alles 5
everywhere ['evriweə] überall 6
evil ['iːvl] böse; *(das)* Böse 7: 2 (26)
exact [ɪg'zækt] genau, exakt 7: 3 (47)
examination *(infml auch* **exam)** [ɪgzæmɪ'neɪʃn], [ɪg'zæm] Prüfung 7: 1 (8/9) **take/do an exam** eine Prüfung machen 7: 1 (8/9)
example [ɪg'zɑːmpl] Beispiel 6 **for example** zum Beispiel 6
exchange [ɪks'tʃeɪndʒ]:
1. austauschen 7: 2 (24/25)
2. (Aus-)Tausch, Schüleraustausch 7: 2 (24/25)
excited [ɪk'saɪtɪd] aufgeregt, gespannt 5
excitement [ɪk'saɪtmənt] Aufregung, Spannung 7: 3 (48)
exciting [ɪk'saɪtɪŋ] aufregend 6
Excuse me, ... [ɪks'kjuːz miː] Entschuldigung, ... / Entschuldigen Sie, ... 5
exercise ['eksəsaɪz] Übung, Aufgabe 6
exercise book ['eksəsaɪz bʊk] (Schul-)Heft 5
°**exist** [ɪg'zɪst] existieren
exit ['eksɪt] Ausgang; Ausfahrt 6
expensive [ɪk'spensɪv] teuer 5
experiment [ɪk'sperɪmənt] Experiment 6
°**expert** ['ekspɜːt] Experte, Expertin
explain sth. to sb. [ɪk'spleɪn] jm. etwas erklären 6
°**explanation** [eksplə'neɪʃn] Erklärung
explode [ɪk'spləʊd] explodieren 7: 3 (48)
explosion [ɪk'spləʊʒn] Explosion 7: 3 (48)
express [ɪk'spres] ausdrücken, zum Ausdruck bringen 7: 2 (36)
expression [ɪk'spreʃn] Ausdruck 7: 2 (36)
°**extra** ['ekstrə] Extra-, zusätzliche(r, s)
extraordinary [ɪk'strɔːdnri] außergewöhnlich 7: 1 (21)
eye [aɪ] Auge 6

F

face [feɪs]:
1. Gesicht 6
2. **face sb./sth.** jm./einer Sache ins Auge sehen, jm./einer Sache entgegentreten 6
facilities *(pl)* [fə'sɪlətiz] Einrichtungen, Geräte 7: 1 (8/9)
fact [fækt] Tatsache 7: 3 (52)
factory ['fæktri] Fabrik 7: 3 (50)
fair [feə] fair 7: 2 (33)
fairy ['feəri] Fee, Elfe 7: 5 (89)
fairy tale ['feəri teɪl] Märchen 7: 5 (89)
fall [fɔːl], **fell, fallen** fallen; hinfallen 5
fallen ['fɔːlən] *siehe* **fall**
°**false** [fɔːls] falsch, unrichtig
fame [feɪm] Ruhm 6
family ['fæməli] Familie 5
°**family tree** [fæməli 'triː] Familienstammbaum
famine ['fæmɪn] Hungersnot 7: 4 (58/59)
famous (for) ['feɪməs] berühmt (für, wegen) 5
fan [fæn] Fan 5
fancy dress [fænsi 'dres] *(no pl)* Kostüm, Verkleidung 5
fancy dress party [fænsi 'dres pɑːti] Kostümparty 5
fantasy ['fæntəsi] Fantasie; Fantasy *(Literatur-, Filmgattung)* 7: 3 (47)
FAQ (= frequently asked questions) [ef eɪ 'kju], [friːkwəntli ɑːskt 'kwestʃənz] häufig gestellte Fragen 6
far [fɑː] weit (entfernt) 6
farm [fɑːm] Bauernhof, Farm 6
farmer ['fɑːmə] Bauer, Bäuerin; Landwirt/in 6
farming ['fɑːmɪŋ] Landwirtschaft 7: 4 (70)
fashion ['fæʃn] Mode 7: 2 (36)
fast [fɑːst] schnell 5
°**fast finisher** [fɑːst 'fɪnɪʃəz] Schüler/in, der/die die Aufgabe(n) schnell(er) schafft
fast food [fɑːst 'fuːd] Fastfood *(schnell zubereitete und verzehrte Gerichte)*; Schnellimbiss 5
father ['fɑːðə] Vater 5
fault [fɔːlt] Fehler; Schuld 5
favourite ['feɪvərɪt] Lieblings- 5
February ['februəri] Februar 5
fed [fed] *siehe* **feed**
feed [fiːd], **fed, fed** füttern; ernähren 6
feedback ['fiːdbæk] *(no pl)* Feedback *(Rückmeldung)* 7: 1 (23)
feel [fiːl], **felt, felt** sich fühlen; fühlen 5
feeling ['fiːlɪŋ] Gefühl 6
fell [fel] *siehe* **fall**
felt [felt] *siehe* **feel**
female ['fiːmeɪl] weiblich; Frau 7: 1 (15)
fence [fens] fechten *(Sport)* 7: 1 (8/9)
ferret ['ferɪt] Frettchen 5
ferry ['feri] Fähre 5
ferryman, *pl* **ferrymen** ['ferimən] Fährmann 6
festival ['festɪvl] Fest 5
few [fjuː]: **a few** ein paar, einige 7: 3 (54)
field [fiːld] Feld; Weide 6 **in the field** auf der Weide 6
fight [faɪt]:
1. Kampf 5
2. **fight, fought, fought** kämpfen, bekämpfen 5
fighter ['faɪtə] Kämpfer/in 7: 2 (26)
figure ['fɪgə]:
1. Figur 6
2. Ziffer, Zahl 7: 4 (61)
°**file** [faɪl] Datei; Ordner, Liste
fill [fɪl] füllen 7: 1 (8/9) **fill sth. in** etwas ausfüllen; etwas einsetzen 7: 1 (8/9)
film [fɪlm]:
1. Film 5
°2. filmen, drehen
final ['faɪnl] Finale 6
°**finally** ['faɪnəli] schließlich, endlich
find [faɪnd], **found, found** finden 5 **find out (about sth.)** herausfinden; sich (über etwas) informieren 7: 2 (36)
fine [faɪn]:
1. gut, in Ordnung; schön 5 **I'm fine.** Mir geht es gut. 5
2. fein *(z. B. Stoff)*; dünn *(z. B. Haar)* 7: 3 (45)

finger ['fɪŋgə] Finger 6 **tap your fingers** mit den Fingern klopfen 7: 4 (68)
finish ['fɪnɪʃ] beenden, zu Ende machen 5
fire ['faɪə] Feuer 6
firework ['faɪəwɜːk] Feuerwerkskörper 5 **fireworks** *(pl)* Feuerwerk 5
first [fɜːst]:
1. erste(r, s) 5
2. zuerst, als Erstes 5
finish first *(im Wettkampf)* Erste/r werden 5
first language [fɜːst 'læŋgwɪdʒ] Muttersprache 7: 1 (16)
first name ['fɜːst neɪm] Vorname 7: 1 (15)
Firstly, ... ['fɜːstli] Erstens ... 7: 5 (79)
fish [fɪʃ] Fisch(e) 5
fish finger [fɪʃ 'fɪŋgə] Fischstäbchen 5
fit [fɪt] fit 6
fit (sth.) [fɪt] passen (zu etwas) 7: 2 (28)
five [faɪv] fünf 5
flag [flæg] Fahne, Flagge 5
flat [flæt] Wohnung 5
flew [fluː] *siehe* **fly**
flight [flaɪt] Flug 6
floor [flɔː]:
1. Fußboden 5
2. Etage, Stock 6
first floor *(AE:)* Erdgeschoss; *(BE:)* 1. Etage 6
flour ['flaʊə] Mehl 7: 4 (67)
flower ['flaʊə] Blume; Blüte 5
flown [fləʊn] *siehe* **fly**
fly [flaɪ], **flew, flown** fliegen 5
flyer ['flaɪə] Flieger/in 7: 3 (54)
fog [fɒg] Nebel 5
foggy ['fɒgi] nebelig 5
follow ['fɒləʊ] (be)folgen; verfolgen 7: 1 (15)
follower ['fɒləʊə] Anhänger/in, Fan 7: 5 (79)
food [fuːd] Essen, Lebensmittel; Futter 5
foot, *pl* **feet** [fʊt], [fiːt] Fuß 6
football ['fʊtbɔːl]:
1. Fußball 5
2. *(AE)* American Football 6
football club (FC) ['fʊtbɔːl klʌb] Fußballverein 5
for [fɔː] für 5 **for 30 years** 30 Jahre (lang) 5 **for example** zum Beispiel 6 **What's for homework?** Was haben wir als Hausaufgabe(n) auf? 6
foreground ['fɔːgraʊnd] Vordergrund 7: 4 (63)
forest ['fɒrɪst] Wald 6
forget [fə'get], **forgot, forgotten** vergessen 6
forgot [fə'gɒt] *siehe* **forget**
forgotten [fə'gɒtn] *siehe* **forget**
fork [fɔːk] Gabel 7: 4 (67)
form [fɔːm] Formular 7: 1 (8/9)
fortunately ['fɔːtʃənətli] zum Glück, glücklicherweise 7: 5 (83)
forward ['fɔːwəd] vorwärts, nach vorne 7: 3 (48) **look forward to doing sth.** sich darauf freuen, etwas zu tun 7: 1 (15) **look forward to sth.** sich auf etwas freuen 7: 1 (15)
fought [fɔːt] *siehe* **fight**
found [faʊnd]:
1. *siehe* **find**
2. gründen 7: 5 (78)
founder ['faʊndə] Gründer/in 7: 5 (78)
four [fɔː] vier 5
fox [fɒks] Fuchs 6
free [friː]:
1. kostenlos 5
2. frei 5
free time Freizeit, freie Zeit 5
freeze [friːz], **froze, frozen** (ge)frieren; erstarren 7: 1 (16)
fresh [freʃ] frisch 5
Friday ['fraɪdeɪ], ['fraɪdi] Freitag 5
fridge [frɪdʒ] Kühlschrank 6
fried [fraɪd] frittiert, gebraten 6
friend [frend] Freund/in 5 **make friends** Freunde finden 7: 1 (10)
friendless ['frendləs] ohne Freunde 6
friendly ['frendli] freundlich 5
friendship ['frendʃɪp] Freundschaft 7: 5 (76/77)
frog [frɒg] Frosch 6
from [frɒm] von, aus 5 **Where are you from?** Wo kommst du her? 5
front [frʌnt] vorderer Teil, Vorderseite 5 **at the front** vorne 5 **in front of** vor 5
front page [frʌnt 'peɪdʒ] Titelseite 6
frown [fraʊn]:
1. die Stirn runzeln 7: 4 (68)
2. Stirnrunzeln 7: 4 (68)
froze [frəʊz] *siehe* **freeze**
frozen ['frəʊzn] *siehe* **freeze**
fruit [fruːt] Obst 5
fry [fraɪ] frittieren, braten 6
full [fʊl] vollständig; voll 7: 1 (15) **full of** voll mit/von, voller 7: 1 (15)
fun [fʌn] Spaß 5 **be fun** Spaß machen 5 **have fun** Spaß haben 5 **it sounds fun** es klingt, als ob es Spaß macht 6 **°for fun** zum Spaß, zum Vergnügen
fund [fʌnd] finanzieren 7: 5 (79)
funding ['fʌndɪŋ] Finanzierung, *(finanzielle)* Mittel 7: 5 (79)
funny ['fʌni] witzig, komisch 5
furniture ['fɜːnɪtʃə] Möbel 6
further ['fɜːðə] weiter (entfernt) 6
furthest ['fɜːðəst] am weitesten (entfernt) 6
future ['fjuːtʃə]:
1. Zukunft 7: 2 (36)
2. zukünftige(r, s) 7: 2 (36)

G

Gaelic ['geɪlɪk] Gälisch *(Sprache)* 7: 4 (58/59)
game [geɪm] Spiel 5
°gameplay ['geɪmpleɪ] Spielen eines Spiels; Spielmechanik
gamer ['geɪmə] Spieler/in, Gamer/in 6
games console [games 'geɪmz kənsəʊl] Spielekonsole 6
gap [gæp] Lücke, Abstand 6
garage ['gærɑːʒ] Garage 5
garden ['gɑːdn] Garten 5
garlic ['gɑːlɪk] Knoblauch 6
gas [gæs] *(AE)* Benzin 6
gas station ['gæs steɪʃn] *(AE)* Tankstelle 6
gate [geɪt] Tor, Gatter 6
gave [geɪv] *siehe* **give**
gay [geɪ] schwul 7: 2 (26)
gender ['dʒendə] Geschlecht *(als soziales Merkmal)* 7: 1 (15)
geocaching ['dʒiːəʊkæʃɪŋ] Geocaching *(GPS-Schnitzeljagd)* 5
geography [dʒi'ɒgrəfi] Geografie, Erdkunde 5
get [get], **got, got:**
1. *(sich etwas)* holen/besorgen; bekommen 5
2. werden 6
get wet nass werden 6
3. get sth. etwas verstehen, mitbekommen 7: 1 (14)
4. get (to) gelangen, (hin)kommen (nach) 6 **get on a plane/bus/train** in ein Flugzeug/einen Bus/einen Zug einsteigen 6 **get off a plane/bus/train** aus einem Flugzeug/Bus/Zug aussteigen 6 **get in(to) a car** in ein Auto einsteigen 7: 2 (30) **get out of a car** aus einem Auto aussteigen 7: 2 (30) **get up** aufstehen 5
ghost [gəʊst] Geist, Gespenst 6
°giant ['dʒaɪənt] Riese/Riesin

giraffe, *pl* **giraffe** *or* **giraffes** [dʒə'rɑːf] Giraffe 7: 5 (78)
girl [gɜːl] Mädchen 5
girlfriend ['gɜːlfrend] (feste) Freundin 7: 1 (14)
give [gɪv], **gave, given** geben 5 **give a talk** einen Vortrag halten 5 **give in (to sb./sth.)** (jm./einer Sache) nachgeben 7: 5 (89)
given ['gɪvn] *siehe* **give**
glass [glɑːs] Glas 7: 2 (35)
glasses *(pl)* ['glɑːsɪz] *(eine)* Brille 6
glove [glʌv] Handschuh 6
go [gəʊ]: **on the go** unterwegs 7: 5 (86)
go [gəʊ], **went, gone** gehen, fahren 5 **go off** klingeln *(Wecker)*; losgehen *(Alarm, Waffe)* 7: 5 (88) **go wrong** schiefgehen 6 **I'm going to ...** ich werde ... *(Plan, Vorhaben)* 6
goal [gəʊl] Tor *(im Sport)* 5
°**gob** [gɒb] *(slang)* Schnauze *(Slang für „Mund")*
gobbledygook ['gɒbldiguːk] *(infml)* Kauderwelsch 7: 1 (20)
°**gobstopper** ['gɒbstɒpə] Riesenbonbon
god [gɒd] Gott 7: 2 (31) **Oh my god!** Oh mein Gott! 7: 2 (31)
gold [gəʊld] Gold 5
gone [gɒn] *siehe* **go be gone** weg sein 7: 1 (20)
°**gonna** *(infml)* ['gɒnə]: **you gonna be ...** du wirst ... sein *(= you're going to be)*
good [gʊd] gut 5 **Good morning.** Guten Morgen. 5
Goodbye. [gʊd'baɪ] Auf Wiedersehen! / Servus. 5
gorilla [gə'rɪlə] Gorilla 6
got [gɒt] *siehe* **get have got** haben 6
government ['gʌvənmənt] Regierung 7: 1 (16)
grade [greɪd]:
1. (Schul-)Note 6
2. *(AE)* Klasse, Schuljahr 6
gram (= g) [græm] Gramm 5
grandad ['grændæd] Opa 5
grandfather ['grænfɑːðə] Großvater 5
grandma ['grænmɑː] Oma 5
grandmother ['grænmʌðə] Großmutter 5
grandparents *(pl)* ['grænpeərənts] Großeltern 5
graph [græf], [grɑːf] Graph, Schaubild 6
grass [grɑːs] Gras; Rasen 6
great [greɪt]:
1. toll, großartig 5
2. groß *(bedeutend, angesehen)* 5
Great Britain [greɪt 'brɪtn] Großbritannien 5
greedy ['griːdi] gierig, habgierig 7: 3 (49)
green [griːn] grün 5
grey [greɪ] grau 5
°**grilled** [grɪld] gegrillt
gross [grəʊs] *(infml)* widerlich 7: 2 (32)
ground [graʊnd] (Erd-)Boden 7: 3 (54)
group [gruːp] Gruppe 5
°**guard** [gɑːd] Wärter/in; Wache; Schutz(vorrichtung)
guardian ['gɑːdiən] Vormund 7: 1 (15)
°**guess** [ges] (er)raten
guest [gest] Gast 7: 2 (35)
guide (to) [gaɪd] Ratgeber (für), Reiseführer *(Buch, Broschüre)* 5
guinea pig ['gɪni pɪg] Meerschweinchen 5
guitar [gɪ'tɑː] Gitarre 5
gum [gʌm] Gummi; Zahnfleisch 7: 5 (78)
guys *(pl)* [gaɪz] Leute *(Anrede)* 5
gym [dʒɪm]:
1. Turnhalle, Sporthalle 5
2. Fitnessstudio 5
gymnastics [dʒɪm'næstɪks] Turnen, Gymnastik 5

H

had [hæd] *siehe* **have**
haggis ['hægɪs] *schottisches Gericht aus gefülltem Schafsmagen* 6
hair [heə] Haar, Haare 5
hairdresser ['heədresə] Friseur/in 6 **hairdresser's** Friseursalon 6
hairstyle ['heəstaɪl] Frisur 7: 5 (85)
half [hɑːf] halbe(r, s) 6 **half an apple** ein halber Apfel 6 **half past 6** halb 7 5
half-brother ['hɑːf brʌðə] Halbbruder 5
half-sister ['hɑːf sɪstə] Halbschwester 5
half-time show ['hɑːftaɪm ʃəʊ] Show in der Halbzeitspause 6
halfway [hɑːf'weɪ] auf halbem Wege, halb(wegs) 7: 3 (55)
hall [hɔːl]:
1. Flur, Diele 5
2. Halle, Saal; Flur 7: 2 (35)
Halloween [hæləʊ'iːn] Halloween *(der Abend des 31. Oktober)* 5
ham [hæm] Schinken 5
hamster ['hæmstə] Hamster 5
hand [hænd] Hand 5 **hold hands** Händchen halten 6 **put up your hand** sich melden, aufzeigen 6
handover ['hændəʊvə] Übergabe 7: 4 (73)
hang [hæŋ], **hung, hung** hängen 6 **hang out** rumhängen, abhängen 6 **hang sth. out** etwas aufhängen *(Wäsche)* 6
°**ha'penny** ['heɪpni] halber Penny *(brit. Münze)*
happen (to sb.) ['hæpən] (jm.) geschehen, passieren 5
happiness ['hæpinəs] Glück, Zufriedenheit 7: 5 (76/77)
happy ['hæpi] glücklich, froh 5
harbour ['hɑːbə] Hafen 5
hard [hɑːd] schwer, schwierig; hart 5 **train hard** hart trainieren 7: 2 (28)
hardly ['hɑːdli] kaum 7: 3 (55)
has [hæz], [həz]: **he/she/it has** er/sie/es hat 5
hat [hæt] Hut, Mütze 6
hate [heɪt] hassen 5
hater ['heɪtə] Verfasser/in von Hasskommentaren *(Internet)* 7: 5 (89)
have [hæv], **had, had** haben 5 **have breakfast/lunch/dinner** frühstücken/(zu) Mittag essen/(zu) Abend essen 5 **have to do sth.** etwas tun müssen 6 **I'll have ...** ich nehme ... *(beim Essen, im Restaurant)* 5
have got [həv 'gɒt] haben 6
he [hiː] er 5 **he's (= he is)** er ist 5
head [hed] Kopf 6
headache ['hedeɪk] Kopfschmerzen 6
heading ['hedɪŋ] Überschrift 7: 2 (36)
°**headphones** *(pl)* ['hedfəʊnz] *(ein)* Kopfhörer
health [helθ] Gesundheit 6
healthy ['helθi] gesund 6
hear [hɪə], **heard, heard** hören 5
heard [hɜːd] *siehe* **hear**
heart [hɑːt] Herz 6
°**heart attack** ['hɑːt ətæk] Herzinfarkt
heavy ['hevi] schwer *(Gewicht)* 6
heck [hek]: **What/Where/... the heck is ...?** *(infml)* Was/Wo/... ist denn nur/bloß ...? 7: 5 (78)
held [held] *siehe* **hold**
°**helicopter** ['helɪkɒptə] Hubschrauber
Hello. [hə'ləʊ] Hallo. / Grüß Gott. 5
°**helmet** ['helmɪt] Helm

help [help]:
1. helfen 5
2. Hilfe 5

her [hɜː], [hə] sie; ihr 5
her mum [hɜː], [hə] ihre Mutter 5
here [hɪə] hier; hierher 5 **Here you are.** Bitte schön. / Hier, bitte. 5
hermit crab ['hɜːmɪt kræb] Einsiedlerkrebs 5
hero, *pl* **heroes** ['hɪərəʊ] Held/in 7: 2 (26)
hers [hɜːz] ihrer, ihre, ihres *(zu „she")* 6
herself [hɜː'self] sie/sich selbst *(zu „she")* 6
Hi. [haɪ] Hallo. 5 **Say hi to everyone.** Grüß/t alle. 7: 1 (10)
hid [hɪd] *siehe* **hide**
hidden ['hɪdn] *siehe* **hide**
hide [haɪd], **hid, hidden** verstecken; sich verstecken 7: 3 (48)
high [haɪ] hoch 6
Highlands ['haɪləndʒ]: **the Highlands** *(pl)* das schottische Hochland *(der bergige Norden Schottlands)* 6
highlight ['haɪlaɪt]:
1. hervorheben, unterstreichen 7: 3 (52)
2. Höhepunkt; Schlaglicht 7: 3 (52)

high-tech [haɪ 'tek] High-Tech-, Hochleistungs- 7: 4 (70)
highway ['haɪweɪ] *(AE)* Fernstraße *(in den USA; oft mit vier oder mehr Spuren)* 6
hike [haɪk] wandern 6
hiking ['haɪkɪŋ] *(das)* Wandern 6
hill [hɪl] Hügel 6
him [hɪm] ihm, ihn 5
himself [hɪm'self] er selbst, ihn/ihm/sich selbst 6
his [hɪz]:
1. sein/e *(zu „he")* 5
2. seiner, seine, seins *(zu „he")* 6

Hispanic [hɪ'spænɪk] hispanisch *(lateinamerikanischer Herkunft)* 6
history ['hɪstri] Geschichte 5
hit [hɪt]:
1. Hit 5
2. **hit, hit, hit** schlagen 5 stoßen gegen, zusammenstoßen mit; treffen auf 5

hobby ['hɒbi] Hobby 5
hockey ['hɒki] Hockey 5
hold [həʊld], **held, held** halten 5 **hold hands** Händchen halten 6 **hold out** *(jm. etwas)* hinhalten 6
hole [həʊl] Loch 6
holiday ['hɒlədeɪ] Urlaub 5 **holidays** Ferien 5 **on holiday** im/in den Urlaub 5
holy ['həʊli] heilig 7: 4 (63)
home [həʊm]:
1. Heim, Zuhause 5 **at home** zu Hause, daheim 5 **dogs' home** Hundeheim 6
2. nach Hause 5 **come home** nach Hause kommen 5

homeless ['həʊmləs] obdachlos 6
home-made [həʊm'meɪd] hausgemacht, selbstgemacht 6
homesick ['həʊmsɪk]: **be/feel homesick** Heimweh haben 7: 1 (10)
°**hometown** [həʊm'taʊn] Heimatstadt
homework ['həʊmwɜːk] Hausaufgabe(n) 5 **do your homework** Hausaufgaben machen 5 **What's for homework?** Was haben wir als Hausaufgabe(n) auf? 6
hood [hʊd] Kapuze 6
hoodie ['hʊdi] Kapuzenpullover 7: 1 (13)
hope [həʊp]:
1. hoffen 6
2. Hoffnung 7: 2 (31)

hopeful ['həʊpfl] zuversichtlich, hoffnungsvoll 7: 2 (31)
hopeless ['həʊpləs] hoffnungslos 6
horrible ['hɒrəbl] schrecklich 5
horror ['hɒrə] Horror(-) 6
horse [hɔːs] Pferd 5 **ride a horse** ein Pferd reiten 5
horse riding ['hɔːs raɪdɪŋ] *(das)* Reiten, Reitsport 5
hospital ['hɒspɪtl] Krankenhaus 5
hostel ['hɒstl] Wohnheim; Hostel *(günstige Unterkunft für Reisende)* 7: 4 (69)
hot [hɒt] heiß, warm 5
hot chocolate [hɒt 'tʃɒklət] Kakao, heiße (Trink-)Schokolade 5
hot dog ['hɒt dɒg] Hot Dog *(heißes Würstchen in einem Brötchen)* 6
hotel [həʊ'tel] Hotel 5
hour ['aʊə] Stunde 5
house [haʊs] Haus 5
how [haʊ] wie 5 **How are you?** Wie geht's? / Wie geht es dir/euch/Ihnen? 5 **How much is/are …?** Was (Wie viel) kostet/kosten …? 5 **how to do sth.** wie man etwas macht 7: 3 (54)
however [haʊ'evə] allerdings, jedoch 7: 5 (79)
hundred ['hʌndrəd]: **a hundred** (ein)hundert 5
hung [hʌŋ] *siehe* **hang**
hungry ['hʌŋgri] hungrig 5
hunt [hʌnt]:
1. Jagd 7: 4 (66)
2. jagen 7: 4 (66)

hurt [hɜːt], **hurt, hurt** verletzen; wehtun 5 **be hurt** verletzt sein 6 **get hurt** sich verletzen 6
husband ['hʌzbənd] Ehemann 7: 3 (45)
hyphen ['haɪfn] Bindestrich, Trennstrich 7: 5 (79)

I

I [aɪ] ich 5 **I'm (= I am)** ich bin 5
ice [aɪs] Eis *(gefrorenes Wasser)* 6
ice cream [aɪs 'kriːm] (Speise-)Eis 5
idea [aɪ'dɪə] Idee 5
identity [aɪ'dentəti] Identität 7: 5 (89)
if [ɪf]:
1. wenn, falls 6 **What if?** Was wäre, wenn? 6
2. ob 7: 1 (10)

ill [ɪl] krank 6
illness ['ɪlnəs] Krankheit 7: 4 (60)
imagine sth. [ɪ'mædʒɪn] sich etwas vorstellen 7: 4 (71)
immigrant ['ɪmɪgrənt] Einwanderer, Einwanderin 7: 1 (16)
immigrate ['ɪmɪgreɪt] einwandern, immigrieren 7: 4 (61)
immigration [ɪmɪ'greɪʃn] Einwanderung 7: 4 (61)
impatient [ɪm'peɪʃnt] ungeduldig 7: 4 (68)
important [ɪm'pɔːtnt] wichtig 5
in [ɪn] in 5 **in 1540** (im Jahre) 1540 5 **in English** auf Englisch 5 **in my picture** auf meinem Bild 5 **in the country** auf dem Land 5 **in the evening** abends, am Abend 5 **in the field** auf der Weide 6 **in the morning** morgens, am Morgen 5 **in the photo** auf dem Foto 5 **in town** in der Stadt 5
°**include** [ɪn'kluːd] (mit) einschließen
independence (from) [ɪndɪ'pendəns] Unabhängigkeit (von) 7: 4 (62)
Independence Day [ɪndɪ'pendəns deɪ] *(US-amerikanischer)* Unabhängigkeitstag *(4. Juli)* 6
independent (of/from) [ɪndɪ'pendənt] unabhängig (von) 7: 1 (20)
°**individually** [ɪndɪ'vɪdʒʊəl] einzeln, individuell

°infographic [ɪnfə'græfɪk] Infografik
°infographic maker [ɪnfə'græfɪk meɪkə] *Programm zur Herstellung von Infografiken*
information [ɪnfə'meɪʃn] Information(en) 5
°injured ['ɪndʒəd] verletzt, verwundet
inside [ɪn'saɪd] innen, auf der Innenseite 6
°inside cover [ɪnsaɪd 'kʌvə] Umschlaginnenseite *(Buch)*
inside out [ɪnsaɪd 'aʊt] verkehrt herum, auf links *(Kleidung)* 7: 1 (20)
turn your T-shirt inside out dein T-Shirt auf links ziehen 7: 1 (20)
instruction [ɪn'strʌkʃn] Anweisung 7: 1 (15)
instrument ['ɪnstrəmənt] Instrument 5
interest (in) ['ɪntrəst] Interesse (an) 7: 3 (57)
°interested (in) ['ɪntrəstɪd] interessiert (an)
interesting ['ɪntrəstɪŋ] interessant 5
international [ɪntə'næʃnəl] international 6
internet ['ɪntənet] Internet 5
interview ['ɪntəvjuː] Interview 5
into ['ɪntu], ['ɪntə] in (... hinein) 5
introduce sb. to sb./sth. [ɪntrə'djuːs] jm. jn./etwas vorstellen, jn. mit jm./etwas bekanntmachen 7: 1 (23)
introduction [ɪntrə'dʌkʃn] Einleitung; Vorstellung *(Bekanntmachen)* 7: 1 (23)
invade [ɪn'veɪd] einmarschieren (in), eindringen (in) 7: 3 (44)
invitation (to) [ɪnvɪ'teɪʃn] Einladung (zu, nach) 5
invite (to) [ɪn'vaɪt] einladen (zu, nach) 5
is [ɪz] *(er/sie/es)* ist 5 **The shirt is £2.** Das Hemd kostet 2 Pfund. 5
island ['aɪlənd] Insel 6
IT (information technology) [aɪ 'tiː], [ɪnfə'meɪʃn teknɒlədʒi] IT (Informationstechnologie) 5
it [ɪt] er, sie, es 5
°italics [ɪ'tælɪks]: **in italics** kursiv (gedruckt)
its [ɪts] sein/seine, ihr/ihre *(besitzanzeigend bei Dingen und Tieren)* 5
itself [ɪt'self] es/sich selbst (zu *„it“*) 6

J

jacket ['dʒækɪt] Jacke, Jackett 6
January ['dʒænjuəri] Januar 5
jeans *(pl)* [dʒiːnz] Jeans 5
°jelly baby ['dʒeli beɪbi] *gummibärchenartige Süßigkeit in der Form eines Babys*
job [dʒɒb] Job, (Arbeits-)Stelle; Aufgabe 5
jobless ['dʒɒbləs] arbeitslos 6
join a club [dʒɔɪn]: in einen Klub eintreten 7: 1 (15)
joke [dʒəʊk] Witz, Scherz 6
journey ['dʒɜːni] Reise 5
judge [dʒʌdʒ]:
1. (be)urteilen 7: 5 (89)
2. Richter/in 7: 5 (89)
juice [dʒuːs] Saft 5
juicy ['dʒuːsi] saftig 6
July [dʒu'laɪ] Juli 5
jump [dʒʌmp] springen 7: 2 (27)
°jumpsuit ['dʒʌmpsuːt] Overall
June [dʒuːn] Juni 5
°jungle ['dʒʌŋgl] Dschungel
junior high (school) [dʒuːniə 'haɪ skuːl] *(AE) Schule für Kinder zwischen 12 und 14* 7: 1 (20)
just [dʒʌst]:
1. nur, bloß; einfach 6
2. gerade (eben) 6

K

karate [kə'rɑːti] Karate 5
keep [kiːp], **kept, kept** halten; behalten 7: 1 (11) **keep sth. out of the oceans** verhindern, dass etwas in die Ozeane gelangt 7: 5 (85)
kept [kept] *siehe* **keep**
kid [kɪd] Kind, Jugendliche/r 5
kill [kɪl] töten 7: 1 (13)
kilometre (km) ['kɪləmiːtə] Kilometer 6
kilt [kɪlt] Kilt *(schottischer Rock für Männer)* 6
kind [kaɪnd] nett, freundlich 6
kind (of) [kaɪnd] Art, Sorte 7: 3 (46)
king [kɪŋ] König 7: 2 (26)
Kingdom ['kɪŋdəm]: **the United Kingdom (= the UK)** das Vereinigte Königreich 5
kitchen ['kɪtʃɪn] Küche 5
knead [niːd] kneten 7: 4 (67)
kneel [niːl], **knelt, knelt** knien 7: 3 (48)
knelt [nelt] *siehe* **kneel**
knew [njuː] *siehe* **know**
knife, *pl* **knives** [naɪf], [naɪvz] Messer 7: 3 (45)
knit [nɪt] stricken 7: 1 (8/9)
knock (at sth.) [nɒk] (an)klopfen (an etwas) 6
know [nəʊ], **knew, known** wissen; kennen 5 **you know** nämlich, weißt du 7: 1 (12)
known [nəʊn] *siehe* **know**
Kurdish ['kɜːdɪʃ] Kurdisch 6

L

LA [el 'eɪ] Los Angeles *(Stadt in Kalifornien)* 6
lacrosse [lə'krɒs] Lacrosse *(Ballspiel, ähnlich wie Hockey)* 7: 1 (8/9)
lady ['leɪdi] Dame 6
lake [leɪk] (Binnen-)See 6
lame [leɪm] lahm, langweilig 7: 5 (83)
lamp [læmp] Lampe 5
land [lænd]:
1. Land *(Grund und Boden)* 7: 3 (42/43)
2. landen 7: 3 (42/43)
language ['læŋgwɪdʒ] Sprache 5
laptop ['læptɒp] Laptop 7: 2 (35)
°large [lɑːdʒ] groß
lasagne [lə'zænjə] Lasagne 6
lasso, *pl* **lassos** *or* **lassoes** [læ'suː] Lasso 7: 2 (26)
last [lɑːst] letzte(r, s) 5 **last week** letzte/vorige Woche 5 **at last** schließlich, endlich 7: 3 (48)
last name ['lɑːst neɪm] Nachname, Familienname 7: 1 (15)
late [leɪt] spät 5 **I'm late.** Ich habe mich verspätet. 5
late-night shopping [leɪt 'naɪt] Einkaufen am späten Abend 6
later ['leɪtə] später 5
laugh [lɑːf] lachen 6
leaflet ['liːflət] Faltblatt, Informationsblatt 6
league [liːg] Liga 6
lean [liːn] lehnen 7: 3 (48)
learn [lɜːn] lernen 5
°least [liːst]: **at least** wenigstens, zumindest
leather ['leðə] Leder 7: 3 (45)
leave [liːv], **left, left** abfahren; (weg)gehen; *(jemanden)* verlassen 5 **leave out** weglassen 7: 1 (16) **leave sth.** etwas (zurück) lassen 5 **leave sth. at home** etwas zu Hause lassen 5
left [left] *siehe* **leave**
left [left] links; nach links 5 **on the left** links, auf der linken Seite 5
leg [leg] Bein 6
lemonade [lemə'neɪd] Limonade 6

lend [lend], **lent, lent** leihen, verleihen 6
length [leŋθ] Länge; Dauer 7: 5 (80)
lent [lent] *siehe* **lend**
°**leprechaun** ['leprəkɔ:n] Kobold
lesson ['lesn] (Unterrichts-) Stunde 5
let [let], **let, let** lassen 5 **Let's ...** Lass(t) uns ... 5 **Let's go!** Auf geht's! / Dann mal los! 5
letter ['letə]:
1. Brief 6
2. Buchstabe 6
library ['laɪbrəri] Bücherei, Bibliothek 5
lie [laɪ]:
1. Lüge 7: 1 (11)
tell a lie/lies lügen 7: 1 (11)
2. **lie (to sb.)** (jn. an)lügen 7: 1 (11)
life, *pl* **lives** [laɪf], [laɪvz] *(das)* Leben 5 **in real life** im echten Leben 7: 2 (26)
lift [lɪft] Lift *(Aufzug)* 6
light [laɪt]:
1. hell 7: 3 (55)
2. leicht 7: 3 (55)
light [laɪt] Licht 7: 1 (11) **lights out** Licht aus 7: 1 (11)
like [laɪk] mögen 5 **I'd like ... (= I would like)** Ich hätte gern ... / Ich möchte ... 5 **I'd like to talk about ... (= I would like to)** Ich würde gern über ... sprechen. 5 **I'd like you to be ...** Ich möchte, dass ihr ... seid. 6 **they like to play ...** sie spielen gern ... 5
like [laɪk] wie 5 **like this** so, auf diese Art 7: 5 (83) **What's ... like?** Wie ist ...? / Wie sieht ... aus? 5
likely ['laɪkli] wahrscheinlich 7: 5 (84)
line [laɪn]:
1. Reihe 5
2. Telefonanschluss; Telefonleitung 7: 1 (21)
The line went dead. Die (Telefon-)Leitung war tot. 7: 1 (21)
3. U-Bahn-Linie 6
4. Zeile 5
°5. Linie
linen ['lɪnɪn] Leinen; Wäsche 7: 3 (45)
link [lɪŋk]:
1. Verbindung; Link 7: 3 (42/43)
2. **link (to/with)** verbinden (mit) 7: 3 (42/43)
lion ['laɪən] Löwe 6
list [lɪst] Liste 6 **to-do list** Aufgabenliste 6
listen ['lɪsn]: **listen (to)** (sich etwas) anhören; zuhören 5 **listen for sth.** auf etwas horchen, *(beim Zuhören)* auf etwas achten 7: 2 (34)
listener ['lɪsənə] Zuhörer/in 6
litter ['lɪtə] Abfall 6
litter bin ['lɪtə bɪn] Mülleimer 6
little ['lɪtl]:
1. klein 5
2. **a little** ein wenig, ein bisschen 7: 4 (67)
live [lɪv] leben, wohnen 5
live [laɪv] live 6
lives [laɪvz] *Plural von* **life** 5
living room ['lɪvɪŋ ru:m] Wohnzimmer 5
load [ləʊd] (be)laden 6 **load the dishwasher** die Spülmaschine einräumen 7: 2 (32)
loch [lɒx] *schottisches Wort für* **lake** 6
locker ['lɒkə] Spind, Schließfach 5
Londoner ['lʌndənə] Londoner/in 6
lonely ['ləʊnli] einsam 7: 4 (68)
long [lɒŋ] lang 5
look [lʊk]:
1. aussehen 5
2. sehen, schauen 5
look at sth. sich etwas anschauen 5 **look for** suchen; Ausschau halten nach 5 **look forward to doing sth.** sich darauf freuen , etwas zu tun 7: 1 (15) **look forward to sth.** sich auf etwas freuen 7: 1 (15) **look after** sich kümmern um; aufpassen auf 6
lorry ['lɒri] Lastwagen, LKW 7: 1 (16)
lose [lu:z], **lost, lost** verlieren 6
lost [lɒst] *siehe* **lose**
lot [lɒt]: **lots (of)** viel/e 5 **a lot (of)** viel/e; sehr 5
loud [laʊd] laut 7: 1 (11)
love [lʌv]:
1. lieben, sehr mögen 5
love to do sth. / love doing sth. etwas sehr gern tun 5
2. Liebe 6
Love ... Liebe Grüße, ... *(Briefschluss)* 5
°**love hearts** *(pl)* ['lʌvhɑ:ts] Liebesherzen *(Süßigkeiten)*
lucky ['lʌki] Glücks-, glücklich 5
ludo ['lu:dəʊ] Mensch ärgere dich nicht *(Spiel)* 7: 5 (82)
luggage ['lʌgɪdʒ] Gepäck 6
lunch [lʌntʃ] Mittagessen 5 **have lunch** (zu) Mittag essen 5 **What's for lunch?** Was gibt es zum Mittagessen? 5

M

macaroni [mækə'rəʊni] Makkaroni 7: 2 (34)
machine [mə'ʃi:n] Automat, Maschine 6
made [meɪd] *siehe* **make**
magazine [mægə'zi:n] Zeitschrift 5
magic ['mædʒɪk]:
1. magisch 7: 1 (10)
2. Zauberei, Magie 7: 1 (10)
3. **by magic** durch Zauberei 7: 1 (10)
main [meɪn] Haupt-, wichtigste(r, s) 7: 3 (52)
main course [meɪn 'kɔ:s] Hauptgericht 6
make [meɪk], **made, made** machen, herstellen 5 **make money)** (Geld) verdienen 6 **make a difference** etwas bewirken, etwas ausmachen 5 **make friends** Freunde finden 7: 1 (10) **make sb. do sth.** jn. dazu bringen, etwas zu tun 7: 2 (36) **make sure that ...** sicherstellen, dass ...; dafür sorgen, dass ... 7: 4 (61)
male [meɪl] männlich; Mann 7: 1 (15)
man, *pl* **men** [mæn], [men] Mann 5
manage (to do sth.) ['mænɪdʒ] (es) schaffen (etwas zu tun) 7: 4 (61)
manager ['mænɪdʒə] Manager/in 7: 2 (36)
many ['mæni] viele 5 **how many?** wie viele? 5
map [mæp] Landkarte, Stadtplan 6
March [mɑ:tʃ] März 5
market ['mɑ:kɪt] Markt 5
°**marriage** ['mærɪdʒ] Hochzeit, Ehe
marry ['mæri] heiraten 7: 1 (13)
mask [mɑ:sk] Maske 7: 2 (26)
°**match** [mætʃ] (passend) zusammenfügen **match with/to** zuordnen
match [mætʃ] Spiel, Wettkampf 6
material [mə'tɪəriəl] Stoff; Material 7: 2 (36)
maths [mæθs] Mathe(matik) 5
May [meɪ] Mai 5
may [meɪ] dürfen 5 **May I ...?** Darf ich ...? 5
maybe ['meɪbi] vielleicht 6
me [mi:] mich; mir 5 **It's me.** Ich bin's. 5
meal [mi:l] Mahlzeit, Essen 5
mean [mi:n], **meant, meant** bedeuten; sagen wollen 6
meaning ['mi:nɪŋ] Bedeutung 7: 5 (86)

meant [ment] *siehe* **mean**
meat [miːt] Fleisch 5
meatball ['miːtbɔːl] Fleischbällchen, Frikadelle 6
media ['miːdiə] Medien 6
°mediation [miːdi'eɪʃn] Vermittlung, Sprachmittlung
medicine ['medsɪn] *(no pl)* Medizin; Medikament(e) 6
meet [miːt], **met, met** kennenlernen; (sich) treffen 5 **Nice to meet you.** Freut mich, dich/euch/Sie kennenzulernen. 5
°member ['membə] Mitglied
meme [miːm] Internet-Mem, Internetphänomen 7: 5 (79)
memorial (to sb./sth.) [mə'mɔːriəl] Denkmal (für jn./etwas), Gedenkstätte 7: 4 (58/59)
Memorial Day [mə'mɔːriəl deɪ] Gedenktag *(zur Erinnerung an Kriegsgefallene und -opfer)* 6
men [men] *Plural von* **man** 5
°mental ['mentl] geistig, psychisch, seelisch
°mental health [mentl 'helθ] psychische/seelische Gesundheit
mentor ['mentə]:
1. betreuen *(als Mentor/in)* 7: 4 (70)
2. Mentor/in *(Ratgeber/in)* 7: 4 (70)
menu ['menjuː] Speisekarte 5
message ['mesɪdʒ]:
1. Nachricht, Mitteilung 5 **message in a bottle** Flaschenpost 6
°2. Botschaft *(Mitteilung)*
met [met] *siehe* **meet**
metal ['metl] Metall 7: 3 (44)
metre ['miːtə] Meter 6
mice [maɪs] *Plural von* **mouse** 5
middle ['mɪdl] Mitte 5 **in the middle** in der Mitte 5
might [maɪt]: **you might find ...** du könntest ... finden, vielleicht findest du ... 7: 4 (66)
milk [mɪlk] Milch 5
million ['mɪljən] Million 6
mime [maɪm] vorspielen, pantomimisch darstellen 7: 2 (28)
°minced beef [mɪnst 'biːf] Rinderhackfleisch
mind [maɪnd]: **Mind the gap ...** Achten Sie auf den Abstand ... 6 **I don't mind doing sth.** Es macht mir nichts aus, etwas zu tun. 6 **Never mind him.** Kümmer dich nicht um ihn. / Er braucht dich nicht zu interessieren. 5 **Never mind.** (Das) macht nichts. / Nicht (so) schlimm. 5
mind [maɪnd]: **change your mind** seine Meinung ändern 7: 5 (83)
mind map ['maɪnd mæp] Gedankenkarte, Wörternetz, Mindmap 5
mine [maɪn] meine, meiner, meins 6
minute ['mɪnɪt] Minute 5 **Wait a minute.** Warte mal. / Einen Moment. 5
mirror ['mɪrə] Spiegel 7: 1 (20)
miss [mɪs]:
1. vermissen 6 **miss doing sth.** vermissen, etwas zu tun 6
2. auslassen 6
3. verpassen 6
°mistake [mɪ'steɪk] Fehler
mix [mɪks] (ver)mischen 5
mobile (phone) [məʊbaɪl 'fəʊn] Handy 5
model ['mɒdl] (Foto-)Modell 5
modern ['mɒdn] modern 6
mom [mɒm] *(AE)* Mama, Mutti 5
moment ['məʊmənt] Moment 5 **at the moment** im Moment, zurzeit 5
Monday ['mʌndeɪ], ['mʌndi] Montag 5
money ['mʌni] Geld 5
monk [mʌŋk] Mönch 6
monster ['mɒnstə] Monster, Ungeheuer 6
month [mʌnθ] Monat 5
monument ['mɒnjumənt] Monument, Denkmal 7: 4 (58/59)
moor [mɔː] Heide(land); Moor 6
more [mɔː] mehr 6 **more than** mehr als 6
morning ['mɔːnɪŋ] Morgen 5 **Good morning.** Guten Morgen. 5 **in the morning** morgens, am Morgen 5
most [məʊst]: **the most ...** die meisten ...; am meisten 5
mother ['mʌðə] Mutter 5
mountain ['maʊntən] Berg 6
mouse, *pl* **mice** [maʊs], [maɪs] Maus 5
mouth [maʊθ] Mund 6
move [muːv] (sich) bewegen; *(etwas)* verschieben, verlegen, versetzen 5 **move (to)** (um)ziehen (nach); *(Schule)* wechseln (auf/zu) 5
movement ['muːvmənt] Bewegung 7: 4 (68)
movie ['muːvi] Film, Spielfilm 6
movie theater ['muːvi θɪətə] *(AE)* Kino 6
Mr ... ['mɪstə] Herr ... 5
Mrs ... ['mɪsɪz] Frau ... *(Anrede für verheiratete Frauen)* 5
Ms ... [mɪz], [məz] Frau ... *(allgemeine Anrede für Frauen)* 5
much [mʌtʃ] viel 5 **How much is/are ...?** Was (Wie viel) kostet/kosten ...? 5 **How much?** Wie viel? 5
muffin ['mʌfɪn] Muffin *(kleiner runder Kuchen)* 5
multicultural [mʌlti'kʌltʃərəl] multikulturell 6
multiplayer [mʌlti'pleɪə] Mehrspieler- 7: 5 (82)
mum [mʌm] Mama, Mutti 5
museum [mju'ziːəm] Museum 5
music ['mjuːzɪk] Musik 5
musical ['mjuːzɪkl]:
1. musikalisch 6
2. Musical 6
musician [mju'zɪʃn] Musiker/in 7: 4 (58/59)
must [mʌst] müssen 5 **mustn't do** nicht tun dürfen 7: 2 (33)
my [maɪ] mein/e 5
myself [maɪ'self] ich/mich/mir (selbst) 6

N

name [neɪm] Name 5 **call sb. names** jn. beschimpfen 7: 5 (89) **first name** Vorname 7: 1 (15) **last name** Nachname, Familienname 7: 1 (15) **What's your name?** Wie heißt du? 5
name day ['neɪm deɪ] Namenstag 5
national ['næʃnəl] national, National- 6
national day [næʃnəl 'deɪ] Nationalfeiertag 7: 4 (63)
national park [næʃnəl 'pɑːk] Nationalpark 6
nationality [næʃə'næləti] Nationalität 6
near [nɪə] nahe (bei), in der Nähe von 5
nearest ['nɪərəst]: **the nearest ...** der/die/das nächstgelegene ... 7: 4 (65)
nearly ['nɪəli] fast 5
need [niːd] brauchen, benötigen 5 **need to do sth.** etwas tun müssen 6 **needn't do** nicht tun brauchen 7: 2 (33)
negative ['negətɪv] negativ 7: 5 (89)
neighbour ['neɪbə] Nachbar/in 5

nervous ['nɜːvəs] nervös, aufgeregt 5
net [net] Netz *(Sport)* 7: 1 (10)
netball ['netbɔːl] Korbball 5
never ['nevə] nie, niemals 5 **Never mind.** (Das) macht nichts. / Nicht (so) schlimm. 5
new [njuː] neu 5
°New World [njuː 'wɜːld] Neue Welt *(europäische Bezeichnung für Amerika nach der Entdeckung durch Kolumbus 1492)*
news [njuːz] Nachrichten 6
newspaper ['njuːzpeɪpə] (Tages-)Zeitung 6
next [nekst] nächste(r, s) 5 **Next ...** Als Nächstes ... 7: 2 (30) **the next day/morning** am nächsten Tag/Morgen 6
next to ['nekst tə] neben 5
nice [naɪs] nett, schön 5
°nickname ['nɪkneɪm] Spitzname
niece [niːs] Nichte 6
night [naɪt] Nacht 5 **at night** nachts, in der Nacht 5 **Good night.** Gute Nacht. 5 **that night** in jener Nacht 6
nine [naɪn] neun 5
no [nəʊ]:
1. nein 5
2. kein, keine; verboten 5
no one ['nəʊ wʌn] niemand 5
nobody ['nəʊbədi] niemand 5
nod [nɒd]:
1. **nod (your head)** (mit dem Kopf) nicken 7: 3 (54) **nod to sb.** jm. zunicken 7: 3 (54)
2. **nod (of your head)** (Kopf-)Nicken 7: 3 (54)
noise [nɔɪz] Geräusch; Lärm 5
noisy ['nɔɪzi] laut, voller Lärm 5
°non- [nɒn] Nicht-
none [nʌn] keine(r, s) 7: 5 (89)
noodles *(pl)* [nuːdlz] Nudeln 5
normal ['nɔːml] normal 7: 1 (20)
Norman ['nɔːmən] Normanne/ Normannin; normannisch 7: 3 (42/43)
north [nɔːθ] Norden; nördlich; Nord- 6 **north-east** Nordosten, nordöstlich 6 **north-west** Nordwesten, nordwestlich 6
northbound ['nɔːθbaʊnd] in Richtung Norden *(Zug, Bus)* 6
northern ['nɔːðən] Nord-, nördlich 7: 4 (62)
nose [nəʊz] Nase 6
not [nɒt] nicht 5 **I'm not a boy.** Ich bin kein Junge. 5
note [nəʊt] Notiz; kurzer Brief 7: 2 (24/25) **make notes** (sich) Notizen machen *(zur Vorbereitung)* 7: 2 (24/25) **take notes** (sich) Notizen machen *(beim Lesen oder Zuhören)* 7: 2 (24/25)
notebook ['nəʊtbʊk] Notizbuch 7: 1 (20)
nothing ['nʌθɪŋ] nichts 6
notice ['nəʊtɪs] (be)merken 7: 1 (21)
notification [nəʊtɪfɪ'keɪʃn] Benachrichtigung, Mitteilung 7: 5 (88)
November [nəʊ'vembə] November 5
now [naʊ] nun, jetzt 5
nowhere ['nəʊweə] nirgendwo(hin) 7: 5 (88)
number ['nʌmbə] Zahl, Ziffer, Nummer 5 **number of** Anzahl (an) 6 **phone number** Telefonnummer 5
nurse [nɜːs] Krankenpfleger/in 6
nut [nʌt] Nuss 7: 1 (10)

O

object ['ɒbdʒɪkt] Objekt, Gegenstand 7: 3 (45)
ocean ['əʊʃn] Ozean 6
o'clock [ə'klɒk]: **at 7 o'clock** um 7 Uhr 5
October [ɒk'təʊbə] Oktober 5
of [ɒv], [əv] von 5 **a cup of ...** eine Tasse ... 5 **the name of the school** der Name der Schule 5
of course [əv 'kɔːs] natürlich, selbstverständlich 7: 1 (21)
off [ɒf]: **go off** klingeln *(Wecker)*; losgehen *(Alarm, Waffe)* 7: 5 (88)
offer ['ɒfə]:
1. (an)bieten 7: 5 (83)
2. Angebot 7: 5 (83)
offline [ɒf'laɪn] offline, nicht übers/ im Internet 7: 5 (76/77)
off-peak [ɒf 'piːk] außerhalb der Stoßzeiten 6
often ['ɒfn], ['ɒftən] oft 5
oh [əʊ] Null *(im gesprochenen Englisch)* 5
oil [ɔɪl] Öl 6
oil rig ['ɔɪl rɪg] Ölbohrinsel 6
oily ['ɔɪli] ölig 6
OK [əʊ'keɪ] okay, gut, in Ordnung 5 **I'm OK.** Es geht mir gut. 5
old [əʊld] alt 5
°ollie ['ɒli] Ollie (Sprung mit dem Skateboard)
°Olympic [ə'lɪmpɪk] olympisch
Olympics [ə'lɪmpɪks] olympische Spiele 5
on [ɒn] auf 5 **on holiday** im/in den Urlaub 5 **on the beach** am Strand 5 **on the bus** im Bus 5 **on TV** im Fernsehen 6 **on Wednesday** am Mittwoch 5 **be on** gezeigt werden *(Kino, Fernsehen)*, stattfinden 6
one [wʌn]:
1. eins 5
one day eines Tages 6
2. **the nearest one** der/die/das Nächstgelegene 7: 4 (65) **the only one** der/die Einzige 7: 2 (31)
°onion ['ʌnjən] Zwiebel
online [ɒn'laɪn] online, Online- 5
only ['əʊnli]:
1. nur, bloß 5
2. erst 5
3. **the only student** der einzige Schüler / die einzige Schülerin 7: 2 (31)
onto ['ɒntu], ['ɒntə]: **onto the rocks** auf die Felsen (hinauf) 6
open ['əʊpən]:
1. öffnen; aufschlagen *(Buch)* 5
2. sich öffnen, aufgehen 6
3. offen, geöffnet 5
opera ['ɒpərə] Oper 6
opinion [ə'pɪnjən] Meinung 6 **in my opinion** meiner Meinung nach 6
or [ɔː] oder; sonst 5
orange ['ɒrɪndʒ]:
1. orange(farben) 5
2. Orange, Apfelsine 5
orange juice ['ɒrɪndʒ dʒuːs] Orangensaft 5
orchestra ['ɔːkɪstrə] Orchester 7: 1 (8/9)
°order ['ɔːdə] Reihenfolge **put in the right order** in die richtige Reihenfolge bringen
order sth. ['ɔːdə] etwas bestellen 5
ordinary ['ɔːdnri] normal, gewöhnlich 7: 1 (21)
other ['ʌðə] andere(r, s) 5 **the others** die anderen 5
ought to ['ɔːt tə]: **you ought to switch off ...** du solltest ... ausschalten 7: 5 (84)
our ['aʊə] unser/e 5
ours [ɑːz], ['aʊəz] unserer, unsere, unseres 6
ourselves [aʊə'selvz] wir/uns selbst 6
out (of ...) [aʊt] aus, heraus/hinaus; aus ... (heraus/hinaus) 5
outdoor ['aʊtdɔː]: **outdoor (sport)** (Sport) für draußen / im Freien 5 **outdoor swimming pool** Freibad 5

out-of-school activities [aʊt əv 'sku:l] Aktivitäten außerhalb der Schule 7: 1 (14)
outside [aʊt'saɪd] draußen; nach draußen 5 **outside (the UK)** außerhalb (des Vereinigten Königreiches) 6
oven ['ʌvn] Backofen 6
over ['əʊvə] über, hinüber 6 **over here** hier herüber; hier drüben 6 **over there** da drüben, dort drüben 6 **So it's car over me?** Also das Auto ist dir wichtiger als ich? 7: 5 (83)
°overeating [əʊvər'i:tɪŋ] übermäßiges Essen
owe sb. sth. [əʊ] jm. etwas schulden, schuldig sein 6
own [əʊn]:
1. **own sth.** etwas besitzen 7: 4 (61)
2. eigene(r, s) 7: 1 (10)
my own room mein/ein eigenes Zimmer 7: 1 (10)
owner ['əʊnə] Besitzer/in 7: 4 (61)
oyster ['ɔɪstə] Auster 7: 4 (66)

P

Pacific Ocean [pəsɪfɪk 'əʊʃn] Pazifischer Ozean, Pazifik 6
°pads *(pl)* [pædz] Protektoren *(z. B. für Knie/Ellbogen beim Sport)*
page (= p.) [peɪdʒ] (Buch-, Heft-)Seite 5 **front page** Titelseite 6
paid [peɪd] *siehe* **pay**
pair [peə] Paar 6
pan [pæn] Pfanne 6
pants *(pl) (AE)* [pænts] (eine) Hose 6 **baggy pants** *(pl)* Schlabberhose 6
paper ['peɪpə] Papier 6 **piece of paper** Stück Papier, Zettel 6
parade [pə'reɪd] Parade, Umzug 6
paragraph ['pærəgrɑ:f] (Text-)Abschnitt 7: 2 (27)
paraphrase ['pærəfreɪz] umschreiben, mit anderen Worten sagen 7: 1 (18)
parents *(pl)* ['peərənts] Eltern 5
park [pɑ:k] Park 5
parking lot ['pɑ:kɪŋ lɒt] *(AE)* Parkplatz 6
°parkour [pɑ:'kʊə] Parkour *(möglichst effiziente Fortbewegungsart von Punkt A zu Punkt B nur mit den Fähigkeiten des eigenen Körpers, z. B. in der Stadt)*
parliament ['pɑ:ləmənt] Parlament 6
part (of) [pɑ:t] Teil (von) 6
partner ['pɑ:tnə] Partner/in 5
party ['pɑ:ti] Party 5
passenger ['pæsɪndʒə] Passagier/in, Fahrgast 6
passport ['pɑ:spɔ:t] (Reise-)Pass 6
past [pɑ:st]:
1. **half past 6** halb 7 5 **quarter past 6** viertel nach 6 5
2. **past (the wood)** (am Wald) vorbei 6
past [pɑ:st] Vergangenheit 6
pasta ['pæstə] Pasta *(italienische Bezeichnung für Teigwaren)* 5
path [pɑ:θ] Weg, Pfad 6
patient ['peɪʃnt] geduldig 7: 4 (68)
pattern ['pætn] *(wiederkehrendes)* Muster, Schema 7: 4 (61)
pavement ['peɪvmənt] Gehweg, Bürgersteig 6
pay (for sth.) [peɪ], **paid, paid** (etwas be)zahlen 6
PE (physical education) [pi: 'i:], [fɪzɪkl edʒu'keɪʃn] (Schul-)Sport 5
pea [pi:] Erbse 6
peace [pi:s] Frieden 7: 2 (26)
°peanut butter ['pi:nʌt] Erdnussbutter
pen [pen] Kugelschreiber, Stift; Füller 5
pence [pens] Pence *(Plural von penny)* 5
pencil ['pensl] Bleistift 5
pencil case ['pensl keɪs] Federmäppchen 5
pencil sharpener ['pensl ʃɑ:pnə] Bleistiftspitzer 5
penknife, *pl* **penknives** ['pennaɪf], ['pennaɪvz] Taschenmesser 6
penny (= p) ['peni], [pi:] Penny *(kleinste britische Münze)* 5
people *(pl)* ['pi:pl] Leute, Menschen 5
pepper ['pepə]:
1. Paprika, Peperoni 6
2. Pfeffer 6
per cent (%) [pə 'sent] Prozent 5
°perform [pə'fɔ:m] auftreten *(Künstler/in)*
period ['pɪəriəd] (Unterrichts-)Stunde 6
person ['pɜ:sn] Person 5
pet [pet] (Haus-)Tier 5
petrol ['petrəl] Benzin 6
petrol station ['petrəl steɪʃn] Tankstelle 6
phone [fəʊn]:
1. anrufen, telefonieren 6
2. Telefon 5
answer the phone ans Telefon gehen 7: 1 (21) **on the phone** am Telefon 5
phone call ['fəʊn kɔ:l] *(oft auch kurz:* call*)* (Telefon-)Anruf 7: 1 (10)
phone number ['fəʊn nʌmbə] Telefonnummer 5
photo ['fəʊtəʊ] Foto 5 **in the photo** auf dem Foto 5 **take a photo** ein Foto machen 5
photographer [fə'tɒgrəfə] Fotograf/in 6
phrase [freɪz] Ausdruck, (Rede-)Wendung 7: 1 (18)
piano [pi'ænəʊ] Klavier 5
pick sth. up [pɪk] etwas aufheben *(vom Boden)*, etwas hochheben 6
picnic ['pɪknɪk] Picknick 6 **have a picnic** ein Picknick machen 6
picture ['pɪktʃə] Bild 5
pie chart ['paɪ tʃɑ:t] Tortendiagramm 6
piece [pi:s] Stück, Teil 6 **piece of paper** Stück Papier 6
pigeon ['pɪdʒɪn] Taube 6
°pilot ['paɪlət] Pilot/in
pink [pɪŋk] rosa 5
pirate ['paɪrət] Pirat/in 5
pizza ['pi:tsə] Pizza 5
place [pleɪs] Ort, Platz 5
°placemat ['pleɪsmæt] Platzdeckchen
plan [plæn]:
1. planen 5
plan to do sth. planen, etwas zu tun 5
2. Plan 5
plane [pleɪn] Flugzeug 5
plastic ['plæstɪk] Plastik, Kunststoff 7: 5 (85)
plate [pleɪt] Teller 7: 3 (48)
platform ['plætfɔ:m] Bahnsteig 6 **at platform 4** auf Gleis 4 6
play [pleɪ]:
1. spielen 5 **play sport(s)** Sport treiben 7: 2 (24/25) **play the piano / the guitar** Klavier / Gitarre spielen 5
2. Schauspiel, Theaterstück 6
player ['pleɪə] Spieler/in 5
playing field ['pleɪɪŋ fi:ld] Sportplatz 7: 1 (8/9)
please [pli:z] bitte 5
pleased [pli:zd] froh, erfreut, zufrieden 7: 4 (62) **Pleased to meet you.** Freut mich Sie kennenzulernen. 7: 4 (62)
plot [plɒt] Handlung(sverlauf) *(z. B. Film/Geschichte)* 7: 2 (30)
plough [plaʊ]:
1. Pflug 7: 3 (48)
2. pflügen 7: 3 (48)

plug [plʌg]:
1. Stecker 7: 1 (20)
2. plug sth. in etwas einstecken, anschließen 7: 1 (20)
plum [plʌm] Pflaume 5
pm [piː'em]: **7 pm** 7 Uhr nachmittags/abends, 19 Uhr 6
poem ['pəʊɪm] Gedicht 5
point [pɔɪnt]:
1. Punkt 6
2. Komma *(Dezimalzeichen)* 6
point [pɔɪnt]: **point (at/to)** zeigen, deuten (auf) 6 **point sth. out** auf etwas hinweisen, aufmerksam machen 7: 3 (52)
police *(pl)* [pə'liːs] Polizei 7: 1 (20)
police officer [pə'liːs ɒfɪsə] Polizeibeamter/-beamtin 6
polite [pə'laɪt] höflich 7: 1 (19)
pony ['pəʊni] Pony 6
pool (= swimming pool) [puːl] (Schwimm-)Bad 5
poor [pɔː], [pʊə] arm 6
pop (music) ['pɒp mjuːzɪk] Pop(musik) 5
pop star ['pɒp stɑː] Popstar 5
popcorn ['pɒpkɔːn] Popcorn 6
popular ['pɒpjələ] beliebt, populär 5
population [pɒpju'leɪʃn] Bevölkerung, Einwohner(zahl) 7: 4 (60)
porridge ['pɒrɪdʒ] Haferbrei 6
positive ['pɒzətɪv] positiv 7: 5 (89)
°possible ['pɒsəbl] möglich
post [pəʊst]:
1. Post [pəʊst] *(Briefe etc.)* Post 5
2. Post *(Eintrag in Blog oder sozialen Medien)* 7: 5 (79)
3. posten *(im Internet veröffentlichen)* 7: 5 (79)
post office ['pəʊst ɒfɪs] Post(amt) 5
postcard ['pəʊstkɑːd] Postkarte 6
postcode ['pəʊstkəʊd] Postleitzahl 7: 5 (87)
poster ['pəʊstə] Poster 5
potato, *pl* **potatoes** [pə'teɪtəʊ] Kartoffel 5
potluck (dinner) [pɒt'lʌk], [pɒtlʌk 'dɪnə] *(AE) (Abend-)Essen, zu dem jeder etwas mitbringt* 7: 2 (34)
pound [paʊnd]:
1. Pfund *(Gewichtseinheit; GB: 454 Gramm)* 7: 3 (48)
2. (£) Pfund *(britische Wärung)* 5
pour [pɔː] strömen; gießen, schütten 7: 5 (88)
power ['paʊə] Kraft, Macht 7: 2 (26)
power line ['paʊə laɪn] Stromleitung 6
practice ['præktɪs]:
1. Übung(en) 6
2. practice *(AE)* üben 6
practise ['præktɪs] üben 6
°prank [præŋk] Streich
pray [preɪ] beten 7: 4 (63)
prayer [preə] Gebet 7: 4 (63)
precious ['preʃəs] wertvoll, kostbar 7: 3 (44)
precious metal [preʃəs 'metl] Edelmetall 7: 3 (44)
prefer sth. to sth. [prɪ'fɜː] etwas einer Sache vorziehen, etwas lieber tun/haben als etwas 7: 5 (76/77) **I'd prefer ...** ich würde ... vorziehen 7: 5 (76/77)
prepare (for) [prɪ'peə] vorbereiten; sich vorbereiten (auf) 7: 1 (23)
present [prɪ'zent] präsentieren, vorstellen 6
present ['preznt] Geschenk 5 **wedding present** Hochzeitsgeschenk 6
presentation [prezn'teɪʃn] Referat, Präsentation 6 **give a presentation** ein Referat halten 6
president ['prezɪdənt] Präsident/in 7: 2 (36)
pressure ['preʃə] Druck 7: 5 (88) **put pressure on sb.** jn. unter Druck setzen 7: 5 (88)
price [praɪs] (Kauf-)Preis 6
priest [priːst] Priester/in 7: 4 (63)
prince [prɪns] Prinz 7: 2 (26)
°princess [prɪn'ses] Prinzessin
principal ['prɪnsəpl] Rektor/in, Schulleiter/in 5
°print sth. (out) [prɪnt] etwas (aus) drucken
private ['praɪvət] privat; persönlich 6
prize [praɪz] Preis, Gewinn 6
probably ['prɒbəbli] wahrscheinlich 6
problem ['prɒbləm] Problem 6
°product ['prɒdʌkt] Produkt
profile ['prəʊfaɪl] Profil; Beschreibung, Portrait 7: 4 (70)
profit ['prɒfɪt] Gewinn *(Profit)* 7: 2 (36) **make a profit** Gewinn/Profit machen 7: 2 (36)
°program ['prəʊgræm] (Computer-)Programm
programme ['prəʊgræm] (Fernseh-)Sendung 6
project ['prɒdʒekt] Projekt 5
pronounce [prə'naʊns] aussprechen 7: 5 (86)
pronunciation [prənʌnsi'eɪʃn] Aussprache 7: 5 (86)
protect (from/against) [prə'tekt] (be)schützen (vor) 7: 5 (86)
Protestant ['prɒtɪstənt] Protestant/in; protestantisch, evangelisch 7: 4 (62)
prove [pruːv] nachweisen, beweisen 6
pub [pʌb] Kneipe 7: 4 (58/59)
public ['pʌblɪk] öffentlich 6
public holiday [pʌblɪk 'hɒlədeɪ] öffentlicher/gesetzlicher Feiertag 6
pug [pʌg] Mops *(Hund)* 7: 5 (80)
pullover ['pʊləʊvə] Pullover 5
purple ['pɜːpl] violett, lila 5
put [pʊt], **put, put** *(etwas wohin)* tun, legen, stellen, stecken 5 **put away** weglegen, zur Seite legen 6 **put in** hineinlegen 5 **put up your hand** sich melden, aufzeigen 6 **°put in the right order** in die richtige Reihenfolge bringen
°puzzle ['pʌzl] Rätsel
puzzled ['pʌzld] verwundert 6

Q

quake [kweɪk] *(infml)* Erdbeben 6
quality ['kwɒləti] Qualität, Qualitäts-; Eigenschaft 7: 5 (78) **be better quality** von besserer Qualität sein 7: 5 (78)
quarter ['kwɔːtə] Viertel 5 **quarter past 6** viertel nach 6 5 **quarter to 7** viertel vor 7 5
queen [kwiːn] Königin 5
question ['kwestʃən] Frage 5
quick [kwɪk] schnell 7: 2 (26)
quiet ['kwaɪət] ruhig, still, leise 5
quite [kwaɪt] ziemlich, ganz 6
quiz, *pl* **quizzes** [kwɪz], ['kwɪzɪz]:
1. Quiz 5
2. Test 7: 1 (21)

R

rabbit ['ræbɪt] Kaninchen 5
°racing ['reɪsɪŋ] Rennsport, Rennen
°radio ['reɪdiəʊ] Radio
raft [rɑːft] Floß 6
rain [reɪn]:
1. Regen 5
2. regnen 5
rain jacket ['reɪn dʒækɪt] Regenjacke 6
rainy ['reɪni] regnerisch 5
ramp [ræmp] Rampe 5
ran [ræn] *siehe* **run**
rang [ræŋ] *siehe* **ring**
°rank [ræŋk] einstufen, anordnen
rap [ræp] Rap 5
raw [rɔː] roh 6

react (to) [ri'ækt] reagieren (auf) 7: 5 (83)
read [red] *siehe* **read**
read [ri:d], **read, read** lesen 5 °**read out** (laut) vorlesen
reader ['ri:də] Leser/in 7: 5 (88)
ready ['redi] fertig, bereit 5 **Get ready.** Bereite dich vor. 5
real [rɪəl] echt, wirklich 6 **in real life** im echten Leben 7: 2 (26)
reality [ri'ælɪti] Realität, Wirklichkeit 6 **reality show** Reality-Show 6
real-life [rɪəl 'laɪf] real *(aus dem echten Leben)* 7: 2 (27)
really ['ri:əli], ['rɪəli] wirklich 5
reason ['ri:zn] Grund, Begründung 6 **for this reason** aus diesem Grund 6
recently ['ri:sntli] in letzter Zeit, neulich 6
recess [rɪ'ses] *(AE)* Pause 6
recipe ['resəpi] (Koch-)Rezept 6
recommend sth. (to sb.) [rekə'mend] (jm.) etwas empfehlen 7: 4 (69)
°**record** [rɪ'kɔ:d] aufnehmen, aufzeichnen
record ['rekɔ:d] Schallplatte 7: 5 (89)
record deal ['rekɔ:d di:l] Plattenvertrag 7: 5 (89)
°**recording** [rɪ'kɔ:dɪŋ] Aufnahme
recycle [ri:'saɪkl] recyceln, wiederverwerten 7: 5 (85)
recycling [rɪ'saɪklɪŋ] Recycling 7: 5 (85)
red [red] rot 5
red deer [red 'dɪə] Rotwild 6
refugee [refju'dʒi:] Flüchtling 7: 1 (16)
registration [redʒɪ'streɪʃn] *Anwesenheitskontrolle und Ankündigung aktueller Ereignisse vor dem Unterricht* 5
°**regular** ['regjələ] regelmäßig; normal
relationship [rɪ'leɪʃnʃɪp] Beziehung, Verhältnis 7: 5 (89) **be in a relationship with sb.** mit jm. eine Beziehung haben 7: 5 (89)
relax [rɪ'læks] sich entspannen 7: 2 (24/25)
remember [rɪ'membə]:
1. daran denken, nicht vergessen 5
remember to do sth. daran denken, etwas zu tun 5
2. sich erinnern an 5
remember doing sth. sich daran erinnern, etwas getan zu haben 5
repeat [rɪ'pi:t] wiederholen 6 **Repeat after me.** Sprich/Sprecht mir nach. 6
report [rɪ'pɔ:t]:
1. Bericht, Referat 6
2. **report (on)** berichten (über) 6
reporter [rɪ'pɔ:tə] Reporter/in 7: 2 (26)
research [rɪ'sɜ:tʃ] Forschung(en), Recherche(n) 6 **do research** recherchieren 6
rest [rest] Rest 7: 1 (20)
restaurant ['restrɒnt] Restaurant 5 **at a restaurant** in einem Restaurant 5
result [rɪ'zʌlt] Ergebnis 6 **as a result** folglich, demzufolge 6
review [rɪ'vju:]:
1. Besprechung, Rezension, Kritik 7: 4 (69)
2. besprechen, rezensieren; überprüfen 7: 4 (69)
revise [rɪ'vaɪz] *(Lernstoff)* wiederholen 7: 5 (86)
revision [rɪ'vɪʒn] Wiederholung *(von Lernstoff)* 7: 5 (86)
rice [raɪs] Reis 5
rich [rɪtʃ] reich 5
ridden ['rɪdn] *siehe* **ride**
ride [raɪd], **rode, ridden** reiten 5 **ride a bike** mit dem Fahrrad fahren 5 **ride a horse** ein Pferd reiten 5
rig [rɪg]: **oil rig** Ölbohrinsel 6
right [raɪt]:
1. richtig 5
be right Recht haben 6
2. rechts; nach rechts 5
on the right rechts, auf der rechten Seite 5
right [raɪt] Recht 7: 5 (89)
ring [rɪŋ] Ring 6
ring [rɪŋ], **rang, rung** läuten, klingeln 7: 1 (21)
rink [rɪŋk]: **(skating) rink** Schlittschuhbahn 5
river ['rɪvə] Fluss 6
road [rəʊd] Straße *(Landstraße zwischen Orten; Straße in Orten)* 6
roast meat [rəʊst 'mi:t] Braten 6
roasted [rəʊstɪd] gebraten, geröstet 6
rock [rɒk]:
1. Rock(musik) 5
2. Felsen 6
°3. Zuckerstange
°**rock and roll** [rɒk ən 'rəʊl] Rock and Roll *(Musikrichtung)*
rode [rəʊd] *siehe* **ride**
°**role** [rəʊl] Rolle *(Film, Theater)*
°**role-play** ['rəʊl pleɪ]:
1. Rollenspiel
2. **role-play sth.** etwas in einem Rollenspiel darstellen
roll [rəʊl] rollen; (sich) verdrehen *(Augen)* 7: 4 (68) **roll your eyes** die Augen verdrehen 7: 4 (68)
°**roller skate** ['rəʊlə skeɪt] Rollschuh
Roman ['rəʊmən] Römer/in; römisch 7: 3 (42/43)
room [ru:m], [rʊm] Raum, Zimmer 5
roommate ['ru:mmeɪt] Zimmergenosse/-genossin 7: 1 (8/9)
root [ru:t] Wurzel 7: 4 (61)
round [raʊnd]:
1. rund 7: 3 (48)
2. Runde 7: 3 (48)
3. **round …** um (… herum), in … umher 7: 3 (48)
turn round (sich) umdrehen 5
royal ['rɔɪəl] königlich 7: 3 (53)
RSVP [ɑ:r es vi: 'pi] um Antwort wird gebeten 5
rubber ['rʌbə] Radiergummi 5
rubbish ['rʌbɪʃ] (Haus-)Müll, Abfall 5
°**ruby red** [ru:bi 'red] Rubinrot
rucksack ['rʌksæk] *(BE)* Rucksack 6
rude [ru:d] unhöflich, frech 7: 3 (55)
rug [rʌg] Teppich, Läufer 7: 3 (54)
rugby ['rʌgbi] Rugby *(Ballsportart)* 5
rule [ru:l] Regel 6
ruler ['ru:lə] Lineal 5
run [rʌn], **ran, run** rennen, laufen 5 **run after sb.** jm. nachlaufen 6
rung [rʌŋ] *siehe* **ring**

S

sad [sæd] traurig 5
sadness ['sædnəs] Traurigkeit 7: 5 (89)
safe [seɪf] sicher *(gefahrlos)* 6
said [sed] *siehe* **say**
sail [seɪl] segeln, *(mit dem Schiff)* fahren 5
salad ['sæləd] Salat *(als Gericht oder Beilage)* 5
salt [sɔ:lt] Salz 6
salty ['sɔ:lti] salzig 6
same [seɪm]: **the same** gleich; derselbe/dieselbe/dasselbe; dieselben 5
sand [sænd] Sand 6
°**sandpaper** ['sændpeɪpə] Schmirgelpapier
sandwich ['sænwɪtʃ], ['sænwɪdʒ] Sandwich 5

sang [sæŋ] *siehe* **sing**
sat [sæt] *siehe* **sit**
Saturday ['sætədeɪ], ['sætədi] Samstag 5
sauce [sɔːs] Soße 5
°**saucer** ['sɔːsə] Untertasse
sausage ['sɒsɪdʒ] (Brat-, Bock-) Würstchen, Wurst 6
save [seɪv]:
1. retten 6
2. sparen 6
saw [sɔː] *siehe* **see**
Saxon ['sæksn] Sachse/Sächsin; sächsisch 7: 3 (42/43)
say [seɪ], **said, said** sagen 5 **Say hi to everyone.** Grüß/t alle. 7: 1 (10) **say sorry to sb.** sich bei jm. entschuldigen 5 **it says that ...** es (be)sagt, dass ... 5
scan (a text for) [skæn] (einen Text) überfliegen (nach), absuchen (nach) 7: 2 (27)
scared [skeəd] ängstlich, verängstigt 5 **be scared (of)** Angst haben (vor) 5
scarf, *pl* **scarves** [skɑːf], [skɑːvz] Schal 7: 2 (26)
scary ['skeəri] unheimlich, beängstigend, gruselig 6
scene [siːn] Szene 7: 2 (24/25)
schedule ['skedʒuːl] *(AE)* Stundenplan 6
°**scholarship** ['skɒləʃɪp] Stipendium
school [skuːl] Schule 5 **at school** in der Schule 5
school club [klʌb] AG *(in der Schule)* 5
schoolbag ['skuːlbæg] Schultasche 5
science ['saɪəns] Naturwissenschaft 5
scientist ['saɪəntɪst] (Natur-)Wissenschaftler/in 7: 4 (63)
scooter ['skuːtə] (Motor-)Roller 5
score [skɔː]:
1. erzielen *(Punkt/Tor/Treffer)* 6
2. Spiel-/Punktestand; *(im Spiel/Sport erzielter)* Punkt 6
scrape [skreɪp] kratzen, schaben 7: 3 (48)
screen [skriːn] Bildschirm 6
script [skrɪpt] Drehbuch 7: 2 (24/25)
sea [siː] Meer, (die) See 5
second ['sekənd] zweite(r, s) 5
Secondly, ... ['sekəndli] Zweitens ... 7: 5 (79)
seconds *(pl)* ['sekəndz] Nachschlag 6
secret ['siːkrət]:
1. Geheimnis 7: 1 (10)
2. geheim 7: 1 (10)
in secret im Geheimen 7: 1 (13)
see [siː], **saw, seen** sehen 5 **See you tomorrow.** Bis morgen. 5
seem (to be/do) [siːm] erscheinen; (zu sein / zu tun) scheinen 6
seen [siːn] *siehe* **see**
self-defence [self dɪ'fens] Selbstverteidigung 7: 1 (8/9)
selfie stick ['selfi stɪk] Selfiestick 7: 2 (35)
sell [sel], **sold, sold** verkaufen 5
send [send], **sent, sent** senden, schicken 5
sent [sent] *siehe* **send**
sentence ['sentəns] Satz 5
September [sep'tembə] September 5
series, *pl* **series** ['sɪəriːz] Serie, Sendereihe 6
serious ['sɪəriəs] ernst 6
set [set]: **(tea) set** Set, Garnitur, (Tee-)Service 5
set [set], **set, set** stellen, legen, setzen 7: 2 (32) **set sth. up** etwas einrichten, aufbauen 7: 4 (71) **set the table** den Tisch decken 7: 2 (32)
setting ['setɪŋ] Schauplatz *(z. B. Film/Geschichte)* 7: 2 (30)
settle ['setl] sich niederlassen, sich ansiedeln 7: 3 (42/43)
settler ['setlə] Siedler/in 7: 3 (42/43)
seven ['sevn] sieben 5
several ['sevrəl] mehrere, einige 7: 5 (79)
sew [səʊ], **sewed, sewn** nähen 7: 2 (36)
sewing machine ['səʊɪŋ məʃiːn] Nähmaschine 7: 2 (36)
sewn [səʊn] *siehe* **sew**
shake [ʃeɪk], **shook, shaken:**
1. schütteln 6
2. zittern 7: 3 (48)
shaken ['ʃeɪkən] *siehe* **shake**
shallow ['ʃæləʊ] flach, seicht; oberflächlich 7: 5 (89)
shamrock ['ʃæmrɒk] Kleeblatt 7: 4 (63)
share [ʃeə] teilen 5 **share a room (with ...)** sich ein Zimmer teilen mit ... 5
shark [ʃɑːk] Hai 7: 4 (60)
sharpener ['ʃɑːpnə] Spitzer 5
she [ʃiː] sie *(weibliche Person)* 5
shelf, *pl* **shelves** [ʃelf], [ʃelvz] Regal 5
sheriff ['ʃerɪf] *(AE)* Sheriff 7: 1 (20)
ship [ʃɪp] Schiff 5
shirt [ʃɜːt] Hemd 5
shoe [ʃuː] Schuh 5 **in sb.'s shoes** an jds. Stelle 7: 5 (83)
shook [ʃʊk] *siehe* **shake**
shop [ʃɒp]:
1. Laden, Geschäft 5
°**2. shop for sth.** etwas kaufen (gehen)
shop assistant ['ʃɒp əsɪstənt] Verkäufer/in 5
shopping ['ʃɒpɪŋ] *(das)* Einkaufen 5 **go shopping** einkaufen gehen 5
shopping centre ['ʃɒpɪŋ sentə] Einkaufszentrum 5
shopping list ['ʃɒpɪŋ lɪst] Einkaufsliste 6
short [ʃɔːt]:
1. kurz 5
2. klein *(Personen)* 6
shorts *(pl)* [ʃɔːts] kurze Hose 5
should [ʃʊd]: **we should ...** wir sollten ... 5
shoulder ['ʃəʊldə] Schulter 6
shout [ʃaʊt] rufen 5
show [ʃəʊ]:
1. Show, Vorführung, Aufführung 5
2. show, showed, shown zeigen 7: 1 (10)
shower ['ʃaʊə] Dusche 5 **have a shower** (sich) duschen 5
shown [ʃəʊn] *siehe* **show**
shrug [ʃrʌg]:
1. Achselzucken 7: 4 (68)
2. shrug (your shoulders) mit den Achseln/Schultern zucken 7: 4 (68)
shy [ʃaɪ] scheu, schüchtern 6
sick [sɪk] krank 6 **be sick** sich übergeben 6 **I feel sick.** Mir ist schlecht 6
side [saɪd] Seite *(z. B. Straßenseite)* 7: 3 (45)
side dish ['saɪd dɪʃ] Beilage 6
sidewalk ['saɪdwɔːk] *(AE)* Bürgersteig 6
sight [saɪt]:
1. Anblick, Bild 6
2. Sehenswürdigkeit 6
sightseeing ['saɪtsiːɪŋ] Besichtigungen *(von Sehenswürdigkeiten)* 6
sign [saɪn] Schild, Zeichen 6
sign language ['saɪn læŋgwɪdʒ] Zeichensprache, Gebärdensprache 7: 1 (8/9)
signature ['sɪgnətʃə] Unterschrift 7: 1 (15)
silly ['sɪli] dumm, blöd; albern 7: 5 (78)
silver ['sɪlvə] Silber 7: 3 (45)

similar (to sb./sth.) ['sɪmələ] (jm./einer Sache) ähnlich 7: 4 (58/59)
simple ['sɪmpl] einfach 6
since [sɪns] seit 6
since then [sɪns 'ðen] seitdem 7: 5 (78)
sing [sɪŋ], **sang, sung** singen 5
singer ['sɪŋə] Sänger/in 5
single ['sɪŋgl] Einzel-, einzelne(r, s) 7: 5 (82)
single room [sɪŋgl 'ru:m] Einzelzimmer 7: 5 (82)
Sir [sɜ:] Sir *(britischer Adelstitel)* 5
sister ['sɪstə] Schwester 5
sit [sɪt], **sat, sat:**
1. sitzen; sich setzen 5
sit down sich (hin)setzen 5 **sit up** sich aufsetzen, sich gerade hinsetzen 7: 1 (21)
2. (herum-)stehen, (herum-)liegen 7: 1 (20)
sitcom ['sɪtkɒm] Sitcom, Comedyserie 6
site [saɪt] *(kurz für)* Website; Stelle, Platz, Stätte 7: 5 (78)
situation [sɪtʃu'eɪʃn] Situation 6
six [sɪks] sechs 5
size [saɪz] Größe 5 **What size do you take?** Welche Größe hast du? 5
skate [skeɪts] Skateboard fahren 7: 5 (76/77)
skate park ['skeɪt pɑ:k] Skatepark 7: 5 (76/77)
skateboard ['skeɪtbɔ:d]:
1. Skateboard 7: 5 (76/77)
2. Skateboard fahren 7: 5 (76/77)
skating ['skeɪtɪŋ] Schlittschuhlaufen; (Inline-)Skaten 5
skating rink ['skeɪtɪŋ rɪŋk] Schlittschuhbahn 5
ski [ski:] Ski laufen, Ski fahren 5
skill [skɪl] Fähigkeit, Fertigkeit 7: 4 (70)
skim a text [skɪm] einen Text überfliegen *(um den Inhalt grob zu erfassen)* 7: 4 (60)
skirt [skɜ:t] Rock 5
skyscraper ['skaɪskreɪpə] Wolkenkratzer 6
slave [sleɪv] Sklave, Sklavin 7: 4 (63)
sleep [sli:p]:
1. Schlaf 6
2. **sleep, slept, slept** schlafen 5
sleepless ['sli:pləs] schlaflos 6
slept [slept] *siehe* **sleep**
slide [slaɪd] Dia(-); Folie *(Präsentationssoftware)* 7: 1 (23)
slogan ['sləʊgən] Slogan 7: 1 (20)
sloppy ['slɒpi] schlabberig; nachlässig, schludrig 7: 2 (34)
slow [sləʊ] langsam 5
small [smɔ:l] klein 5
small talk ['smɔ:l tɔ:k] Smalltalk *(oberflächliche, leichte Konversation)* 7: 3 (51)
smart [smɑ:t] schick 5
smartphone ['smɑ:tfəʊn] Smartphone 5
smell [smel]:
1. riechen; schlecht riechen 5
2. Geruch; Gestank 6
smile [smaɪl]:
1. lächeln 5
2. *(ein/das)* Lächeln 5
snack [snæk] Snack, kleine Mahlzeit 6
snake [sneɪk] Schlange 7: 4 (63)
snapshot ['snæpʃɒt] Schnappschuss 7: 4 (58/59)
snow [snəʊ]:
1. Schnee 5
2. schneien 6
snowy ['snəʊi] schneebedeckt; verschneit 5
so [səʊ]:
1. so 6
so many so viele 6
2. also, daher 5
3. **so (that)** sodass 7: 2 (26)
soap [səʊp] Seife 6 **soap (opera)** Seifenoper, Soap 6
soccer ['sɒkə] Fußball 6
social [səʊʃl] sozial
social media *(pl)* [səʊʃl 'mi:diə] soziale Medien 7: 5 (79) **on social media** in den sozialen Medien 7: 5 (79)
°soda bread ['səʊdə bred] Sodabrot *(hergestellt mit Backpulver statt Hefe)*
sofa ['səʊfə] Sofa 7: 2 (33)
soft [sɒft] weich; *(Stimme)* leise 7: 3 (48) **in a soft voice** mit leiser Stimme 7: 3 (48)
sold [səʊld] *siehe* **sell**
soldier ['səʊldʒə] Soldat/in 7: 3 (45)
°solid ['sɒlɪd] fest, solide, stabil
solution (to a problem) [sə'lu:ʃn] Lösung (eines Problems) 7: 5 (88)
some [sʌm], [səm] einige, ein paar; etwas, ein wenig 5 **Would you like some tea/potatoes?** Möchtest du (etwas) Tee / (ein paar) Kartoffeln? 5
somebody ['sʌmbədi] jemand 6
someone ['sʌmwʌn] jemand 6
something ['sʌmθɪŋ] etwas 5
sometimes ['sʌmtaɪmz] manchmal 5
somewhere ['sʌmweə] irgendwo(hin) 6
son [sʌn] Sohn 7: 3 (45)
song [sɒŋ] Lied 5
songwriter ['sɒŋraɪtə] Songwriter/in, Liedermacher/in 6
soon [su:n] bald 5
sore [sɔ:]: **a sore throat** Halsschmerzen 6
sorry ['sɒri]: **Sorry. / I'm sorry.** Tut mir leid. / Entschuldigung. 5 **say sorry to sb.** sich bei jm. entschuldigen 5 **°feel sorry for sb.** Mitleid haben mit jm.
sound [saʊnd]:
1. Geräusch; Klang, Laut 6
2. klingen 6
it sounds fun es klingt, als ob es Spaß macht 6
soundtrack ['saʊndtræk] Filmmusik; Tonspur 7: 2 (31)
soup [su:p] Suppe 6
sour [saʊr] sauer 6
sour cream ['saʊr kri:m] saure Sahne 6
source [sɔ:s] Quelle *(z. B. Website, Text)* 7: 3 (52)
south [saʊθ] Süden; südlich; Süd- 6 **south-east** Südosten, südöstlich 6 **south-west** Südwesten, südwestlich 6
southbound ['saʊθbaʊnd] in Richtung Süden *(Zug, Bus)* 6
southern ['sʌðən] südlich, Süd- 7: 4 (62)
spade [speɪd] Spaten, Schaufel 7: 3 (48)
spaghetti [spə'geti] Spaghetti 6
speak [spi:k], **spoke, spoken** sprechen 5
speaker ['spi:kə] Sprecher/in 7: 3 (52)
special ['speʃl]:
1. besondere(r, s) 5
2. Sonderausgabe *(Magazin)*, Sondersendung *(Fernsehen)* 6
specific [spə'sɪfɪk] bestimmte(r, s), spezielle(r, s); genau, präzise 7: 3 (46)
speech bubble ['spi:tʃ bʌbl] Sprechblase 5
spell [spel] buchstabieren 5
spelling ['spelɪŋ] Schreibweise, Rechtschreibung 5
spend [spend], **spent, spent:**
1. ausgeben 5
spend 235 euros (on) 235 Euro ausgeben (für) 5
2. **spend time** Zeit verbringen 5
spent [spent] *siehe* **spend**
spice [spaɪs] Gewürz 6

spicy ['spaɪsi] würzig 6
spider ['spaɪdə] Spinne 5
spin [spɪn], **spun, spun** (sich) drehen 7: 3 (54)
spoke [spəʊk] *siehe* **speak**
spoken ['spəʊkən] *siehe* **speak**
sponsor ['spɒnsə]:
1. sponsern 7: 5 (78)
2. Sponsor/in 7: 5 (78)
spoon [spu:n] Löffel 7: 4 (67)
sport [spɔ:t] Sport; Sportart 5 **do sport** Sport treiben 5 **play sport(s)** Sport treiben 7: 2 (24/25)
sporty ['spɔ:ti] sportlich 7: 2 (36)
spread (sth.) [spred], **spread, spread** (etwas) verbreiten *(Virus, Krankheit)*; sich ausbreiten 7: 4 (60)
spun [spʌn] *siehe* **spin**
square [skweə] Kästchen, Spielfeld; Platz *(in der Stadt)* 7: 5 (82)
St = Saint [seɪnt] St = Sankt 7: 4 (58/59)
stadium ['steɪdiəm] Stadion 6
stand [stænd], **stood, stood** stehen; sich (hin)stellen 6 **stand up** aufstehen 5 **stand up (straight)** (gerade) stehen; sich (gerade) hinstellen 7: 4 (68)
star [stɑ:]:
1. (Film-/Pop-)Star 5
2. Stern 5
start [stɑ:t]:
1. Anfang, Start 7: 3 (42/43)
2. beginnen, anfangen (mit) 5
start a business ein Geschäft aufmachen, einen Betrieb gründen/eröffnen 7: 2 (36)
starting point ['stɑ:tɪŋ pɔɪnt] Ausgangspunkt 7: 5 (80)
starve [stɑ:v] verhungern 7: 4 (60)
state [steɪt] (Bundes-)Staat 6
°**statement** ['steɪtmənt] Aussage(satz)
station ['steɪʃn] Bahnhof 5
statistics *(pl)* [stə'tɪstɪks] Statistik(en) 7: 5 (86)
statue ['stætʃu:] Statue 7: 4 (58/59)
stay [steɪ] bleiben; übernachten 5
steal [sti:l], **stole, stolen** stehlen, rauben 7: 2 (30)
step [step] Stufe; Schritt 5 **step by step** Schritt für Schritt 7: 1 (18)
stepbrother ['stepbrʌðə] Stiefbruder 5
stepdad ['stepdæd] Stiefvater 5
stepfather ['stepfɑ:ðə] Stiefvater 5
stepmother ['stepmʌðə] Stiefmutter 5
stepmum ['stepmʌm] Stiefmutter 5
stepsister ['stepsɪstə] Stiefschwester 5
stew [stju:] Eintopf(gericht) 7: 4 (58/59)
stick [stɪk] Stock; Schläger *(Sport)* 7: 1 (10)
°**stick** [stɪk], **stuck, stuck** kleben
°**sticky dot** ['stɪki dɒt] Klebepunkt
still [stɪl] (immer) noch; trotzdem 6
stole [stəʊl] *siehe* **steal**
stolen ['stəʊlən] *siehe* **steal**
stomach ['stʌmək] Bauch; Magen 6
stomach ache ['stʌmək eɪk] Bauchschmerzen, Magenschmerzen 6
stone [stəʊn] Stein 6
stone circle [stəʊn 'sɜ:kl] Steinkreis 6
stood [stʊd] *siehe* **stand**
stop [stɒp]:
1. (an)halten; stoppen; aufhören (mit) 5
stop sb. doing sth. jn. davon abhalten, etwas zu tun 7: 5 (86)
2. Halt, Haltepunkt 6
bus stop Bushaltestelle 6
storm [stɔ:m] Sturm; Gewitter 5
stormy ['stɔ:mi] stürmisch 5
story ['stɔ:ri] Geschichte 5
straight [streɪt] gerade; *(Haare)* glatt 6
straight on [streɪt 'ɒn] geradeaus (weiter) 5
strange [streɪndʒ] seltsam, sonderbar 6
stranger ['streɪndʒə] Fremde/r 7: 3 (51)
strategy ['strætədʒi] Strategie 7: 5 (76/77)
strawberry ['strɔ:bəri] Erdbeere 5
street [stri:t] Straße *(in Ortschaften)* 5
°**stress** [stres] Betonung
strict [strɪkt] streng 5
strong [strɒŋ] stark 6
structure ['strʌktʃə]:
1. strukturieren, aufbauen 7: 3 (52)
2. Struktur 7: 3 (52)
°**stuck** [stʌk] *siehe* **stick**
student ['stju:dnt] Schüler/in; Student/in 5
study ['stʌdi] studieren; lernen *(z. B. für Prüfungen)* 7: 4 (63)
stupid ['stju:pɪd] dumm, blöd 5
style [staɪl] Stil; Art 7: 2 (36)
subject ['sʌbdʒɪkt]:
1. (Schul-)Fach 5
2. Thema 6
subscribe to sth. [səb'skraɪb] etwas abonnieren 7: 5 (78)
subscriber [səb'skraɪbə] Abonnent/in 7: 5 (78)
successful [sək'sesfl] erfolgreich 7: 2 (36)
suddenly ['sʌdənli] plötzlich, auf einmal 6
sugar ['ʃʊgə] Zucker 6
sugary ['ʃʊgəri] zuckrig, zuckerhaltig 6
suggest [sə'dʒest] vorschlagen 7: 4 (71)
suit [su:t] (Herren-)Anzug; (Damen-)Kostüm 7: 2 (26)
suit (sb.) [su:t] geeignet sein für, passen (zu); jm. stehen *(Frisur, Kleidung)* 7: 5 (85)
sum sth. up [sʌm 'ʌp] etwas zusammenfassen 7: 3 (52) **To sum up,** Um (es) zusammenzufassen, ... / Zusammenfassend kann man sagen, ... 7: 3 (52)
summer ['sʌmə] Sommer 5
summer camp ['sʌmə kæmp] Ferienlager *(im Sommer)* 6
sun [sʌn] Sonne 5
Sunday ['sʌndeɪ], ['sʌndi] Sonntag 5
sung [sʌŋ] *siehe* **sing**
sunglasses *(pl)* ['sʌnglɑ:sɪz] Sonnenbrille 6
sunny ['sʌni] sonnig 5
super ['su:pə] super 6
Super Bowl ['su:pə bəʊl] Super Bowl *(Endspiel der American National Football League)* 6
supercool ['su:pəku:l] supercool 7: 2 (26)
superhero, *pl* **superheroes** ['su:pəhɪərəʊ] Superheld/in 7: 2 (26)
supermarket ['su:pəmɑ:kɪt] Supermarkt 5
superpower ['su:pəpaʊə] Superkraft 7: 2 (26)
superstrong [su:pə'strɒŋ] superstark 7: 2 (26)
support [sə'pɔ:t] unterstützen 6
sure [ʃʊə], [ʃɔ:] sicher *(ohne Zweifel)* 6 **make sure that ...** sicherstellen, dass ...; dafür sorgen, dass ... 7: 4 (61)
surfer ['sɜ:fə] Surfer/in 6
surfing ['sɜ:fɪŋ]: **go surfing** surfen gehen 5
surprise [sə'praɪz]:
1. überraschen 7: 4 (66)
2. Überraschung 7: 4 (66)
surprised [sə'praɪzd] überrascht 6
survey ['sɜ:veɪ] Umfrage 6 **do a survey** eine Umfrage durchführen 6

sushi ['suːʃi] Sushi 5
swam [swæm] *siehe* **swim**
swap [swɒp] tauschen 5
sweet [swiːt] süß 7: 5 (83)
sweets *(pl)* [swiːts] Süßigkeiten 5
swim [swɪm], **swam, swum** schwimmen 5
swimming costume ['swɪmɪŋ kɒstjuːm] Badeanzug 6
swimming pool ['swɪmɪŋ puːl] Schwimmbad 5
swimming trunks *(pl)* ['swɪmɪŋ trʌŋks] Badehose 6
switch [swɪtʃ]:
1. Schalter 7: 5 (84)
2. **switch sth. on/off** etwas einschalten/ausschalten 7: 5 (84)
swum [swʌm] *siehe* **swim**
symbol (of) ['sɪmbl] Symbol (für) 7: 3 (53)

T

table ['teɪbl]:
1. Tisch 5
2. Tabelle 6
table tennis ['teɪbl tenɪs] Tischtennis 5
tablet ['tæblət] Tablet(computer) 6
taco ['tækəʊ] Taco *(Maistortilla)* 6
take [teɪk], **took, taken:**
1. (mit)nehmen; bringen 5 **take a break** Pause machen, abschalten 7: 4 (58/59) **take notes** sich Notizen machen 7: 2 (24/25) **take off** ausziehen, ablegen 6 **take off** wegnehmen, aus dem Spiel nehmen 7: 5 (82) °**take turns** sich abwechseln **take a photo** ein Foto machen 5
2. dauern, *(Zeit)* brauchen, in Anspruch nehmen 5
takeaway ['teɪkəweɪ] Schnellrestaurant; Essen zum Mitnehmen 6
taken ['teɪkn] *siehe* **take**
tale [teɪl] Erzählung, Geschichte 7: 5 (89)
talk [tɔːk]:
1. Vortrag, Rede; Gespräch 5 **give a talk** einen Vortrag halten 5
2. **talk (to)** sprechen, reden (mit) 5
tall [tɔːl] groß *(Person)*; hoch *(Gebäude)* 6
tap sth. [tæp] (leise) klopfen, tippen an etwas 7: 4 (68) **tap your fingers** mit den Fingern klopfen 7: 4 (68)
task [tɑːsk] Aufgabe 5
taste [teɪst]:
1. schmecken; kosten, probieren 6
2. Geschmack 6
tasty ['teɪsti] schmackhaft, lecker 6
taught [tɔːt] *siehe* **teach**
taxi ['tæksi] Taxi 6
tea [tiː] Tee 5
teach [tiːtʃ], **taught, taught** lehren, unterrichten 6 **teach sb. to do sth.** jm. beibringen, etwas zu tun 6
teacher ['tiːtʃə] Lehrer/in 5 **My dad is a teacher.** Mein Papa ist Lehrer (von Beruf). 5
team [tiːm] Team, Mannschaft 5
teamwork ['tiːmwɜːk] Teamwork, Zusammenarbeit 6
tear [tɪə] Träne 7: 5 (88)
teaspoon ['tiːspuːn] Teelöffel 7: 4 (67)
tech [tek] *(infml)* Technik 7: 4 (70)
°**technical** ['teknɪkl] technisch
technology [tek'nɒlədʒi] Technik(unterricht); Technologie 5
teen [tiːn] Teenager 6
teenager ['tiːneɪdʒə] Teenager 6
teeth [tiːθ] *Plural von* **tooth** 6
tell [tel], **told, told** sagen, erzählen, berichten 5 **tell about** erzählen von, berichten über 5 **tell sb. (not) to do sth.** jn. auffordern, etwas (nicht) zu tun; jm. sagen, dass er/sie etwas (nicht) tun soll 6
temperature ['temprətʃə] Temperatur; Fieber 6 **have a temperature** Fieber haben 6
temple ['templ] Tempel 7: 3 (44)
ten [ten] zehn 5
tennis ['tenɪs] Tennis 5
tennis court ['tenɪs kɔːt] Tennisplatz 7: 1 (8/9)
tent [tent] Zelt 6
terminal ['tɜːmɪnl] Terminal, Abfertigungsgebäude 6
terrible ['terəbl] schrecklich, fürchterlich 5
terror ['terə] (panische) Angst 7: 5 (88)
test [test]:
1. Klassenarbeit, Test 6
2. testen 6
text [tekst]:
1. Text 5
2. SMS 5
3. **text sb.** jm. eine SMS schicken 7: 2 (24/25)
text message ['tekst mesɪdʒ] *(kurz auch:* **text***)* SMS 5
than [ðən]: **more than** mehr als 6
thank you ['θæŋk juː] danke (schön) 5
thanks [θæŋks] danke (schön) 5
Thanksgiving Day [θæŋks'gɪvɪŋ deɪ] Erntedankfest 6
that [ðæt], [ðət]:
1. das (dort) 5 **that night** in jener Nacht 6 **That's £2.** Das macht 2 Pfund. 5
2. dass 5 **it says that ...** es (be)sagt, dass ... 5 **so that** sodass 7: 2 (26)
3. der, die, das *(Relativpronomen)* 7: 1 (10) **sports that I've never done before** Sportarten, die ich noch nie gemacht habe 7: 1 (10)
the [ðə] der, die, das 5
theatre ['θɪətə] Theater 5
their [ðeə] ihr/e *(Plural)* 5
theirs [ðeəz] ihrer, ihre, ihrs *(zu „they")* 6
them [ðem], [ðəm] sie, ihnen 5
themselves [ðəm'selvz] sie/sich selbst *(Plural)* 6
then [ðen] dann, danach 5
there [ðeə] da, dort; dahin, dorthin 5 **there are** es sind ... / es gibt ... 5 **there's (= there is)** es ist ... / es gibt ... 5
these [ðiːz] diese (hier) 5
they [ðeɪ] sie *(Plural)* 5
°**thin** [θɪn] schlank, dünn
thing [θɪŋ] Ding, Sache 5
think [θɪŋk], **thought, thought** denken, meinen, glauben 5 **think of** denken an 5 **What do they think of/about ...?** Was halten sie von ...? / Wie denken sie über ...? 7: 5 (83) °**think of sth.** sich etwas überlegen, ausdenken
third [θɜːd] dritte(r, s) 5 **one third** ein Drittel 7: 1 (16)
Thirdly, ... ['θɜːdli] Drittens ... 7: 5 (79)
this [ðɪs] dies; diese(r, s) 5 **this evening** heute Abend 6 **This is ...** Dies ist ... / Das ist ... 5
those [ðəʊz] die dort, jene (dort) 5
though [ðəʊ] obwohl 7: 3 (48)
thought [θɔːt] *siehe* **think**
thousand ['θaʊznd] tausend 6
three [θriː] drei 5
threw [θruː] *siehe* **throw**
throat [θrəʊt] Hals 6 **a sore throat** Halsschmerzen 6
through [θruː] durch 6
throw [θrəʊ], **threw, thrown** werfen 7: 3 (48)
thrown [θrəʊn] *siehe* **throw**
thunder ['θʌndə] Donner 7: 2 (30)

Thursday ['θɜːzdeɪ], ['θɜːzdi] Donnerstag 5
°tick [tɪk] Häkchen
ticket ['tɪkɪt] Eintrittskarte, Fahrkarte 5 **child ticket** Kinderfahrschein 6
ticket gate ['tɪkɪt geɪt] Sperre *(zur Fahrkartenkontrolle)* 6
ticket office ['tɪkɪt ɒfɪs] Kartenschalter, Kartenverkaufsstelle 7: 2 (35)
tidy ['taɪdi]:
1. ordentlich 5
2. aufräumen 5
tie [taɪ]:
1. binden, schnüren 7: 2 (37)
2. Krawatte 5
time [taɪm]:
1. Zeit; Uhrzeit 5
have a good time Spaß haben, sich vergnügen 6 **on time** pünktlich 7: 3 (51) **What time is it?** Wie spät ist es? 5
2. Mal 6
timetable ['taɪmteɪbl]:
1. Stundenplan 5
2. Fahrplan, Zeitplan 5
tip [tɪp] Tipp 5
tired ['taɪəd] müde 5
°title ['taɪtl] Titel, Überschrift
to [tu], [tə]:
1. zu, nach 5
upload sth. to the internet etwas ins Internet (hoch)laden 7: 5 (78)
2. bis 5
7 to 12 (von) 7 bis 12 5
3. vor *(Uhrzeiten)* 5
quarter to 7 viertel vor 7 5
4. (um) zu 5
how to do sth. wie man etwas macht 7: 3 (54) **I didn't know what to say.** Ich wusste nicht, was ich sagen sollte. 7: 3 (54)
time to go Zeit, zu gehen 5
toast [təʊst] Toast 5
today [tə'deɪ] heute 5
to-do list [tu 'duː lɪst] To-Do-Liste 6
together [tə'geðə] zusammen 5
toilet ['tɔɪlət] Toilette 5
token ['təʊkən] Spielfigur; Chip (Wertmarke); (Geschenk-)Gutschein 7: 5 (82)
told [təʊld] *siehe* **tell**
tomato, *pl* **tomatoes** [tə'mɑːtəʊ] Tomate 5
tomorrow [tə'mɒrəʊ] morgen 5
See you tomorrow. Bis morgen. 5
°tongue-twister ['tʌŋ twɪstə] Zungenbrecher
too [tuː] auch 5 **from Berlin too** auch aus Berlin 5
too expensive [tuː] zu teuer 6
took [tʊk] *siehe* **take**
tooth, *pl* **teeth** [tuːθ], [tiːθ] Zahn 6
top [tɒp] Spitze, das obere Ende 6 **the top ten tips** die zehn besten Tipps 5
°topic ['tɒpɪk] Thema
torch [tɔːtʃ] Taschenlampe 6
total ['təʊtl]:
1. Gesamt-; total 7: 5 (78)
2. Gesamtmenge, Gesamtzahl 7: 5 (78)
touch [tʌtʃ] anfassen, berühren 7: 3 (48)
tour (of) [tʊə] Tour, Reise, Rundgang/Rundfahrt 5
tourist ['tʊərɪst] Tourist/in 6
toward(s) [tə'wɔːdz] nach, auf ... zu, in Richtung (von) 7: 3 (54)
towel ['taʊəl] Handtuch 6
tower ['taʊə] Turm 5
town [taʊn] Stadt 5
trade [treɪd]:
1. Handel 7: 3 (44)
2. handeln, Handel (be)treiben 7: 3 (44)
tradition [trə'dɪʃn] Tradition 7: 4 (63)
traditional [trə'dɪʃənl] traditionell 6
train [treɪn] Zug, Eisenbahn 5
train [treɪn] trainieren; ausbilden 7: 2 (28)
training ['treɪnɪŋ] Training; Ausbildung, Dressur 6
tram [træm] Straßenbahn 5
trampolining ['træmpəliːnɪŋ] Trampolinspringen/-turnen 5
transport ['trænspɔːt] *(no pl)* Fortbewegungsmittel; Beförderung 5
trash [træʃ] *(AE)* Abfall, Müll 7: 2 (32)
travel ['trævl] reisen 5
treasure ['treʒə] Schatz 5
tree [triː] Baum 5
tribe [traɪb] (Volks-)Stamm 7: 3 (42/43)
trick [trɪk] List, Streich 7: 1 (21) **play a trick on sb.** jm. einen Streich spielen 7: 1 (21)
trip [trɪp] Ausflug; Reise 5 **class trip** Klassenausflug 5 **school trip** Schulausflug 5
trouble ['trʌbl] Ärger, Schwierigkeiten 5 **be in trouble** Ärger haben, in Schwierigkeiten sein 5 **°the Troubles** die Unruhen in Nordirland
°troubleshoot ['trʌblʃuːt] Fehler beheben, Probleme lösen
trousers *(pl)* ['traʊzəz] Hose 5
truck [trʌk] Last(kraft)wagen, LKW 7: 2 (35)
true [truː] wahr, richtig 6
trust [trʌst]:
1. vertrauen 6
2. *(das)* Vertrauen 6
truth [truːθ] Wahrheit 7: 2 (26)
try [traɪ] versuchen, (aus)probieren 5 **try sth. on** anprobieren *(Kleidung)* 5 **try to do sth.** versuchen, etwas zu tun 5
T-shirt ['tiː ʃɜːt] T-Shirt 5
tube [tjuːb]: **the Tube** *(infml)* die Londoner U-Bahn 6
Tuesday ['tjuːzdeɪ], ['tjuːzdi] Dienstag 5
tunnel ['tʌnl] Tunnel 7: 1 (16)
turkey ['tɜːki] Truthahn, Pute; Putenfleisch 6
turn [tɜːn]:
1. (sich) umdrehen 7: 3 (48)
turn (a)round (sich) umdrehen 5
turn sth. (over) etwas umdrehen 7: 3 (48) **turn sth. down** etwas leise(r) stellen, herunterregeln 7: 5 (83) **turn your T-shirt inside out** dein T-Shirt auf links ziehen 7: 1 (20)
2. turn right/left (nach) rechts/links abbiegen 5
3. turn to sth. zu etwas werden 6
°turns ['tɜːnz]: **take turns** sich abwechseln
turtle ['tɜːtl] (Wasser-)Schildkröte 5
°tutorial [tjuː'tɔːriəl] Anleitung
TV [tiː'viː] Fernseher 5
twelve [twelv] zwölf 5
twenty ['twenti] zwanzig 5
twin [twɪn]: **twin brother/sister** Zwillingsbruder/-schwester 7: 2 (32) **twins** *(pl)* Zwillinge 7: 2 (32)
two [tuː] zwei 5
type (of) [taɪp] Art, Sorte 6
typical (of) ['tɪpɪkl] typisch (für) 7: 2 (30)

U

UK [juː 'keɪ] das Vereinigte Königreich 5
umbrella [ʌm'brelə] (Regen-)Schirm 6
°unchanging [ʌn'tʃeɪndʒɪŋ] unveränderlich
uncle ['ʌŋkl] Onkel 5
unclear [ʌn'klɪə] unklar 7: 5 (91)
under ['ʌndə] unter 5
underground ['ʌndəgraʊnd] U-Bahn 6

understand [ʌndə'stænd], **understood, understood** verstehen 5
understood [ʌndə'stʊd] *siehe* **understand**
underwater [ʌndə'wɔːtə] unter Wasser, Unterwasser- 7: 5 (78)
unfortunately [ʌn'fɔːtʃənətli] unglücklicherweise, leider 7: 5 (83)
°**unfriend** [ʌn'frend] entfreunden *(in sozialen Medien)*
unfriendly [ʌn'frendli] unfreundlich 6
unhappy [ʌn'hæpi] unglücklich 6
unhealthy [ʌn'helθi] ungesund 6
uniform ['juːnɪfɔːm] Uniform 5
unit ['juːnɪt] Lektion, Kapitel *(Schulbuch)* 5
United Kingdom (= the UK) [junaɪtɪd 'kɪŋdəm] das Vereinigte Königreich 5
university [juːnɪ'vɜːsəti] Universität 5
unlikely [ʌn'laɪkli] unwahrscheinlich 7: 5 (84)
unpopular (with) [ʌn'pɒpjələ] unbeliebt (bei) 6
unsafe [ʌn'seɪf] unsicher 6
unspecified [ʌn'spesɪfaɪd] nicht angegeben, keine Angabe *(Formular)* 7: 1 (15)
unsure [ʌn'ʃʊə] unsicher 7: 4 (68)
untidy [ʌn'taɪdi] unordentlich 6
until [ən'tɪl] bis *(zeitlich)* 6 **not … until** erst, wenn … 6
up [ʌp] hinauf, hoch 5
upload [ʌp'ləʊd] hochladen 6
upset [ʌp'set]:
1. aufgebracht, verärgert 7: 3 (49)
2. **upset sb., upset, upset** jn. aufregen, ärgern, erschüttern 7: 3 (49)
upstairs [ʌp'steəz] (nach) oben *(die Treppe hoch)* 5
us [ʌs], [əs] uns 5
USA [juː es 'eɪ] USA (= die Vereinigten Staaten von Amerika) 5
use [juːz] benutzen, verwenden 5
°**use** [juːs] Gebrauch, Verwendung
useful ['juːsfl] nützlich, hilfreich 7: 1 (18)
useless ['juːsləs] nutzlos 6
username [juːzəneɪm] Benutzername 7: 5 (89)
usual ['juːʒuəl] üblich, gewöhnlich 6
usually ['juːʒuəli] normalerweise, meistens 5

V

vacation [və'keɪʃn] *(AE)* Urlaub, Ferien 6
vacuum ['vækjuəm] Staubsaugen 7: 2 (32)
vacuum cleaner ['vækjuəm kliːnə] Staubsauger 7: 2 (32)
°**vampire** ['væmpaɪə] Vampir
vegetables *(pl)* ['vedʒtəblz] Gemüse 5
vegetarian [vedʒə'teəriən] vegetarisch; Vegetarier/in 5
very ['veri] sehr 5
vet [vet] Tierarzt/-ärztin 6
video ['vɪdiəʊ] Video(-) 5
video game ['vɪdiəʊ geɪm] Videospiel 7: 2 (24/25)
view [vjuː]:
1. Aufruf *(eines Videos im Internet)*; (An-)Blick, (Aus-)Sicht 7: 5 (78) **in my view** meiner Ansicht nach 6
2. anschauen 7: 5 (78)
Viking ['vaɪkɪŋ] Wikinger/in 7: 3 (42/43)
village ['vɪlɪdʒ] Dorf 5
°**vinegar** ['vɪnɪgə] Essig
violence ['vaɪələns] Gewalt; Gewalttätigkeit 7: 4 (62)
violent ['vaɪələnt] gewalttätig; gewaltsam 7: 4 (62)
violin [vaɪə'lɪn] Geige, Violine 7: 5 (81)
viral ['vaɪrəl] Virus-, viral 7: 5 (79) **go viral** sich *(im Internet)* rasend schnell verbreiten 7: 5 (79)
°**virtual** ['vɜːtʃuəl] virtuell
visit ['vɪzɪt]:
1. besuchen 5
2. Besuch 7: 3 (54)
visitor ['vɪzɪtə] Besucher/in; Gast 7: 3 (54)
vocabulary *(infml auch* **vocab***)* [və'kæbjələri], ['vəʊkæb] Vokabeln; Vokabelverzeichnis; Wortschatz 7: 1 (20)
voice [vɔɪs] Stimme 6 **in a loud voice** mit lauter Stimme 7: 1 (11)
voice message ['vɔɪs mesɪdʒ] Sprachnachricht 7: 2 (35)
volleyball ['vɒlibɔːl] Volleyball 5
volunteer [vɒlən'tɪə] Freiwillige/r 6
volunteer organisation [vɒləntɪər ɔːgənaɪ'zeɪʃn] Freiwilligenorganisation 6
vote [vəʊt]:
1. Abstimmung, Votum 7: 2 (39) **have a vote (on)** abstimmen (über) 7: 2 (39)
2. **vote (on sth.)** wählen; abstimmen (über etwas) 7: 2 (39)

W

wait (for) [weɪt] warten (auf) 5 **Wait a minute.** Warte mal. / Einen Moment. 5
wake up [weɪk 'ʌp], **woke, woken** aufwachen 5
wake-up time ['weɪk ʌp taɪm] Weckzeit 7: 1 (11)
walk [wɔːk] wandern, (zu Fuß) gehen 5 **walk around** umhergehen 6
wall [wɔːl] Wand, Mauer 5
want [wɒnt] wollen 5 **want to do sth.** etwas tun wollen 5 **I didn't want them to know …** Ich wollte nicht, dass sie … wussten. 7: 1 (11)
wardrobe ['wɔːdrəʊb] Kleiderschrank 5
warm [wɔːm] warm 5
was [wɒz], [wəz]: **I/he/she/it was** *Vergangenheitsform von* **be** 5
wash [wɒʃ] (sich) waschen 6
washing ['wɒʃɪŋ] Wäsche 6
watch [wɒtʃ] *(sich etwas)* anschauen; beobachten 5 **watch TV** fernsehen 5
water ['wɔːtə] Wasser 5
waterfall ['wɔːtəfɔːl] Wasserfall 6
°**wave** [weɪv] Welle
way [weɪ]:
1. Weg 7: 3 (48)
2. Art und Weise 7: 3 (48)
No way! Auf keinen Fall! 6
we [wiː] wir 5
weak [wiːk] schwach 7: 5 (89)
weapon ['wepən] Waffe 7: 2 (26)
wear [weə], **wore, worn** tragen, anhaben *(Kleidung)* 5
weather ['weðə] Wetter 5
web [web] Netz 5
webpage ['webpeɪdʒ] Webseite 7: 5 (76/77)
website ['websaɪt] Website 5
wedding ['wedɪŋ] Hochzeit 6
wedding present ['wedɪŋ preznt] Hochzeitsgeschenk 6
Wednesday ['wenzdeɪ], ['wenzdi] Mittwoch 5
week [wiːk] Woche 5
weekday ['wiːkdeɪ] Werktag, Wochentag 7: 2 (24/25)
weekend [wiːk'end] Wochenende 5 **at the weekend** am Wochenende 5
welcome ['welkəm]:
1. **Welcome to …** Willkommen in/an … 5
2. **You're welcome.** Bitte, gern geschehen. / Nichts zu danken. 5

well [wel]**:** gut *(Adv.)* 7: 2 (26) **Well, ...** Nun, ... / Also, ... / Na ja, ... 6 **°... as well as ...** sowohl ... als auch ...
went [went] *siehe* **go**
were [wɜː], [wə]**:** **we/you/they were** *Vergangenheitsform von* **be** 5
west [west] Westen; westlich; West- 6
westbound ['westbaʊnd] in Richtung Westen *(Zug, Bus)* 6
western ['westən] westlich, West- 7: 4 (62)
wet [wet] nass 6
wetsuit ['wetsuːt] Taucheranzug, Neoprenanzug 6
whale [weɪl] Wal 6
what [wɒt]**:**
1. was 5
What about you? Und du? / Was ist mit dir? 5 **What's your name?** Wie heißt du? 5
2. welche(r, s) 5
What time is it? Wie spät ist es? 5
wheel [wiːl] Rad 6 **big wheel** Riesenrad 6
wheelchair ['wiːltʃeə] Rollstuhl 5
wheelchair accessible [wiːltʃeər ək'sesəbl] rollstuhlgerecht *(mit dem Rollstuhl zu erreichen)* 7: 2 (35)
when [wen]**:**
1. als *(zeitlich)* 5
2. wann 5
When's your birthday? Wann hast du Geburtstag? 5
3. wenn *(zeitlich)* 5
where [weə] wo; wohin 5 **Where are you from?** Wo kommst du her? 5
which [wɪtʃ]**:**
1. welche(r, s) 5
2. der, die, das; die *(Relativpronomen)* 7: 1 (12)
a film which has ... ein Film, der ... hat 7: 1 (12)
while [waɪl] während 6
white [waɪt] weiß 5
who [huː]**:**
1. wer 5
2. wem; wen 6
3. der, die *(Relativpronomen, Person)* 7: 1 (12)
a girl who ... ein Mädchen, das ... 7: 1 (12)
whole [həʊl] ganze(r, s) 6
wholemeal ['həʊlmiːl] Vollkorn- 7: 4 (67)
whose [huːz]**:**
1. wessen 5
2. dessen, deren *(Relativpronomen)* 7: 1 (12)
why [waɪ] warum 5
Wi-Fi ['waɪ faɪ] WLAN, kabellose Datenübertragung 7: 1 (8/9)
will [wɪl]**:** **you'll (= you will) fall** du wirst fallen 6
win [wɪn]**, won, won** gewinnen 6
wind [wɪnd] Wind 5
window ['wɪndəʊ] Fenster 5
windy ['wɪndi] windig 5
°wine [waɪn] Wein
°wine gum ['waɪn gʌm] Weingummi, Gummibonbon
winner ['wɪnə] Gewinner/in, Sieger/in 6
winter ['wɪntə] Winter 5
wish [wɪʃ]**:**
1. wünschen 5
2. Wunsch 5
Best wishes Viele Grüße ... *(Briefschluss)* 5 **make a wish** sich etwas wünschen 5
with [wɪð]**:**
1. mit 5
2. bei 5
with us bei uns 5
without [wɪ'ðaʊt] ohne 6
woke [wəʊk] *siehe* **wake up**
woken ['wəʊkən] *siehe* **wake up**
°wolf, *pl* **wolves** [wʊlf], [wʊlvz] Wolf, Wölfe
woman, *pl* **women** ['wʊmən], ['wɪmɪn] Frau 5
won [wʌn] *siehe* **win**
won't [wəʊnt]**:** **you won't need (= you will not need) ...** du wirst ... nicht brauchen 6
wood [wʊd] Holz; Wald 6
wool [wʊl] Wolle 7: 3 (45)
word [wɜːd] Wort 5
word building ['wɜːd bɪldɪŋ] das Bilden von Wörtern 7: 5 (79)
word web ['wɜːd web] Wortnetz 5
wore [wɔː] *siehe* **wear**
work [wɜːk]**:**
1. Arbeit 5
at work bei der Arbeit, am Arbeitsplatz 5
2. arbeiten; funktionieren 5
worker ['wɜːkə] Arbeiter/in 6
world [wɜːld] Welt 5 **the best place in the world** der beste Ort der Welt / auf der Welt 5
worn [wɔːn] *siehe* **wear**
worried ['wʌrid]**:** **be worried (about)** beunruhigt sein, besorgt sein (wegen) 5
worry ['wʌri]**:** **worry (about)** sich Sorgen machen (wegen, um) 6 **worry sb.** jn. beunruhigen 6
worse [wɜːs] schlechter, schlimmer 6
worst [wɜːst] der/die/das schlechteste, schlimmste; am schlechtesten, am schlimmsten 6
would [wʊd]**:** **Would you like some tea/potatoes?** Möchtest du (etwas) Tee / (ein paar) Kartoffeln? 5 **I'd like ... (= I would like)** Ich hätte gern ... / Ich möchte ... 5 **I'd like to talk about ...(= I would like to)** Ich würde gern über ... sprechen. 5
°wrist [rɪst] Handgelenk
°wristwatch ['rɪstwɒtʃ] Armbanduhr
write [raɪt]**, wrote, written** schreiben 5 **write sth. down** etwas aufschreiben 7: 3 (52)
writer ['raɪtə] Autor/in, Verfasser/in 6
writing ['raɪtɪŋ] Schrift 6
written ['rɪtn] *siehe* **write**
wrong [rɒŋ] falsch 5 **be wrong** Unrecht haben 6 **go wrong** schiefgehen 6 **What's wrong?** Was fehlt dir/Ihnen? *(beim Arzt)* 6
wrote [rəʊt] *siehe* **write**

Y

year [jɪə] Jahr(gang) 5
yellow ['jeləʊ] gelb 5
yes [jes] ja 5
yesterday ['jestədeɪ] gestern 5
yet [jet]**:** **... yet?** ... schon ...? 6 **not ... yet** noch nicht ... 6
yoga ['jəʊgə] Yoga 7: 1 (8/9)
you [ju], [jə] du; dich; dir; ihr; euch; Sie; Ihnen 5
young [jʌŋ] jung 6
your [jɔː], [jə] dein/e; euer/eure; Ihr/e 5
yours [jɔːz] deine, deiner, deins; eurer, eure, eures; Ihrer, Ihre, Ihres *(zu „you")* 6
yourself [jə'self] du/dir/dich (selbst) 6
yourselves [jɔː'selvz], [jə'selvz] ihr/euch selbst 6
yum [jʌm] *(infml)* lecker 7: 5 (87)

Z

zero ['zɪərəʊ] Null 5
zone [zəʊn] Zone 6
zoo [zuː] Zoo 6

Das **German – English dictionary** enthält den **Lernwortschatz** der Bände 5 bis 7 von *Go Ahead*. Es kann dir eine erste Hilfe sein, wenn du vergessen hast, wie etwas auf Englisch heißt.

Wenn du wissen möchtest, wo das englische Wort zum ersten Mal in *Go Ahead 7* vorkommt, dann kannst du im **English – German dictionary** (S. 194–218) nachschlagen.

Es werden folgende **Abkürzungen** und **Symbole** verwendet:
pl = plural (Mehrzahl) • *AE = American English* • *BE = British English* • *infml = informal* (umgangssprachlich)
sb. = somebody • *sth. = something* • *jn.* = jemanden • *jm.* = jemandem

A

abbiegen: (nach) rechts/links abbiegen turn right/left [tɜːn]
Abend evening ['iːvnɪŋ] **am Abend** in the evening **(zu) Abend essen** have dinner ['dɪnə]
Abendessen dinner ['dɪnə]
abends in the evening ['iːvnɪŋ] **19 Uhr abends** 7 pm [piː'em]
aber but [bʌt], [bət]
abfahren leave [liːv]
Abfall litter ['lɪtə]; rubbish ['rʌbɪʃ]; trash *(AE)* [træʃ]
abhalten: jn. davon abhalten, etwas zu tun stop sb. doing sth. [stɒp]
abhängen *(sich entspannen)* chill out [tʃɪl 'aʊt]; hang out [hæŋ 'aʊt]
abkühlen cool [kuːl]
ablegen take off [teɪk 'ɒf]
Abonnent/in subscriber [səb'skraɪbə]
abonnieren subscribe to [səb'skraɪb]
abschalten take a break [teɪk ə 'breɪk]
abschneiden: besser abschneiden do better ['betə]
Abschnitt *(Text)* paragraph ['pærəgrɑːf]
abschreiben copy ['kɒpi]
Abstand gap [gæp]
abstimmen (über) have a vote (on) [vəʊt]; vote (on)
Abstimmung vote [vəʊt]
Absturz crash [kræʃ]
abstürzen (lassen) crash [kræʃ]
absuchen: (einen Text) absuchen (nach) scan (a text for) [skæn]
Abwasch dishes *(pl)* ['dɪʃɪz]
Achseln: mit den Achseln zucken shrug your shoulders
Achselzucken shrug [ʃrʌg]
acht eight [eɪt]
achten (auf) *(aufpassen)* pay attention (to) [peɪ ə'tenʃn] **achten auf** *(beachten)* mind [maɪnd] **achten auf etwas** *(beim Zuhören)* listen for sth.
addieren add [æd]
Adresse address [ə'dres]
AG *(in der Schule)* (school) club [klʌb]; *(freiwillige Veranstaltung in der Schule nach Unterrichtsschluss)* after-school activitiy [æk'tɪvəti]
ähnlich: (jm./einer Sache) ähnlich similar (to sb./sth.) ['sɪmələ]
Aktion action ['ækʃn]
Aktivität activity [æk'tɪvəti] **Aktivitäten außerhalb der Schule** out-of-school activities
albern silly ['sɪli]
Album album ['ælbəm]
alias aka (= also known as) [eɪ keɪ 'eɪ]
alle(s) all [ɔːl] **alle** *(jeder)* everybody, everyone ['evribɒdi], ['evriwʌn] **alles** everything ['evriθɪŋ]
allein alone [ə'ləʊn]
allerdings however [haʊ'evə]
Alphabet alphabet ['ælfəbet]
alphabetisches Wörterverzeichnis dictionary ['dɪkʃənri]
als as [æz], [əz]; *(zeitlich)* when [wen] **als Sänger/in** as a singer **mehr als** more than ['mɔː ðən]
also so [səʊ] **Also, ...** Well, ... [wel]
alt old [əʊld]; *(historisch)* ancient ['eɪnʃənt]
Alter age [eɪdʒ] **im Alter von 12 (Jahren)** at the age of 12 **in jedem Alter** at any age
am: am Arbeitsplatz at work [æt], [ət] **am besten** best [best] **am Meer** by the sea [baɪ] **am Mittwoch** on Wednesday [ɒn] **am Morgen/Abend** in the morning/evening [ɪn] **am Wochenende** at the weekend
American Football football *(AE)* ['fʊtbɔːl]
an at [æt], [ət] **das Gute/Schlechte an Fahrrädern** the good/bad thing about bikes [ə'baʊt]
anbieten offer ['ɒfə]
Anblick sight [saɪt]; view [vjuː]
andere(r, s) other ['ʌðə] **alle anderen** everyone else [els] **ein(e) andere(r, s)** another [ə'nʌðə]
ändern; sich ändern change [tʃeɪndʒ] **seine Meinung ändern** change your mind [tʃeɪndʒ jə 'maɪnd]
anders different ['dɪfrənt]
Anfang beginning [bɪ'gɪnɪŋ]; start [stɑːt]
anfangen (mit) start [stɑːt]
anfassen touch [tʌtʃ]
anfeuern *(Sportler/innen)* cheer [tʃɪə]
Angabe: keine Angabe *(Formular)* unspecified [ʌn'spesɪfaɪd]
angeben: nicht angegeben *(Formular)* unspecified [ʌn'spesɪfaɪd]
Angebot offer ['ɒfə]
Angeln *(germanisches Volk)* Angles ['æŋglz]
angreifen attack [ə'tæk]
Angriff attack [ə'tæk]
Angst: Angst haben (vor) be scared (of) [skeəd] **(panische) Angst** terror ['terə]
ängstlich scared [skeəd]
anhaben *(Kleidung)* wear [weə]
anhalten *(stoppen)* stop [stɒp]
Anhänger/in follower ['fɒləʊə]
anhören: (sich etwas) anhören listen to ['lɪsn]
anklopfen (an etwas) knock (at sth.) [nɒk]
ankommen arrive [ə'raɪv]
Ankunft arrival [ə'raɪvl]
anlügen: jn. anlügen lie to sb. [laɪ]
anprobieren *(Kleidung)* try sth. on [traɪ 'ɒn]
Anruf *(Telefon)* (phone) call ['fəʊn kɔːl]
anrufen call [kɔːl]; phone [fəʊn]
Anrufer/in caller ['kɔːlə]
anschauen view [vjuː] **sich etwas anschauen** look at sth. ['lʊk ət]; *(Fernsehen)* watch [wɒtʃ]
anschließen: etwas anschließen *(an Strom)* plug sth. in [plʌg 'ɪn]
Ansicht: meiner Ansicht nach in my view [vjuː]
ansiedeln: sich ansiedeln settle ['setl]

Anspruch: *(Zeit)* **in Anspruch nehmen** take [teɪk]
Antrag application [æplɪ'keɪʃn]
Antragsformular application form [æplɪ'keɪʃn fɔːm]
antreiben *(Tiere)* drive [draɪv]
Antwort (auf) answer (to) ['ɑːnsə]
um Antwort wird gebeten RSVP
antworten (auf) answer ['ɑːnsə]
Anweisung instruction [ɪn'strʌkʃn]
Anwesenheitskontrolle registration [redʒɪ'streɪʃn]
Anzahl (an) number of
anziehen: sich anziehen get dressed [get 'drest]
Anzug *(Herrenanzug)* suit [suːt]
Apfel apple ['æpl]
Apfelsine orange ['ɒrɪndʒ]
App app [æp]
April April ['eɪprəl]
Aquarium aquarium [ə'kweəriəm]
arabisch; Arabisch Arabic ['ærəbɪk]
Arbeit work [wɜːk] **bei der Arbeit** at work
arbeiten work [wɜːk]
Arbeiter/in worker ['wɜːkə]
arbeitslos jobless ['dʒɒbləs]
Arbeitsplatz: am Arbeitsplatz at work [ət 'wɜːk]
Arbeitsstelle job [dʒɒb]
Ärger trouble ['trʌbl] **Ärger haben** be in trouble
ärgerlich *(unangenehm)* annoying [ə'nɔɪɪŋ]; *(verärgert)* annoyed [ə'nɔɪd]
ärgern: jn. ärgern annoy sb. [ə'nɔɪ]; upset sb. [ʌp'set]
Mensch ärgere dich nicht *(Spiel)* ludo ['luːdəʊ]
Argument argument ['ɑːgjumənt]
Arm arm [ɑːm]
arm poor [pɔː], [pʊə]
Armband bracelet ['breɪslət]
Armee army ['ɑːmi]
Ärmelkanal (English) Channel [ɪŋglɪʃ 'tʃænl]
Art kind (of) [kaɪnd]; type (of) [taɪp]; *(Stil)* style [staɪl] **Art und Weise** way [weɪ] **auf diese Art** like this [laɪk 'ðɪs]
Artikel article ['ɑːtɪkl]
Arzt, Ärztin doctor ['dɒktə]
atlantischer Ozean, Atlantik Atlantic Ocean [ətlæntɪk 'əʊʃn]
atmen breathe [briːð]
auch also ['ɔːlsəʊ]; too [tuː]
auf on [ɒn]; at [æt], [ət] **auf dem Feld** in the field **auf dem Foto** in the photo [ɪn] **auf dem Land** in the country **auf die Felsen (hinauf)** onto the rocks ['ɒntu], ['ɒntə] **auf Englisch** in English
auf (etwas) zu toward(s) [tə'wɔːd], [tə'wɔːdz] **auf meinem Bild** in my picture **Auf Wiedersehen!** Goodbye. [gʊd'baɪ]
aufbauen set up [set 'ʌp]; *(strukturieren)* structure ['strʌktʃə]
auffordern: jn. auffordern, etwas (nicht) zu tun tell sb. (not) to do sth. [tel]
aufführen act [ækt]
Aufführung show [ʃəʊ]
Aufgabe task [tɑːsk]; exercise ['eksəsaɪz]; job [dʒɒb]
Aufgabenliste to-do list [tə 'duː lɪst]
aufgebracht upset [ʌp'set]
aufgehen *(sich öffnen)* open ['əʊpən]
aufgeregt excited [ɪk'saɪtɪd]; *(nervös)* nervous ['nɜːvəs]
aufhaben: Was haben wir als Hausaufgabe(n) auf? What's for homework?
aufhängen *(Wäsche)* hang out [hæŋ 'aʊt]
aufheben *(vom Boden)* pick up [pɪk 'ʌp]
aufhören (mit) stop [stɒp]
aufladen *(Mobiltelefon)* charge [tʃɑːdʒ]
aufmerksam careful ['keəfl] **aufmerksam machen auf etwas** point sth. out [pɔɪnt 'aʊt]
Aufmerksamkeit attention [ə'tenʃn]
aufpassen: aufpassen (auf) *(achten auf)* pay attention (to) [peɪ ə'tenʃn] **aufpassen auf** *(sich kümmern um)* look after [lʊk 'ɑːftə]
aufräumen tidy ['taɪdi]
aufregen: jn. aufregen upset sb. [ʌp'set]
aufregend exciting [ɪk'saɪtɪŋ]
Aufregung excitement [ɪk'saɪtmənt]
Aufruf *(eines Videos im Internet)* view [vjuː]
aufschlagen *(Buch)* open ['əʊpən]
aufschreiben write down
aufsetzen: sich aufsetzen *(sich gerade hinsetzen)* sit up [sɪt 'ʌp]
aufstehen get up [get 'ʌp]; stand up [stænd 'ʌp]
auftauchen appear [ə'pɪə]
aufteilen (in) divide (up) (into) [dɪ'vaɪd]
aufwachen wake up [weɪk 'ʌp]
aufzeigen put up your hand [pʊt 'ʌp]
Aufzug lift [lɪft]; elevator *(AE)* ['elɪveɪtə]
Auge eye [aɪ] **die Augen verdrehen** roll your eyes [rəʊl] **jm./einer Sache ins Auge sehen** face sb./sth. [feɪs]
August August ['ɔːgəst]
aus from [frɒm] **aus ... (heraus/hinaus)** out (of ...) [aʊt]
ausatmen breathe out [briːð 'aʊt]
ausbilden train [treɪn]
Ausbildung training ['treɪnɪŋ]
ausbreiten: sich ausbreiten spread [spred]
Ausdruck expression [ɪk'spreʃn]; phrase [freɪz] **zum Ausdruck bringen** express [ɪk'spres]
ausdrücken express [ɪk'spres]
Ausfahrt exit ['eksɪt]
Ausflug trip [trɪp] **(Tages-)Ausflug** day out
ausfüllen fill in [fɪl 'ɪn]
Ausgang exit ['eksɪt]
Ausgangspunkt starting point ['stɑːtɪŋ pɔɪnt]
ausgeben (für) *(Geld)* spend (on) [spend]
auslassen miss [mɪs]
ausleihen: sich (aus)leihen borrow ['bɒrəʊ]
ausmachen: Es macht mir nichts aus ... I don't mind ... [maɪnd] **etwas ausmachen** make a difference [meɪk ə 'dɪfrəns]
ausprobieren try [traɪ]
Ausrüstung equipment *(no pl)* [ɪ'kwɪpmənt]
ausschalten switch off [swɪtʃ 'ɒf]
Ausschau halten nach look for ['lʊk fə]
aussehen look [lʊk]
außergewöhnlich extraordinary [ɪk'strɔːdnri]
außerhalb: außerhalb der Stoßzeiten off-peak [ɒf 'piːk] **außerhalb des Vereinigten Königreiches** outside the UK [aʊt'saɪd]
Aussicht view [vjuː]
Aussprache pronunciation [prənʌnsi'eɪʃn]
aussprechen pronounce [prə'naʊns]
aussteigen: aus einem Auto aussteigen get out of a car **aus einem Flugzeug/Bus/Zug aussteigen** get off a plane/bus/train
Austausch exchange [ɪks'tʃeɪndʒ]
austauschen exchange [ɪks'tʃeɪndʒ]
Auster oyster ['ɔɪstə]
Auswahl choice [tʃɔɪs]

auswählen choose [tʃuːz]
Auswanderer/Auswanderin emigrant ['emɪgrənt]
auswandern emigrate ['emɪgreɪt]
Auswanderung emigration [emɪ'greɪʃn]
Auswirkung effect [ɪ'fekt]
ausziehen take off [teɪk 'ɒf]
Auto car [kɑː]
Automat machine [mə'ʃiːn]
Autor/in writer ['raɪtə]
Avocado avocado [ævə'kɑːdəʊ]
Axt axe [æks]

B

Baby baby ['beɪbi]
Backblech baking sheet ['beɪkɪŋ ʃiːt]
backen bake [beɪk]
Back-Natron baking soda ['beɪkɪŋ səʊdə]
Backofen oven ['ʌvn]
Backsoda baking soda ['beɪkɪŋ səʊdə]
Bad: *(Badezimmer)* bathroom ['bɑːθruːm]; *(in der Badewanne)* bath [bɑːθ]; *(Schwimmbad)* (swimming) pool ['swɪmɪŋ puːl] **ein Bad nehmen** *(in der Badewanne)* have/take a bath
Badeanzug swimming costume ['swɪmɪŋ kɒstjuːm]
Badehose swimming trunks ['swɪmɪŋ trʌŋks]
baden *(in der Badewanne)* have/ take a bath [bɑːθ]
Badewanne bath [bɑːθ]
Badminton badminton ['bædmɪntən]
Bahnhof station ['steɪʃn]
Bahnsteig platform ['plætfɔːm]
bald soon [suːn]
Balkon balcony ['bælkəni]
Ball ball [bɔːl]
Ballon balloon [bə'luːn]
Banane banana [bə'nɑːnə]
Band *(Musikgruppe)* band [bænd]
Bank *(Geldinstitut)* bank [bæŋk]
Bar bar [bɑː]
Bär bear [beə]
Barkeeper barkeeper *(AE)* ['bɑːkiːpə]
Bart beard [bɪəd]
Basketball basketball ['bɑːskɪtbɔːl]
Bauarbeiter/in builder ['bɪldə]
Bauch stomach ['stʌmək]
Bauchschmerzen stomach ache ['stʌmək eɪk]
bauen build [bɪld]
Bauer, Bäuerin farmer ['fɑːmə]
Bauernhof farm [fɑːm]
Baum tree [triː]
Bayern Bavaria [bə'veəriə]
beachten mind [maɪnd]
beängstigend scary ['skeəri]
beantworten answer ['ɑːnsə]
bedecken cover ['kʌvə]
bedeuten mean [miːn]
Bedeutung meaning ['miːnɪŋ]
beenden end [end]; finish ['fɪnɪʃ]
befolgen follow ['fɒləʊ]
befördern carry ['kæri]
beginnen (mit) start [stɑːt]
Begründung reason ['riːzn]
behalten keep [kiːp]
bei at [æt], [ət]; with [wɪð] **bei Ben zu Hause/daheim** at Ben's house **bei der Arbeit** at work **bei uns** with us
beide both [bəʊθ]
Beil axe [æks]
Beilage side dish ['saɪd dɪʃ]
Bein leg [leg]
Beispiel example [ɪg'zɑːmpl] **zum Beispiel** for example
bekämpfen fight [faɪt]
bekannt: auch bekannt als aka (= also known as) [eɪ keɪ 'eɪ]
bekanntmachen: jn. mit jm./etwas bekanntmachen introduce sb. to sb./sth. [ɪntrə'djuːs]
bekommen get [get]
beladen load [ləʊd]
belebt busy ['bɪzi]
beliebt popular ['pɒpjələ]
bellen: (jn. an)bellen bark (at sb.) [bɑːk]
bemerken notice ['nəʊtɪs]
Benachrichtigung notification [nəʊtɪfɪ'keɪʃn]
benehmen: sich benehmen behave [bɪ'heɪv]
benötigen need [niːd]
benutzen use [juːz]
Benutzername username [juːzəneɪm]
Benzin petrol ['petrəl]; gas *(AE)* [gæs]
beobachten watch [wɒtʃ]
bequem comfortable ['kʌmftəbl]
Bereich area ['eəriə]
bereit ready ['redi]
Berg mountain ['maʊntən]
Bericht report [rɪ'pɔːt]
berichten (über) report (on) [rɪ'pɔːt]; tell (about) [tel]
berühmt (für, wegen) famous (for) ['feɪməs]
berühren touch [tʌtʃ]
beschäftigt sein be busy ['bɪzi]
beschimpfen: jn. beschimpfen call sb. names [kɔːl 'neɪmz]
beschließen etwas zu tun choose to do sth. [tʃuːz]; decide to do sth. [dɪ'saɪd]
beschreiben describe [dɪ'skraɪb]
Beschreibung description [dɪ'skrɪpʃn]; *(Profil)* profile ['prəʊfaɪl]
beschützen (vor) protect (from/ against) [prə'tekt]
Besichtigungen *(von Sehenswürdigkeiten)* sightseeing ['saɪtsiːɪŋ]
besiegen beat [biːt]
besitzen: etwas besitzen own sth. [əʊn]
Besitzer/in owner ['əʊnə]
besondere(r, s) special ['speʃl]
besorgen: (sich) etwas besorgen get sth. [get]
besorgt sein (wegen) be worried (about) ['wʌrid]
besprechen *(rezensieren)* review [rɪ'vjuː] **etwas besprechen** discuss sth. [dɪ'skʌs]
Besprechung review [rɪ'vjuː]
besser better ['betə] **besser abschneiden** do better
beste(r, s) best [best]
bestellen order ['ɔːdə]
bestimmt: ganz bestimmt definitely ['defɪnətli]
bestimmte(r, s) specific [spə'sɪfɪk]
Besuch visit ['vɪzɪt]
besuchen visit ['vɪzɪt]
Besucher/in visitor ['vɪzɪtə]
beten pray [preɪ]
betonen emphasize ['emfəsaɪz]
betreuen *(als Mentor/in)* mentor ['mentə]
Betrieb *(Geschäft)* business ['bɪznəs] **einen Betrieb gründen/ eröffnen** start a business
Bett bed [bed] **ins Bett gehen** go to bed
beunruhigen: jn. beunruhigen worry sb. ['wʌri]
beunruhigt sein (wegen) be worried (about) ['wʌrid]
beurteilen judge [dʒʌdʒ]
Bevölkerung population [pɒpju'leɪʃn]
bevor before [bɪ'fɔː]
bewegen: sich bewegen move [muːv]
Bewegung movement ['muːvmənt]
beweisen prove [pruːv]
Bewerbung application [æplɪ'keɪʃn]
Bewerbungsformular application form [æplɪ'keɪʃn fɔːm]

bewirken: etwas bewirken make a difference [meɪk ə 'dɪfrəns]
bezahlen pay (for) [peɪ]
Beziehung relationship [rɪ'leɪʃnʃɪp] **mit jm. eine Beziehung haben** be in a relationship with sb.
Bibliothek library ['laɪbrəri]
Bier beer [bɪə]
bieten *(anbieten)* offer ['ɒfə]
Bild picture; *(Anblick)* sight [saɪt]
Bildschirm screen [skriːn]
Bildunterschrift caption ['kæpʃn]
billig *(preiswert)* cheap [tʃiːp]
binden tie [taɪ]
Bindestrich hyphen ['haɪfn]
Binnensee lake [leɪk]
bis *(zeitlich)* until [ən'tɪl] **Bis morgen.** See you tomorrow. ['siː juː] **(von) 7 bis 12** (from) 7 to 12 [tu], [tə]
bisschen: ein bisschen a bit [bɪt]; a little
bitte *(in Fragen und Aufforderungen)* please [pliːz] **Bitte, gern geschehen.** *(Nichts zu danken.)* You're welcome. ['welkʌm] **Bitte schön. / Hier, bitte.** Here you are. [hɪə juː 'ɑː]
bitten: jn. bitten, etwas zu tun ask sb. to do sth. **um etwas bitten** ask for sth. ['ɑːsk fə]
blasen blow [bləʊ]
blau blue [bluː]
Blazer blazer ['bleɪzə]
bleiben stay [steɪ]
Bleistift pencil ['pensl]
Bleistiftspitzer pencil sharpener ['pensl ʃɑːpnə]
Blick *(Anblick)* view [vjuː]
Block block [blɒk]
blöd silly ['sɪli]; stupid ['stjuːpɪd]
Blog *(Internet-Tagebuch)* blog [blɒg]
blond blond [blɒnd]
bloß just [dʒʌst]; only ['əʊnli] **Was/Wo/... ist denn nur/bloß ...?** What/Where/... the heck is ...? *(infml)* [hek]
Blume flower ['flaʊə]
Blüte flower ['flaʊə]
Boden *(Erdboden)* ground [graʊnd]
Bonbon sweet [swiːt]; candy *(AE)* ['kændi]
boomen *(Wirtschaft, Geschäft)* boom [buːm]
Boot boat [bəʊt]
Bord: an Bord gehen board [bɔːd]
Bordkarte boarding card ['bɔːdɪŋ kɑːd]
borgen: sich borgen borrow ['bɒrəʊ]
böse; *(das)* **Böse** evil ['iːvl]
Boss boss [bɒs]
Bowling bowling ['bəʊlɪŋ]
Braten roast meat [rəʊst 'miːt]
braten fry [fraɪ]
Brathähnchen chicken ['tʃɪkɪn]
brauchen need [niːd] *(Zeit)* **brauchen** take [teɪk] **nicht tun brauchen** needn't do ['niːdnt]
braun brown [braʊn]
brechen break [breɪk]
brennen burn [bɜːn]
Brett board [bɔːd]
Brettspiel board game ['bɔːd geɪm]
Brief letter ['letə] **kurzer Brief** note [nəʊt]
Briefumschlag envelope ['envələʊp]
Brille glasses ['glɑːsɪz]
bringen bring [brɪŋ]; take [teɪk] **jn. dazu bringen, etwas zu tun** make sb. do sth. [meɪk]
Brite/Britin Briton ['brɪtn]
britisch British ['brɪtɪʃ]
Brot bread [bred]
Brücke bridge [brɪdʒ]
Bruder brother ['brʌðə]
Bub boy [bɔɪ]
Buch book [bʊk]
Bücherei library ['laɪbrəri]
Buchhalter/in accountant [ə'kaʊntənt]
Buchstabe letter ['letə]
buchstabieren spell [spel]
Büfett buffet ['bʊfeɪ]
Bundesstaat state [steɪt]
Burg castle ['kɑːsl]
Bürgersteig pavement ['peɪvmənt]; sidewalk *(AE)* ['saɪdwɔːk]
Bus bus [bʌs]; *(Reisebus)* coach [kəʊtʃ] **im Bus** on the bus **mit dem Bus fahren** go by bus
Bushaltestelle bus stop ['bʌs stɒp]
Butter butter ['bʌtə]
Buttermilch buttermilk ['bʌtəmɪlk]

C

Café cafe ['kæfeɪ]
campen gehen go camping ['kæmpɪŋ]
Camping camping ['kæmpɪŋ]
Cape *(Umhang)* cape [keɪp]
Cent cent [sent]
Chance chance [tʃɑːns]
Charakter character ['kærəktə]
Chat chat [tʃæt]
chatten (mit) chat (with) [ʃæt]
Check check [tʃek]
Chef/in boss [bɒs]
Chip (Wertmarke) token ['təʊkən]
Chips crisps [krɪsps]
Chor choir ['kwaɪə]
Code code [kəʊd]
Cola cola ['kəʊlə]
Collage collage ['kɒlɑːʒ]
Comedyserie sitcom ['sɪtkɒm]
Comic comic ['kɒmɪk]
Computer computer [kəm'pjuːtə]
cool cool [kuːl]
Cornflakes cornflakes *(pl)* ['kɔːnfleɪks]
Cousin/e cousin ['kʌzn]
Creme cream [kriːm]
Crowdfunding *(Schwarmfinanzierung)* crowdfunding ['kraʊdfʌndɪŋ]
Curry curry ['kʌri]

D

da(hin) there [ðeə] **da drüben** over there
daheim at home [ət 'həʊm] **bei Ben daheim** at Ben's house
daher so [səʊ]
Dame lady ['leɪdi]
danach then [ðen]
danke (schön) thank you ['θæŋk juː]; thanks [θæŋks]
danken: Nichts zu danken. *(Gern geschehen.)* You're welcome. ['welkʌm]
dann then [ðen]
das *(Artikel)* the [ðə]; *(Relativpronomen)* that [ðæt]; *(Relativpronomen, Dinge/Tiere)* which [wɪtʃ] **das (da) ist** that's (= that is) [ðæts], [ðæt 'ɪz] **Ist das ...?** Is that ...?
dass that [ðət] **es (be)sagt, dass ...** it says that ...
dasselbe the same [seɪm]
Datum date [deɪt]
Dauer length [leŋθ]
dauern take [teɪk]
Deck deck [dek] **an Deck** on deck
decken: den Tisch decken set the table [leɪ]
dein/e *(vor Nomen)* your [jɔː], [jə]
deine/r, deins yours [jɔːz]
dekorieren decorate ['dekəreɪt]
Delfin dolphin ['dɒlfɪn]
demzufolge as a result [rɪ'zʌlt]
denken think [θɪŋk] **denken an** think of **daran denken** remember [rɪ'membə] **Wie denken sie über ...?** What do they think of/about ...?

Denkmal monument ['mɒnjumənt] **Denkmal (für jn./etwas)** memorial (to sb./sth.) [mə'mɔːriəl]
der *(Artikel)* the [ðə]; *(Relativpronomen)* that [ðæt]; *(Relativpronomen, Person)* who [huː]; *(Relativpronomen, Dinge/Tiere)* which [wɪtʃ]
deren *(Relativpronomen)* whose [huːz]
derselbe the same [seɪm]
dessen *(Relativpronomen)* whose [huːz]
Dessert dessert [dɪ'zɜːt]
Detektiv/in detective [dɪ'tektɪv]
deuten (auf) point (at/to) [pɔɪnt]
deutlich clear [klɪə] **deutlich machen** emphasize ['emfəsaɪz] **deutlich sprechen** speak clearly
Dezember December [dɪ'sembə]
Dia(-) slide [slaɪd]
Diagramm chart [tʃɑːt]
Dialog dialogue ['daɪəlɒg]
dich (selbst) yourself [jə'self]
dick *(Person)* big [bɪg]
die *(Artikel)* the [ðə]; *(Relativpronomen)* that [ðæt]; *(Relativpronomen, Dinge/Tiere)* which [wɪtʃ]; *(Relativpronomen, Person)* who [huː] **die dort** *(Plural)* those [ðəʊz]
Diele hall [hɔːl]
Dienstag Tuesday ['tjuːzdeɪ], ['tjuːzdi]
dies this [ðɪs]
diese(r, s) this [ðɪs] **diese (hier)** *(Plural)* these [ðiːz]
dieselbe(n) the same [seɪm]
digital digital ['dɪdʒɪtl]
Ding thing [θɪŋ]
dir (selbst) yourself [jə'self]
Disco disco ['dɪskəʊ]
diskutieren: über etwas diskutieren discuss sth. [dɪ'skʌs]
Distanz distance ['dɪstəns]
Dock dock [dɒk]
Dokumentarfilm documentary [dɒkju'mentri]
Dollar dollar ($) ['dɒlə]
Dom *(Kathedrale)* cathedral [kə'θiːdrəl]
Donner *(bei Gewitter)* thunder ['θʌndə]
Donnerstag Thursday ['θɜːzdeɪ], ['θɜːzdi]
Dorf village ['vɪlɪdʒ]
dort(hin) there [ðeə] **dort drüben** over there
draußen: (nach) draußen outside [aʊt'saɪd] **Sport für draußen, im Freien** outdoor sport ['aʊtdɔː]
Drehbuch script [skrɪpt]
drehen: (sich) drehen spin [spɪn] **sich drehen** *(immer wieder)* go around and around
drei three [θriː]
Dressur training ['treɪnɪŋ]
dritte(r, s) third [θɜːd]
Drittel third [θɜːd]
Drittens ... Thirdly, ... ['θɜːdli]
Droge drug [drʌg]
drüben: da/dort drüben over there [əʊvə 'ðeə] **hier drüben** over here [əʊvə 'hɪə]
Druck pressure ['preʃə] **jn. unter Druck setzen** put pressure on sb.
du you [juː], [jə] **du selbst** yourself [jə'self]
du solltest ... ausschalten you ought to switch off ... ['ɔːt tə]
Dudelsack bagpipes *(pl)* ['bægpaɪps]
dumm silly ['sɪli]; stupid ['stjuːpɪd]
dunkel dark [dɑːk]
dünn *(z. B. Haar)* fine [faɪn]
durch through [θruː]
dürfen may [meɪ] **Darf ich ...?** May I ...? **nicht tun dürfen** mustn't do ['mʌsnt]
Dusche shower ['ʃaʊə]
duschen have a shower ['ʃaʊə]
DVD DVD [diːviː'diː]

E

echt real [rɪəl]
Edelmetall precious metal [preʃəs 'metl]
Effekt effect [ɪ'fekt]
effektiv effective [ɪ'fektɪv]
egal: Du bist mir nicht egal. I care about you. [keə] **Es ist mir egal.** I don't care.
Ehemann husband ['hʌzbənd]
Ei egg [eg]
eigene(r, s): mein/ein eigenes Zimmer my own room [əʊn] own
Eigenschaft quality ['kwɒləti]
eigentlich actually ['æktʃuəli]
Eimer bucket ['bʌkɪt]; *(Mülleimer)* bin [bɪn]
ein/e *(Artikel)* a, an [ə], [ən]
einander each other [iːtʃ 'ʌðə]
einatmen breathe in [briːð 'ɪn]
Einbrecher/in burglar ['bɜːglə]
eindringen (in) invade [ɪn'veɪd]
einfach simple ['sɪmpl]; *(leicht)* easy ['iːzi]; *(nur, bloß)* just [dʒʌst]
einfangen catch [kætʃ]
Einfluss effect [ɪ'fekt]
einige a few [fjuː]; several ['sevrəl]; some [sʌm], [səm]
einkaufen: einkaufen gehen go shopping ['ʃɒpɪŋ] *(das)* **Einkaufen** shopping
Einkaufsliste shopping list ['ʃɒpɪŋ lɪst]
Einkaufszentrum shopping centre ['ʃɒpɪŋ sentə]
einladen (zu, nach) invite (to) [ɪn'vaɪt]
Einladung (zu, nach) invitation (to) [ɪnvɪ'teɪʃn]
Einleitung introduction [ɪntrə'dʌkʃn]
einmal: auf einmal suddenly ['sʌdənli] **(noch) nicht einmal** not even [nɒt 'iːvn] **noch einmal** again [ə'gen] **schon einmal** ever ['evə]
einmarschieren (in) invade [ɪn'veɪd]
einräumen: die Spülmaschine einräumen load the dishwasher [ləʊd]
einrichten set up [set 'ʌp]
Einrichtungen facilities [fə'sɪlətiz]
eins one [wʌn]
einsam lonely ['ləʊnli]
einschalten switch on [swɪtʃ 'ɒn]
einsetzen fill in [fɪl 'ɪn]
Einsiedlerkrebs hermit crab ['hɜːmɪt kræb]
einstecken: etwas einstecken *(z. B. in eine Steckdose)* plug sth. in [plʌg 'ɪn]
einsteigen: in ein Auto einsteigen get in(to) a car [get 'ɪn] **in ein Flugzeug/einen Bus/einen Zug einsteigen** get on a plane/bus/train
einteilen (in) divide (up) (into) [dɪ'vaɪd]
Eintopf(gericht) stew [stjuː]
Eintrag *(Tagebuch)* entry ['entri]
eintreten: in einen Klub eintreten join a club [dʒɔɪn]
Eintritt entry ['entri]
Eintrittskarte ticket ['tɪkɪt]
einverstanden sein mit etwas agree with sth. [ə'griː]
Einwanderer/Einwanderin immigrant ['ɪmɪgrənt]
einwandern immigrate ['ɪmɪgreɪt]
Einwanderung immigration [ɪmɪ'greɪʃn]

Einwohner(zahl) population [pɒpju'leɪʃn]
Einzelzimmer single room [sɪŋgl 'ruːm]
einzige(r, s): der/die einzige ... the only ... ['əʊnli]
Eis *(gefrorenes Wasser)* ice [aɪs]; *(Speiseeis)* ice cream [aɪs 'kriːm]
Eisenbahn train [treɪn]
Elefant elephant ['elɪfənt]
elf eleven [ɪ'levən]
Elfe fairy ['feəri]
Ellbogen elbow ['elbəʊ]
Eltern parents *(pl)* ['peərənts]
E-Mail email ['iːmeɪl]
E-Mail-Freund/in e-friend ['iːfrend]
emigrieren emigrate ['emɪgreɪt]
empfehlen: (jm.) etwas empfehlen recommend sth. (to sb.) [rekə'mend]
Ende end [end] **das obere Ende** top [tɒp] **das untere Ende** bottom ['bɒtəm] **zu Ende machen** finish ['fɪnɪʃ]
enden end [end]
endlich at last [ət 'lɑːst]
endlos endless ['endləs]
englischsprachig English-speaking ['ɪŋglɪʃ spiːkɪŋ]
entdecken discover [dɪ'skʌvə]
Ente duck [dʌk]
Entfernung distance ['dɪstəns]
entgegentreten: jm./einer Sache entgegentreten face sb./sth. [feɪs]
entkommen (aus) escape (from) [ɪ'skeɪp]
entlang: den Weg entlang along the path [ə'lɒŋ]
entscheiden: sich entscheiden etwas zu tun choose to do sth. [tʃuːz]; decide to do sth. [dɪ'saɪd]
Entscheidung decision [dɪ'sɪʒn] **eine Entscheidung fällen** make a decision
entschuldigen: sich bei jm. entschuldigen say sorry to sb. [seɪ 'sɒri]
Entschuldigung. *(Darf ich mal stören?)* Excuse me, ... [ɪks'kjuːz miː]; *(Tut mir leid.)* Sorry. / I'm sorry. ['sɒri]
entspannen: sich entspannen chill out [tʃɪl 'aʊt]; relax [rɪ'læks]
enttäuschen disappoint [dɪsə'pɔɪnt]
enttäuschend disappointing [dɪsə'pɔɪntɪŋ]
enttäuscht (von) disappointed (with) [dɪsə'pɔɪntɪd]
entwerfen design [dɪ'zaɪn]
entwickeln; sich entwickeln develop [dɪ'veləp]
er he [hiː]; *(Dinge, Tiere)* it [ɪt] **er/sich selbst** himself [hɪm'self]
Erbse pea [piː]
Erdbeben earthquake ['ɜːθkweɪk]; quake *(infml)* [kweɪk]
Erdbeere strawberry ['strɔːbəri]
Erdboden ground [graʊnd]
Erde earth [ɜːθ]
Erdkunde geography [dʒi'ɒgrəfi]
Ereignis event [ɪ'vent]
erfolgreich successful [sək'sesfl]
erfreut pleased [pliːzd]
Ergebnis result [rɪ'zʌlt]
erkältet sein have a cold [kəʊld]
Erkältung cold [kəʊld]
erklären: jm. etwas erklären explain sth. to sb. [ɪk'spleɪn]
erlaubt allowed [ə'laʊd]
ernähren feed [fiːd]
ernst serious ['sɪəriəs]
Erntedankfest Thanksgiving Day [θæŋks'gɪvɪŋ deɪ]
erobern conquer ['kɒŋkə]
erreichbar (für) accessible (to) [ək'sesəbl]
erschaffen create [kri'eɪt]
erscheinen appear [ə'pɪə]; seem [siːm]
erschüttern: jn. erschüttern upset sb. [ʌp'set]
erst only ['əʊnli] **erst, wenn ...** not ... until [nɒt ən'tɪl]
erstarren freeze [friːz]
erstaunlich amazing [ə'meɪzɪŋ]
erste(r, s) first [fɜːst] *(im Wettkampf)* **Erste/r werden** finish first **als Erstes** first
erstellen create [kri'eɪt]
Erstens ... Firstly, ... ['fɜːstli]
Erwachsene/r adult ['ædʌlt]
erwischen catch [kætʃ]
erzählen (von) tell (about) [tel]
Erzählung tale [teɪl]
erzielen *(Punkt/Tor/Treffer)* score [skɔː]
es it [ɪt] **es/sich selbst** itself [ɪt'self]
Essen food [fuːd]; *(Mahlzeit)* meal [miːl]
essen eat [iːt]
Esszimmer dining room ['daɪnɪŋ ruːm]
Etage floor [flɔː]
etwas something ['sʌmθɪŋ]; *(ein bisschen)* some [sʌm], [səm]
EU (Europäische Union) EU (= European Union) [iː 'juː]
euch (selbst) yourselves [jɔː'selvz], [jə'selvz]
euer/eure *(vor Nomen)* your [jɔː], [jə]
eure/r, eures yours [jɔːz]
Euro euro, *pl* euros ['jʊərəʊ]
Europäische Union European Union [jʊərəpiːən 'juːniən]
evangelisch Protestant ['prɒtɪstənt]
exakt exact [ɪg'zækt]
Exemplar *(Kopie)* copy ['kɒpi]
Experiment experiment [ɪk'sperɪmənt]
explodieren explode [ɪk'spləʊd]
Explosion explosion [ɪk'spləʊʒn]

F

Fabrik factory ['fæktri]
Fach *(Schulfach)* subject ['sʌbdʒɪkt]
Fähigkeit skill [skɪl]
Fahne flag [flæg]
Fähre ferry ['feri]
fahren go [gəʊ]; *(mit dem Auto)* drive [draɪv]; *(mit dem Schiff)* sail [seɪl] **mit dem Bus fahren** go by bus **mit dem Fahrrad fahren** ride a bike [raɪd]
Fahrer/in driver ['draɪvə]
Fahrgast passenger ['pæsɪndʒə]
Fahrkarte ticket ['tɪkɪt]
Fährmann ferryman, *pl* ferrymen ['ferimən]
Fahrplan timetable ['taɪmteɪbl]
Fahrrad bike [baɪk]
fair fair [feə]
Fall: auf jeden Fall definitely ['defɪnətli] **Auf keinen Fall!** No way! [nəʊ 'weɪ]
fallen drop [drɒp]; fall [fɔːl] **(sich) fallen lassen** drop
fällen: eine Entscheidung fällen make a decision [dɪ'sɪʒn]
falls if [ɪf]
falsch wrong [rɒŋ]
Faltblatt leaflet ['liːflət]
Familie family ['fæməli]
Familienname last name ['lɑːst neɪm]
Fan fan [fæn]; follower ['fɒləʊə]
fangen catch [kætʃ]
Fantasie fantasy ['fæntəsi]
Fantasy *(Literatur-, Filmgattung)* fantasy ['fæntəsi]
Farbe colour ['kʌlə] **Welche Farbe hat ...?** What colour is ...?
Farm farm [fɑːm]
fast nearly ['nɪəli]
Februar February ['februəri]
fechten *(Sport)* fence [fens]
Federball badminton ['bædmɪntən]

Federmäppchen pencil case ['pensl keɪs]
Fee fairy ['feəri]
Feedback *(Rückmeldung)* feedback ['fiːdbæk]
Fehler fault [fɔːlt]
feiern celebrate ['selɪbreɪt]
Feiertag: öffentlicher/gesetzlicher Feiertag public holiday [pʌblɪk 'hɒlədeɪ]
fein *(z. B. Stoff)* fine [faɪn]
Feind/in enemy ['enəmi]
Feld field [fiːld] **auf dem Feld** in the field
Felsen rock [rɒk]
Fenster window ['wɪndəʊ]
Ferien holidays ['hɒlədeɪz]; vacation *(AE)* [və'keɪʃn]
Ferienlager *(im Sommer)* summer camp ['sʌmə kæmp]
Ferne: in der Ferne in the distance ['dɪstəns]
fernsehen watch TV [wɒtʃ tiː'viː]
Fernseher TV [tiː'viː]
Fernsehsendung programme ['prəʊgræm]
Fernstraße highway *(AE)* ['haɪweɪ]
fertig ready ['redi]
Fertigkeit skill [skɪl]
Fest festival ['festɪvl]
Feuer fire ['faɪə]
Feuerwerk fireworks *(pl)* ['faɪəwɜːks]
Feuerwerkskörper firework ['faɪəwɜːk]
Fieber temperature ['temprətʃə] **Fieber haben** have a temperature
Figur figure ['fɪgə]; *(aus einer Geschichte)* character ['kærəktə]
Film film [fɪlm]; movie ['muːvi]
Filmmusik soundtrack ['saʊndtræk]
Finale final ['faɪnl]
finanzielle Mittel funding ['fʌndɪŋ]
finanzieren fund [fʌnd]
Finanzierung funding ['fʌndɪŋ]
finden find [faɪnd] **Freunde finden** make friends [meɪk 'frendz]
Finger finger ['fɪŋgə]
Firma company ['kʌmpəni]
Fisch(e) fish [fɪʃ]
Fischstäbchen fish finger [fɪʃ 'fɪŋgə]
fit fit [fɪt]
Fitnessstudio gym [dʒɪm]
flach shallow ['ʃæləʊ]
Flagge flag [flæg]
Flasche bottle ['bɒtl]
Flaschenpost message in a bottle
Fledermaus bat [bæt]
Fleisch meat [miːt]
Fleischbällchen meatball ['miːtbɔːl]
Fliege *(Krawatte)* bow tie [bəʊ 'taɪ]
fliegen fly [flaɪ]
Flieger/in flyer ['flaɪə]
fliehen (vor/aus) escape (from) [ɪ'skeɪp]
Floß raft [rɑːft]
Flucht escape [ɪ'skeɪp]
Flüchtling refugee [refju'dʒiː]
Flug flight [flaɪt]
Flughafen airport ['eəpɔːt]
Flugzeug plane [pleɪn]
Flur *(Diele)* hall [hɔːl]
Fluss river ['rɪvə]
folgen follow ['fɒləʊ]
folglich as a result [rɪ'zʌlt]
Folie *(bei Präsentation m. Computerprogramm)* slide [slaɪd]
Formular form [fɔːm]
Forschung(en) research [rɪ'sɜːtʃ]
fort away [ə'weɪ]
Fortbewegungsmittel transport ['trænspɔːt]
fortfahren continue [kən'tɪnjuː]
fortsetzen; sich fortsetzen continue [kən'tɪnjuː]
Foto photo ['fəʊtəʊ] **ein Foto machen** take a photo
Fotoapparat camera ['kæmərə]
Fotograf/in photographer [fə'tɒgrəfə]
Fotomodell model ['mɒdl]
Frage question ['kwestʃən]
fragen ask [ɑːsk] **nach etwas fragen** ask for sth. ['ɑːsk fə]
Frau female ['fiːmeɪl]; woman, *pl* women ['wʊmən], ['wɪmɪn], *(Anrede für verheiratete Frauen)* Mrs ... ['mɪsɪz] **Frau ...** *(allgemeine Anrede für Frauen)* Ms ... [mɪz], [məz]
frech rude [ruːd]
frei free [friː] **freie Zeit** free time [friː 'taɪm]
Freitag Friday ['fraɪdeɪ], ['fraɪdi]
Freiwillige/r volunteer [vɒlən'tɪə]
Freiwilligenorganisation volunteer organisation [vɒləntɪər ɔːgənaɪ'zeɪʃn]
Freizeit free time [friː 'taɪm]
Fremde/r stranger ['streɪndʒə]
fressen eat [iːt]
Frettchen ferret ['ferɪt]
freuen: Freut mich, dich/euch/Sie kennenzulernen. Nice to meet you. **Freut mich Sie kennenzulernen.** Pleased to meet you. [pliːzd] **sich auf etwas freuen / sich darauf freuen, etwas zu tun** look forward to sth. / to doing sth. [lʊk 'fɔːwəd]
Freund/in friend [frend]; *(feste Freundin)* girlfriend ['gɜːlfrend]; *(fester Freund)* boyfriend ['bɔɪfrend] **Freunde finden** make friends
freundlich friendly ['frendli]; *(nett)* kind [kaɪnd]
Freundschaft friendship ['frendʃɪp]
Frieden peace [piːs]
frieren be cold ['kəʊld]; freeze [friːz]
Frikadelle meatball ['miːtbɔːl]
frisch fresh [freʃ]
Friseur/in hairdresser ['heədresə]
Friseursalon hairdresser's ['heədresəz]
Frisur hairstyle ['heəstaɪl]
frittieren fry [fraɪ]
frittiert fried [fraɪd]
froh happy ['hæpi]; pleased [pliːzd]
Frosch frog [frɒg]
früh early ['ɜːli]
Frühstück breakfast ['brekfəst]
Fuchs fox [fɒks]
fühlen; sich fühlen feel [fiːl]
füllen fill [fɪl]
Füller pen [pen]
fünf five [faɪv]
funktionieren work [wɜːk]
für for [fɔː] **Schritt für Schritt** step by step
fürchterlich terrible ['terəbl]
Fuß foot, *pl* feet [fʊt], [fiːt]
Fußball football ['fʊtbɔːl]; soccer ['sɒkə]
Fußballverein football club (FC) ['fʊtbɔːl klʌb]
Fußboden floor [flɔː]
Futter food [fuːd]
füttern feed [fiːd]

G

Gabel fork [fɔːk]
Gälisch *(Sprache)* Gaelic ['geɪlɪk]
Gamer/in gamer ['geɪmə]
ganz: ganze(r, s) whole [həʊl]
ganz (gut) quite (good) [kwaɪt]
ganze(r, s): auf der ganzen Welt all over the world [ɔːl 'əʊvə] **das ganze Jahr (über)** all year [ɔːl 'jɪə]
Garage garage ['gærɑːʒ]
Gardine curtain ['kɜːtn]
Garnitur set [set]
Garten garden ['gɑːdn]
Gast guest [gest]; visitor ['vɪzɪtə]
Gatter gate [geɪt]

Gebärdensprache sign language ['saın læŋgwıdʒ]
Gebäude building ['bıldıŋ]
geben give [gıv] **es gibt** there are ['ðeər ɑː]; there's [ðeəz]
Gebet prayer [preə]
geboren: er wurde geboren he was born [bɔːn]
gebraten fried [fraıd]; roasted [rəʊstıd]
Geburt birth [bɜːθ]
Geburtsdatum date of birth [deıt əv 'bɜːθ]
Geburtstag birthday ['bɜːθdeı] **Wann hast du Geburtstag?** When's your birthday?
Gedankenkarte mind map ['maınd mæp]
Gedenkstätte memorial [mə'mɔːriəl]
Gedicht poem ['pəʊım]
geduldig patient ['peıʃnt]
geeignet sein für suit [suːt]
Gefahr danger ['deındʒə]
gefährlich dangerous ['deındʒərəs]
gefrieren freeze [friːz]
Gefühl feeling ['fiːlıŋ]
gegen against [ə'genst]
Gegend area ['eəriə]
Gegenstand *(Objekt)* object ['ɒbdʒıkt]
geheim secret ['siːkrət] **im Geheimen** in secret
Geheimnis secret ['siːkrət]
gehen go [gəʊ]; *(weggehen, verlassen)* leave [liːv]; *(zu Fuß)* walk [wɔːk] **ans Telefon gehen** answer the phone ['ɑːnsə] **Auf geht's!** Let's go. **Es geht nicht nur darum, Spiele zu spielen.** It isn't only about playing games. **Wie geht's (dir/euch/Ihnen)?** How are you? [haʊ 'ɑː ju]
gehören belong [bı'lɒŋ]
Gehweg pavement ['peıvmənt]
Geige violin [vaıə'lın]
Geist ghost [gəʊst]
gekocht boiled [bɔıld]
gelangen (nach) get (to) [get]
gelangweilt bored [bɔːd]
gelb yellow ['jeləʊ]
Geld money ['mʌni]
Gelegenheit chance [tʃɑːns]
Gemüse vegetables *(pl)* ['vedʒtəblz]
gemütlich comfortable ['kʌmftəbl]
genau *(exakt)* exact [ıg'zækt]; *(präzise)* specific [spə'sıfık]
genauso gut wie as good as
genießen enjoy [ın'dʒɔı]
genug enough [ı'nʌf]

Geocaching *(GPS-Schnitzeljagd)* geocaching ['dʒiːəʊkæʃıŋ]
geöffnet open ['əʊpən]
Geografie geography [dʒi'ɒgrəfi]
Gepäck luggage ['lʌgıdʒ]; baggage *(AE)* ['bægıdʒ]
gerade straight [streıt] **gerade (eben)** just [dʒʌst] **sich gerade hinsetzen** sit up [sıt 'ʌp]
geradeaus (weiter) straight on [streıt 'ɒn]
Geräte facilities [fə'sılətiz]
Geräusch sound [saʊnd]; *(Lärm)* noise [nɔız]
Gericht *(Mahlzeit)* dish [dıʃ]
gern: etwas sehr gern tun love to do sth. / love doing sth. [lʌv] **Ich hätte gern / Ich möchte** I'd like [laık] **ich würde gern über ... sprechen.** I'd like to (= I would like to) talk about **sie spielen gern ...** they like to play ...
geröstet roasted [rəʊstıd]
Geruch smell [smel]
Gesamt- total ['təʊtl]
Gesamtmenge total ['təʊtl]
Gesamtzahl total ['təʊtl]
Geschäft shop [ʃɒp]; *(Betrieb)* business ['bıznəs]; *(Vereinbarung)* deal [diːl] **ein Geschäft aufmachen** start a business
Geschäftsführer/in CEO (Chief Executive Officer) [siː iː'əʊ], [tʃiːf ıgzekjətıv 'ɒfısə]
Geschäftsmann businessman, *pl* businessmen ['bıznəsmən]
geschehen happen ['hæpən] **Bitte, gern geschehen.** You're welcome. ['welkʌm]
Geschenk present ['preznt]
Geschenkgutschein token ['təʊkən]
Geschichte *(Erzählung)* story ['stɔːri]; tale [teıl]; *(vergangene Zeiten)* history ['hıstri]
geschieden divorced [dı'vɔːst]
Geschirrspülmaschine dishwasher ['dıʃwɒʃə]
Geschlecht *(als soziales Merkmal)* gender ['dʒendə]
geschlossen closed [kləʊzd]
Geschmack taste [teıst]
Gesellschaft company ['kʌmpəni]
Gesicht face [feıs]
gespannt excited [ık'saıtıd]
Gespenst ghost [gəʊst]
Gespräch conversation [kɒnvə'seıʃn]; talk [tɔːk]
gestalten design [dı'zaın]
Gestank smell [smel]
gestern yesterday ['jestədeı]

gesund healthy ['helθi]
Gesundheit health [helθ]
Getränk drink [drıŋk]
Gewalt(tätigkeit) violence ['vaıələns]
gewaltsam violent ['vaıələnt]
gewalttätig violent ['vaıələnt]
Gewinn *(Preis)* prize [praız]; *(Profit)* profit ['prɒfıt] **Gewinn/Profit machen** make a profit
gewinnen win, won, won [wın]
Gewinner/in winner ['wınə]
Gewitter storm [stɔːm]
gewöhnlich ordinary ['ɔːdnri]
Gewürz spice [spaıs]
gezeigt werden *(Kino, Fernsehen)* be on [ɒn]
gierig greedy ['griːdi]
gießen pour [pɔː]
Giraffe giraffe, *pl* giraffe *or* giraffes [dʒə'rɑːf]
Gitarre guitar [gı'tɑː]
Glas glass [glɑːs]
glatt *(Haare)* straight [streıt]
glatzköpfig bald [bɔːld]
glauben think [θıŋk]; *(an etwas)* believe (in sth.) [bı'liːv]
gleich *(dasselbe)* the same [seım]
Gleis *(Bahnsteig)* platform ['plætfɔːm] **auf Gleis 4** at platform 4
Glocke bell [bel]
Glück *(Zufriedenheit)* happiness ['hæpinəs] **Glück haben** be lucky ['lʌki] **zum Glück** fortunately ['fɔːtʃənətli]
glücklich happy ['hæpi]; *(Glück haben)* lucky ['lʌki]
glücklicherweise fortunately ['fɔːtʃənətli]
Glückwunsch: Herzlichen Glückwunsch zum Geburtstag. Happy birthday. [hæpi 'bɜːθdeı]
Gold gold [gəʊld]
Gorilla gorilla [gə'rılə]
Gott god [gɒd] **Oh mein Gott!** Oh my god!
graben dig [dıg]
Gramm gram (= g) [græm]
Graph graph [græf], [grɑːf]
Gras grass [grɑːs]
grau grey [greı]
Grillen barbecue ['bɑːbıkjuː]
Grillfest barbecue ['bɑːbıkjuː]
groß big [bıg]; *(bedeutend, angesehen)* great [greıt]; *(Person)* tall [tɔːl]
großartig amazing [ə'meızıŋ]; great [greıt]; awesome *(AE, infml)* ['ɔːsəm]

Großbritannien (Great) Britain ['brɪtn]
Großbuchstabe capital (letter) ['kæpɪtl]
Größe size [saɪz] **Welche Größe hast du?** What size do you take?
Großeltern grandparents ['grænpeərənts]
Großmutter grandmother ['grænmʌðə]
Großstadt city ['sɪti]
Großvater grandfather ['grænfɑːðə]
grün green [griːn]
Grund *(Begründung)* reason ['riːzn] **aus diesem Grund** for this reason
gründen found [faʊnd]
Gründer/in founder ['faʊndə]
Gruppe group [gruːp]
gruselig scary ['skeəri]
Grüße: Liebe Grüße, ... *(Briefschluss)* Love ... [lʌv] **Viele Grüße ...** Best wishes ['wɪʃɪz]
grüßen: Grüß/t alle. Say hi to everyone. **Grüß Gott.** Hello. [hə'ləʊ]
Gummi gum [gʌm]
gut good [gʊd]; *(Adv.)* well [wel]; *(in Ordnung)* fine [faɪn]; *(okay)* OK [əʊ'keɪ] **Gute Nacht.** Good night. **Guten Morgen.** Good morning. **gut in etwas sein** be good at sth. **Mir geht es gut.** I'm OK. / I'm fine.
Gymnastik gymnastics [dʒɪm'næstɪks]

H

Haar(e) hair [heə]
haben have [hæv]; have got [həv 'gɒt] **Ich hätte gern** I'd like [laɪk] **viel zu tun haben** be busy ['bɪzi]
habgierig greedy ['griːdi]
Hafen harbour ['hɑːbə]; *(Dock)* dock [dɒk]
Haferbrei porridge ['pɒrɪdʒ]
Hähnchen chicken ['tʃɪkɪn]
Hai shark [ʃɑːk]
halb(wegs) halfway [hɑːf'weɪ]
halb 7 half past 6 [pɑːst]
Halbbruder half-brother ['hɑːf brʌðə]
halbe(r, s) half [hɑːf] **auf halbem Wege** halfway [hɑːf'weɪ] **ein halber Apfel** half an apple
Halbschwester half-sister ['hɑːf sɪstə]
Halle hall [hɔːl]
Hallo. Hello. [hə'ləʊ]; Hi. [haɪ]
Halloween *(der Abend des 31. Oktober)* Halloween [hæləʊ'iːn]
Hals throat [θrəʊt]
Halsschmerzen a sore throat [sɔː 'θrəʊt]
halten hold [həʊld]; keep [kiːp]; *(stoppen)* stop [stɒp] **Was halten sie von ...?** What do they think of/about ...? [θɪŋk]
Haltestelle, -punkt stop [stɒp]
Hamburger *(Frikadelle)* burger ['bɜːgə]
Hamster hamster ['hæmstə]
Hand hand [hænd] **Händchen halten** hold hands
Handel trade [treɪd]
handeln *(Handel treiben)* trade [treɪd]
Handlung action ['ækʃn]
Handlung(sverlauf) *(z. B. Film/ Geschichte)* plot [plɒt]
Handschuh glove [glʌv]
Handtuch towel ['taʊəl]
Handy mobile (phone) [məʊbaɪl 'fəʊn]
hängen hang [hæŋ]
hart *(Adj. und Adv.)* hard [hɑːd] **hart trainieren** train hard
hassen hate [heɪt]
Hasser/in hater ['heɪtə]
Hasskommentare: Verfasser/in von Hasskommentaren *(Internet)* hater ['heɪtə]
häufig gestellte Fragen FAQ (= frequently asked questions) [ef eɪ 'kjuː], ['friːkwəntli ɑːskt 'kwestʃənz]
Haupt- main [meɪn]
Hauptgericht main course [meɪn 'kɔːs]
Hauptstadt capital (city) ['kæpɪtl]
Haus house [haʊs] **nach Hause** home [həʊm] **zu Hause** at home [ət 'həʊm]
Hausarbeit chore [tʃɔː] **Hausarbeiten erledigen** do chores
Hausaufgabe(n) homework ['həʊmwɜːk] **Was haben wir als Hausaufgabe(n) auf?** What's for homework?
hausgemacht home-made [həʊm'meɪd]
Haustier pet [pet]
Heft exercise book ['eksəsaɪz bʊk]
Heide(land) moor [mɔː]
heilig holy ['həʊli]
Heim home [həʊm]
Heimweh haben be/feel homesick ['həʊmsɪk]
heiraten marry ['mæri]
heiß hot [hɒt]
heißen be called [kɔːld] **Wie heißt du?** What's your name? [wɒts jɔː 'neɪm]
hektisch busy ['bɪzi]
Held/in hero, *pl* heroes ['hɪərəʊ]
helfen help [help]
hell light [laɪt]
Hemd shirt [ʃɜːt]
heraus out [aʊt]
herausfinden find out [faɪnd 'aʊt]
Herr Taylor Mr Taylor ['mɪstə]
herstellen make [meɪk]
herüber: hier herüber over here [əʊvə 'hɪə]
herumliegen sit [sɪt]
herumstehen sit [sɪt]
herunter down [daʊn]
herunterladen download [daʊn'ləʊd]
herunterregeln turn down [tɜːn 'daʊn]
hervorheben highlight ['haɪlaɪt]
Herz heart [hɑːt] **Du liegst mir am Herzen.** I care about you. [keə]
heute today [tə'deɪ]
hier(her) here [hɪə] **hier drüben / hier herüber** over here [əʊvə 'hɪə]
High-Tech- high-tech [haɪ 'tek]
Hilfe help [help]
hilfreich useful ['juːsfl]
hinauf up [ʌp] **auf die Felsen hinauf** onto the rocks ['ɒntu], ['ɒntə]
hinaus out [aʊt]
hineinlegen put in [pʊt 'ɪn]
hinfallen fall [fɔːl]
hingehören belong [bɪ'lɒŋ]
hinhalten *(ausstrecken)* hold out [həʊld]
hinkommen (nach) *(gelangen nach)* get (to) [get]
hinsetzen: sich gerade hinsetzen sit up [sɪt 'ʌp] **sich hinsetzen** sit down [sɪt 'daʊn]
hinstellen: sich (gerade) hinstellen stand up (straight) [stænd 'ʌp] **sich (hin)stellen** stand [stænd]
hinten at the back [bæk]
hinter behind [bɪ'haɪnd]
hinterer Teil back [bæk]
Hintergrund background ['bækgraʊnd]
hinüber over ['əʊvə]; *(Straße, Brücke)* across [ə'krɒs]
hinunter down [daʊn]
hinweisen auf point out [pɔɪnt 'aʊt]
hinzufügen add [æd]
Hirsch(e) deer [dɪə]

hispanisch *(lateinamerikanischer Herkunft)* Hispanic [hɪ'spænɪk]
historisch ancient ['eɪnʃənt]
Hit hit [hɪt]
Hobby hobby ['hɒbi]
hoch high [haɪ]; *(Gebäude)* tall [tɔːl]; *(hinauf)* up [ʌp]
hochheben pick up [pɪk 'ʌp]
hochladen upload [ʌp'ləʊd]
Hochland: das schottische Hochland the Highlands *(pl)* ['haɪləndz]
Hochleistungs- high-tech [haɪ 'tek]
Hochschule college ['kɒlɪdʒ]
Hochzeit wedding ['wedɪŋ]
Hochzeitsgeschenk wedding present ['wedɪŋ preznt]
Hockey hockey ['hɒki]
hoffen hope [həʊp]
Hoffnung hope [həʊp]
hoffnungslos hopeless ['həʊpləs]
hoffnungsvoll hopeful ['həʊpfl]
höflich polite [pə'laɪt]
Höhepunkt highlight ['haɪlaɪt]
Höhle cave [keɪv]; cavern ['kævən]
holen: (sich) etwas holen get sth. [get]
Holz wood [wʊd]
horchen auf etwas listen for sth.
hören hear [hɪə]
Horror(-) horror ['hɒrə]
Hose pants *(pl) (AE)* [pænts]; trousers *(pl)* ['traʊzəz] **kurze Hose** shorts *(pl)* [ʃɔːts]
Hostel *(günstige Unterkunft für Reisende)* hostel ['hɒstl]
Hot Dog *(heißes Würstchen in einem Brötchen)* hot dog ['hɒt dɒg]
Hotel hotel [həʊ'tel]
Hügel hill [hɪl]
Huhn chicken ['tʃɪkɪn]
Hund dog [dɒg]
Hundeheim dogs' home
hundert a hundred ['hʌndrəd]
Hunger haben be hungry ['hʌŋgri]
Hungersnot famine ['fæmɪn]
hungrig hungry ['hʌŋgri]
Husten; husten cough [kʌf]
Hut hat [hæt]

I

ich I [aɪ] **ich bin** I'm (= I am) [aɪm], [aɪ 'æm] **Ich bin's.** It's me. [ɪts 'miː] **ich (selbst)** myself [maɪ'self]
Idee idea [aɪ'dɪə]
Identität identity [aɪ'dentəti]
ihm him [hɪm]
ihn him [hɪm]
ihnen them [ðem], [ðəm]
ihr *(Plural von „du")*: **ihr selbst** yourselves [jɔː'selvz], [jə'selvz]
ihr *(zu „she")* her [hɜː], [hə] **Hilf ihr.** Help her.
Ihr/e *(besitzanzeigend zur höflichen Anrede „Sie")* your [jɔː], [jə]
ihr/e *(besitzanzeigend bei Dingen und Tieren)* its [ɪts]; *(besitzanzeigend zu „she")* her [hɜː], [hə]; *(besitzanzeigend zu „they")* their [ðeə]
Ihre/r, Ihres yours [jɔːz]
ihre/r, ihrs *(zu „she")* hers [hɜːz]
ihre/r, ihrs *(zu „they")* theirs [ðeəz]
im: im Alter von 12 Jahren at the age of 12 **im Bus** on the bus [ɒn] **im echten Leben** in real life **im Fernsehen** on TV **im Jahre 1540** in 1540 [ɪn] **im Kino/Supermarkt** at the cinema/supermarket [æt], [ət]
immer always ['ɔːlweɪz] **immer noch** still [stɪl]
immigrieren immigrate ['ɪmɪgreɪt]
Imperium empire ['empaɪə]
in at [æt], [ət]; in [ɪn] **in (... hinein)** into ['ɪntu], ['ɪntə] **in der Nacht** at night **in der Schule** at school **in jedem Alter** at any age **etwas ins Internet hochladen** upload sth. to the internet
Information(en) information [ɪnfə'meɪʃn]
Informationsblatt leaflet ['liːflət]
informieren: sich informieren über find out about [faɪnd 'aʊt]
Ingenieur/in engineer [endʒɪ'nɪə]
Inlineskaten skating ['skeɪtɪŋ]
innen inside [ɪn'saɪd]
Innenseite: auf der Innenseite inside [ɪn'saɪd]
insbesondere especially [ɪ'speʃəli]
Insel island ['aɪlənd]
Instrument instrument ['ɪnstrəmənt]
interessant interesting ['ɪntrəstɪŋ]
Interesse (an) interest (in) ['ɪntrəst]
interessieren: Er braucht dich nicht zu interessieren. Never mind him. [nevə 'maɪnd] **Wen interessiert das?** Who cares? [keəz]
Internat boarding school ['bɔːdɪŋ skuːl] **Wohngebäude eines Internats** boarding house ['bɔːdɪŋ haʊs]
international international [ɪntə'næʃnəl]
Internatsschüler/in boarder ['bɔːdə]
Internet internet ['ɪntənet] **nicht übers/im Internet** offline [ɒf'laɪn]
Interview interview ['ɪntəvjuː]
irgendetwas *(in Fragen)* anything ['eniθɪŋ]
irgendjemand anybody ['enibɒdi]; anyone ['eniwʌn]
irgendwelche: Gibt es irgendwelche ...? Are there any ...? ['eni]
irgendwo(hin) somewhere ['sʌmweə]; anywhere ['eniweə] **irgendwo anders** anywhere else [eniweər 'els]
IT (Informationstechnologie) IT (information technology) [aɪ 'tiː], [ɪnfə'meɪʃn teknɒlədʒi]

J

ja yes [jes]
Jacke jacket ['dʒækɪt]
Jackett jacket ['dʒækɪt]
Jagd hunt [hʌnt]
jagen hunt [hʌnt]
Jahr(gang) year [jɪə] **im Jahre 1540** in 1540
Jahrhundert century ['sentʃəri]
Januar January ['dʒænjuəri]
Jeans jeans *(pl)* [dʒiːnz]
jede(r, s) *(alle)* everybody ['evribɒdi]; *(vor Nomen)* every ['evri] **jede/r andere** everybody/everyone else [els] **jede/r (beliebige)** anybody ['enibɒdi]; anyone ['eniwʌn] **jeder/jede/jedes (einzelne)** each [iːtʃ]
jedoch however [haʊ'evə]
jemals ever ['evə]
jemand somebody, someone ['sʌmbədi], ['sʌmwʌn]; *(irgendjemand, jeder beliebige)* anybody ['enibɒdi]; *(irgendjemand, jeder beliebige)* anyone ['eniwʌn]
jene(r, s) that [ðæt] **jene (dort)** those [ðəʊz] **in jener Nacht** that night
jetzt now [naʊ]
Job job [dʒɒb]
jubeln *(anfeuern)* cheer [tʃɪə]
Jugendliche/r kid [kɪd]
Juli July [dʒu'laɪ]
jung young [jʌŋ]
Junge boy [bɔɪ]
Juni June [dʒuːn]

K

Käfig cage [keɪdʒ]
kahl bald [bɔːld]

Kaiser emperor ['empərə]
Kaiserin empress ['emprəs]
Kakao hot chocolate [hɒt 'tʃɒklət]
Kalender calendar ['kælɪndə]
Kalifornien California [kælə'fɔːniə]
kalt cold [kəʊld]
Kälte cold [kəʊld]
Kamera camera ['kæmərə]
Kampf fight [faɪt]
kämpfen fight [faɪt]
Kämpfer/in fighter ['faɪtə]
Kanal channel ['tʃænl]
Kaninchen rabbit ['ræbɪt]
Kantine canteen [kæn'tiːn]
Kapelle *(kleiner kirchlicher Raum)* chapel ['tʃæpl]
Kapitän/in captain ['kæptɪn]
Kapitel *(Schulbuch)* unit ['juːnɪt]
Kapsel capsule ['kæpsjuːl]
kaputt broken ['brəʊkən]
kaputtgehen break [breɪk]
kaputtmachen break [breɪk]
Kapuze hood [hʊd]
Kapuzenpullover hoodie ['hʊdi]
Karate karate [kə'rɑːti]
Karibik; karibisch Caribbean [kærɪ'biːən]
Karneval carnival ['kɑːnɪvl]
Karotte carrot ['kærət]
Karriere career [kə'rɪə]
Karte card [kɑːd]
Kartenschalter ticket office ['tɪkɪt ɒfɪs]
Kartenverkaufsstelle ticket office ['tɪkɪt ɒfɪs]
Kartoffel potato, *pl* potatoes [pə'teɪtəʊ]
Kartoffelchips crisps [krɪsps]
Käse cheese [tʃiːz]
Kästchen box [bɒks]; square [skweə]
Kasten box [bɒks]
Kathedrale cathedral [kə'θiːdrəl]
Katholik/in Catholic ['kæθlɪk]
katholisch Catholic ['kæθlɪk]
Katze cat [kæt]
Kauderwelsch gobbledygook *(infml)* ['gɒbldiguːk]
kauen chew [tʃuː]
kaufen buy [baɪ]
Kaufhaus department store [dɪ'pɑːtmənt stɔː]
Kaufpreis price [praɪs]
Kaugummi chewing gum ['tʃuːɪŋ gʌm]
kaum hardly ['hɑːdli]
Kegeln *(Bowling)* bowling ['bəʊlɪŋ]
kein/e no [nəʊ] **es gibt kein/keine/keinen** there aren't any ['eni] **ich bin kein/e ...** I'm not ... [nɒt]
keine(r, s) none [nʌn]
Keks biscuit ['bɪskɪt]
Keller cellar ['selə]
kennen know [nəʊ]
kennenlernen meet [miːt] **Freut mich, dich/euch/Sie kennenzulernen.** Nice to meet you.
Kerze candle ['kændl]
Kilometer kilometre (km) ['kɪləmiːtə]
Kilt *(schottischer Rock für Männer)* kilt [kɪlt]
Kind child, *pl* children [tʃaɪld], ['tʃɪldrən]; kid [kɪd]
Kinderfahrschein child ticket [tʃaɪld 'tɪkɪt]
Kino cinema ['sɪnəmə]; movie theater *(AE)* ['muːvi θɪətə] **im Kino** at the cinema
Kirche church [tʃɜːtʃ]
Kiste box [bɒks]
Klang sound [saʊnd]
klar clear [klɪə]
Klasse class [klɑːs]; grade *(AE)* [greɪd]
klasse *(großartig)* awesome *(AE, infml)* ['ɔːsəm]
Klassenarbeit test [test]
Klassenausflug class trip ['klɑːs trɪp]
Klassenlehrer/in class teacher ['klɑːs tiːtʃə]
Klassenraum classroom ['klɑːsruːm]
Klaue claw [klɔː]
Klavier piano [pi'ænəʊ]
Kleeblatt shamrock ['ʃæmrɒk]
Kleid dress [dres]
Kleiderordnung dress code ['dres kəʊd]
Kleiderschrank wardrobe ['wɔːdrəʊb]
Kleidung(sstücke) clothes *(pl)* [kləʊðz]
klein little ['lɪtl]; small [smɔːl]; *(Personen)* short [ʃɔːt]
klicken (auf) click (on) [klɪk]
klingeln ring [rɪŋ]; *(Wecker)* go off [gəʊ 'ɒf]
klopfen (an etwas) knock (at sth.) [nɒk] **leise klopfen an etwas** tap sth. [tæp] **mit den Fingern klopfen** tap your fingers
Klotz block [blɒk]
Klub club [klʌb] **in einen Klub eintreten** join a club [dʒɔɪn]
klug clever ['klevə]
knacken *(z. B. Code)* crack [kræk]
Kneipe pub [pʌb]
kneten knead [niːd]
knien kneel [niːl]
Knoblauch garlic ['gɑːlɪk]
Knochen bone [bəʊn]
knochenlos boneless ['bəʊnləs]
Koch, Köchin cook [kʊk]
kochen cook [kʊk]; *(in Wasser)* boil [bɔɪl]
Kochrezept recipe ['resəpi]
kodieren *(Computer)* code [kəʊd]
Kodierer/in *(Programmierer/in)* coder ['kəʊdə]
komisch funny ['fʌni]
Komma *(Dezimalzeichen)* point [pɔɪnt]
kommen come [kʌm] **(hin) kommen (nach)** *(gelangen nach)* get (to) [get] **Wo kommst du her?** Where are you from?
Kommentar comment ['kɒment]
kommentieren comment on ['kɒment ɒn]
Kommode chest of drawers, *pl* chests of drawers [tʃest əv 'drɔːz]
komplett complete [kəm'pliːt]
König king [kɪŋ]
Königin queen [kwiːn]
königlich royal ['rɔɪəl]
Königreich: das Vereinigte Königreich the United Kingdom (UK) [junaɪtɪd 'kɪŋdəm]
können can [kæn], [kən] **du könntest ... finden** you might find ... [maɪt] **es kann nicht spielen** it can't (= cannot) play [kɑːnt], ['kænɒt] **etwas gut können** be good at sth. [bi 'gʊd æt] **ich konnte, ich könnte** I could [kʊd]
Kontakt contact ['kɒntækt] **Kontakt aufnehmen mit jm.** contact sb.
Kontrolle check [tʃek]
kontrollieren check [tʃek]
Konzentration concentration [kɒnsn'treɪʃn]
konzentrieren: sich konzentrieren (auf) concentrate (on) ['kɒnsntreɪt]
Konzert concert ['kɒnsət]
Kopf head [hed]
Kopfschmerzen headache ['hedeɪk]
Kopfsprung: einen Kopfsprung machen dive [daɪv]
Kopie copy ['kɒpi]
kopieren copy ['kɒpi]
Korbball netball ['netbɔːl]
Körper body ['bɒdi]
Körpersprache body language ['bɒdi læŋgwɪdʒ]
kostbar precious ['preʃəs]

kosten *(Geld)* cost [kɒst]; *(probieren)* taste [teɪst] **Das Hemd kostet 2 Pfund.** The shirt is £2. **Die Hemden kosten 6 Pfund.** The shirts are £6. **Was (Wie viel) kostet/kosten?** How much is/are ...?
kostenlos free [friː]
Kostüm costume ['kɒstjuːm]; *(Damenkostüm)* suit [suːt]; *(Verkleidung)* fancy dress [fænsi 'dres]
Kostümparty fancy dress party [fænsi 'dres pɑːti]
krachen crash [kræʃ]
Kraft power ['paʊə]
Kralle claw [klɔː]
krank ill [ɪl]; sick [sɪk]
Krankenhaus hospital ['hɒspɪtl]
Krankenpfleger/in nurse [nɜːs]
Krankheit disease [dɪ'ziːz]; illness ['ɪlnəs]
kratzen scrape [skreɪp]
Krawatte tie [taɪ]
kreativ creative [kri'eɪtɪv]
Krebs crab [kræb]
Kreis circle ['sɜːkl]
Kreuz cross [krɒs]
kreuzen cross [krɒs]
Krimi crime film ['kraɪm fɪlm]
Kriminalität crime [kraɪm]
Krimiserie detective series [dɪ'tektɪv sɪəriːz]
Kritik *(Rezension)* review [rɪ'vjuː]
Küche kitchen ['kɪtʃɪn]
Kuchen cake [keɪk]
Kugelschreiber pen [pen]
kühl cool [kuːl]
kühlen cool [kuːl]
Kühlschrank fridge [frɪdʒ]
Kultur culture ['kʌltʃə]
kümmern: Kümmer dich nicht um ihn Never mind him. [nevə 'maɪnd] **sich kümmern um** look after [lʊk 'ɑːftə]
Kunde, Kundin customer ['kʌstəmə]
Kunst art [ɑːt]
Künstler/in artist ['ɑːtɪst]
Kunststoff plastic ['plæstɪk]
Kurdisch Kurdish ['kɜːdɪʃ]
Kurs class [klɑːs]
kurz short [ʃɔːt]
kurze Hose shorts *(pl)* [ʃɔːts]
Küste coast [kəʊst]

L

lächeln; *(ein)* Lächeln smile [smaɪl]
lachen; *(ein)* Lachen laugh [lɑːf]
Lacrosse *(Ballspiel, ähnlich wie Hockey)* lacrosse [lə'krɒs]
Laden shop [ʃɒp]
laden load [ləʊd]
Lager *(Zeltlager)* camp [kæmp]
lahm *(langweilig)* lame [leɪm]
Lampe lamp [læmp]
Land country ['kʌntri]; *(Grund und Boden)* land [lænd] **auf dem Land** in the country
landen land [lænd]
Landkarte map [mæp]
Landstraße road [rəʊd]
Landwirt/in farmer ['fɑːmə]
Landwirtschaft farming ['fɑːmɪŋ]
lang long [lɒŋ] **30 Jahre lang** for 30 years [fɔː]
Länge length [leŋθ]
langsam slow [sləʊ]
langweilig boring ['bɔːrɪŋ]; lame [leɪm] **mir ist langweilig** I'm bored [bɔːd]
Laptop laptop ['læptɒp]
Lärm noise [nɔɪz]
Lasagne lasagne [lə'zænjə]
lassen leave [liːv]; let [let] **etwas zu Hause lassen** leave sth. at home **Lass(t) uns ...** Let's ... [lets]
Lasso lasso, *pl* lassos *or* lassoes [læ'suː]
Last(kraft)wagen lorry ['lɒri]; truck [trʌk]
laufen run [rʌn]
Läufer *(Teppich)* rug [rʌg]
Laut sound [saʊnd]
laut loud [laʊd]; *(voller Lärm)* noisy ['nɔɪzi] **laut ...** *(... zufolge)* according to [ə'kɔːdɪŋ] **mit lauter Stimme** in a loud voice [vɔɪs]
läuten ring [rɪŋ]
Leben life, *pl* lives [laɪf], [laɪvz]
leben live [lɪv]
Lebensmittel food [fuːd]
lecker yum *(infml)* [jʌm]; tasty ['teɪsti]
Leder leather ['leðə]
leer empty ['empti]
leeren empty ['empti]
legen put [pʊt]; set [set] **zur Seite legen** put away
lehnen lean [liːn]
lehren teach [tiːtʃ]
Lehrer/in teacher ['tiːtʃə]
leicht *(einfach)* easy ['iːzi]; *(Gewicht, Arbeit)* light [laɪt]
leider unfortunately [ʌn'fɔːtʃənətli]
leidtun: Tut mir leid. Sorry. / I'm sorry. ['sɒri]
leihen lend [lend] **sich (aus) leihen** borrow ['bɒrəʊ]
Leinen linen ['lɪnɪn]
leise quiet ['kwaɪət]; *(Stimme)* soft [sɒft] **leise(r) stellen** turn down [tɜːn 'daʊn] **mit leiser Stimme** in a soft voice
leisten: (es) sich leisten (können) afford [ə'fɔːd]
Lektion *(Schulbuch)* unit ['juːnɪt]
lernen learn [lɜːn]; *(z. B. für Prüfungen)* study ['stʌdi]
lesen read [riːd]
Leser/in reader ['riːdə]
letzte(r, s) last [lɑːst] **letzte Woche** last week
Leute people ['piːpl]; *(als Anrede verwendet)* guys *(pl)* [gaɪz]
Licht light [laɪt] **Licht aus** lights out
Liebe love [lʌv]
Liebe/r ... Dear ... [dɪə]
lieben love [lʌv]
lieber: etwas lieber mögen like sth. better ['betə] **etwas lieber tun/haben als etwas** prefer sth. to sth. [prɪ'fɜː]
Lieblings- favourite ['feɪvərɪt]
Lied song [sɒŋ]
Liedermacher songwriter ['sɒŋraɪtə]
Liga league [liːg]
lila purple ['pɜːpl]
Limonade lemonade [lemə'neɪd]
Lineal ruler ['ruːlə]
Link link [lɪŋk]
links, nach links left [left] **auf der linken Seite** on the left **auf links** *(Kleidung)* inside out [ɪnsaɪd 'aʊt] **dein T-Shirt auf links ziehen** turn your T-shirt inside out
List trick [trɪk]
Liste list [lɪst]
live live [laɪv]
LKW lorry ['lɒri]; truck [trʌk]
Loch hole [həʊl]
lockig curly ['kɜːli]
Löffel spoon [spuːn]
Londoner/in Londoner ['lʌndənə]
los: Dann mal los! Go ahead. [ə'hed]; Let's go. [lets 'gəʊ]
löschen delete [dɪ'liːt]
lösen *(z. B. Problem)* crack [kræk]
losgehen *(Alarm, Waffe)* go off [gəʊ 'ɒf]
Lösung (eines Problems) solution (to a problem) [sə'luːʃn]
Löwe lion ['laɪən]
Lücke gap [gæp]
Luft air [eə]
Lüge lie [laɪ]
lügen lie [laɪ]; tell a lie/lies

M

machen *(herstellen)* make [meɪk]; *(tun)* do [duː] **Das macht 2 Pfund.** That's £2. **eine Prüfung machen** take/do an exam [ɪɡ'zæm] **ein Foto machen** take a photo [teɪk ə 'fəʊtəʊ] **sich Sorgen machen (wegen, um)** worry (about) ['wʌri] **wie man etwas macht** how to do sth.
Macht power ['paʊə]
Mädchen girl [ɡɜːl]
Magen stomach ['stʌmək]
Magenschmerzen stomach ache ['stʌmək eɪk]
Magie magic ['mædʒɪk]
magisch magic ['mædʒɪk]
mähen *(Rasen)* cut [kʌt]
Mahlzeit meal [miːl] **kleine Mahlzeit** snack [snæk]
Mai May [meɪ]
Makkaroni macaroni [mækə'rəʊni]
Mal time [taɪm] **viele Male** lots of times
Mama mum [mʌm]; *(AE)* mom [mɒm]
Manager/in manager ['mænɪdʒə]
manchmal sometimes ['sʌmtaɪmz]
Mann male [meɪl]; man, *pl* men [mæn], [men]
männlich male [meɪl]
Mannschaft team [tiːm]
Märchen fairy tale ['feəri teɪl]
Markt market ['mɑːkɪt]
März March [mɑːtʃ]
Maschine machine [mə'ʃiːn]
Maske mask [mɑːsk]
Material material [mə'tɪəriəl]
Mathe(matik) maths [mæθs]
Mauer wall [wɔːl]
Maus mouse, *pl* mice [maʊs], [maɪs]
Medien media ['miːdiə]
Medikament(e) medicine ['medsɪn]
Medizin medicine ['medsɪn]
Meer sea [siː]
Meerschweinchen guinea pig ['ɡɪni pɪɡ]
Mehl flour ['flaʊə]
mehr more [mɔː] **mehr als** more than ['mɔː ðən] **nicht mehr** not (...) any more [eni 'mɔː]
mehrere several ['sevrəl]
Mehrspieler- multiplayer [mʌlti'pleɪə]
mein/e *(vor Nomen)* my [maɪ]
meine/r, meins mine [maɪn]
meinen *(denken, glauben)* think [θɪŋk]; *(sagen wollen)* mean [miːn]
Meinung opinion [ə'pɪnjən] **meiner Meinung nach** in my opinion **seine Meinung ändern** change your mind [tʃeɪndʒ jə 'maɪnd]
meiste(r, s): die meisten; am meisten (the) most [məʊst]
meistens usually ['juːʒuəli]
Meisterschaft championship ['tʃæmpiənʃɪp]
melden: sich melden *(aufzeigen)* put up your hand [pʊt 'ʌp]
Menge *(Menschenmenge)* crowd [kraʊd]
Mensa canteen [kæn'tiːn]
Mensch: Mensch ärgere dich nicht *(Spiel)* ludo ['luːdəʊ] **Menschen** people ['piːpl]
Menschenmenge crowd [kraʊd]
Mentor/in *(Ratgeber/in)* mentor ['mentə]
merken *(bemerken)* notice ['nəʊtɪs]
Messer knife, *pl* knives [naɪf], [naɪvz]
Metall metal ['metl]
Meter metre ['miːtə]
mich me [miː] **mich (selbst)** myself [maɪ'self]
Milch milk [mɪlk]
Milliarde billion ['bɪliən]
Million million ['mɪljən]
Mindmap mind map ['maɪnd mæp]
Minute minute ['mɪnɪt]
mir me [miː] **mir (selbst)** myself [maɪ'self]
mischen mix [mɪks]
mit with [wɪð] **mit 12 Jahren** at the age of 12 **mit dem Fahrrad/Auto/...** by bike/car/... [baɪ]
mitbekommen: etwas mitbekommen *(verstehen, richtig hören)* get sth. [ɡet]
mitbringen bring [brɪŋ]
mitkommen come [kʌm]
mitnehmen take [teɪk] **Essen zum Mitnehmen** takeaway ['teɪkəweɪ]
Mitschüler/in classmate ['klɑːsmeɪt]
Mittag: (zu) Mittag essen have lunch [lʌntʃ]
Mittagessen lunch [lʌntʃ] **Was gibt es zum Mittagessen?** What's for lunch?
Mitte middle ['mɪdl] **in der Mitte** in the middle
Mitteilung message ['mesɪdʒ]; notification [nəʊtɪfɪ'keɪʃn]
Mittwoch Wednesday ['wenzdeɪ], ['wenzdi]
mobben bully ['bʊli]
Mobber/in bully ['bʊli]
Möbel furniture ['fɜːnɪtʃə]
möchte: Ich möchte ... I'd like ... [laɪk] **Ich möchte, dass ihr ... seid.** I'd like you to be ... **ich möchte gern über ... sprechen.** I'd like to (= I would like to) talk about
Mode fashion ['fæʃn]
Modell model ['mɒdl]
modern modern ['mɒdn]
mögen like [laɪk] **etwas am liebsten mögen** like sth. best **sehr mögen** love [lʌv]
Möhre carrot ['kærət]
Moment moment ['məʊmənt] **Einen Moment.** Wait a minute. ['weɪt ə mɪnɪt] **im Moment** at the moment
Monat month [mʌnθ]
Mönch monk [mʌŋk]
Monster monster ['mɒnstə]
Montag Monday ['mʌndeɪ], ['mʌndi]
Monument monument ['mɒnjumənt]
Moor moor [mɔː]
Mops *(Hund)* pug [pʌɡ]
Morgen morning ['mɔːnɪŋ] **am Morgen** in the morning **Guten Morgen.** Good morning.
morgen tomorrow [tə'mɒrəʊ] **Bis morgen.** See you tomorrow.
morgens in the morning ['mɔːnɪŋ] **9 Uhr morgens** 9 am [eɪ'em]
Motorroller scooter ['skuːtə]
müde tired ['taɪəd]
Muffin *(kleiner runder Kuchen)* muffin ['mʌfɪn]
Müll rubbish ['rʌbɪʃ]; trash *(AE)* [træʃ]
Mülleimer bin [bɪn]
multikulturell multicultural [mʌlti'kʌltʃərəl]
Mund mouth [maʊθ]
Münze coin [kɔɪn]
Museum museum [mju'ziːəm]
Musical musical ['mjuːzɪkl]
Musik music ['mjuːzɪk]
musikalisch musical ['mjuːzɪkl]
Musiker/in musician [mju'zɪʃn]
Musikgruppe band [bænd]
müssen must [mʌst] **etwas tun müssen** have to do sth.; need to do sth. [niːd]
Muster *(wiederkehrend)* pattern ['pætn]
mutig brave [breɪv]
Mutter mother ['mʌðə]
Muttersprache first language [fɜːst 'læŋɡwɪdʒ]

Mutti mum [mʌm]; *(AE)* mom [mɒm]
Mütze hat [hæt]

N

na: Na ja, ... Well, ... [wel] **Na und?** Who cares? [keəz]
nach *(auf etwas zu)* toward(s) [tə'wɔːd], [tə'wɔːdz]; *(örtlich)* to [tu], [tə]; *(zeitlich)* after [ɑːftə] **nach Hause** home [həʊm] **400 n. Chr.** 400 AD [eɪ 'diː] **viertel nach 6** quarter past 6 [pɑːst]
Nachbar/in neighbour ['neɪbə]
nachdenken über think about
nachgeben: (jm./einer Sache) nachgeben give in (to sb./sth.) [gɪv 'ɪn]
nachlässig sloppy ['slɒpi]
nachlaufen: jm. nachlaufen run after sb.
Nachmittag afternoon [ɑːftə'nuːn]
nachmittags: 5 Uhr nachmittags 5 pm [piː'em]
Nachname last name ['lɑːst neɪm]
Nachricht message ['mesɪdʒ]
Nachrichten news [njuːz]
Nachschlag seconds *(pl)* ['sekəndz]
Nachsitzen detention [dɪ'tenʃn]
Nachspeise dessert [dɪ'zɜːt]
nächste(r, s) next [nekst] **am nächsten Tag/Morgen** the next day/morning
Nächstes: als Nächstes next
nächstgelegene: der/die/das nächstgelegene ... the nearest ... ['nɪərɪst]
Nacht night [naɪt] **Gute Nacht.** Good night. **in der Nacht** at night **in jener Nacht** that night
Nachteil disadvantage [dɪsəd'vɑːntɪdʒ] **im Nachteil** at a disadvantage
nachts at night [naɪt]
nachweisen prove [pruːv]
nahe (bei) near [nɪə]
Nähe: in der Nähe von near [nɪə]
nähen sew [səʊ]
Nähmaschine sewing machine ['səʊɪŋ məʃiːn]
Name name [neɪm]
Namenstag name day ['neɪm deɪ]
nämlich you know
Nase nose [nəʊz]
nass wet [wet]
national, National- national ['næʃnəl]
Nationalfeiertag national day [næʃnəl 'deɪ]
Nationalität nationality [næʃə'nælətі]
Nationalpark national park [næʃnəl 'pɑːk]
natürlich of course [əv 'kɔːs]
Naturwissenschaft science ['saɪəns]
Naturwissenschaftler/in scientist ['saɪəntɪst]
Nebel fog [fɒg]
nebelig foggy ['fɒgi]
neben next to ['nekst tə]
negativ negative ['negətɪv]
nehmen take [teɪk]; *(z. B. Zug, Bus)* catch [kætʃ] **aus dem Spiel nehmen** take off [teɪk 'ɒf] **ich nehme ...** *(beim Essen, im Restaurant)* I'll have ... [aɪl 'hæv]
nein no [nəʊ]
nennen call [kɔːl]
Neoprenanzug wetsuit ['wetsuːt]
nervös nervous ['nɜːvəs]
nett nice [naɪs]; *(freundlich)* kind [kaɪnd]
Netz web [web]; *(Sport)* net [net]
neu new [njuː]
neulich recently ['riːsntli]
neun nine [naɪn]
nicht not [nɒt] **nicht mehr** not (...) any more [eni 'mɔː] **ich bin nicht ...** I'm not ... **ich mochte ... nicht** I didn't like ... **noch nicht ...** not ... yet [jet]
Nichte niece [niːs]
nichts nothing ['nʌθɪŋ]; not (...) anything ['eniθɪŋ] **Nichts zu danken.** You're welcome. ['welkʌm]
Nicken *(Kopfnicken)* nod (of your head) [nɒd]
nicken: (mit dem Kopf) nicken nod (your head) [nɒd]
nie(mals) never ['nevə]
niederlassen: sich niederlassen settle ['setl]
niedlich cute [kjuːt]
niemand no one ['nəʊ wʌn]; nobody ['nəʊbədi]
nirgends not (...) anywhere
nirgendwo(hin) nowhere ['nəʊweə]
noch *(immer noch)* still [stɪl] **noch ein/e** another [ə'nʌðə] **noch einmal** again [ə'gen] **noch nicht** not ... yet [jet]
Nord-, nördlich northern ['nɔːðən]
Norden, Nord- north [nɔːθ] **in Richtung Norden** northbound ['nɔːθbaʊnd]
nördlich north [nɔːθ]
Nordosten, nordöstlich north-east [nɔːθ'iːst]
Nordwesten, nordwestlich north-west [nɔːθ'west]
normal normal ['nɔːml]; *(gewöhnlich)* ordinary ['ɔːdnri]
normalerweise usually ['juːʒuəli]
Normanne/Normannin Norman ['nɔːmən]
normannisch Norman ['nɔːmən]
Note: (Schul-)Note grade [greɪd]
Notfall emergency [i'mɜːdʒənsi]
Notiz note [nəʊt] **sich Notizen machen** *(beim Lesen oder Zuhören)* take notes [teɪk 'nəʊts]; *(zur Vorbereitung)* make notes
Notizbuch notebook ['nəʊtbʊk]
November November [nəʊ'vembə]
Nudeln noodles [nuːdlz]; noodles *(pl)*
Null zero ['zɪərəʊ]; *(im gesprochenen Englisch)* oh [əʊ]
Nummer number ['nʌmbə]
nun now [naʊ] **Nun, ...** Well, ... [wel]
nur just [dʒʌst]; only ['əʊnli] **Was/Wo/... ist denn nur/bloß ...?** What/Where/... the heck is ...? *(infml)* [hek]
Nuss nut [nʌt]
nützlich useful ['juːsfl]
nutzlos useless ['juːsləs]

O

ob if [ɪf]
obdachlos homeless ['həʊmləs]
oben *(die Treppe hoch)* upstairs [ʌp'steəz] **das obere Ende** top [tɒp]
oberflächlich shallow ['ʃæləʊ]
Objekt object ['ɒbdʒɪkt]
Obst fruit [fruːt]
obwohl although [ɔːl'ðəʊ]; though [ðəʊ]
oder or [ɔː]
offen open ['əʊpən]
öffentlich public ['pʌblɪk]
offline offline [ɒf'laɪn]
öffnen, sich öffnen open ['əʊpən]
oft often ['ɒfn], ['ɒftən]
ohne without [wɪ'ðaʊt] **ohne Freunde** friendless ['frendləs]
Ohr ear [ɪə]
Ohrenschmerzen earache ['ɪəreɪk]
okay OK [əʊ'keɪ]
Oktober October [ɒk'təʊbə]
Öl oil [ɔɪl]
Ölbohrinsel oil rig ['ɔɪl rɪg]
ölig oily ['ɔɪli]

olympische Spiele Olympics [ə'lɪmpɪks]
Oma grandma ['grænmɑː]
Onkel uncle ['ʌŋkl]
online, Online- online [ɒn'laɪn]
Opa grandad ['grændæd]
Oper opera ['ɒpərə]
Orange orange ['ɒrɪndʒ]
orange(farben) orange ['ɒrɪndʒ]
Orangensaft orange juice ['ɒrɪndʒ dʒuːs]
Orchester orchestra ['ɔːkɪstrə]
ordentlich tidy ['taɪdi]
Ordnung: in Ordnung fine [faɪn]; OK [əʊ'keɪ]
Ort place [pleɪs]
Osten, Ost- east [iːst] **in Richtung Osten** *(Zug, Bus)* eastbound ['iːstbaʊnd]
Ostern Easter ['iːstə]
östlich east [iːst]
östlich, Ost- eastern ['iːstən]
Ozean ocean ['əʊʃn]

P

Paar couple ['kʌpl]; pair [peə] **ein paar; ein Paar** a couple of
paar: ein paar a few [fjuː]; some [sʌm], [səm] **Möchtest du ein paar Kartoffeln?** Would you like some potatoes?
pantomimisch darstellen mime [maɪm]
Papa dad [dæd]
Papier paper ['peɪpə] **Stück Papier** piece of paper [piːs əv 'peɪpə]
Paprika pepper ['pepə]
Parade parade [pə'reɪd]
Park park [pɑːk]
Parkplatz car park ['kɑː pɑːk]; parking lot *(AE)* ['pɑːkɪŋ lɒt]
Parlament parliament ['pɑːləmənt]
Partner/in partner ['pɑːtnə]
Party party ['pɑːti]
Pass *(Reisepass)* passport ['pɑːspɔːt]
Passagier/in passenger ['pæsɪndʒə]
passen (zu) fit [fɪt]; *(geeignet sein)* suit [suːt]
passieren happen ['hæpən]
Pasta pasta ['pæstə]
Pause break [breɪk]; recess *(AE)* [rɪ'ses] **Pause machen** take a break [teɪk ə 'breɪk]
Pazifischer Ozean, Pazifik Pacific Ocean [pəsɪfɪk 'əʊʃn]
Pence: fünfzig Pence 50p [piː]
Peperoni pepper ['pepə]
Person person ['pɜːsn]
persönlich private ['praɪvət]
Pfad path [pɑːθ]
Pfanne pan [pæn]
Pfeffer pepper ['pepə]
Pferd horse [hɔːs] **ein Pferd reiten / auf einem Pferd reiten** ride a horse [raɪd]
Pflaume plum [plʌm]
Pflicht *(lästige Pflicht)* chore [tʃɔː]
Pflug plough [plaʊ]
pflügen plough [plaʊ]
Pfund *(britische Währung)* pound: (£) [paʊnd]; *(Gewichtseinheit)* pound
Picknick picnic ['pɪknɪk] **ein Picknick machen** have a picnic
Pirat/in pirate ['paɪrət]
Pizza pizza ['piːtsə]
Plan plan [plæn]
planen plan [plæn]
Plastik plastic ['plæstɪk]
Plattenvertrag record deal ['rekɔːd diːl]
Platz site [saɪt]; *(in der Stadt)* square [skweə]; *(Ort)* place [pleɪs]
Plätzchen *(Keks)* biscuit ['bɪskɪt]
plötzlich suddenly ['sʌdənli]
Polizei police *(pl)* [pə'liːs]
Polizeibeamter/-beamtin police officer [pə'liːs ɒfɪsə]
Pommes frites chips *(pl)* [tʃɪps]
Pony pony ['pəʊni]
Pop(musik) pop (music) ['pɒp mjuːzɪk]
Popcorn popcorn ['pɒpkɔːn]
Popstar pop star ['pɒp stɑː]
populär popular ['pɒpjələ]
Portrait *(Profil)* profile ['prəʊfaɪl]
positiv positive ['pɒzətɪv]
Post *(Briefe etc.)* post [pəʊst]
Post *(Eintrag in Blog oder sozialen Medien)* post [pəʊst]
Post(amt) post office ['pəʊst ɒfɪs]
posten *(im Internet veröffentlichen)* post [pəʊst]
Poster poster ['pəʊstə]
Postkarte postcard ['pəʊstkɑːd]
Postleitzahl postcode ['pəʊstkəʊd]
Präsentation presentation [prezn'teɪʃn]
präsentieren present [prɪ'zent]
Präsident/in president ['prezɪdənt]
präzise specific [spə'sɪfɪk]
Preis *(Auszeichnung)* award [ə'wɔːd]; *(Gewinn)* prize [praɪz]; *(Kaufpreis)* price [praɪs]
preisgekrönt award-winning [ə'wɔːd wɪnɪŋ]
Preisträger/in award-winner [ə'wɔːd wɪnə]
preiswert cheap [tʃiːp]
Priester/in priest [priːst]
Prinz prince [prɪns]
privat private ['praɪvət]
pro: dreimal pro Woche three times a week
probieren try [traɪ]
Problem problem ['prɒbləm]
Profil profile ['prəʊfaɪl]
programmieren *(Computer)* code [kəʊd]
Programmierer/in coder ['kəʊdə]
Projekt project ['prɒdʒekt]
Promi celebrity [sə'lebrəti]
Prominente/r celebrity [sə'lebrəti]
Protestant/in Protestant ['prɒtɪstənt]
protestantisch Protestant ['prɒtɪstənt]
Prozent per cent [pə 'sent]
prüfen check [tʃek]
Prüfung examination *(infml. auch* exam) [ɪgzæmɪ'neɪʃn], [ɪg'zæm] **eine Prüfung machen** take/do an exam
Pullover pullover ['pʊləʊvə]
Punkt point [pɔɪnt]; *(im Spiel/Sport erzielt)* score [skɔː]
punkten *(im Sport)* score [skɔː]
Punktestand score [skɔː]
pünktlich on time [ɒn 'taɪm]
pusten blow [bləʊ]
Pute; Putenfleisch turkey ['tɜːki]
putzen do the cleaning [du ðə 'kliːnɪŋ]; clean [kliːn]

Q

Qualität(s-) quality ['kwɒləti] **von besserer Qualität sein** be better quality
Quelle *(z. B. Website, Text)* source [sɔːs]
Quiz quiz, *pl* quizzes [kwɪz], ['kwɪzɪz]

R

Rad wheel [wiːl]; *(Fahrrad)* bike [baɪk]
Rad fahren: *(das)* **Radfahren** biking
Radiergummi rubber ['rʌbə]
Rampe ramp [ræmp]
Rap rap [ræp]
Rasen grass [grɑːs]
Rat(schlag), Ratschläge advice [əd'vaɪs]
Ratgeber (für) *(Buch, Broschüre)* guide (to) [gaɪd]
rauben steal [stiːl]
Raum room [ruːm], [rʊm]

Rauschgift drug [drʌg]
reagieren (auf) react (to) [ri'ækt]
real *(aus dem echten Leben)* real-life [rɪəl 'laɪf]
Realität reality [ri'æləti]
Recherche(n) research [rɪ'sɜːtʃ]
recherchieren do research [rɪ'sɜːtʃ]
Recht right
Recht haben be right [raɪt]
rechts, nach rechts right [raɪt] **auf der rechten Seite** on the right
Rechtschreibung spelling ['spelɪŋ]
recyceln recycle [ri'saɪkl]
Recycling recycling [rɪ'saɪklɪŋ]
Rede talk [tɔːk]
reden (mit) talk (to) [tɔːk]
Redewendung phrase [freɪz]
Referat presentation [prezn'teɪʃn]; report [rɪ'pɔːt] **ein Referat halten** give a presentation
Regal shelf, *pl* shelves [ʃelf], [ʃelvz]
Regel rule [ruːl]
Regen rain [reɪn]
Regenjacke rain jacket ['reɪn dʒækɪt]
Regenschirm umbrella [ʌm'brelə]
Regierung government ['gʌvənmənt]
Regisseur/in director [də'rektə]
regnen rain [reɪn]
regnerisch rainy ['reɪni]
Reh(e) deer [dɪə]
Reich *(Imperium)* empire ['empaɪə]
reich rich [rɪtʃ]
Reihe line [laɪn]
Reinigungskraft cleaner ['kliːnə]
Reis rice [raɪs]
Reise journey ['dʒɜːni]; tour [tʊə]; trip [trɪp]
Reiseführer (für) *(Buch, Broschüre)* guide (to) [gaɪd]
reisen travel ['trævl]
Reisepass passport ['pɑːspɔːt]
Reiten *(Reitsport)* horse riding ['hɔːs raɪdɪŋ]
reiten ride [raɪd] **ein Pferd reiten / auf einem Pferd reiten** ride a horse
Reklame advertising ['ædvətaɪzɪŋ]
Rektor/in principal ['prɪnsəpl]
rennen run [rʌn]
Reporter/in reporter [rɪ'pɔːtə]
Rest rest [rest]
Restaurant restaurant ['restrɒnt] **in einem Restaurant** at a restaurant
retten save [seɪv]
rezensieren review [rɪ'vjuː]
Rezension review [rɪ'vjuː]
Rezept *(Kochrezept)* recipe ['resəpi]
Richter/in judge [dʒʌdʒ]
richtig right [raɪt]; *(wahr)* true [truː]
Richtung direction [də'rekʃn] **in Richtung Norden** *(Zug, Bus)* northbound ['nɔːθbaʊnd] **in Richtung Osten** *(Zug, Bus)* eastbound ['iːstbaʊnd] **in Richtung Süden** *(Zug, Bus)* southbound ['saʊθbaʊnd] **in Richtung (von)** toward(s) [tə'wɔːd], [tə'wɔːdz] **in Richtung Westen** *(Zug, Bus)* westbound ['westbaʊnd]
riechen *(schlecht riechen)* smell [smel]
Riesenrad big wheel [bɪg 'wiːl]
Rindfleisch beef [biːf]
Ring ring [rɪŋ]
Rock skirt [skɜːt]; *(Musik)* rock [rɒk]
roh raw [rɔː]
rollen roll [rəʊl]
Roller scooter ['skuːtə]
Rollstuhl wheelchair ['wiːltʃeə]
rollstuhlgerecht *(mit dem Rollstuhl zu erreichen)* wheelchair accessible [wiːltʃeər ək'sesəbl]
Rolltreppe escalator ['eskəleɪtə]
Römer/in Roman ['rəʊmən]
römisch Roman ['rəʊmən]
rosa pink [pɪŋk]
rot red [red]
Rote Beete beetroot ['biːtruːt]
Rotwild red deer [red 'dɪə]
Rücken back [bæk]
Rucksack rucksack *(BE)* ['rʌksæk]
Rückseite back [bæk]
rufen shout [ʃaʊt]; call [kɔːl]
Rugby *(Ballsportart)* rugby ['rʌgbi]
ruhig quiet ['kwaɪət]
Ruhm fame [feɪm]
rumhängen hang out [hæŋ 'aʊt]
rund round [raʊnd]
Runde round [raʊnd]
Rundfahrt/-gang (durch) tour (of) [tʊə]
runzeln: die Stirn runzeln frown [fraʊn]

S

Saal hall [hɔːl]
Sache thing [θɪŋ]
Sachse/Sächsin Saxon ['sæksn]
sächsisch Saxon ['sæksn]
sackig *(Kleidung)* baggy ['bægi]
Saft juice [dʒuːs]
saftig juicy ['dʒuːsi]
sagen say [seɪ]; tell [tel]
Sahne cream [kriːm] **saure Sahne** sour cream
Salat *(als Gericht oder Beilage)* salad ['sæləd]
Salz salt [sɔːlt]
salzig salty ['sɔːlti]
Samstag Saturday ['sætədeɪ], ['sætədi]
Sand sand [sænd]
Sandwich sandwich ['sænwɪtʃ], ['sænwɪdʒ]
Sänger/in singer ['sɪŋə]
Sarg coffin ['kɒfɪn]
Satz sentence ['sentəns]
sauber clean [kliːn]
sauber machen clean [kliːn]
sauer sour [saʊr] **saure Sahne** sour cream ['saʊr kriːm]
schaben scrape [skreɪp]
Schach chess [tʃes]
schaffen: (es) schaffen (etwas zu tun) manage (to do sth.) ['mænɪdʒ]
schaffen *(erschaffen)* create [kri'eɪt]
Schal scarf, *pl* scarves [skɑːf], [skɑːvz]
Schale bowl [bəʊl]; dish [dɪʃ]
Schallplatte record ['rekɔːd]
Schalter switch [swɪtʃ]
Schatz treasure ['treʒə]
Schaubild graph [græf], [grɑːf]
Schaufel *(Spaten)* spade [speɪd]
Schauplatz *(z. B. Film/Geschichte)* setting ['setɪŋ]
Schauspiel drama ['drɑːmə]; play [pleɪ]
Schauspieler/in actor ['æktə]
scheinen seem [siːm] **zu sein/tun scheinen** appear to be/do [ə'pɪə]
Schema pattern ['pætn]
Scherz joke [dʒəʊk]
scheu shy [ʃaɪ]
schick smart [smɑːt]
schicken send [send] **jm. eine SMS schicken** textsb. [tekst]
schiefgehen go wrong [gəʊ 'rɒŋ]
Schiff ship [ʃɪp]; boat [bəʊt]
Schild sign [saɪn]
Schildkröte *(Wasserschildkröte)* turtle ['tɜːtl]
Schinken ham [hæm]
Schirm umbrella [ʌm'brelə]
Schlabberhose baggy pants [bægi 'pænts]
schlabberig *(nachlässig)* sloppy ['slɒpi]
Schlaf sleep [sliːp]
schlafen sleep [sliːp]
Schlafenszeit bedtime ['bedtaɪm]
schlaflos sleepless ['sliːpləs]
Schlafzimmer bedroom ['bedruːm]

schlagen hit [hɪt]; *(besiegen)* beat [biːt]
Schläger *(Sport)* stick [stɪk]
Schlaglicht highlight ['haɪlaɪt]
Schlange snake [sneɪk]
schlau clever ['klevə]
schlecht bad [bæd] **schlechter** worse [wɜːs] **schlecht riechen** smell [smel] **der/die/das schlechteste, am schlechtesten** worst [wɜːst] **Mir ist schlecht** I feel sick. [sɪk]
Schleife bow [bəʊ]
schlicht simple ['sɪmpl]
schließen *(zumachen)* close [kləʊz]
Schließfach locker ['lɒkə]
schließlich at last [ət 'lɑːst]
schlimm bad [bæd] **schlimmer** worse [wɜːs] **der/die/das schlimmste, am schlimmsten** worst [wɜːst]
Schlittschuhbahn (skating) rink [rɪŋk]
Schlittschuhlaufen skating ['skeɪtɪŋ]
schludrig sloppy ['slɒpi]
Schluss end [end]
schmackhaft tasty ['teɪsti]
schmecken taste [teɪst]
Schmerz(en) ache [eɪk]
schmücken decorate ['dekəreɪt]
schmutzig dirty ['dɜːti]
Schnappschuss snapshot ['snæpʃɒt]
Schnee snow [snəʊ]
schneebedeckt snowy ['snəʊi]
schneiden cut [cʌt]
schneien snow [snəʊ]
schnell fast [fɑːst]; quick [kwɪk]
Schnellimbiss fast food
Schnellrestaurant *(Essen zum Mitnehmen)* takeaway ['teɪkəweɪ]
Schnuller dummy ['dʌmi]
schnüren tie [taɪ]
Schokolade chocolate ['tʃɒklət] **heiße (Trink-)Schokolade** hot chocolate
schon already [ɔːl'redi] **schon einmal** ever ['evə] **... schon ...?** ... yet? [jet]
schön fine [faɪn]; nice [naɪs]
Schrank *(Kleiderschrank)* wardrobe ['wɔːdrəʊb]; *(Küchenschrank)* cupboard ['kʌbəd]
schrecklich horrible ['hɒrəbl]; terrible ['terəbl]
schreiben write [raɪt]
Schreibtisch desk [desk]
Schreibweise spelling ['spelɪŋ]
Schrift writing ['raɪtɪŋ]

Schritt step [step] **Schritt für Schritt** step by step
schüchtern shy [ʃaɪ]
Schuh shoe [ʃuː]
Schulausflug school trip ['skuːl trɪp]
Schuld fault [fɔːlt]
schulden: jm. etwas schulden owe sb. sth. [əʊ]
schuldig: jm. etwas schuldig sein owe sb. sth. [əʊ]
Schule school [skuːl] **in der Schule** at school
Schüler/in student ['stjuːdnt]
Schüleraustausch exchange [ɪks'tʃeɪndʒ]
Schulfach subject ['sʌbdʒɪkt]
Schulheft exercise book ['eksəsaɪz bʊk]
Schuljahr year [jɪə]; grade *(AE)* [greɪd]
Schulleiter/in principal ['prɪnsəpl]
Schulmensa canteen [kæn'tiːn]
Schulnote grade [greɪd]
Schulsport PE (physical education) [piː 'iː], [fɪzɪkl edʒu'keɪʃn]
Schultasche schoolbag ['skuːlbæg]
Schulter shoulder ['ʃəʊldə] **mit den Schultern zucken** shrug your shoulders
Schulversammlung assembly [ə'sembli]
Schüssel bowl [bəʊl]; dish [dɪʃ]
schütteln shake [ʃeɪk]
schütten pour [pɔː]
schützen (vor) protect (from/against) [prə'tekt]
schwach weak [wiːk]
schwarz black [blæk]
schwer *(Gewicht)* heavy ['hevi]; *(Person)* big [bɪg]; *(schwierig)* hard [hɑːd]
Schwester sister ['sɪstə]
schwierig hard [hɑːd]
Schwierigkeiten trouble ['trʌbl] **in Schwierigkeiten sein** be in trouble
Schwimmbad swimming pool ['swɪmɪŋ puːl]
schwimmen swim [swɪm]
schwul gay [geɪ]
sechs six [sɪks]
See *(Binnensee)* lake [leɪk]; *(Meer)* sea [siː]
segeln sail [seɪl]
sehen see [siː]
Sehenswürdigkeit sight [saɪt]
sehr very ['veri]; a lot [ə 'lɒt]
seicht shallow ['ʃæləʊ]
Seife soap [səʊp]

Seifenoper soap [səʊp]
sein be [biː]
sein/e *(besitzanzeigend bei Dingen und Tieren)* its [ɪts]; *(zu „he“)* his [hɪz]
seine/r, seins his [hɪz]
seit since [sɪns]
seitdem since then [sɪns 'ðen]
Seite *(Buchseite, Heftseite)* page [peɪdʒ]; *(z. B. Straßenseite)* side [saɪd] **auf der linken/rechten Seite** on the left/right
selbst even ['iːvn]
selbstgemacht home-made [həʊm'meɪd]
selbstsicher confident ['kɒnfɪdənt]
selbstverständlich of course [əv 'kɔːs]
Selbstverteidigung self-defence [self dɪ'fens]
Selfiestick selfie stick ['selfi stɪk]
seltsam strange [streɪndʒ]
senden send [send]
Sendung *(Radio, Fernsehen)* programme ['prəʊgræm]
September September [sep'tembə]
Serie series ['sɪəriːz]
Service *(Teeservice)* (tea) set [set]
Servus. Goodbye. [gʊd'baɪ]
Set *(Garnitur)* set [set]
setzen set [set] **sich (hin)setzen** sit (down) [sɪt 'daʊn]
Sheriff sheriff *(AE)* ['ʃerɪf]
Show show [ʃəʊ]
sich *(sich gegenseitig, einander)* each other [iːtʃ 'ʌðə] **sich (selbst)** *(zu „he“)* himself [hɪm'self]; *(zu „she“)* herself [hɜː'self]
sicher *(gefahrlos)* safe [seɪf]; *(ohne Zweifel)* sure [ʃʊə], [ʃɔː]; *(selbstsicher)* confident ['kɒnfɪdənt]
sicherstellen, dass ... make sure that ... [meɪk 'ʃʊə]
Sicht *(Aussicht)* view [vjuː]
Sie *(höfliche Anrede)* you [ju], [jə] **Sie/sich selbst** *(Plural)* yourselves [jɔː'selvz], [jə'selvz]; *(Singular)* yourself [jə'self]
sie *(Plural)* they [ðeɪ] **für sie** for them [ðem], [ðəm] **mit ihnen** with them **sie/sich selbst** themselves [ðəm'selvz]
sie *(Singular; Dinge und Tiere)* it [ɪt]
sie *(weibliche Person)* she [ʃiː] **Frag sie.** Ask her. [hɜː], [hə] **sie/sich selbst** herself [hɜː'self]
sieben seven ['sevn]
sieden boil [bɔɪl]
Siedler/in settler ['setlə]
Sieger/in winner ['wɪnə]
Silber silver ['sɪlvə]

simpel simple ['sɪmpl]
singen sing [sɪŋ]
sinken drop [drɒp]
Sir *(britischer Adelstitel)* Sir [sɜː]
Sitcom sitcom ['sɪtkɒm]
Situation situation [sɪtʃu'eɪʃn]
sitzen sit [sɪt]
Skateboard skateboard ['skeɪtbɔːd]
Skateboard fahren skate [skeɪts]; skateboard ['skeɪtbɔːd]
Skatepark skate park ['skeɪt pɑːk]
Ski laufen/fahren ski [skiː]
Sklave, Sklavin slave [sleɪv]
Slogan slogan ['sləʊgən]
Smalltalk *(oberflächliche, leichte Konversation)* small talk ['smɔːl tɔːk]
Smartphone smartphone ['smɑːtfəʊn]
SMS text (message) ['tekst mesɪdʒ] **jm. eine SMS schicken** text sb.
Snack snack [snæk]
so like this [laɪk 'ðɪs]; so [səʊ]
Socke sock [sɒk]
sodass so (that) [səʊ], ['səʊ ðət]
Sofa sofa ['səʊfə]
sogar even ['iːvn]
Sohn son [sʌn]
Soldat/in soldier ['səʊldʒə]
sollen: Was soll's? Who cares? [keəz] **wir sollten ...** we should ... [ʃʊd]
Sommer summer ['sʌmə]
Sonderausgabe *(Magazin)* special ['speʃl]
sonderbar strange [streɪndʒ]
Sondersendung *(Fernsehen)* special ['speʃl]
Songwriter songwriter ['sɒŋraɪtə]
Sonne sun [sʌn]
Sonnenbrille sunglasses *(pl)* ['sʌnglɑːsɪz]
sonnig sunny ['sʌni]
Sonntag Sunday ['sʌndeɪ], ['sʌndi]
sonst or [ɔː] **sonst irgendwo(hin)** anywhere else [eniweər 'els] **sonst noch etwas** anything else [eniθɪŋ 'els]
Sorgen: sich Sorgen machen (wegen, um) worry (about) ['wʌri]
sorgen: dafür sorgen, dass ... make sure that ... [meɪk 'ʃʊə]
sorgfältig careful ['keəfl]
Sorte kind (of) [kaɪnd]; type (of) [taɪp]
Soße sauce [sɔːs]
sozial social [səʊʃl]
soziale Medien social media *(pl)* [səʊʃl 'miːdiə] **in den sozialen Medien** on social media
Spaghetti spaghetti [spə'geti]
Spannung excitement [ɪk'saɪtmənt]
sparen save [seɪv]
Spaß fun [fʌn] **Spaß haben** have a good time; have fun **Spaß machen** be fun **es klingt, als ob es Spaß macht** it sounds fun
spät late [leɪt] **Einkaufen am späten Abend** late-night shopping **Wie spät ist es?** What time is it?
Spaten spade [speɪd]
später later ['leɪtə]
Speck bacon ['beɪkən]
Speiseeis ice cream [aɪs 'kriːm]
Speisekarte menu ['menjuː]
Sperre *(zur Fahrkartenkontrolle)* ticket gate ['tɪkɪt geɪt]
spezielle(r, s) specific [spə'sɪfɪk]
Spiegel mirror ['mɪrə]
Spiel game [geɪm]; *(Wettkampf)* match [mætʃ] **aus dem Spiel nehmen** take off [teɪk 'ɒf]
Spielekonsole games console [kən'səʊl]
spielen play [pleɪ]; *(aufführen)* act [ækt] **jm. einen Streich spielen** play a trick on sb. [trɪk] **Klavier spielen** play the piano
Spieler/in player ['pleɪə]; gamer ['geɪmə]
Spielfeld square [skweə]
Spielfigur token ['təʊkən]
Spielfilm movie ['muːvi]
Spielstand score [skɔː]
Spind locker ['lɒkə]
Spinne spider ['spaɪdə]
Spitze top [tɒp]
Spitzer sharpener ['ʃɑːpnə]
sponsern sponsor ['spɒnsə]
Sponsor/in *(Geldgeber/in)* sponsor ['spɒnsə]
Sport(art) sport [spɔːt] **Sport treiben** do sport; play **Sport(unterricht)** PE (physical education) [piː 'iː], [fɪzɪkl edʒu'keɪʃn]
Sporthalle gym [dʒɪm]
sportlich sporty ['spɔːti]
Sportplatz playing field ['pleɪɪŋ fiːld]
Sprache language ['læŋgwɪdʒ]
Sprachnachricht voice message ['vɔɪs mesɪdʒ]
Sprechblase speech bubble ['spiːtʃ bʌbl]
sprechen speak [spiːk] **sprechen (mit)** talk (to) [tɔːk] **Sprich/ Sprecht mir nach.** Repeat after me. [rɪ'piːt]
Sprecher/in speaker ['spiːkə]
springen jump [dʒʌmp]; *(ins Wasser)* dive [daɪv]
Spülmaschine dishwasher ['dɪʃwɒʃə] **die Spülmaschine einräumen** load the dishwasher [ləʊd]
St = Sankt St = Saint [seɪnt]
Staat state [steɪt]
Stadion stadium ['steɪdiəm]
Stadt *(Großstadt)* city ['sɪti]; *(Kleinstadt)* town [taʊn] **in der Stadt** in town
Stadtplan map [mæp]
Stamm *(Volksstamm)* tribe [traɪb]
Star *(Film-, Popstar)* star [stɑː]
stark strong [strɒŋ]; *(großartig)* awesome *(AE, infml)* ['ɔːsəm]
Start start [stɑːt]
Statistik(en) statistics *(pl)* [stə'tɪstɪks]
Stätte site [saɪt]
stattfinden be on [ɒn]
Statue statue ['stætʃuː]
Staub saugen vacuum ['vækjuəm]
Staubsauger vacuum cleaner ['vækjuəm kliːnə]
stecken *(etwas wohin tun)* put [pʊt]
Stecker plug [plʌg]
stehen stand [stænd] **(gerade) stehen** stand up (straight) [stænd 'ʌp] **jm. stehen** *(Kleidung)* suit sb. [suːt]
stehlen steal [stiːl]
Stein stone [stəʊn]
Steinkreis stone circle [stəʊn 'sɜːkl]
Stelle *(Arbeitsstelle)* job [dʒɒb] **an js. Stelle** in sb.'s shoes [ʃuːz]
stellen put [pʊt]; set [set] **sich (hin)stellen** stand [stænd]
sterben die [daɪ]
Stern star [stɑː]
Stiefbruder stepbrother ['stepbrʌðə]
Stiefel boot [buːt]
Stiefmutter stepmum ['stepmʌm]; stepmother ['stepmʌðə]
Stiefschwester stepsister ['stepsɪstə]
Stiefvater stepdad ['stepdæd]; stepfather ['stepfɑːðə]
Stift *(zum Schreiben)* pen [pen]
Stil style [staɪl]
still quiet ['kwaɪət]
Stimme voice [vɔɪs] **mit lauter Stimme** in a loud voice
Stirn: die Stirn runzeln frown [fraʊn]
Stirnrunzeln frown [fraʊn]

Stock stick [stɪk]; *(Etage)* floor [flɔː]
Stoff material [mə'tɪəriəl]
stoppen stop [stɒp]
stoßen gegen hit [hɪt]
Stoßzeiten: außerhalb der Stoßzeiten off-peak [ɒf 'piːk]
Strand beach [biːtʃ] **am Strand** on the beach
Straße road [rəʊd]; *(in Ortschaften)* street [striːt]
Straßenbahn tram [træm]
Strategie strategy ['strætədʒi]
Streich trick [trɪk] **jm. einen Streich spielen** play a trick on sb.
Streit argument ['ɑːgjumənt] **in Streit geraten mit jm.** get into an argument with sb.
streng strict [strɪkt]
stricken knit [nɪt]
strömen pour [pɔː]
Stromleitung power line ['paʊə laɪn]
Struktur structure ['strʌktʃə]
strukturieren structure ['strʌktʃə]
Stück piece [piːs]
Stück(chen) bit [bɪt]
Student/in student ['stjuːdnt]
studieren study ['stʌdi]
Stufe step [step]
Stuhl chair [tʃeə]
Stunde hour ['aʊə]; *(Schulstunde)* lesson ['lesn]; period ['pɪəriəd]
Stundenplan schedule *(AE)* ['skedʒuːl]; timetable ['taɪmteɪbl]
Sturm storm [stɔːm]
stürmisch stormy ['stɔːmi]
suchen look for ['lʊk fə]
Süden, Süd- south [saʊθ] **in Richtung Süden** *(Zug, Bus)* southbound ['saʊθbaʊnd]
südlich south [saʊθ]
südlich, Süd- southern ['sʌðən]
Südosten, südöstlich south-east [saʊθ'iːst]
Südwesten, südwestlich south-west [saʊθ'west]
super super ['suːpə]
supercool supercool ['suːpəkuːl]
Superheld/in superhero, *pl* superheroes ['suːpəhɪərəʊ]
Superkraft superpower ['suːpəpaʊə]
Supermarkt supermarket ['suːpəmɑːkɪt] **im Supermarkt** at the supermarket
superstark superstrong [suːpə'strɒŋ]
Suppe soup [suːp]
surfen gehen go surfing ['sɜːfɪŋ]
Surfer/in surfer ['sɜːfə]
Sushi sushi ['suːʃi]
süß sweet [swiːt]; *(niedlich)* cute [kjuːt]
Süßigkeiten sweets *(pl)* [swiːts]; candy *(AE)* ['kændi]
Symbol (für) symbol (of) ['sɪmbl]
Szene scene [siːn]

T

Tabelle chart [tʃɑːt]; table ['teɪbl]
Tablet(computer) tablet ['tæblət]
Taco *(Maistortilla)* taco ['tækəʊ]
Tafel *(Schule)* board [bɔːd]
Tag day [deɪ] **eines Tages** one day
Tagebucheintrag diary entry ['daɪəri entri]
Tagesausflug day out
Tageszeitung newspaper ['njuːzpeɪpə]
täglich daily ['deɪli]
Talkshow chat show ['tʃæt ʃəʊ]
Tankstelle gas station *(AE)* ['gæs steɪʃn]; petrol station ['petrəl steɪʃn]
Tante aunt [ɑːnt]
tanzen dance [dɑːns]
Tänzer/in dancer ['dɑːnsə]
Taschenlampe torch [tɔːtʃ]
Taschenmesser penknife, *pl* penknives ['pennaɪf], ['pennaɪvz]
Tasse cup [kʌp] **eine Tasse ...** a cup of ...
Tätigkeit activity [æk'tɪvəti]
Tatsache fact [fækt]
tatsächlich actually ['æktʃuəli]
Taube pigeon ['pɪdʒɪn]
Taucheranzug wetsuit ['wetsuːt]
Tausch exchange [ɪks'tʃeɪndʒ]
tauschen swap [swɒp]
tausend thousand ['θaʊznd]
Taxi cab *(AE)* [kæb]; taxi ['tæksi]
Team team [tiːm]
Teamwork teamwork ['tiːmwɜːk]
Technik tech *(infml)* [tek]
Technik(unterricht) technology [tek'nɒlədʒi]
Techniker/in engineer [endʒɪ'nɪə]
Technologie technology [tek'nɒlədʒi]
Tee tea [tiː]
Teelöffel teaspoon ['tiːspuːn]
Teenager teen [tiːn]; teenager ['tiːneɪdʒə]
Teil bit [bɪt]; part [pɑːt]; *(Stück)* piece [piːs]
teilen share [ʃeə] **sich ein Zimmer teilen mit** share a room with
Telefon phone [fəʊn] **am Telefon** on the phone **ans Telefon gehen** answer the phone ['ɑːnsə]
Telefonanruf (phone) call ['fəʊn kɔːl]
Telefonanschluss line [laɪn]
telefonieren phone [fəʊn]
Telefonleitung line [laɪn] **Die (Telefon-)Leitung war tot.** The line went dead. [ded]
Telefonnummer phone number ['fəʊn nʌmbə]
Teller plate [pleɪt]
Tempel temple ['templ]
Temperatur temperature ['temprətʃə]
Tennis tennis ['tenɪs]
Tennisplatz tennis court ['tenɪs kɔːt]
Teppich carpet ['kɑːpɪt]; rug [rʌg]
Test quiz [kwɪz]; test [test]
testen test [test]
teuer expensive [ɪk'spensɪv]
Text text [tekst]
Textabschnitt paragraph ['pærəgrɑːf]
Theater theatre ['θɪətə]
Theaterstück play [pleɪ]
Thema subject ['sʌbdʒɪkt]
tief deep [diːp]
Tier animal ['ænɪml]; *(Haustier)* pet [pet]
Tierarzt/-ärztin vet [vet]
Tipp tip [tɪp]
tippen an etwas *(leise klopfen)* tap sth. [tæp]
Tisch table ['teɪbl]
Tischtennis table tennis ['teɪbl tenɪs]
Titelseite front page [frʌnt 'peɪdʒ]
Toast toast [təʊst]
Tochter daughter ['dɔːtə]
Tod death [deθ]
Todesdatum date of death [deɪt əv 'deθ]
To-Do-Liste to-do list [tu 'duː lɪst]
Toilette toilet ['tɔɪlət]
toll great [greɪt]
Tomate tomato, *pl* tomatoes [tə'mɑːtəʊ]
Tonspur soundtrack ['saʊndtræk]
Tor gate [geɪt]; *(im Sport)* goal [gəʊl]
Torte cake [keɪk]
Tortendiagramm pie chart ['paɪ tʃɑːt]
tot dead [ded] **Die (Telefon-)Leitung war tot.** The line went dead.
total total ['təʊtl]
töten kill [kɪl]
Tour tour [tʊə]
Tourist/in tourist ['tʊərɪst]
Tradition tradition [trə'dɪʃn]

traditionell traditional [trə'dɪʃənl]
tragen carry ['kæri]; *(Kleidung)* wear [weə]
Trainer/in coach [kəʊtʃ]
trainieren train [treɪn]
Trampolinspringen/-turnen trampolining ['træmpəli:nɪŋ]
Träne tear [tɪə]
transportieren carry ['kæri]
Traum(-) dream [dri:m]
traurig sad [sæd]
Traurigkeit sadness ['sædnəs]
treffen: treffen auf hit [hɪt] **(sich) treffen** meet [mi:t]
treiben *(Tiere)* drive [draɪv] **Sport treiben** do sport; play sport(s)
Trennstrich hyphen ['haɪfn]
trinken drink [drɪŋk]
trotzdem still [stɪl]
Truthahn turkey ['tɜ:ki]
Tschüs. Bye. [baɪ]
T-Shirt T-shirt ['ti: ʃɜ:t]
tun do [du:]; *(etwas wohin tun)* put [pʊt] **viel zu tun haben** be busy ['bɪzi]
Tunnel tunnel ['tʌnl]
Tür door [dɔ:] **die Tür aufmachen, zur/an die Tür gehen** answer the door ['ɑ:nsə]
Turm tower ['taʊə]
Turnen gymnastics [dʒɪm'næstɪks]
Turnhalle gym [dʒɪm]
typisch (für) typical (of) ['tɪpɪkl]
Tyrann/in bully ['bʊli]
tyrannisieren bully ['bʊli]

U

U-Bahn underground ['ʌndəgraʊnd]; *(London)* (the) Tube [tju:b]
U-Bahn-Linie line [laɪn]
üben practise ['præktɪs]; practice *AE*
über about [ə'baʊt]; over ['əʊvə] **über die Geschichte** about the story **über eine Brücke** across a bridge [ə'krɒs]
überall everywhere ['evriweə] **überall auf der Welt** all over the world [ɔ:l 'əʊvə] **überall(hin)** anywhere [eniweə]
überfliegen: (einen Text) überfliegen (nach) scan (a text for) [skæn] *(Text, um den Inhalt grob zu erfassen)* skim [skɪm]
überfüllt crowded ['kraʊdɪd]
Übergabe handover ['hændəʊvə]
übergeben: sich übergeben be sick [sɪk]
überhaupt: überhaupt (nicht) (not) at all [ət 'ɔ:l] **ohne überhaupt zu checken ...** without even checking ... ['i:vn]
übernachten stay [steɪ]
überprüfen check [tʃek]; review [rɪ'vju:]
überqueren cross [krɒs]
überraschen surprise [sə'praɪz]
überrascht surprised [sə'praɪzd]
Überraschung surprise [sə'praɪz]
Überschrift heading ['hedɪŋ]
Übung(en) practice ['præktɪs]; exercise(s) ['eksəsaɪz]
Uhr *(Wanduhr, Standuhr, Turmuhr)* clock [klɒk] **7 Uhr nachmittags/abends, 19 Uhr** 7 pm [pi:'em] **9 Uhr morgens/vormittags** 9 am [eɪ'em] **um 7 Uhr** at 7 o'clock [ə'klɒk]
Uhrzeit time [taɪm]
um: um ... % gesunken sein be down (by) ... % **um (... herum)** around ... [ə'raʊnd]; round ... [raʊnd] **um 7 Uhr** at 7 o'clock [ə'klɒk] **um etwas zu tun** to do sth.
umdrehen: etwas umdrehen turn sth. (over) [tɜ:n] **(sich) umdrehen** turn; turn (a)round [tɜ:n ə'raʊnd]
Umfeld environment [ɪn'vaɪrənmənt]
Umfrage survey ['sɜ:veɪ] **eine Umfrage durchführen** do a survey
Umgebung environment [ɪn'vaɪrənmənt]
umher: in ... umher round ... [raʊnd]
umhergehen walk around [wɔ:k ə'raʊnd]
Umschlag *(Briefumschlag)* envelope ['envələʊp]
umschreiben paraphrase ['pærəfreɪz]
umsteigen change [tʃeɪndʒ]
Umwelt environment [ɪn'vaɪrənmənt]
Umwelt- environmental [ɪnvaɪrən'mentl]
umziehen: umziehen (nach) move (to) [mu:v] **sich umziehen** change [tʃeɪndʒ]
Umzug parade [pə'reɪd]
unabhängig (von) independent (of/from) [ɪndɪ'pendənt]
Unabhängigkeit (von) independence (from) [ɪndɪ'pendəns]
unbeliebt (bei) unpopular (with) [ʌn'pɒpjələ]
und and [ænd], [ənd] **Na und?** Who cares? [keəz]
Unfall accident ['æksɪdənt]; crash [kræʃ] **einen Unfall haben (mit)** crash (into)
unfreundlich unfriendly [ʌn'frendli]
ungeduldig impatient [ɪm'peɪʃnt]
ungefähr about [ə'baʊt]
Ungeheuer monster ['mɒnstə]
ungesund unhealthy [ʌn'helθi]
unglücklich unhappy [ʌn'hæpi]
unglücklicherweise unfortunately [ʌn'fɔ:tʃənətli]
unheimlich *(beängstigend)* scary ['skeəri]
unhöflich rude [ru:d]
Uniform uniform ['ju:nɪfɔ:m]
Universität university [ju:nɪ'vɜ:səti]
unklar unclear [ʌn'klɪə]
unordentlich untidy [ʌn'taɪdi]
Unrecht haben be wrong [rɒŋ]
uns us [ʌs], [əs] **uns selbst** ourselves [aʊə'selvz]
unser/e *(vor Nomen)* our ['aʊə]
unsere/r, unseres ours [ɑ:z], ['aʊəz]
unsicher unsafe [ʌn'seɪf]; unsure [ʌn'ʃʊə]
unten below [bɪ'ləʊ]; *(die Treppe hinunter)* downstairs [daʊn'steəz] **das untere Ende** bottom ['bɒtəm]
unter under ['ʌndə]
unter(halb von) below [bɪ'ləʊ]
unterhalten: sich unterhalten (mit) chat (with) [tʃæt] **jn. unterhalten** entertain sb. [entə'teɪn]
Unterhaltung *(Gespräch)* chat [tʃæt]
Unterricht class [klɑ:s]
unterrichten teach [ti:tʃ]
Unterrichtsstunde lesson ['lesn]; period ['pɪəriəd]
Unterschied difference ['dɪfrəns]
Unterschrift signature ['sɪgnətʃə]
unterstreichen *(hervorheben)* highlight ['haɪlaɪt]
unterstützen support [sə'pɔ:t]
Unterwasser- underwater [ʌndə'wɔ:tə]
unterwegs on the go [ɒn ðə 'gəʊ]
unwahrscheinlich unlikely [ʌn'laɪkli]
uralt ancient ['eɪnʃənt]
Urlaub holiday ['hɒlədeɪ]; vacation *(AE)* [və'keɪʃn] **im/in den Urlaub** on holiday
urteilen judge [dʒʌdʒ]
usw. (und so weiter) etc. *(aus dem Lateinischen)* [et'setərə]

V

Vater father ['fɑːðə]
Vati dad [dæd]
Vegetarier/in vegetarian [vedʒə'teəriən]
vegetarisch vegetarian [vedʒə'teəriən]
Verabredung date [deɪt]
verändern; sich verändern (zu/in) change (into) [tʃeɪndʒ]
Veränderung change [tʃeɪndʒ]
verängstigt scared [skeəd]
verärgert annoyed [ə'nɔɪd]; upset [ʌp'set]
verbieten ban [bæn]
verbinden (mit) link (to/with) [lɪŋk]
Verbindung link [lɪŋk] **sich in Verbindung setzen mit jm.** contact sb. ['kɒntækt]
Verbot (von) ban (on) [bæn]
verboten: verboten sein/werden be banned [bænd] **Hunde verboten!** No dogs! [nəʊ]
Verbrechen crime [kraɪm]
verbreiten: sich *(im Internet)* **rasend schnell verbreiten** *(viral = wie ein Virus)* go viral ['vaɪrəl] **sich verbreiten** spread [spred]
verbrennen burn [bɜːn]
verbringen: Zeit verbringen spend time [spend]
verdienen *(Geld)* make (money); *(Geld, durch Arbeit)* earn [ɜːn]
verdrehen: die Augen verdrehen roll your eyes
Verein club [klʌb]
Vereinbarung deal [diːl]
vereinigt: das Vereinigte Königreich the United Kingdom (UK) [junaɪtɪd 'kɪŋdəm]
Verfasser/in writer ['raɪtə] **Verfasser/in von Hasskommentaren** *(Internet)* hater ['heɪtə]
verfolgen follow ['fɒləʊ]
Vergangenheit past [pɑːst]
vergessen forget [fə'get] **nicht vergessen** remember [rɪ'membə]
vergleichen (mit) compare (to/with) [kəm'peə]
vergnügen: sich vergnügen have a good time
verhalten: sich verhalten behave [bɪ'heɪv]
Verhältnis relationship [rɪ'leɪʃnʃɪp]
verhindern, dass etwas in die Ozeane gelangt keep sth. out of the oceans [kiːp]
verhungern starve [stɑːv]
verkaufen sell [sel]
Verkäufer/in (shop) assistant [ə'sɪstənt]
Verkehrsmittel transport ['trænspɔːt]
verkehrt herum inside out [ɪnsaɪd 'aʊt]
Verkleidung costume ['kɒstjuːm]; *(Kostüm)* fancy dress [fænsi 'dres]
verlassen: jemanden verlassen leave sb. [liːv] **sich auf jn. verlassen** count on sb.
verlegen embarrassed [ɪm'bærəst] **etwas verlegen** *(bewegen)* move sth. [muːv]
verleihen lend [lend]
verletzen hurt [hɜːt] **sich verletzen** get hurt **verletzt sein** be hurt
verlieren lose [luːz]
vermischen mix [mɪks]
vermissen miss [mɪs]
verpassen miss [mɪs]
verrückt crazy ['kreɪzi]
verschieben: etwas verschieben move sth. [muːv]
verschieden different ['dɪfrənt]
verschneit snowy ['snəʊi]
verschwinden disappear [dɪsə'pɪə]
versetzen: etwas versetzen move sth. [muːv]
verspäten: sich verspäten be late [leɪt]
verspätet delayed [dɪ'leɪd] **Ich habe mich verspätet.** I'm late. [leɪt]
verstecken; sich verstecken hide [haɪd]
verstehen understand [ʌndə'stænd] **etwas verstehen** *(mitbekommen)* get sth. [get]
versuchen try [traɪ]
Verteidigung defence [dɪ'fens]
vertrauen; *(das)* **Vertrauen** trust [trʌst]
vervollständigen complete [kəm'pliːt]
verwandeln: (sich) verwandeln (in) change (into) [tʃeɪndʒ]
Verwandlung change [tʃeɪndʒ]
verwenden use [juːz]
verwundert puzzled ['pʌzld]
Video(-) video ['vɪdiəʊ]
Videospiel video game ['vɪdiəʊ geɪm]
viel a lot (of) [ə 'lɒt]; lots of [lɒts]; much [mʌtʃ] **viele** a lot (of); lots of; many ['mæni] **Viele Grüße ...** *(Briefschluss)* Best wishes ['wɪʃɪz] **Wie viel?** How much?
vielleicht maybe ['meɪbi] **vielleicht findest du ...** you might find ... [maɪt]
vier four [fɔː]
Viertel quarter ['kwɔːtə] **viertel nach 6** quarter past 6 [pɑːst] **viertel vor 7** quarter to 7 [tu], [tə]
violett purple ['pɜːpl]
Violine violin [vaɪə'lɪn]
viral viral ['vaɪrəl]
Virus- viral ['vaɪrəl]
Vogel bird [bɜːd]
Vokabeln vocabulary (*infml auch* vocab) [və'kæbjələri], ['vəʊkæb]
Vokabelverzeichnis vocabulary (*infml auch* vocab) [və'kæbjələri], ['vəʊkæb]
voll full [fʊl]; *(von Menschen)* crowded ['kraʊdɪd] **voll mit/von** full of
voller ... full of ... [fʊl]
Volleyball volleyball ['vɒlibɔːl]
Vollkorn- wholemeal ['həʊlmiːl]
vollständig complete [kəm'pliːt]; full [fʊl]
von from [frɒm]
vor *(örtlich)* in front of [ɪn 'frʌnt əv]; *(zeitlich)* before [bɪ'fɔː] **vor vielen Jahren** many years ago [ə'gəʊ] **750 v. Chr.** 750 BC [biː 'siː] **viertel vor 7** quarter to 7 [tu], [tə]
vorbei past [pɑːst]
vorbereiten prepare [prɪ'peə] **sich vorbereiten (auf)** get ready (for) ['redi]; prepare (for)
vorderer Teil front [frʌnt]
Vordergrund foreground ['fɔːgraʊnd]
Vorderseite front [frʌnt]
Vorführung show [ʃəʊ]
Vorhang curtain ['kɜːtn]
vorher before [bɪ'fɔː]
vorige Woche last week [lɑːst 'wiːk]
vormittags: 9 Uhr vormittags 9 am [eɪ'em]
Vormund guardian ['gɑːdiən]
Vorname first name ['fɜːst neɪm]
vorne at the front [frʌnt] **nach vorne** forward ['fɔːwəd]
vorschlagen suggest [sə'dʒest]
vorsichtig careful ['keəfl]
vorspielen mime [maɪm]
vorstellen present [prɪ'zent] **jm. jn./etwas vorstellen** introduce sb. to sb./sth. [ɪntrə'djuːs] **sich etwas vorstellen** imagine sth. [ɪ'mædʒɪn]
Vorstellung *(Bekanntmachen)* introduction [ɪntrə'dʌkʃn]
Vorteil advantage [əd'vɑːntɪdʒ]
Vortrag talk [tɔːk] **einen Vortrag halten** give a talk

vorwärts forward ['fɔːwəd]
vorziehen: etwas einer Sache vorziehen prefer sth. to sth. [prɪ'fɜː] **ich würde ... vorziehen** I'd prefer ...
Votum vote [vəʊt]

W

Waffe weapon ['wepən]
Wahl choice [tʃɔɪs]
wählen *(auswählen)* choose [tʃuːz]; *(polit. Wahl)* vote [vəʊt]
wahr true [truː]
während while [waɪl]; as [æz], [əz]
Wahrheit truth [truːθ]
wahrscheinlich likely ['laɪkli]; probably ['prɒbəbli]
Wal whale [weɪl]
Wald forest ['fɒrɪst]; wood [wʊd]
Wand wall [wɔːl]
wandern walk [wɔːk] **(das) Wandern** hiking ['haɪkɪŋ]
wann? when? [wen] **Wann hast du Geburtstag?** When's (= when is) your birthday?
warm warm [wɔːm]; hot [hɒt]
warten (auf) wait (for) [weɪt] **Warte mal.** Wait a minute.
warum? why? [waɪ]
was? what? [wɒt] **Was ist mit dir?** What about you? [wɒt əbaʊt 'juː] **Was kostet/kosten ...?** How much is/are ...? [haʊ 'mʌtʃ]
Wäsche washing ['wɒʃɪŋ]; linen ['lɪnɪn]
waschen: (sich) waschen wash [wɒʃ]
Wasser water ['wɔːtə] **unter Wasser** underwater [ʌndə'wɔːtə]
Wasserfall waterfall ['wɔːtəfɔːl]
Wasserschildkröte turtle ['tɜːtl]
Webseite webpage ['webpeɪdʒ]
Website website ['websaɪt]; *(Kurzform)* site [saɪt]
Wechsel change [tʃeɪndʒ]
wechseln change [tʃeɪndʒ] **wechseln (auf/zu)** *(Schule)* move (to) [muːv]
Weckzeit wake-up time ['weɪk ʌp taɪm]
Weg path [pɑːθ]; way [weɪ] **den Weg beschreiben** give directions [də'rekʃnz] **nach dem Weg fragen** ask for directions
weg away [ə'weɪ] **weg sein** be gone [gɒn]
Wegbeschreibung(en) directions [də'rekʃnz]
wegen because of [bɪ'kɒz əv] **wegen etwas (an)fragen** ask about sth. [ə'baʊt]
weggehen leave [liːv]
weglassen leave out [liːv 'aʊt]
weglegen put away
wegnehmen take off [teɪk 'ɒf]
wehen blow [bləʊ]
wehtun hurt [hɜːt] **Mir tut der Hals weh.** I have a sore throat. [sɔː 'θrəʊt]
weiblich female ['fiːmeɪl]
weich soft [sɒft]
Weide field [fiːld] **auf der Weide** in the field
Weihnachten Christmas ['krɪsməs]
weil because [bɪ'kɒz]
weinen cry [kraɪ]
Weise way [weɪ]
weiß white [waɪt]
weit: weit (entfernt) far [fɑː] **weiter (entfernt)** further ['fɜːðə] **am weitesten (entfernt)** furthest ['fɜːðəst] **weit (geschnitten)** *(Kleidung)* baggy ['bægi]
weiterführende Schule *(BE)* community college [kə'mjuːnəti kɒlɪdʒ]
weitergehen continue [kən'tɪnjuː]
weitermachen continue [kən'tɪnjuː]
welche(r, s)? what? [wɒt]; which? [wɪtʃ]
Welt world [wɜːld] **der beste Ort der Welt / auf der Welt** the best place in the world
wem? who? [huː]
wen? who? [huː]
Wendung *(Redewendung)* phrase [freɪz]
wenig: ein wenig a little; some [sʌm], [səm]
wenn *(falls)* if [ɪf]; *(zeitlich)* when [wen]
wer? who? [huː]
Werbung advertising ['ædvətaɪzɪŋ] **Werbung machen (für)** advertise ['ædvətaɪz]
Werdegang *(schulisch/beruflich)* career [kə'rɪə]
werden *(Futur)*: **du wirst nicht brauchen** you won't need (= you will not need) [wəʊnt] **ich werde ... mitbringen** *(Plan, Vorhaben)* I'm going to bring ... ['gəʊɪŋ tə] **du wirst fallen** you'll (= you will) fall [wɪl]
werden *(Veränderung)* become [bɪ'kʌm] **nass werden** get wet [get] **werden zu** change into [tʃeɪndʒ] **zu etwas werden** turn to sth.
werfen throw [θrəʊ]
Werktag weekday ['wiːkdeɪ]
wertvoll precious ['preʃəs]
wessen? whose? [huːz]
Westen, West- west [west] **in Richtung Westen** *(Zug, Bus)* westbound ['westbaʊnd]
westlich west [west]
westlich, West- western ['westən]
Wettbewerb competition [kɒmpə'tɪʃn]
Wetter weather ['weðə]
Wettkampf match [mætʃ]
wichtig important [ɪm'pɔːtnt] **wichtigste(r, s)** main [meɪn] **etwas wichtig nehmen** care about sth. [keə]
widerlich gross *(infml)* [grəʊs]
widersprechen *(nicht zustimmen)* disagree [dɪsə'griː]
wie *(ähnlich/so wie)* like [laɪk]; *(Präp. & Konj.)* as [æz], [əz] **genauso gut wie** as good as **nicht so gut wie** not as good as
wie? how? [haʊ] **Wie alt bist du?** How old are you? **Wie geht es dir/euch/Ihnen?** How are you? **Wie ist ...? / Wie sieht ... aus?** What's ... like? [wɒts 'laɪk] **wie man etwas macht** how to do sth. **Wie spät ist es?** What time is it?
wieder again [ə'gen]
wiederholen repeat [rɪ'piːt]; *(Lernstoff)* revise [rɪ'vaɪz]
Wiederholung *(von Lernstoff)* revision [rɪ'vɪʒn]
Wiedersehen: Auf Wiedersehen! Goodbye. [gʊd'baɪ]
wiederverwerten recycle [riˈsaɪkl]
Wikinger/in Viking ['vaɪkɪŋ]
Willkommen in/an ... Welcome to ... ['welkəm]
Wind wind [wɪnd]
windig windy ['wɪndi]
Winter winter ['wɪntə]
wir we [wiː] **wir selbst** ourselves [aʊə'selvz]
wirklich really ['riːəli], ['rɪəli]; real [rɪəl]
Wirklichkeit reality [ri'æləti]
wirksam effective [ɪ'fektɪv]
Wirkung effect [ɪ'fekt]
Wirtschaft *(Volkswirtschaft)* economy [ɪ'kɒnəmi]
wirtschaftlich, Wirtschafts- economic [iːkə'nɒmɪk]
wissen know [nəʊ] **Ich wusste nicht, was ich sagen sollte.** I didn't know what to say. **weißt du** *(nämlich)* you know
Wissenschaftler/in scientist ['saɪəntɪst]
Witz joke [dʒəʊk]

witzig funny ['fʌni]
WLAN *(kabellose Datenübertragung)* Wi-Fi ['waɪ faɪ]
wo? where? [weə] **Wo kommst du her?** Where are you from?
Woche week [wi:k]
Wochenende weekend [wi:k'end]
Wochentag weekday ['wi:kdeɪ]
wohin? where? [weə]
wohltätige Organisation charity ['tʃærəti]
wohnen live [lɪv]
Wohnheim hostel ['hɒstl]
Wohnung flat [flæt]; *(AE)* apartment [ə'pɑ:tmənt]
Wohnzimmer living room ['lɪvɪŋ ru:m]
Wolkenkratzer skyscraper ['skaɪskreɪpə]
Wolle wool [wʊl]
wollen want [wɒnt] **etwas tun wollen** want to do sth. **wollen, dass jd. etwas tut** want sb. to do sth.
Wort word [wɜ:d] **das Bilden von Wörtern** word building ['wɜ:d bɪldɪŋ] **mit anderen Worten sagen** paraphrase ['pærəfreɪz]
Wörterbuch dictionary ['dɪkʃənri]
Wörternetz mind map ['maɪnd mæp]
Wörterverzeichnis *(alphabetisch)* dictionary ['dɪkʃənri]
Wortnetz word web ['wɜ:d web]
wunderschön beautiful ['bjuːtɪfl]
Wunsch wish [wɪʃ]
wünschen wish [wɪʃ] **sich etwas wünschen** make a wish
Würfel dice, *pl* dice [daɪs]
Wurst sausage ['sɒsɪdʒ]
Würstchen sausage ['sɒsɪdʒ]
Wurzel root [ru:t]
würzig spicy ['spaɪsi]
Wüste desert ['dezət]
wütend angry ['æŋgri]

Y

Yoga yoga ['jəʊgə]

Z

Zahl number ['nʌmbə]; *(Ziffer)* figure ['fɪgə]
zahlen pay [peɪ]
zählen count [kaʊnt]
Zahn tooth, *pl* teeth [tu:θ], [ti:θ]
Zahnarzt/-ärztin dentist ['dentɪst]
Zahnfleisch gum [gʌm]
Zahnklammer braces *(pl)* ['breɪsɪz]
Zahnspange braces *(pl)* ['breɪsɪz]
Zauberei magic ['mædʒɪk] **durch Zauberei** by magic
zehn ten [ten]
Zeichen sign [saɪn]
Zeichensprache sign language ['saɪn læŋgwɪdʒ]
Zeichnung drawing ['drɔ:ɪŋ]
zeigen show [ʃəʊ] **zeigen (auf)** point (at/to) [pɔɪnt]
Zeile line [laɪn]
Zeit time [taɪm] **Zeit verbringen** spend time [spend] **in letzter Zeit** recently ['ri:sntli]
Zeitplan timetable ['taɪmteɪbl]
Zeitschrift magazine [mægə'zi:n]
Zeitung newspaper ['nju:zpeɪpə]
Zelt tent [tent]
zelten gehen go camping ['kæmpɪŋ]
Zentrum centre ['sentə]
zerbrechen break [breɪk]
zerbrochen broken ['brəʊkən]
Zettel piece of paper [pi:s əv 'peɪpə]
ziehen: ziehen (nach) *(umziehen)* move (to) [mu:v] **dein T-Shirt auf links ziehen** turn your T-shirt inside out [tɜ:n ɪnsaɪd 'aʊt]
Ziel aim [eɪm]
zielen auf etwas aim at sth. ['eɪm ət]
ziemlich quite [kwaɪt]
Ziffer figure ['fɪgə]; number ['nʌmbə]
Zimmer room [ru:m], [rʊm]
Zimmergenosse/-genossin roommate ['ru:mmeɪt]
zittern shake [ʃeɪk]
Zone zone [zəʊn]
Zoo zoo [zu:]
zu *(örtlich)* to [tu], [tə] **zu Hause** at home [ət 'həʊm] **zum Frühstück/Mittagessen/Abendessen** for breakfast/lunch/dinner [fɔ:], [fə] **zu teuer** too expensive [tu:] **auf (etwas) zu** toward(s) [tə'wɔ:d], [tə'wɔ:dz] **bei Ben zu Hause** at Ben's house [haʊs] **Nur zu!** Go ahead. [ə'hed] **Zeit, zu gehen** time to go [taɪm tu 'gəʊ]
zubereiten *(Essen)* cook [kʊk]
zucken: mit den Achseln/Schultern zucken shrug (your shoulders)
Zucker sugar ['ʃʊgə]
zuckerhaltig sugary ['ʃʊgəri]
zuckrig sugary ['ʃʊgəri]
zuerst first [fɜ:st]
Zufahrt *(z. B. zu einer Garage)* drive [draɪv]
zufolge according to [ə'kɔ:dɪŋ]
zufrieden pleased [pli:zd]
Zufriedenheit happiness ['hæpinəs]
Zug *(Eisenbahn)* train [treɪn]
zugänglich (für) accessible (to) [ək'sesəbl]
Zuhause home [həʊm]
zuhören listen ['lɪsn]
Zuhörer/in listener ['lɪsənə]
Zukunft future ['fju:tʃə]
zukünftige(r, s) future ['fju:tʃə]
zumachen close [kləʊz]
zunicken: jm. zunicken nod to sb. [nɒd]
zurück back [bæk]
zurücklassen: etwas zurücklassen leave sth. [li:v]
zurzeit at the moment ['məʊmənt]
zusammen together [tə'geðə]
Zusammenarbeit teamwork ['ti:mwɜ:k]
zusammenbrechen crash [kræʃ]
zusammenfassen sum up [sʌm 'ʌp] **Um (es) zusammenzufassen, ...** To sum up, ...
Zusammenstoß crash [kræʃ]
zusammenstoßen mit crash into [kræʃ]; hit [hɪt]
Zusammensturz crash [kræʃ]
zustimmen: jm. zustimmen agree with sb. [ə'gri:] **nicht zustimmen** disagree [dɪsə'gri:]
Zutritt entry ['entri]
zuversichtlich confident ['kɒnfɪdənt]; hopeful ['həʊpfl]
zuvor before [bɪ'fɔ:]
zwanzig twenty ['twenti]
zwei two [tu:]
zweite(r, s) second ['sekənd]
Zweitens ... Secondly, ... ['sekəndli]
Zwillinge twins *(pl)* [twɪnz]
Zwillingsbruder/-schwester twin brother/sister [twɪn]
zwischen between [bɪ'twi:n]
zwölf twelve [twelv]

ENGLISH SOUNDS & ALPHABET

English sounds

[iː]	green, he, sea
[ɑː]	ask, class, car, park
[ɔː]	or, ball, door, four, morning
[uː]	ruler, blue, too, two, you
[ɜː]	early, her, girl, work, T-shirt
[ɪ]	in, big, expensive
[e]	yes, bed, again, breakfast
[æ]	animal, apple, black, cat
[ʌ]	mum, bus, colour
[ɒ]	song, on, dog, what
[ʊ]	book, good, pullover
[ə]	again, today, a sister
[i]	happy, Turkey, coffee
[u]	museum, you, to
[eɪ]	name, eight, play, great
[aɪ]	I, time, right, my
[ɔɪ]	boy, toilet, noise
[əʊ]	old, no, boat, yellow
[aʊ]	now, house
[eə]	where, hair, share, their
[ʊə]	tour
[ɪə]	here, theatre, zero
[b]	bike, table, crab
[p]	pen, popular, shop
[d]	day, window, good
[t]	ten, butter, at
[g]	go, again, bag
[k]	kitchen, car, back
[m]	man, remember, mum
[n]	no, one, ten
[ŋ]	wrong, uncle, thanks
[l]	like, old, small
[r]	ruler, friend, sorry
[w]	we, where, one
[j]	yes, you, uniform
[f]	family, after
[v]	very, seven, have
[s]	six, poster, yes
[z]	quiz, his, music, please
[ʃ]	she, station, English
[ʒ]	usually, treasure, garage
[tʃ]	child, teacher, watch
[dʒ]	job, German, project, orange
[θ]	thing, three, bathroom, month
[ð]	the, father, with
[h]	house, who, behind
[x]	loch

Am besten kannst du dir die Aussprache der einzelnen Lautzeichen einprägen, wenn du dir zu jedem Zeichen ein einfaches Wort merkst – das [eɪ] ist der *name*-Laut usw.

The English alphabet

a	[eɪ]	**g**	[dʒiː]	**m**	[em]	**s**	[es]	**y**	[waɪ]
b	[biː]	**h**	[eɪtʃ]	**n**	[en]	**t**	[tiː]	**z**	[zed]
c	[siː]	**i**	[aɪ]	**o**	[əʊ]	**u**	[juː]		
d	[diː]	**j**	[dʒeɪ]	**p**	[piː]	**v**	[viː]		
e	[iː]	**k**	[keɪ]	**q**	[kjuː]	**w**	['dʌbljuː]		
f	[ef]	**l**	[el]	**r**	[ɑː]	**x**	[eks]		

COUNTRIES AND CONTINENTS

Country/Continent	Adjective	Person	People
Afghanistan [æf'gænɪstæn] *Afghanistan*	**Afghan** ['æfgæn]	**an Afghan**	**the Afghans**
Africa ['æfrɪkə] *Afrika*	**African** ['æfrɪkən]	**an African**	**the Africans**
America [ə'merɪkə] *Amerika*	**American** [ə'merɪkən]	**an American**	**the Americans**
Asia ['eɪʃə, 'eɪʒə] *Asien*	**Asian** ['eɪʃn, 'eɪʒn]	**an Asian**	**the Asians**
Australia [ɒ'streɪliə] *Australien*	**Australian** [ɒ'streɪliən]	**an Australian**	**the Australians**
Austria ['ɒstriə] *Österreich*	**Austrian** ['ɒstriən]	**an Austrian**	**the Austrians**
Bangladesh [bæŋglə'deʃ] *Bangladesch*	**Bangladesh**	**a Bangladeshi** [bæŋglə'deʃi]	**the Bangladeshis**
Belgium ['beldʒəm] *Belgien*	**Belgian** ['beldʒən]	**a Belgian**	**the Belgians**
Brazil [brə'zɪl] *Brasilien*	**Brasilian** [brə'zɪliən]	**a Brasilian**	**the Brasilians**
Bulgaria [bʌl'geəriə] *Bulgarien*	**Bulgarian** [bʌl'geəriən]	**a Bulgarian**	**the Bulgarians**
Canada ['kænədə] *Kanada*	**Canadian** [kə'neɪdiən]	**a Canadian**	**the Canadians**
China ['tʃaɪnə] *China*	**Chinese** [tʃaɪ'ni:z]	**a Chinese**	**the Chinese**
Croatia [krəʊ'eɪʃə] *Kroatien*	**Croatian** [krəʊ'eɪʃn]	**a Croatian**	**the Croatians**
the Czech Republic [ˌtʃek rɪ'pʌblɪk] *Tschechien, die Tschechische Republik*	**Czech** [tʃek]	**a Czech**	**the Czechs**
Denmark ['denmɑ:k] *Dänemark*	**Danish** ['deɪnɪʃ]	**a Dane** [deɪn]	**the Danes**
England ['ɪŋglənd] *England*	**English** ['ɪŋglɪʃ]	**an Englishman/-woman**	**the English**
Europe ['jʊərəp] *Europa*	**European** [ˌjʊərə'pi:ən]	**a European**	**the Europeans**
Finland ['fɪnlənd] *Finnland*	**Finnish** ['fɪnɪʃ]	**a Finn** [fɪn]	**the Finns**
France [frɑ:ns] *Frankreich*	**French** [frentʃ]	**a Frenchman/-woman**	**the French**
Germany ['dʒɜ:məni] *Deutschland*	**German** ['dʒɜ:mən]	**a German**	**the Germans**
(Great) Britain ['brɪtn] *Großbritannien*	**British** ['brɪtɪʃ]	**a Briton** ['brɪtn]	**the British**
Greece [gri:s] *Griechenland*	**Greek** [gri:k]	**a Greek**	**the Greeks**
Hungary ['hʌŋgəri] *Ungarn*	**Hungarian** [hʌŋ'geəriən]	**a Hungarian**	**the Hungarians**
India ['ɪndiə] *Indien*	**Indian** ['ɪndiən]	**an Indian**	**the Indians**
Iran [ɪ'rɑ:n] *Iran*	**Iranian** [ɪ'reɪniən]	**an Iranian**	**the Iranians**
Iraq [ɪ'rɑ:k] *Irak*	**Iraqi** [ɪ'rɑ:ki]	**an Iraqi**	**the Iraqis**
Ireland ['aɪələnd] *Irland*	**Irish** ['aɪrɪʃ]	**an Irishman/-woman**	**the Irish**
Italy ['ɪtəli] *Italien*	**Italian** [ɪ'tæliən]	**an Italian**	**the Italians**
Jamaica [dʒə'meɪkə] *Jamaika*	**Jamaican** [dʒə'meɪkən]	**a Jamaican**	**the Jamaicans**
Japan [dʒə'pæn] *Japan*	**Japanese** [ˌdʒæpə'ni:z]	**a Japanese**	**the Japanese**
Kenya ['kenjə] *Kenia*	**Kenyan** ['kenjən]	**a Kenyan**	**the Kenyans**
Lesotho [lə'su:tu:] *Lesotho*	**Sotho** ['su:tu:]	**a Mosotho** [mə'su:tu:]	**the Basotho**
the Netherlands ['neðələndz] *die Niederlande, Holland*	**Dutch** [dʌtʃ]	**a Dutchman/-woman**	**the Dutch**
New Zealand [ˌnju: 'zi:lənd] *Neuseeland*	**New Zealand** [ˌnju: 'zi:lənd]	**a New Zealander**	**the New Zealanders**
Norway ['nɔ:weɪ] *Norwegen*	**Norwegian** [nɔ:'wi:dʒən]	**a Norwegian**	**the Norwegians**
Pakistan [pækɪ'stæn] *Pakistan*	**Pakistani** [pækɪ'stæni]	**a Pakistani**	**the Pakistanis**
Poland ['pəʊlənd] *Polen*	**Polish** ['pəʊlɪʃ]	**a Pole** [pəʊl]	**the Poles**
Portugal ['pɔ:tʃʊgl] *Portugal*	**Portuguese** [ˌpɔ:tʃu'gi:z]	**a Portuguese**	**the Portuguese**
Romania [ru'meɪniə] *Rumänien*	**Romanian** [ru'meɪniən]	**a Romanian**	**the Romanians**
Russia ['rʌʃə] *Russland*	**Russian** ['rʌʃn]	**a Russian**	**the Russians**
Scotland ['skɒtlənd] *Schottland*	**Scottish** ['skɒtɪʃ]	**a Scotsman/-woman,**	**the Scots**
Serbia ['sɜ:biə] *Serbien*	**Serbian** ['sɜ:biən]	**a Serb** [sɜ:b]	**the Serbs**
Slovakia [slə'vækiə] *die Slowakei*	**Slovak** ['sləʊvæk]	**a Slovakian** [slə'vækiən]	**the Slovakians**
Slovenia [slə'vi:niə] *Slowenien*	**Slovene** ['sləʊvi:n]	**a Slovenian** [slə'vi:niən]	**the Slovenians**
Spain [speɪn] *Spanien*	**Spanish** ['spænɪʃ]	**a Spaniard** ['spænɪəd]	**the Spaniards**
Sweden ['swi:dn] *Schweden*	**Swedish** ['swi:dɪʃ]	**a Swede** [swi:d]	**the Swedes**
Switzerland ['swɪtsələnd] *die Schweiz*	**Swiss** [swɪs]	**a Swiss**	**the Swiss**
Syria ['sɪriə] *Syrien*	**Syrian** ['sɪriən]	**a Syrian**	**the Syrians**
Turkey ['tɜ:ki] *die Türkei*	**Turkish** ['tɜ:kɪʃ]	**a Turk** [tɜ:k]	**the Turks**
the United Kingdom (the UK) [juˌnaɪtɪd 'kɪŋdəm, ˌju:'keɪ] *das Vereinigte Königreich (Großbritannien und Nordirland)*	**British** ['brɪtɪʃ]	**a Briton** ['brɪtn]	**the British**
the United States of America (the USA) *die Vereinigten Staaten von Amerika*	**American** [ə'merɪkən]	**an American**	**the Americans**
Wales [weɪlz] *Wales*	**Welsh** [welʃ]	**a Welshman/-woman**	**the Welsh**

infinitive	simple past	past participle	
(to) **be**	I/he/she/it **was**; you/we/you/they **were**	**been**	sein
(to) **beat**	**beat**	**beaten**	schlagen, besiegen
(to) **become**	**became**	**become**	werden
°(to) **bite** [aɪ]	**bit** [ɪ]	**bitten** [ɪ]	beißen
(to) **blow**	**blew** [uː]	**blown**	pusten, blasen; wehen
(to) **break** [eɪ]	**broke**	**broken**	brechen
(to) **bring**	**brought**	**brought**	bringen, mitbringen
(to) **build** [ɪ]	**built** [ɪ]	**built** [ɪ]	bauen
(to) **burn**	**burnt**	**burnt**	brennen, verbrennen
(to) **buy**	**bought**	**bought**	kaufen
(to) **catch**	**caught**	**caught**	(ein)fangen; erwischen
(to) **choose**	**chose**	**chosen**	wählen, auswählen
(to) **come**	**came**	**come**	kommen
(to) **cost**	**cost**	**cost**	kosten
(to) **cut**	**cut**	**cut**	schneiden; *(Rasen)* mähen
(to) **do**	**did**	**done** [ʌ]	tun, machen
(to) **dig**	**dug**	**dug**	graben
°(to) **draw**	**drew**	**drawn**	zeichnen
(to) **drink**	**drank**	**drunk**	trinken
(to) **drive** [aɪ]	**drove** [əʊ]	**driven** [ɪ]	fahren
(to) **eat** [iː]	**ate** [et, eɪt]	**eaten** [iː]	essen
(to) **fall**	**fell**	**fallen**	fallen
(to) **feed**	**fed**	**fed**	füttern
(to) **feel**	**felt**	**felt**	fühlen, sich fühlen
(to) **fight**	**fought**	**fought**	kämpfen, bekämpfen
(to) **find**	**found**	**found**	finden
(to) **fly**	**flew**	**flown**	fliegen
(to) **forget**	**forgot**	**forgotten**	vergessen
(to) **freeze**	**froze**	**frozen**	(ge)frieren; erstarren
(to) **get**	**got**	**got**	bekommen; (sich etw.) besorgen, holen
(to) **give** [ɪ]	**gave**	**given** [ɪ]	geben
(to) **go**	**went**	**gone**	gehen, fahren
°(to) **grow**	**grew**	**grown**	wachsen
(to) **hang**	**hung** [ʌ]	**hung**	hängen
(to) **have**	**had**	**had**	haben
(to) **hear** [ɪə]	**heard** [ɜː]	**heard**	hören
(to) **hide**	**hid**	**hidden**	(sich) verstecken
(to) **hit**	**hit**	**hit**	treffen auf, schlagen, prallen, stoßen
(to) **hold**	**held**	**held**	halten
(to) **hurt**	**hurt**	**hurt**	verletzen; wehtun
(to) **keep**	**kept**	**kept**	(be)halten
(to) **kneel**	**knelt**	**knelt**	knien
(to) **know** [nəʊ]	**knew** [njuː]	**known** [nəʊn]	wissen; kennen

infinitive	simple past	past participle	
(to) **leave**	**left**	**left**	lassen, zurücklassen, verlassen
(to) **lend**	**lent**	**lent**	(ver)leihen
(to) **let**	**let**	**let**	lassen
(to) **lose** [uː]	**lost**	**lost**	verlieren
(to) **make**	**made**	**made**	machen, herstellen
(to) **mean** [iː]	**meant** [e]	**meant** [e]	bedeuten; sagen wollen
(to) **meet**	**met**	**met**	treffen
(to) **pay**	**paid**	**paid**	(be)zahlen
(to) **put**	**put**	**put**	legen, stellen, stecken
(to) **read** [iː]	**read** [e]	**read** [e]	lesen
(to) **ride** [aɪ]	**rode**	**ridden** [ɪ]	reiten; *(Rad)* fahren
(to) **ring**	**rang**	**rung**	läuten, klingeln
(to) **run**	**ran**	**run**	rennen, laufen
(to) **say**	**said** [sed]	**said** [sed]	sagen
(to) **see**	**saw**	**seen**	sehen
(to) **sell**	**sold**	**sold**	verkaufen
(to) **send**	**sent**	**sent**	senden, schicken
(to) **set**	**set**	**set**	stellen, legen, setzen
(to) **sew**	**sewed**	**sewn**	nähen
(to) **shake**	**shook**	**shaken**	schütteln
(to) **show**	**showed**	**shown**	zeigen
(to) **sing**	**sang**	**sung**	singen
(to) **sit**	**sat**	**sat**	sitzen; sich setzen
(to) **sleep**	**slept**	**slept**	schlafen
(to) **speak** [iː]	**spoke**	**spoken**	sprechen
(to) **spend**	**spent**	**spent**	*(Geld)* ausgeben, *(Zeit)* verbringen
(to) **spin**	**spun**	**spun**	(sich) drehen
(to) **spread**	**spread**	**spread**	verbreiten, sich ausbreiten
(to) **stand**	**stood**	**stood**	stehen
(to) **steal**	**stole**	**stolen**	stehlen, rauben
°(to) **stick**	**stuck**	**stuck**	kleben
(to) **swim**	**swam**	**swum**	schwimmen
(to) **take**	**took**	**taken**	(mit)nehmen; bringen
(to) **teach** [iː]	**taught** [ɔː]	**taught** [ɔː]	lehren, unterrichten
(to) **tell**	**told**	**told**	sagen; erzählen, berichten
(to) **think**	**thought**	**thought**	denken, glauben, meinen
(to) **throw**	**threw**	**thrown**	werfen
(to) **understand**	**understood**	**understood**	verstehen
(to) **wake up**	**woke up**	**woken up**	aufwachen
(to) **wear** [eə]	**wore** [ɔː]	**worn** [ɔː]	tragen *(Kleidung)*
(to) **win**	**won** [ʌ]	**won** [ʌ]	gewinnen
(to) **write** [aɪ]	**wrote**	**written** [ɪ]	schreiben

°Mit diesem Kringel sind Wörter markiert, die nicht zum Lernwortschatz gehören.

First names (Vornamen)

Aaron ['eərən]
Abby ['æbi]
Alex ['ælɪks]
Alice ['ælɪs]
Ari ['ɑ:ri]
Asha ['ʌʃʌ]
Barack [bə'ræk], [bə'rɑ:k]
Barbie ['bɑ:bi]
Bobby ['bɒbi]
Bram [bræm]
Camilla [kə'mɪlə]
Carly ['kɑ:li]
Cartimandua [kɑ:tɪ'mændʊə]
Catherine ['kæθrɪn]
Charles [tʃɑ:lz]
Charlie ['tʃɑ:li]
Charlotte ['ʃɑ:lət]
Chelsea ['tʃelsi]
Chris [krɪs]
Christ [kraɪst]
Christina [krɪ'sti:nə]
Chuck [tʃʌk]
Claire [kleə]
Clancy, Clance ['klænsi], [klæns]
Clark [klɑ:k]
Conor ['kɒnə]
Constantine ['kɒnstəntaɪn]
D'Angelo [di'ændʒələʊ]
Danny ['dæni]
David ['deɪvɪd]
Dexter ['dekstə]
Diana [daɪ'ænə]
Diego [di'eɪgəʊ]
Dingle ['dɪŋgl]
Doris ['dɒrɪs]
Dorothy ['dɒrəθi]
Ed [ed]
Ella ['elə]
Elton ['eltən]
Elvis ['elvɪs]
Eric ['erɪk]
Ethan ['i:θən]
Fara ['færə]
Finn [fɪn]
Fred [fred]
Freddie ['fredi]
George [dʒɔ:dʒ]
Gordon ['gɔ:dn]
Graham ['greɪəm]
Grover ['grəʊvə]
Guinevere ['gwɪnɪvɪə]
Hadrian ['heɪdriən]
Hailee ['heɪli]
Hamlet ['hæmlət]
Harald ['hærəld]
Harry ['hæri]
Ian ['i:ən]
Ivar ['aɪvə], ['i:və]
James [dʒeɪmz]
Jamie ['dʒeɪmi]
Jawed ['dʒɑ:ved]
Jeanie ['dʒi:ni]
Jesse ['dʒesi]
Joshua ['dʒɒʃuə]
Josie ['dʒəʊsi]
Juliet ['dʒu:liət]
Jumana [dʒu'mɑ:nə]
Justin ['dʒʌstɪn]
Kaitlin ['keɪtlɪn]
Kamala [kə'mɑ:lə]
Kara ['kɑ:rə]
Kate [keɪt]
Kayla ['keɪlə]
Keela ['ki:lə]
Kimani [kɪ'mɑ:ni]
Lancelot ['lɑ:nsəlɒt]
Landon ['lændən]
Latifa [lə'ti:fə]
Lauren ['lɔ:rən]
Lewis ['lu:ɪs]
Liam ['li:əm]
Lindsey ['lɪndzi]
Louis ['lu:i]
Lucia ['lu:siə]
Lucy ['lu:si]
Lukas ['lu:kəs]
Maewyn ['meɪwɪn]
Marilyn ['mærəlɪn]
Matt [mæt]
Meghan ['megən]
Mo [məʊ]
Mohamad [məʊ'hæmɪd]
Molly ['mɒli]
Moziah [məʊ'zaɪə]
Nancy ['nænsi]
Nicholas ['nɪkələs]
Noah ['nəʊə]
Oliver ['ɒlɪvə]
Oscar ['ɒskə]
Owen ['əʊɪn]
Paddy ['pædi]
Patrick ['pætrɪk]
Percy ['pɜ:si]
Pete [pi:t]
Rachel ['reɪtʃəl]
Rick [rɪk]
Riku ['ri:ku]
Riya ['raɪə]
Roald ['rəʊəld]
Romeo ['rəʊmiəʊ]
Roxy ['rɒksi]
Roy [rɔɪ]
Ruby ['ru:bi]
Ryan ['raɪən]
Sabina [sə'bi:nə]
Sami ['sæmi]
Sarah ['seərə]
Selena [sə'li:nə]
Sitara [sɪ'tɑ:rə]
Sydney ['sɪdni]
T'Challa [tə'tʃɑ:lə]
Tara ['tɑ:rə]
Theo ['θi:əʊ]
Vapona [və'pəʊnə]
Victoria [vɪk'tɔ:rɪə]
William ['wɪljəm]
Zahid [zʌ'hi:d]
Zainab ['zeɪnæb]
Zoe ['zəʊi]
Zoella [zəʊ'elə]

Family names / Surnames (Familiennamen)

Arthur ['ɑ:θə]
Begwell ['begwəl]
Bobofit ['bɒbəfɪt]
Brunner ['brʌnə]
Butcher ['bʊtʃə]
Camden ['kæmdən]
Capulet ['kæpjʊlet]
Crew [kru:]
Dahl [dɑ:l]
Danes [deɪnz]
de la Mare [delə'meə]
Dodds [dɒdz]
Donovan ['dɒnəvən]
Drake [dreɪk]
Finehair ['faɪnheə]
Gomez ['gəʊmez]
Haraldsson ['hærəldsən]
Harding ['hɑ:dɪŋ]
Harrington ['hærɪŋtən]
Harris ['hærɪs]
Jackson ['dʒæksən]
John [dʒɒn]
Johnston ['dʒɒnstən]
Karim [kə'ri:m]
Kent [kent]
Khan [kɑ:n]
Malone [mə'ləʊn]
Markle ['mɑ:kl]
Marvel ['mɑ:vl]
McCool [mə'ku:l]
McKenzie [mə'kenzi]
Middleton ['mɪdltən]
Monroe [mən'rəʊ]
Montague ['mɒntəgju:]
O'Brien [əʊ'braɪən]
Obama [əʊ'bɑ:mə]
Planter ['plɑ:ntə]
Porter ['pɔ:tə]
Potter ['pɒtə]
Presley ['presli]
Redfort ['redfət]
Riordan ['rɪədən]
Rowling ['rəʊlɪŋ]
Ryal ['raɪəl]
Scott [skɒt]
Shakespeare ['ʃeɪkspɪə]
Sharma ['ʃɑ:mə]
Steinfeld ['staɪnfeld]
Stephens ['sti:vnz]
Stirling ['stɜ:lɪŋ]
Stoker ['stəʊkə]
Sugg [sʌg]
Thun [tu:n]
Zellner ['zelnə]
Zor-El [zɒ'rel]

Place names (Ortsnamen)

Abbey Theatre [æbi 'θɪətə]
America [ə'merɪkə]
Antrim ['æntrɪm]
Beale Street ['bi:l stri:t]
Beijing [beɪ'dʒɪŋ]
Belfast ['belfɑ:st], [bel'fɑ:st]
Berlin [bɜ:'lɪn]
Blarney ['blɑ:ni]
Bradford ['brædfəd]
Britannia [brɪ'tænjə]
Brooklyn ['brʊklɪn]
Buckingham ['bʌkɪŋəm]
Carlingford ['kɑ:lɪŋfəd]
Connemara [kɒnɪ'mɑ:rə]
Constantinople [kɒnstæntɪ'nəʊpl]
Copenhagen [kəʊpən'heɪgən]
Dublin ['dʌblɪn]
Dublin Bay [dʌblɪn 'beɪ]
Eoforwic ['eɪəʊvəwɪtʃ]
Eton ['i:tən]
Forum ['fɔ:rəm]
Germantown ['dʒɜ:məntaʊn]
Giant's Causeway [dʒaɪənts 'kɔ:zweɪ]
Graceland ['greɪslænd]
Grafton Street ['grɑ:ftən stri:t]
Hampshire ['hæmpʃə]
Hogwarts ['hɒgwɔ:ts]
Hollywood ['hɒliwʊd]
Istanbul [ɪstæn'bʊl]
Jefferson Avenue [dʒefəsən 'ævənju:]
Jersey ['dʒɜ:zi]
Jorvik ['jɔ:vɪk]
Kensington Palace [kensɪŋtən 'pæləs]
Kilimanjaro [kɪlɪmən'dʒɑ:rəʊ]
Leinster Street ['lenstə stri:t]
Los Angeles [lɒs 'ændʒəli:z]

Manhattan [mən'hætn]
Mars [mɑːz]
Memphis ['memfɪs]
Metropolitan Museum of Art [metrəpɒlɪtən mjuziːəm əv 'ɑːt]
Mildenhall ['mɪldənhɔːl]
Mississippi [mɪsɪ'sɪpi]
Moore Street ['mʊə striːt]
Nassau ['næsɔː]
Norfolk ['nɔːfək]
O'Connell Street [əʊ'kɒnl striːt]
Paris ['pærɪs]
Post Museum ['pəʊst mjuziːəm]
Renton Grange [rentən 'greɪndʒ]
Rome [rəʊm]
San Francisco Bay [sæn frən'sɪskəʊ beɪ]
Seattle [si'ætl]
Siberia [saɪ'bɪəriə]
Silicon Docks [sɪlɪkən 'dɒks]
Sligo ['slaɪgəʊ]
Southampton [saʊ'θæmptən]
St Andrews [sənt 'ændruːz]
St Stephen's Green [sənt stiːvnz 'griːn]
St. Paul's Cathedral [sənt pɔːlz kə'θiːdrəl]
Trinity College ['trɪnəti kɒlɪdʒ]
Twinford ['twɪnfəd]
Verona [və'rəʊnə]
Wakanda [wə'kɑːndə]
Wales [weɪlz]
Washington ['wɒʃɪŋtən]
Westminster Abbey [wəstmɪnstər 'æbi]
Wilton ['wɪltən]
Yancy Academy [jænsi ə'kædəmi]
York [jɔːk]
Yorkshire ['jɔːkʃə]

Other names
(Andere Namen)

Banshee [bæn'ʃiː], ['bænʃiː]
Black Panther [blæk 'pænθə]
Brigantes ['brɪgəntəs]
CoderDojo [kəʊdə'dəʊdʒəʊ]
Cosplay ['kɒspleɪ]
Dearg-due [dɑːrʊg'duːə]
Dracula ['drækjʊlə]
Dullahan ['dʌləhən]
EEC (European Economic Community) [jʊərəpiːən iːkə'nɒmɪk kə'mjuːnəti]
enchiladas [entʃɪ'lɑːdəz]
Eurovision Song Contest [jʊərəʊvɪʒn 'sɒŋ kɒntest]
Fungie ['fʌŋgi]
Harley ['hɑːli]
Kait123 [keɪtwʌntu'θriː]
Kronos ['krəʊnəs]
Liffey ['lɪfi]
Lord of the Rings [lɔːd əv ðə 'rɪŋz]
Mandarin ['mændərɪn]
Quidditch ['kwɪdɪtʃ]
skype [skaɪp]
Thames [temz]
wiki ['wɪki]
Wonder Woman ['wʌndə wʊmən]

English-speaking countries

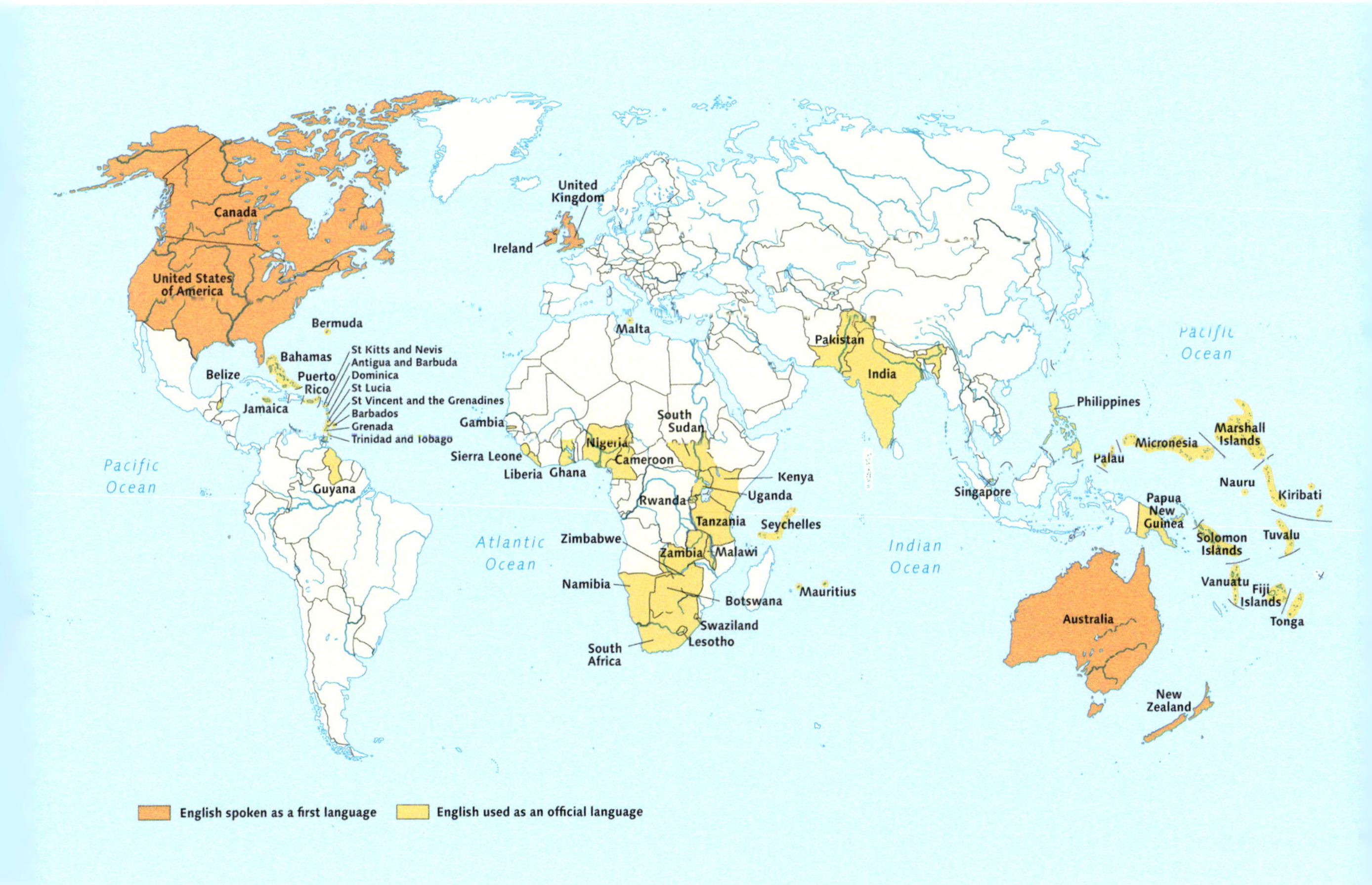

Du und dein Lehrer / deine Lehrerin	You and your teacher
Guten Morgen, Herr / Frau ...	**Good morning, Mr / Mrs / Miss ... (bis 12 Uhr)**
Guten Tag, Herr ...	**Good afternoon, Mr ... (ab 12 Uhr)**
Entschuldigung, dass ich zu spät komme.	**Sorry, I'm late.**
Kann ich bitte das Fenster öffnen / zumachen?	**Can I open / close the window, please?**
Kann ich bitte zur Toilette gehen?	**Can I go to the toilet, please?**
Auf Wiedersehen! / Bis morgen.	**Goodbye. / See you tomorrow.**

Hausaufgaben und Übungen	Homework and exercises
Es tut mir leid, ich habe mein Schulheft nicht dabei.	**Sorry, I have no exercise book.**
Ich verstehe diese Übung nicht.	**I don't understand this exercise.**
Ich kann Nummer 3 nicht lösen.	**I can't do number 3.**
Entschuldigung, ich bin noch nicht fertig.	**Sorry, I haven't finished.**
Ich habe ... Ist das richtig?	**I have ... Is that right?**
Es tut mir leid, das weiß ich nicht.	**Sorry, I don't know.**
Was haben wir (als Hausaufgabe) auf?	**What's for homework?**

Du brauchst Hilfe	You need help
Können Sie mir bitte helfen?	**Can you help me, please?**
Auf welcher Seite sind wir / steht das?	**What page is it, please?**
Was heißt ... auf Englisch / Deutsch?	**What's ... in English / German?**
Können Sie das bitte an die Tafel schreiben?	**Can you write it on the board, please?**
Kann ich das auf Deutsch sagen?	**Can I say it in German?**
Können Sie / Kannst du bitte lauter sprechen?	**Can you speak louder, please?**
Können Sie das bitte noch einmal sagen / abspielen?	**Can you say / play that again, please?**

Partnerarbeit	Work with a partner
Kann ich mit Julian arbeiten?	**Can I work with Julian?**
Du bist dran.	**It's your turn.**
Lass uns ein ... machen / zeichnen.	**Let's make / draw a ...**
Lass uns die Geschichte / den Dialog spielen.	**Let's act the story / dialogue.**

What your teacher says	Was dein Lehrer / deine Lehrerin sagt
Listen, please. / Quiet, please.	**Hört bitte zu. / Ruhe bitte.**
Open your books at page 24.	**Schlagt bitte Seite 24 auf.**
Do exercise 5 for homework, please.	**Macht bitte Übung 5 als Hausaufgabe.**
Where's your book, David?	**Wo ist dein Buch, David?**
Try again!	**Versuche es noch einmal!**
That's really good!	**Das ist wirklich gut!**
That's all for today. You can go.	**Das ist alles für heute. Ihr könnt gehen.**

Diese Arbeitsanweisungen findest du in diesem Buch:

Add drawings/information/...	Füge Zeichnungen/Informationen/... hinzu.
Ask and answer with a partner.	Stelle Fragen und beantworte sie mit einem/r Partner/in.
Answer the questions / Partner B's questions.	Beantworte die Fragen / Partner Bs Fragen.
Check your language/vocabulary/speaking/writing.	Überprüfe deine Sprache / deinen Wortschatz / dein Sprechen / dein Schreiben.
Choose the right answer/captions/...	Wähle die richtige Antwort/Bildunterschrift/... aus.
Compare the headings/ideas/...	Vergleiche die Überschriften/Ideen/...
Complete the questions / sentences / dialogue.	Vervollständige die Fragen / die Sätze / den Dialog.
Copy the table/chart/diagram/...	Schreibe die Tabelle / das Diagramm /... ab.
Correct the mistakes.	Berichtige die Fehler.
Describe the characters/feelings/setting/...	Beschreibe die Figuren / Gefühle / den Schauplatz /...
Discuss your ideas/opinions/...	Diskutiert eure Ideen/Meinungen/...
Finish the lines.	Vervollständige die Zeilen.
Look at page ...	Schlage Seite ... auf. / Schau Seite ... an.
Look at the photos/examples/map/comments.	Sieh dir die Fotos / die Beispiele / die Karte / die Kommentare an.
Listen and check / complete.	Höre zu und überprüfe / vervollständige.
Listen to the interview/pronunciation/...	Hör dir das Interview / die Aussprache /... an.
Make a mind map / notes / a word web.	Fertige eine Mindmap / Notizen / ein Wortnetz an.
Match the sentence parts.	Verbinde die Satzhälften.
Practise the conversation/presentation/...	Übe die Unterhaltung/Präsentation/...
Prepare your part/talk/...	Bereite deinen Teil / deinen Vortrag /... vor.
Put the sentences / recipe in the right order.	Bringe die Sätze / das Rezept in die richtige Reihenfolge.
Read about ...	Lies über ...
Read the text / story / article.	Lies den Text / die Geschichte / den Artikel.
Share your ideas with ...	Teile deine Ideen mit ...
Swap roles/stories/...	Tausche Rollen/Geschichten/...
Take turns.	Wechselt euch ab.
Talk to a partner.	Sprich mit einem/r Partner/in.
Tell your partner / the class.	Erzähle / Sage es deinem/r Partner/in / der Klasse.
True or false? / True, false or not in the text?	Wahr oder falsch? / Wahr, falsch oder nicht im Text?
Turn the book around.	Dreh das Buch um.
Use your notes / the words in a.	Benutze deine Notizen / die Wörter aus Aufgabe a.
Walk around.	Gehe herum.
Watch part 1 / the video.	Sieh Teil 1 / den Film an.
Work with a partner / in groups.	Arbeite mit einem/r Partner/in in Gruppen.
Write words / sentences / questions / answers.	Schreibe Wörter / Sätze / Fragen / Antworten.
Write about ...	Schreibe über ...
Write ... in your exercise book.	Schreibe ... in dein Übungsheft.
Put it in My file.	Hefte es in deinem Dossier ab.

Unit 1 | p. 22

1 Check your vocabulary

a 6 points

1 Self-defence is a) when you fight back to stop others from hurting you.
2 A choir is f) a group of people who sing together.
3 Coding is b) when you write a computer programme.
4 Fencing is e) a sport where two people fight.
5 An orchestra is c) a group that plays instruments together.
6 Sign language is d) using your hands to 'talk' to people who can't hear.

b 5 points

So, your (1) gender is female. What's your date of (2) birth? I need your (3) contact information. What's your address and phone number? Do you live with a parent or with a (4) guardian/ relative? That's it. Could you please write your (5) signature here?

2 Check your language 6 points

Ella is a London girl (1) whose parents are in Africa. She's really enjoying all the activities (2) (–) she is doing and she's started two sports (3) that are new for her. Ella is very happy in Wilton house (4) where she is a boarder and she loves the room (5) which/ (–) she shares with Roxy. Ella would like to say thank you to all the students in Wilton house (6) who have been very friendly to her.

3 Check your speaking 6 points

4 Hi, you're Noah, right? Ethan's brother.
1 Yes, I am. How do you know Ethan?
3 We're in the football team together. I'm Ari.
6 Sorry, I didn't get your name. Could you say it again, please?
2 Sorry, it's Ari.
5 Nice to meet you, Ari.

4 Check your writing 10 points

(1) Dear Ella
(2) How are you? (3) Thanks for your letter. I'm (4) fine, thanks. Here's some school (5) news: we have a new (6) teacher. His name is Mr Planter and he (7) teaches history. He's very nice and (8) doesn't give (9) us too much homework.
Write (10) soon!
Love Riya

Für jede richtige Antwort bekommst du **einen Punkt**. Zähle die Punkte zusammen.

33–25 points	24–16 points	15–0 points
☺ Very good!	😐 OK, but you can do better. Which exercise wasn't easy for you? Practise and try again.	☹ You should practise more. Ask your teacher for help.

Unit 2 | p. 38

1 Check your vocabulary

a 5 points

1 catch 2 save 3 have 4 fight
5 escape

b 5 points

1 Please vacuum e) the living room carpet.
2 Don't forget to set a) the table for dinner.
3 Have you cut d) the grass?
4 You need to take out b) the trash.
5 Remember to make c) your bed.

c 4 points

1 needn't 2 mustn't 3 mustn't
4 needn't

2 Check your language

a 5 points

1 carefully 2 quietly 3 sadly
4 quickly 5 happily

b 5 points

1 You sat down too fast.
c) You must do it slowly.
2 You don't have to cry.
e) Just look unhappy.
3 We have to do the scene again.
d) We need to get it right this time.
4 But we must have lunch first.
a) I need to eat something.
5 I got up late this morning.
b) I had to leave without breakfast.

3 Check your speaking (example) 24 points

A: Hello, is this XYZ cinema?
B: Yes, how can I help?
A: I was wondering how much the tickets cost/are?
B: It's £4 for children until the age of 14 and £6 for adults.
A: OK, thanks. And is it possible to visit the cinema in a wheelchair?
B: Yes, that's not a problem.
A: Are we allowed to take our own drinks into the cinema?
B: I'm afraid you're not allowed to do that. But you can buy drinks inside.
A: Sorry, I didn't get that. Could you say it again, please?
B: Sorry, you're not allowed to take your own drinks inside.
A: OK, thanks for the information. Bye!
B: Bye!

4 Check your writing (example) 16 points

A good friend: She is loyal and friendly. You can always count on her. She doesn't like to wait. She's a happy person and she laughs a lot.
Mum: She's a caring and warm person. She's very clever too and never forgets an appointment. Her family is the most important thing to her. She is always there for us.

Ex. 1–2: Für jede richtige Antwort bekommst du **einen Punkt**.
Ex. 3–4: Für jeden sprachlich und inhaltlich korrekten Satz oder jede korrekte Frage bekommst du **zwei Punkte**.
Zähle die Punkte zusammen.

64–53 points	52–32 points	31–0 points
☺ Very good!	😐 OK, but you can do better. Which exercise wasn't easy for you? Practise and try again.	☹ You should practise more. Ask your teacher for help.

Unit 3 | p. 56

1 Check your vocabulary

a 12 points

1 The Britons were many different tribes.
2 The Romans invaded Britain in 43 AD. They built roads so that they could travel.
3 The Angles and Saxons settled in Britain because of the land.
4 The Vikings conquered the city of York.
5 The Normans built lots of churches and castles.

b 6 points

1 a silver ring
2 a linen shirt
3 a wooden spoon
4 a metal knife
5 a wool sock
6 a leather bag

2 Check your language

a 6 points

1 Have you ever visited Rome?
2 Did you have nice weather?
3 What did you see while you were visiting Rome?
4 Have you ever found 'treasure' in the street?
5 What did you find?
6 What did you do with it?

b 6 points

1 isn't it
2 don't you
3 weren't you
4 do you
5 didn't you
6 did they

3 Check your speaking (example) 20 points

A: In my opinion, we don't need teachers. Computers can do their job.
B: I don't agree with you! Teachers are very important and sometimes I only like a class because of a specific teacher. They can help each person individually.
A: That's true, but I think computers are a better source. We have all the learning materials on our computers and we can learn more in less time.
B: I can't believe that's how you feel. Teachers talk to their students, which is important.
A: I feel that in the future computers will play a big part in how people learn at school. That doesn't mean that we stop talking to other people.
B: I don't think that's going to happen. But if we start learning everything from computers, it's not necessary to go to school every day and we will hardly talk to other students.

4 Check your writing (example) 8 points

When his family moved into their new home, he found an old map in one of the cupboards. It looked like a treasure map, so he started searching for the treasure. The map lead him into the garden, where he had to dig a hole. He found a box, and in it there was a lot of silver and gold!

Ex. 1–2: Für jede richtige Antwort oder Frage bekommst du **einen Punkt**.
Ex. 3–4: Für jeden sprachlich und inhaltlich korrekten Satz bekommst du **zwei Punkte**.
Zähle die Punkte zusammen.

58–46 points	45–29 points	28–0 points
☺ Very good!	😐 OK, but you can do better. Which exercise wasn't easy for you? Practise and try again.	☹ You should practise more. Ask your teacher for help.

Unit 4 | p. 72

1 Check your vocabulary

a 6 points

1 pub
2 leprechaun
3 soda bread
4 the (Great) Famine
5 the Troubles
6 Gaelic

b 5 points

1 You can get this T-shirt in orange or pink. I'll buy the orange one for my sister.
2 My little sister loves funny socks. I'll take these ones for her.
3 Mum might like the blue gloves. But I think she'll love the green ones.
4 A book is a good present for Dad. I'll take this one for him.
5 Mmm, sweets. I'll buy these ones for me!

c 5 points

1 d 2 e 3 c 4 a 5 b

d 6 points

1 using
2 coding
3 to develop
4 to work
5 listening
6 to see

2 Check your language

a 5 points

1 had already learned
2 had seen
3 spent
4 didn't want
5 had enjoyed

b 5 points

1 If you like food, c) try Irish stew.
2 If you like music, d) you'll like Irish pubs.
3 If you like boats, e) visit the Jeanie Johnston.
4 If you like the country, a) go to Connemara.
5 If you believe in leprechauns, b) you might see one!

3 Check your speaking (example) 14 points

Okay, let's start at Custom House. Turn left on Custom House Quay and then turn right to walk across the bridge. Go straight on until you get to Townsend Street. Turn left and go along the street. Then turn right on Lombard Street East. Go past Pearse Street and walk down Westland Row. Then make a right turn and you have arrived at your destination! (Lincoln Place)

4 Check your writing (example) 16 points

1 Enjoying some live music at a pub in Temple Bar in Dublin. Traditional Irish music is the best! Everyone's dancing and having a good time.
2 I've made it to Galway! I will enjoy the city and beautiful Connemara for the next few days.
3 Spent the day at the Cliffs of Moher! One of the most beautiful places I've seen. I'll be back for another visit!

Ex. 1–2: Für jede richtige Antwort oder Frage bekommst du **einen Punkt**.
Ex. 3–4: Für jeden sprachlich und inhaltlich richtigen Satz bekommst du **zwei Punkte**.
Zähle die Punkte zusammen.

62–51 points	50–31 points	30–0 points
🙂 Very good!	😐 OK, but you can do better. Which exercise wasn't easy for you? Practise and try again.	☹ You should practise more. Ask your teacher for help.

Unit 5 | p. 90

1 Check your vocabulary

a 6 points

1 board c) game (2)
2 foot d) ball (1)
3 skate a) park (1)
4 hair f) style (1)
5 post b) code (1)
6 side e) walk (1)

b 6 points

1 posted
2 viral
3 shared
4 subscribed
5 facts
6 switch

c 5 points

1 change
2 call
3 chill
4 give
5 give in

2 Check your language

a 10 points

1 have been hanging out 2 since 3 has been living
4 for 5 have been writing 6 since 7 have been working
8 for 9 haven't been working 10 Have you all been having

b 3 points

1 didn't work
2 'd buy
3 needed

3 Check your speaking (example) 12 points

1 I'm always late for school.
– You ought to get up earlier in the morning.
2 I always forget English vocabulary.
– You ought to practise the new vocabulary every day.
3 Somebody is posting horrible comments about me.
– You ought to talk to that person and tell your teacher/s and/or parents.
4 My parents don't listen to me.
– You ought to write them a letter.
5 I have problems with English pronunciation.
– You ought to practise your pronunciation. You can listen to new words and repeat them.
6 I want to be happy.
– You ought to spend more time with friends/do more things that make you feel happy.

4 Check your writing (example) 10 points

Hi everybody!
Sorry for not posting for a long time! I've been very busy. Last week I went to a workshop and learned all about songwriting. It was really interesting! Also, I have been busy practicing for my band's upcoming concert. We're going to perform live at the youth club on Saturday! Hope to see as many of you as possible there, it's going to be great!

Ex. 1–2: Für jede richtige Antwort oder Frage bekommst du **einen Punkt**.
Ex. 3–4: Für jeden sprachlich und inhaltlich richtigen Satz bekommst du **zwei Punkte**.
Zähle die Punkte zusammen.

52–40 points	39–26 points	25–0 points
☺ Very good!	😐 OK, but you can do better. Which exercise wasn't easy for you? Practise and try again.	☹ You should practise more. Ask your teacher for help.

Quellenverzeichnis

Titelbild: shutterstock / Noradoa (Kylemore Abbey, Ireland)

Illustrationen

Cornelsen / Carlos Borrell Eiköter: Umschlaginnenseiten / vorn und hinten; Karten S. 9, 42, 44, 58, 64, 95, 247 – **Cornelsen / Bildbad:** S. 9, 10, 11, 14, 15, 20, 21, 22, 29, 32, 38, 49, 50, 51, 56, 60, 62, 64, 65, 67, 68, 72, 75, 81, 82, 83, 84, 88, 92, 93, 96, 101, 105, 106, 109, 118 (oben Mitte), 119, 125, 130 bis 138; 141, 142 – **Cornelsen / Tam-An Nguyen, Erlangen:** S. 29 / unten rechts – **Cornelsen / Bernd Kissel:** S. 54, 55, 100, 120 bis 124

Bilder

S. 8 / Mädchen Vordergrund: shutterstock / stockyimages; **/ 1 und 2:** Cornelsen / Trevor Burrows – **S. 9 / Mitte links:** Cornelsen / Trevor Burrows; **/ unten links:** shutterstock / Brian McEntire – **S. 10 / oben (Flaggen):** stock.adobe.com / picoStudio; **/ oben rechts (Münzhaufen):** Cornelsen / Petra Eberhard – **S. 11:** Cornelsen / Daniel Meyer – **S. 12 / oben rechts:** Cornelsen / Trevor Burrows; **/ unten:** shutterstock / ecco – **S. 13 / oben rechts:** Getty Images/ David Livingston; **/ Mitte rechts:** caiaimages / Fotofinder / Tom Merton – **S. 16:** shutterstock / ZouZou – **S. 17 / oben:** shutterstock / Rawpixel.com – **S. 18 / Mitte (Illus):** shutterstock / fad82; **/ unten links:** Cornelsen / Daniel Meyer – **S. 19 / alle:** mauritius images / Alamy / Chris Pearsall, – **S. 20:** Reprinted by permission of HarperCollins Publishers Ltd © (2015) (Lauren Child) – **S. 22:** mauritius images / Alamy / Chris Pearsall – **S. 23 / oben rechts:** shutterstock / tele52; **/ Mitte links:** mauritius images / Alamy / IanDagnall Computing; **/ Mitte:** interfoto e.k. / Writer Pictures Ltd / Facundo Arrizabalaga, **/ Mitte rechts:** mauritius images / Alamy / Ovidiu Hrubaru – **S. 24:** 1) Cornelsen / Trevor Burrows; 2) shutterstock / petch one; 3) stock.adobe.com / SeanPavonePhoto; 4) und 5) Cornelsen / Trevor Burrows – **S. 25:** 6) shutterstock / sirtravelalot; 7) mauritius images / Alamy / Paul Carstairs – **S. 25 / unten rechts (Icons):** Cornelsen / Petra Eberhard – **S. 26 / alle:** shutterstock / vitasunny – **S. 27 / Mitte rechts:** shutterstock / NWM; **/ unten links:** shutterstock / Macrovector; **/ unten rechts:** ddp images / Breuel-Bild – **S. 28:** stock.adobe.com / Robert Kneschke – **S. 30 / beide:** The Red Thunder / Seariders Entertainment / interfilm Berlin Management GmbH – **S. 32 / Icon Daumen:** stock.adobe.com / nezezon; **S. 32 / (Icon Vogel):** Cornelsen / Petra Eberhard – **S. 33 / oben rechts:** stock.adobe.com/ Arpad Nagy-Bagoly; **/ unten rechts:** Cornelsen / Thomas Schulz – **S. 34 / rechts:** shutterstock / Cabeca de Marmore; **/ links:** 1) shutterstock / Elena Shashkina; 2) shutterstock / Brent Hofacker; 3) shutterstock / Bartosz Luczak; 4) shutterstock / Charles Brutlag – **S. 35 / oben rechts:** stock.adobe.com / Antonioguillem; **/ unten rechts:** stock.adobe.com / erika8213 – **S. 36 / Mitte links:** Mo's Bows / Annabella Charles Photography; **/ unten rechts:** Mo's Bows / privat – **S. 37/alle:** Mo can tie a bow / ZDF und Telekult Film- und Medienproduktion GmbH / interfilm Berlin Management GmbH – **S. 39:** Cornelsen / Thomas Schulz – **S. 40 / unten links:** shutterstock / HappyPictures; **/ unten rechts:** shutterstock / HappyPictures – **S. 41 / oben** rechts (Person): shutterstock/anythings, (Hintergrund): shutterstock / KUPRYNENKO ANDRII – **S. 42 und 43** / Bridgeman Images / Look and Learn – **S. 43 / oben links:** Blend Images LLC/Getty Images/Jose Luis Pelaez Inc – **S. 44:** shutterstock / Monkey Business Images – **S. 45 / oben rechts:** bpk | The Trustees of the British Museum (Detail); **/ oben links und unten rechts:** shutterstock / Nejron Photo; **/ Mitte rechts:** shutterstock/johnbraid; **/ Mitte links:** shutterstock / Fernando Cortes **/ unten:** 1) shutterstock/phiseksit; 2) shutterstock / TY Lim; 3) shutterstock / rozdesign; 4) shutterstock / mahey; 5) shutterstock / SOKUR SVITLANA; 6) shutterstock / Ewais; 7) shutterstock / Evannovostro – **S. 46 / alle:** Reprinted by permission of York Archaeological Trust – **S. 47 / oben rechts:** Reprinted by permission of York Archaeological Trust – **S. 47 / Mitte rechts:** shutterstock / Bogdan Sonjachnyj – **S. 48 / oben rechts:** Artwork: Ralph Steadman; From: The Mildenhall Treasure; by: Roald Dahl; Published by: Jonathan Cape. Reprinted by permission of The Random House Group Limited. © 1999; **/ Mitte:** bpk | The Trustees of the British Museum – **S. 50:** shutterstock / Monkey Business Images – **S. 51:** Cornelsen / Thomas Schulz – **S. 52:** Cornelsen / Daniel Meyer – **S. 53 / Mitte rechts:** mauritius images / Alamy / EDB Image Archive; **/ unten rechts:** mauritius images / Alamy stock photo / Jada Images – **S. 57:** 1, 2 und 4) Cornelsen / Daniel Meyer, 3) shutterstock / HomeStudio – **S. 58:** 1) shutterstock / DGLimages; 2) (Flagge): shutterstock / opicobello; 3) shutterstock / Michael Steden; 4) Bridgeman Images/The Irish Image Collection/ Design Pics; 5) (Band): shutterstock / fred goldstein, (Hintergrund): shutterstock / massimofusaro; 6) mauritius images / Alamy / jackie ellis; 7) (Kleeblatt) shutterstock / Bunphot Kliaphuangph – **S. 59 / oben links:** shutterstock / anyaivanova; **/ Mitte links:** shutterstock / Gorodenkoff; **/ unten links:** shutterstock / CKP1001; **/ Mitte rechts:** Cornelsen / Rockfinch / Claire Cunningham – **S. 60 / oben rechts:** shutterstock / IZZARD; **/ unten rechts:** shutterstock / Elenarts – **S. 61:** shutterstock / Leonid Andronov – **S. 63 / Mitte links:** shutterstock / Bunphot Kliaphuangph; **/ unten links:** CartoonStock / Paul Mahoney – **S. 66 / oben links:** shutterstock / Victor Moussa; **/ oben Mitte:** shutterstock / S K Chavan; **/ oben rechts:** mauritius images/Alamy / Ros Drinkwater – **S. 67 / unten rechts:** shutterstock / Laura Adamache – **S. 69 / alle:** Yu Ming is ainm dom / Dough Productions / Daniel Ò Hara – **S. 70:** shutterstock / Cookie Studio – **S. 71:** shutterstock / SpeedKingz – **S. 73 / oben rechts:** shutterstock / Mr. Tobin; **/ Mitte:** shutterstock / DarkBird; **/ Mitte links:** shutterstock / Beto Chagas – **S. 74 / oben rechts:** shutterstock / all_is_magic; **/ unten links (Delfin):** Cornelsen / Petra Eberhard, **(Boot):** mauritius images / Alamy / Mark Henderson; **/ unten rechts:** shutterstock / Ian R Wong – **S. 75:** shutterstock / Mr. Sergey Olegovich – **S. 76 / oben und Mitte links:** shutterstock / KPG_Payless; **/ (Hintergrundkarte):** shutterstock / Juliann; **/ Mitte:** shutterstock / sezer66; **/ unten links:** shutterstock / oneinchpunch; / Rahmen (Tablet): shutterstock / Andrey Mertsalov – **S. 77 / Mitte links:** shutterstock / SpeedKingz; **/ unten links:** shutterstock / ALPA PROD – **S. 78 und 79:** Matt Harding / Seattle – **S. 80 / oben links:** shutterstock / Lisa Charbonneau; **/ oben rechts:** shutterstock / Ezzolo – **S. 81:** shutterstock / marcinswiostek – **S. 82:** 1) shutterstock / Alistair McDonald; 2) shutterstock / Arttury; 3) shutterstock / PERLA BERANT WILDER; 4) shutterstock / Alexey Broslavets – **S. 83:** Coach / *Fluxus Films* / interfilm – **S. 84 und 85 / (Icons):** Cornelsen / Petra Eberhard – **S. 85:** shutterstock / AJR_photo – **S. 86 / oben links:** shutterstock / Golubovy; **/ Mitte links:** shutterstock / yanik88 – **S. 87:** shutterstock / IB Photography – **S. 88:** WENN Ltd / Alamy Stock Photo/ Phil Lewis/ Sarah Edwards – **S. 90:** shutterstock / oneinchpunch – **S. 91 / oben rechts:** shutterstock / Happy monkey; **/ Mitte rechts:** shutterstock / YanLev; **/ unten links:** shutterstock / tomas del amo; **/ unten rechts:** shutterstock / Ebtikar – **S. 92 / Mitte rechts:** stock.adobe.com / i-picture – **S. 94 / oben rechts:** action press / SIPA PRESS; **/ Mitte rechts:** shutterstock / Featureflash Photo Agency – **S. 95 / Mitte rechts:** shutterstock / Laura Adamache – **S. 99:** stock.adobe.com / Andrey Popov – **S. 101 / oben rechts:** CartoonStock / Paul Mahoney – **S. 104 / (Handschriften und Drachenkopf):** Cornelsen / Petra Eberhard; **/ Mitte links:** mauritius images / Alamy / Elena Chaykina; **/ unten:** A) stock.adobe.com / lucielang; B) shutterstock / StudioPortoSabbia; C) shutterstock / Brent Hofacker; D) shutterstock / D. Pimborough; E) shutterstock / mikecphoto; F) shutterstock / Christopher Hall – **S. 105:** interfoto e.k. / Friedrich – **S. 106:** shutterstock / gritsalak karalak – **S. 107 / oben rechts:** shutterstock / Blablo101; **/ (Schilder):** 1) mauritius images / Alamy / richard sowersby; 2) mauritius images / Alamy / Tim Graham; 3) mauritius images / Alamy / Kevin George; 4) stock.adobe.com / Stephen; 5) shutterstock / dleeming69; 6) imago stock&people / Daniela SchMitter; **/ unten links:** shutterstock / Captblack76; **/ unten rechts:** shutterstock / Thomas Barrat – **S. 108 / oben (Illu):** shutterstock / pikepicture;

/unten links: shutterstock/Lapina; **/unten Mitte:** shutterstock/Romariolen; **/unten rechts:** shutterstock/Annette Shaff – **S. 109:** 1) shutterstock/mimagephotography; 2) shutterstock/Alena Ozerova; 3) shutterstock/tommaso79; 4) shutterstock/STUDIO GRAND OUEST – **S. 110/oben links:** 1) shutterstock/Blend Images; 2) shutterstock/Iakov Filimonov; 3) shutterstock/Monkey Business Images; **/oben rechts:** 1) shutterstock/Africa Studio; 2) shutterstock/Prostockstudio; **/Mitte links:** shutterstock/Africa Studio; **/Mitte rechts:** shutterstock/AtiwatPhotography; **/unten links:** 1) shutterstock/Ben Schonewille; 2) shutterstock/LightField Studios; **/unten rechts:** 1) shutterstock/Yellow Door Studios; 2) shutterstock/gabriel12 – **S. 111 (alle):** Bridgeman Images/Look and Learn – **S. 112:** 1 und 2) shutterstock/Treter; 3) shutterstock/Gilmanshin; 4) shutterstock/OliveTree; 5) shutterstock/Evgeniy Isaychev; 6) shutterstock / Gilmanshin; 7) shutterstock/Hedzun Vasyl; 8) shutterstock/Chantal de Bruijne; 9) shutterstock/Eric Isselee; 10) shutterstock/Pina Suthaphan; 11) shutterstock/ChrisVanLennepPhoto; 12) shutterstock/Viliam.M; 13) shutterstock/Susan Schmitz; 14) shutterstock/Pimonpim w; 15 und 16) shutterstock/Olha Insight; 17) shutterstock/Ondrej; 18) shutterstock/James Webb; 19) shutterstock/Africa Studio; 20) shutterstock/Videologia; 21) shutterstock/S. Kuelcue; 22) shutterstock/Vladimir Wrangel; 23) shutterstock/GOLFX; 24) shutterstock/Julija Sh; 25) shutterstock/Nekrasov Andrey; 26) shutterstock/Kristi Blokhin; 27) shutterstock/prapann; 28) shutterstock/Yulia Mayorova; 29) shutterstock/Phonlamai Photo; 30) shutterstock/3Dsculptor; 31) shutterstock/SergeyKlopotov – **S. 113/oben links:** shutterstock/REDPIXEL. PL; **/oben rechts:** shutterstock/MK photograp55; **/Mitte:** shutterstock/Maxx-Studio; **/unten links:** shutterstock/Anan Chincho; **/unten rechts:** shutterstock/Mooshny – **S. 114:** 1) shutterstock/ValeryMinyaev; 2) shutterstock/Josep Suria; 3) shutterstock/Ppictures; 5) shutterstock/Kalamurzing; 6) shutterstock/marigo20; 7) shutterstock/GertjanVH; 8) shutterstock/Monkey Business Images; 9) shutterstock/A3pfamily; 10) shutterstock/bokan; 11) shutterstock/FamVeld; 12) shutterstock/michaeljung; 13) shutterstock/AstroStar; 14) shutterstock/wavebreakmedia; 15) shutterstock/Michael715; 16) shutterstock/Dragon Images – **S. 115/im Uhrzeigersinn:** 1) shutterstock/Daniel Fung; 2) shutterstock/Victoria M Gardner; 3) shutterstock/Saran_Poroong; 4) shutterstock/NcikName; 5) shutterstock/gresei; 6) shutterstock/Khakimullin Aleksandr; 7) shutterstock/PRESSLAB; 8) shutterstock/bildfokus.se; 9) shutterstock / AdamXery; 10) shutterstock/Karen Struthers; 11) shutterstock/supercavie; 12) shutterstock/Iryna Tiumentseva; 13) shutterstock/Nushaba Afandiyeva – **S. 116:** shutterstock/Ruben Martinez Barricarte – **S. 118 (Illu Ameisenbär):** shutterstock/natchapohn – **S. 126 (Schmuckrahmen):** Cornelsen/Petra Eberhard – **S. 127:** REUTERS/Andrew Kelly – **S. 129/oben:** shutterstock/Istvan Hajas; **/unten:** shutterstock/Lorelyn Medina – **S. 133/oben rechts:** Cornelsen/Petra Eberhard – **S. 140:** shutterstock/Pavel_Voitukovic – **S. 143/oben rechts:** shutterstock/Joyseulay; **/alle anderen:** Cornelsen/Petra Eberhard – **S. 147:** shutterstock/stockfour – **S. 149:** Mo can tie a bow/ZDF und Telekult Film- und Medienproduktion GmbH/interfilm Berlin Management GmbH – **S. 150/oben rechts:** shutterstock/Antonio Guillem; **/unten Mitte:** shutterstock/Tom Wang – **S. 151:** shutterstock/Dragon Images – **S. 153/(Flaggen):** stock.adobe.com/pico – **S. 157/beide:** shutterstock/pathdoc – **S. 158:** shutterstock/Billion Photos – **S. 159:** mauritius images/Hero Images – **S. 160:** bpk | The Trustees of the British Museum – **S. 161/Flaggen:** stock.adobe.com/pico – **S. 161/unten rechts:** shutterstock/Iakov Filimonov – **S. 164:** 1) shutterstock/SurfsUp; 2, 3, 5) shutterstock/hanss; 4) Cornelsen/Petra Eberhard; 6) shutterstock/MicroOne – **S. 165/oben:** BBC Worldwide/*Are our kids tough enough? The school that turned Chinese* – **S. 165/unten:** Yu Ming is ainm dom/Dough Productions/Daniel Ò Hara – **S. 166/oben:** shutterstock/rawf8; **/unten:** shutterstock/GrayCatAca – **S. 167/oben:** shutterstock/Macrovector; **/unten:** shutterstock/raevas – **S. 168:** shutterstock/Rtstudio – **S. 170:** shutterstock/Nerthuz – **S. 171:** shutterstock/Min C. Chiu – **S. 172:** shutterstock/Fenton one – **S. 173/oben:** shutterstock/Bildagentur Zoonar GmbH – **/unten:** shutterstock/Yury Gulakov – **S. 174/oben:** shutterstock/rawf8; **/Mitte:** shutterstock/GrayCatAca; **/unten:** shutterstock/NicoElNino – **S. 177:** shutterstock/Tatyana Vyc – **S. 178:** shutterstock/meunierd – **S. 179:** 1) shutterstock/sirtravelalot; 2) shutterstock/schab; 3) shutterstock/lasha; 4) shutterstock/Shutter Baby photo; 5) shutterstock/eddo – **S. 180/oben:** shutterstock/Pressmaster; **/Mitte:** shutterstock/Dragon Images; **/unten:** shutterstock/AlinaMD – **S. 181/oben:** shutterstock/Africa Studio; **/unten:** shutterstock/Red Deer – **S. 182/oben:** shutterstock/donatas1205; **/unten:** shutterstock/Piotr Kamionka – **S. 183:** shutterstock/Tampo – **S. 184 /oben:** shutterstock/rawf8; **/Mitte:** shutterstock/Damir Khabirov; **/unten:** shutter-stock/Kletr – **S. 185/Mitte rechts:** shutterstock/Brothers Good; **/unten:** shutterstock/kamnuan – **S. 186/Mitte:** shutterstock/JIANG HONGYAN; **/unten:** shutterstock/Jambals – **S. 187:** shutterstock/ffolas – **S. 188:** shutterstock/Pannochka – **S. 189:** shutterstock/Natthapong Ponepormmarat – **S. 190/oben:** shutterstock/gualtiero boffi; **/unten:** shutterstock/MIA Studio – **S. 191:** shutterstock/flight of imagination – **S. 192:** shutterstock/Freebird7977 – **S. 193:** shutterstock/TravnikovStudio

Liedtext

S. 127: Mama said. Text: Forchhammer, Lukas/Forrest, Stefan/JENSEN, MORTEN RISTORP/Pilegaard, Morten/Brown, Christopher/Strouse, Charles/Charnin, Martin, copyright: Charles Strouse Publ./W B Music Corp/Warner Bros Inc./Morten Pilegaard Pub Designee/Late 80's Music/Thou Art the Hunger/Southside Independent Music Pub./Westside Independent Music Publ./Big Dreams Aps/Halla!Halla! Publ./Stefmusic/Neue Welt Musikverlag GmbH, Hamburg Morris-Edwin-H-Co Inc./Chappell-Morris Ltd./Warner Chappell Music Inter. Ltd/Chappell & Co. GmbH & Co. KG, Hamburg

Textquellen

◈ Texte mit diesem Zeichen wurden aus didaktischen Gründen gekürzt und vereinfacht. Genaue Informationen stehen in diesem Quellenverzeichnis bei den betreffenden Texten.

S. 20 bis 21: Auszug aus Lauren Child: *Ruby Redfort: Look Into My Eyes.* (◈ Ausschnitt, gekürzt und vereinfacht) HarperCollins Publishers Ltd New York 2015 – **S. 48:** Auszug aus: Roald Dahl: *The Mildenhall Treasure* (◈ Ausschnitt, gekürzt und vereinfacht). Jonathan Cape Ltd. London 1999 – **S. 54 bis 55:** Auszug aus: Christina de la Mare: *Time Flyer.* Cornelsen 2013 – **S. 88 bis 89:** Auszug aus: Zoe Sugg: *Girl Online* (◈ Ausschnitt, gekürzt und vereinfacht). Penguin Books, 2014 – **S. 116 bis 117:** Rick Riordan: *Percy Jackson and the Lightning Thief.* (◈ Ausschnitt, gekürzt und vereinfacht) Puffin – Penguin Books 2005 – **S. 118:** Roald Dahl: *The Ant-Eater.* Jonathan Cape Ltd. 1983 – **S. 120 bis 124:** Auszug aus: Bernd Kissel, Doris Ertel-Zellner, Reinhold Zellner: *The Bridge of Swords*. Cornelsen, 2013